JAMES FRAZER
STIRLING

JAMES STIR

NOTES F
ARC

FRAZER LING ROM THE HIVE

Anthony Vidler

Canadian Centre for Architecture
Yale Center for British Art
in association with
Yale University Press, New Haven and London

This publication accompanies the exhibition *Notes from the Archive: James Frazer Stirling,* on view at the Yale Center for British Art, New Haven (14 October 2010–2 January 2011); Tate Britain (spring/summer 2011); Staatsgalerie, Stuttgart (October–January 2012); and the Canadian Centre for Architecture, Montreal (May–October 2012).

This publication and the exhibition that it accompanies have been generously supported by the Graham Foundation for Advanced Studies in the Fine Arts.

Front Cover: James Frazer Stirling, House for the Architect: model case, probably
late autumn 1948 or early 1949; ink, graphite, paper, cardboard and metal fasteners; 9 x 28 x 28 cm
(3 ⁹⁄₁₆ x 11 x 11 in); AP140.S1.SS1.D3.P3
James Stirling/Michael Wilford fonds, Canadian Centre for Architecture, Montréal

Back Cover: Giovanni Chiaramonte, photographer
B. Braun Melsungen AG Headquarters and Industrial Complex, Melsungen, Germany
negative exposed 1993; chromogenic colour print; 30.4 x 42.5 cm (11 ¹⁵⁄₁₆ x 16 ¾ in)
PH2007:0010:006; Canadian Centre for Architecture, Montréal; Gift of Giovanni Chiaramonte, Mirko Zardini, and Giovanna Borasi on the occasion of Phyllis Lambert's 80th birthday
© Giovanni Chiaramonte

Library of Congress
Cataloging-in-Publication Data

Vidler, Anthony.
James Frazer Stirling : notes from the archive / Anthony Vidler.
    p. cm.
Includes bibliographical references and index.
ISBN 978-0-300-16723-8 (alk. paper)
1. Stirling, James (James Frazer)--Criticism and interpretation. 2. Modern movement (Architecture)
3. James Stirling, Michael Wilford, and Associates--Archives. I. Stirling, James (James Frazer) II. Title.
III. Title: James Frazer Stirling.
NA997.S78V53 2010
720.92--dc22
2010016222

Designed by Michael Bierut and Yve Ludwig, Pentagram.

Set in Serifa and National.

Printed in Italy.

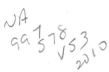

Contents

Project Credits

Guest Curator and Author: Anthony Vidler

Canadian Centre for Architecture

Project Direction: Giovanna Borasi,
Daria Der Kaloustian
Project Management: Elspeth Cowell, Laura Killam
Coordination: Anders Bell, Theodora Doulamis
Research: Howard Shubert
Photography: Michel Boulet, François Gagné,
Michel Legendre
Project Development: Iglika Avramova,
Louise Beauregard, Isabelle Huiban,
Sébastien Larivière, Karen Potje

The Canadian Centre for Architecture (CCA) is
an international research centre and museum
founded on the conviction that architecture
is a public concern. Based on its extensive
collection, exhibitions, programs and research
opportunities, the CCA is a leading voice in
advancing knowledge, promoting public understanding, and widening thought and debate
on the art of architecture, its history, theory,
practice, and role in society today.

Board of Trustees

Yale Center for British Art

Project Direction and Management:
Eleanor Hughes
Project Advancement: Beth Miller
Coordination: Craig Canfield, Anna Magliaro
Project Development: Kevin Derkin, Timothy
Goodhue, Elena Grossman, Richard F. Johnson,
Amy McDonald, Corey Myers, Lyn Rose,
Greg Shea

The Yale Center for British Art (YCBA) houses
the largest and most comprehensive collection
of British art outside the United Kingdom.
Presented to the university by Paul Mellon
(Yale College Class of 1929), the collection
of paintings, sculpture, drawings, prints,
rare books and manuscripts reflects the
development of British art, life and thought
from the Elizabethan period to the present.
The Center offers a number of opportunities
for scholarly research, such as residential
fellowships. Academic resources include the
reference library, conservation laboratories
and study room for examining prints, drawings,
rare books and manuscripts from the
collection. An affiliated institution in London,
the Paul Mellon Centre for Studies in British
Art, awards grants and fellowships, publishes
academic titles and sponsors Yale's first
credit-granting undergraduate study abroad
program, Yale-in-London. Opened to the
public in 1977, the Yale Center for British Art is
the last building designed by the internationally
acclaimed American architect Louis I. Kahn.

The James Stirling/Michael Wilford fonds contains 39,582 drawings, 103.77 linear meters of textual records, and 17.85 linear meters of photographic materials dating from about 1947 to about 2004, embracing most of the work of the various incarnations of the firm: Stirling and Gowan (1956–1963), James Stirling (1963–1971), James Stirling and Partner (1971–1980), James Stirling, Michael Wilford, and Associates (1980–1993) and Michael Wilford and Partners (1993–2004). Also represented in the archive is the work of the successor firms of Michael Wilford Architects and Michael Wilford GmbH. The fonds, as is the usual archival practice, takes its title from the names of the principals on the projects that form the bulk of the archive. The CCA acquired the archive in 2000 and, with the help of a grant from the Andrew W. Mellon Foundation, processed and catalogued it in 2006–2008. The guide to the archive is available on the CCA website: www.cca.qc.ca/stirling/findingaid.

The preservation of an archive, especially the large and complex records of an architecture practice, is a long-term commitment and labour-intensive task. In the beginning, however, someone has to understand the historical value of an archive and assure its protection. In this case we have the wisdom and commitment of Mary Stirling and Michael Wilford to thank for finding a home for the extant records that document James Stirling's legacy. This publication and the accompanying exhibition would not have been possible without their efforts.

Directors' Foreword

One of the most brilliant figures of twentieth-century architecture, James Frazer Stirling occupies a place of particular importance both at the Canadian Centre for Architecture and at Yale University. Stirling's years as a Professor at Yale (1959; 1966–84) had a deep and lasting influence upon his students at the School of Architecture; for Stirling teaching was an opportunity to pursue his work as an architect in order to expand and reformulate the vocabulary of modern architecture. Thanks to the generosity and vision of Mary Stirling and his former partner and friend, Michael Wilford, Stirling's archive has, since 2000, resided at the Canadian Centre for Architecture. This remarkable collection of drawings, models, documents and photographs provides an invaluable resource through which to understand an architect whose buildings have defied easy description and generic classification. Forever controversial, Stirling's work has too often been pigeonholed into numerous stylistic categories, from Modernism through Constructivism to Eclecticism, Neo-Classicism and Post-Modernism. Together, the Canadian Centre for Architecture and the Yale Center for British Art are honoured to present *James Frazer Stirling: Notes from the Archive*, which, through an exploration of his archive, presents a new understanding of Stirling as well as much needed clarification of the conflicting narratives which surrounded his career.

This journey into the world of James Stirling has been carried out with exceptional intelligence and unfailing enthusiasm by Anthony Vidler, Dean and Professor of the Irwin S. Chanin School of Architecture at The Cooper Union. He has been tireless in his work as the author of this publication, and as curator of the exhibition which it accompanies. He has been careful to explain elsewhere in this volume that *Notes from the Archive* is only a beginning; the impressive size and heterogeneous nature of the archive makes this project by necessity "only a very preliminary survey." However, the rich discoveries that Anthony Vidler has made offer encouragement and guidance to future scholars and students of Stirling's work.

The Canadian Centre for Architecture first presented material from the James Stirling/Michael Wilford fonds to the public in 2003–04, with *out of the box: price rossi stirling + matta-clark,* an exhibition which explored the contents of four newly acquired archives. While *out of the box* offered a first look at material only recently removed from the studios of these major figures in twentieth-century architecture, *Notes from the Archive* now presents a more considered reflection upon Stirling, his oeuvre and his archive.

Within this volume, Anthony Vidler has convincingly refuted the supposed inconsistency in Stirling's work. Although each successive building was received through changing frames, Vidler uses the archive to trace the continuity of Stirling's thought and of his designs: "There emerges a noticeable and fundamental continuity throughout his career—one based on compositional strategies, volumetric assemblages and disassemblages, programmatic responses, and, finally, stubbornly held personal preferences." The archival evidence that Vidler has unearthed is particularly authoritative where it demonstrates Stirling's "reluctance to leave a good invention behind and [his] continuing desire to build in one scheme what had to be abandoned in a former." Anthony Vidler identifies Stirling's engagement with certain themes throughout his career. An emphasis on the urban is clear from Stirling's earliest projects, including his thesis, in which he presented not one single building, but a complete urban proposition for a New Town. A preoccupation with specific formal devices, as well as a general interest in revitalizing the language of Modernism, is evident throughout Stirling's buildings. Above all, Vidler contextualizes Stirling's work (viewed through his archive) "in the struggle of Stirling and his generation to overcome the already academicized versions of modern architecture inherited from the masters of what Peter Smithson called 'the Heroic Period of Modern Architecture,' a struggle that, in Manfredo Tarfuri's words, characterizes the dilemma of the architects of the postwar period, forced to choose between "continuity and crisis."

While James Stirling is most commonly recognized as a practitioner, Anthony Vidler argues that "Stirling's 'theory' was no less intellectual or theorized than that of his more verbal contemporaries," who included Colin Rowe and Robert Maxwell, among others. Stirling's deep reflection upon his oeuvre is clear from the archive; his designs show a continuous effort to reveal their "relations with the ongoing, and for Stirling, unbroken tradition of architecture." Stirling's archive is his theory—to follow his thinking through successive iterations of a project, and across each new project, is to discover the remarkable imagination which drove Stirling's career.

Any discussion of Stirling as an architect, and especially as a theoretician, would be incomplete without noting the important role he played as an educator, at the Architectural Association and the Institute of Contemporary

Arts in London, and later at Yale, where Stirling first taught in 1959. From 1966 until 1984, he held the William B. and Charlotte Shepherd Davenport Visiting Professorship of Architectural Design at the Yale University School of Architecture. Stirling's influence at Yale was profound; he inspired a generation of students to experiment with new formal possibilities in the late modern age. His lectures provide a remarkable window on Stirling's thoughts about his own work. His buildings were presented with little comment, their images juxtaposed with famous buildings from the history of architecture. As an accompaniment to *Notes from the Archive* when it is on view at the Yale Center for British Art, the Yale School of Architecture has crafted an exhibition presenting the work of seventy five of Stirling's students from his days as a professor at the school. Curated by Emmanuel Petit, Associate Professor at the Yale School of Architecture, this project demonstrates Stirling's influence on successive generations of Yale students and it illuminates the ways in which he worked out his architectural concepts through teaching.

The preparation of *Notes from the Archive*, both as a publication and as an exhibition, would not have been possible without the support and encouragement of a number of people. First and foremost, our institutions wish to thank Mary Stirling, who has graciously supported this project at every stage, and has generously lent many important objects for the exhibition. Michael Wilford, partner in the office of James Stirling, has been equally forthcoming with his collaboration. It is thanks to the foresight of Mary Stirling and Michael Wilford that the James Stirling/Michael Wilford fonds is being conserved and made available for public presentation at the Canadian Centre for Architecture. Additionally, Kurt Forster, Phyllis Lambert, Robert Maxwell and Robert A.M. Stern have contributed their advice and patient guidance, which has been of great assistance in the process of realizing this project. A number of staff at both our institutions have contributed to its success; while they are thanked separately in the acknowledgements, we would like to record our gratitude for the dedication, expertise, and creativity with which they worked to make this possible. Finally, we must sincerely thank Anthony Vidler. It is due to him that we are able to offer this "inside view" of the world of James Stirling, through his archive, which we sincerely hope will capture the provocative brilliance of his life.

Amy Meyers, Director, Yale Center for British Art
Mirko Zardini, Director, Canadian Centre for Architecture

Acknowledgements

My thanks go first to the Advisory Committee that selected me to organize a symposium and exhibition dedicated to the James Stirling/Michael Wilford fonds at the Canadian Centre for Architecture (CCA), and to write the accompanying book: Phyllis Lambert and Mirko Zardini of the CCA; Amy Meyers of the Yale Center for British Art (YCBA); Robert Stern and Kurt Forster of the School of Architecture, Yale University, and Robert Maxwell. I thank Mary Stirling for her hospitality and support, and for her generous loan of furniture, documents and archival material for the present exhibition. I am also grateful to Michael Wilford, Stirling's former partner, who has been so willing to share freely his memories of the work and his insight into the archive.

In the preparation of the book and exhibition I owe an enormous debt of gratitude to the staffs of the CCA and the YCBA. At the CCA, Giovanna Borasi, Elspeth Cowell, Daria Der Kaloustian and Theodora Doulamis have organized the process of book and exhibition production with graciousness and efficiency; Howard Schubert's deep knowledge of the archive has been indispensable to my research, while the work of Anders Bell has allowed me to collect, select and reproduce countless drawings; Laura Killam and Sébastien Larivière have been tireless in coordinating the ordering and preparation of the over three hundred objects for display. The entire staff of Collections, Conservation, Library, and Programs at the CCA have made my work in the archive over the last six years both pleasurable and memorable.

At the YCBA my thanks go to Amy Meyers for her consistent belief in and enthusiasm for this project; to Eleanor Hughes for her administrative efficiency and curatorial advice; to Beth Miller and Amy McDonald, for their work in making the exhibition and book public. Martina Droth, Linda Friedlaender, and Jane Nowosadko have worked hard to organize a series of programs that introduces the exhibition to the wider community. I am indebted to the preliminary designs of Lindy Roy, and the discussions that helped frame the initial concept of the exhibition. The exhibition owes its dramatic and didactic form to independent designer Stephen Saitas. It has been a pleasure to work with him on the exhibition at Yale, where he has shaped the presentation of the models and drawings with a deep sensitivity to the nature of Stirling's work. Lyn Rose and Elena Grossman have developed the elegant graphic displays and Richard Johnson and his installation team have provided their always judicious and inventive solutions.

At the Irwin S. Chanin School of Architecture, The Cooper Union, I have been helped by the bibliographic work of Emmy Mikelson, the dedicated support of Elizabeth O'Donnell during a particularly active year, and the enthusiasm of the students who gave me the sense that Stirling's ideas were by no means without contemporary significance. The Archive, led by Steven Hillyer, with model-makers Jeremy Jacinth, Andres Larrauri, and Harry Murzyn has enriched the exhibition and the collection of the CCA with an accurate site model of the Staatsgalerie, Stuttgart.

I wish to thank all the participants in the symposium "James Frazer Stirling Architect and Teacher", held at the Yale University School of Architecture in May 2009. Their recollections of working in the office, their critical assessments and their scholarly research offered many insights that allowed me to further develop the exhibition and book.

I am indebted to Sally Salvesen at Yale University Press for her delight in the project and her editorial incisiveness. Yve Ludwig at Pentagram has produced a design for the book that is both lively and evocative of the acts of discovery that take place in an archive. My greatest debt is to Mirko Zardini for his friendship, constant encouragement, deep knowledge of the subject, editorial wisdom and unsurpassed author/curator-management skills.

I dedicate the book and exhibition to the memory of a former teacher and friend, Jim Stirling.

Anthony Vidler

Preface

With each project, there were usually a bundle of drawings, small sketches, which were marvelous. They were marvelous little drawings, tiny little things, and they were very unusual and very characteristic. And a year later I found that he had thrown them all away. It was a tragedy. There were hundreds and hundreds of drawings, and he just threw them away.

Léon Krier on his return to the Stirling office, 1969[1]

My title, "Notes from the Archive," indicates that I have in no way written a full biographical or monographic account of Stirling's life and work; this will be the task of generations of present and future scholars who now have access to a more or less complete archive of Stirling and his office between 1949 and 1992, held at the Canadian Centre for Architecture. Rather, I have selected projects and themes as they have emerged from a study of the archive as an instrument to view Stirling and his office at work, concentrating on the process by which designs were developed and the strategies used to accommodate different contexts and programs. Thus I have concentrated on preliminary sketches and sequential iterations rather than investigating individual commissions in depth. In this sense, I have tried to give the visitor to an exhibition, or the intending scholar, a sense of the potentials inherent in an architect's archive, as well as a taste of the contents of the James Stirling/ Michael Wilford fonds.

In this context, "Notes from the Archive" contextualizes the work as participating in the struggle of Stirling and his generation to overcome the already academicized versions of modern architecture inherited from the masters of what Peter Smithson called "The Heroic Period of Modern Architecture," a struggle that, in Manfredo Tafuri's words, characterizes the dilemma of the architects of the postwar period, forced to choose between "continuity and crisis." While concentrating on the interpretation of the contents of the archive, I have always held the memory, sharp for Stirling, more distanced for myself, of

1. Mark Girouard, *Big Jim: The Life and Work of James Stirling* (London: Chatto and Windus, 1998), 188.

the traumas of the Second World War that had radically devalued the implied utopianism of the universalist, technologically progressivist architecture and urbanism championed by the participants of the Congress of International Modern Architecture (CIAM) in the 1930s. After 1945, and perhaps still today in the context of subsequent wars and natural disasters, the questions posed for architecture were less those of "form and function" than, as Stirling himself noted, of "context and association," by which he signaled the demand for architecture to situate itself in a social and cultural context and endow it with recognizable meaning. This did not mean that the ethics of a socially attuned architecture were thereby thrown away, but more that the implied role of architecture in the social field had been trimmed and redirected.

The Stirling/Wilford fonds at the CCA contains the complete extant records of the office of James Stirling, Michael Wilford and Associates with contents from the very beginning of Stirling's career, including his student work at the Liverpool University School of Architecture, his work in partnership with James Gowan, and then with Michael Wilford and Associates through to his death in 1992. It includes over 40,000 drawings and 50 models, 103 linear meters of documents, and 18 linear meters of photographic materials. The Library of the Canadian Centre also holds that portion of the library of the Stirling/Wilford office not duplicated in the main collection, including annotated books, catalogs and journals, together with a listing of the original contents of the office library. I have also had access, through the generosity of Mary Stirling, to the notebooks in her possession, notably the "Bird Watching Notebook" from the 1940s and the so-called "Black Notebook" kept by Stirling from 1950 to 1954. This latter proved exceptionally important in documenting Stirling's reading and developing thoughts on modernism, and on Le Corbusier in particular, during the important period of his post-school self-formation.

I began work in this archive some six years ago when invited by the CCA to work with curator Mirko Zardini on a small exhibition of James Stirling's work for the exhibition, *out of the box: price rossi stirling + matta-clark* held at the CCA from October 2003 to September 2004. This exhibition took the opportunity presented by these four recently acquired archives to examine and contrast the work of four prominent figures from the 1970s. In the section on James Stirling I chose to concentrate on one aspect of his career that had given rise to controversy: his apparent radical shift towards a modern "neo-classicism" after the mid-1970s. On the evidence of the archive, including his early work, interest in furniture collection, and readings, it became clear that on the one hand, his interest in late eighteenth- and early nineteenth-century classicism had been continuous from the outset, and on the other, his approach to designing was, far from broken by radical shifts, internally consistent and concerned to advance modernism rather than break with it.

These perceptions, and many more, have been developed further in the ensuing years of work towards the present book and exhibition. I have been able to study a vast range of drawings and models; examine his notes for lectures, many stuffed in the pages of the Black Notebook; his reading notes; his drafts for published articles; and his annotations and corrections of drawings, as well as the critical assessment of his work throughout his career. Mary Stirling's invitation to study and photograph the Black Notebook before its valuable transcription and recent publication by Mark Crinson was especially vital in launching my inquiries. There are of course limitations even to this extensive body of work: the CCA archive does not include the personal archive of James Gowan, an important collaborator in the early period; nor does it contain Stirling's large personal library and the possible reading annotations it might contain; finally, his collection of furniture and art is dispersed, with major works at the Art Institute of Chicago, on loan to the National Trust for Scotland, and in the personal collection of Mary Stirling. I was, however, again thanks to her hospitality, able to visit and photograph the Stirling house and its idiosyncratic and thoroughly Stirling-esque contents, spatial layout, and decoration.

It is obvious that the mining of this archive will take the work of a great number of scholars over many years. What I have attempted to provide is an essay that inquires into the potential held by the collection for work in three different areas. The first is that of understanding Stirling's early formation as an architect: his school studies and design projects, and especially his Fifth Year Thesis, offer fascinating insights into what was already a process of intense self-creation. The designs immediately following Stirling's move to London and his theoretical interrogation and experience of the work of Le Corbusier and other contemporary modernists, evince his struggle with, on the one hand, what he felt were becoming the platitudes of the International Style, and, on the other, the increasing "irrationalism" of buildings such as Ronchamp. The experiments with the "vernacular" and "regional" architecture, culminating in the rehousing at Preston, linked his rewriting of the modernist canon to his enthusiasm for the "functional tradition," attested to by the dozens of photographs of factory, warehouse, and rural buildings from this early period.

The second area is that of contextualizing the work from the 1970s to the 1990s, as the archive enables us to see the continuing themes and approaches, developed in the early period, but in a wide range of different contexts and programmatic conditions. Here I have selected a restricted number of projects, commencing with the Engineering Building for the University of Leicester, continuing with the Runcorn Housing, the projects for Olivetti, the German museums, and the university buildings in the United States, beginning the necessary comparative analysis of archive evidence and critical reception, as a way of opening the possibility for a revised assessment of the assumed phases of his career and their place in the general history of contemporary architecture.

Thirdly, I have chosen three projects, one built and two unbuilt, that in the exhaustiveness of their documentation and intensity of design preoccupation offer the potential of analyzing the process of design itself, Stirling's demands for multiple iterations of possible alternative solutions, the working out of these iterations and the selection and deepening of the final project design. One has the sense that, with forensic care over a long period of time, one might even be able to tabulate every stage of these designs chronologically and thereby infer the ongoing debates in the office, as well as register the extraordinary fertility of Stirling's spatial imagination, for his little thumbnail axonometrics at the bottom of sheet after sheet are resonant with so many fruitful avenues not followed.

I conclude with a selection of lecture notes prepared to introduce his studio classes and his work; the lectures, of course, get longer and longer as new projects are added, but they provide a fascinating insight into the working mind of an architect not generally known as a "theorist," and indeed resistant to the appellation, but who with his laconic one-word descriptions of the works reveals the driving ideas behind projects that, as he wished, embodied these ideas in space.

The following book, then, does not pretend to be comprehensive in any way; it is selective and thematic—a preliminary response to an archival encounter. Here, the selection of projects I have chosen to examine has of necessity been strategic, and formulated both with respect to material available in the archive and to the general aims described above. The absence of primary documentation for many of the projects dating before 1974, and especially for the Leicester University Engineering Building and Cambridge University History Faculty Building, has limited research in these cases. But I have also felt it necessary to go beyond the conventional concentration on apparent "phases" of his work: the "red-brick" period of Leicester, Cambridge, and Oxford; the "high-tech" period of Dorman Long, Siemens and Olivetti; the "contextual" period of the German museums; and what is normally understood as his "postmodern" period after Stuttgart. For in the process of research I have, I believe, found a very different James Stirling to that normally presented, either by critics through his career, or by historians after his death. This is a Stirling never wavering in the search for what he called the right balance between the "context" and the "associational" values of the architecture, between the rigorous analysis of the programme and its disaggregation and re-composition into volumetric elements; the insistence on achieving an architecture that can appeal not only to a limited circle of those "in the know" but to the general population of users.

To this end, I have concentrated on a number of projects not generally brought into discussion: the Thesis in its totality as a New Town design and not simply as the single one-off building of the Community Centre; Sheffield as a programmatic and formal rewriting of the Corbusian slab; Preston as a heroic attempt to address questions of regionalism, the vernacular, and new housing conditions, against the restrictions of the new "by-laws"; Runcorn as a continuation of his preoccupation with New Town design, allied to his understanding of the spatial limitations of previous New Towns and the need to bring back the scale of traditional public spaces while not giving up on technological innovation; the competition for "Roma Interrotta," that so often like much of Stirling's work is attributed to the influence of Colin Rowe, but which on examination is revealed to take its distance from the "Collage City" model; and finally the projects for the Wissenschaftszentrum and the Bibliothèque de France that both exemplify his mature formal strategies and radically challenge the received dogmas of "form" and "function." I have, of course, included many more projects and illustrated them from the archive, but, as will become clear, my affection is reserved for those that do not necessarily fit any established pattern for "explaining" an architect whose central force remained consistent within many only apparent inconsistencies.

In this regard a new look at Stirling through the lens of the archive opens up the problem of his apparent lack of interest in "theory" and his single-minded focus on design, a focus that in Robert Maxwell's estimation made him perhaps the greatest British architect of the twentieth century—comparable to the artist Francis Bacon—but that seemingly left him without a thoroughly articulated position towards design, in comparison, say, to that of Robert Venturi or the Smithsons, or those of a slightly younger generation, Aldo Rossi or Peter Eisenman. On one level, his apparent rejection of theory can be explained by the fact that from his time in school he was surrounded by theorists at the centre of an extremely talkative group that included Colin Rowe, Thomas ("Sam") Stevens, Reyner Banham, John Summerson, Alan Colquhoun, Kenneth Frampton, Alvin Boyarsky and Robert Maxwell himself. On the other, his obvious debt to certain aspects of Rowe's ideas has allowed many critics to find, so to speak, Stirling's theory as Rowe's, and certainly one cannot deny the influence at moments in his career. And if for Stirling himself it seemed sufficient to claim, with Summerson, the "programme" as the sole source of unity in modern architecture and leaving it to the critics to say the rest, the archive affords some evidence to the contrary.

Robert Maxwell himself undertook the first step in revealing the continuity of Stirling's thought about architecture, in collecting the writings in a very useful compendium published in 1998. Here one can trace the development of Stirling's ideas from the early articles through to his later reminiscences in interviews. But again, it is in the archive that we get a glimpse of a different kind of "theory," that special thought process that we call somewhat mechanically "the design process." For it is in this process, exemplified in thousands of drawings, models and photographs, notebooks, lecture notes, reports to clients, competition briefs, and even the odd notation on a sketch drawing, that we can identify what is truly theoretical about Stirling's architecture, what, that is to say, we might take away from it today, both for a deeper understanding of it, and for its potential interest for our own practice.

For the archive reveals a very different kind of process than that generally understood as the "history" of a design—the identification of sources, historical and contemporary, the chronology of projects, and the tracing of a supposed evolution of the final design. While one can, of course, find all the evidence for this kind of interpretation—one generally finds what one looks for—the archive, taken as a whole, resists any easy linear narrative of cause and effect, origin and development, source and imitation, theory to practice—the sorts of narrative that we have been led to construct in the absence of any other evidence. Perhaps the single most important aspect of the archive, however, and especially for the period up to 1975, is that it provides a counterpoint to the effect of the redrawing for publication that became a practice of the office with the elegant, unifying drawings of Léon Krier. It is out of this "resistance of the archive" to commonplace views that I attempt to extract a working understanding of what I have called Stirling's theory. In a way, this resistance mirrors his own; the laconic one-liners with which he rebuffed most questions as to his motives are in a way blocks to simplistic interpretation, as is the multiplicity and heterogeneity of the archive.

Bibliographic Note and A Note on the Illustrations

In the case of Stirling, the archive is of especial importance, owing to the relative paucity of comprehensive publications on his work. Most criticism on Stirling has, until recently, been based on the two publications from his office, the so-called "Black" and "White" volumes; the informative Rizzoli book edited by Arnell and Bickford with an introduction by Colin Rowe; Robert Maxwell's Birkhaüser book on James Stirling and Michael Wilford, together with the fleeting presence of Robert Maxwell's anthology of Stirling's writings in the Skira series of "Theories and Works of Contemporary Architects."[2] These may be completed by the moving, and often very personal, account of Stirling's career by his friend the historian Mark Girouard, perhaps the first work to be based on a preliminary examination of the private and office archives.[3] None of the perceptions of his work that we gain from these publications, as well as from the numerous articles written by critics and historians (pro and con) over the years are, necessarily, denied or falsified by the archive. But they *are* made more dense and complicated, and expanded in remarkable ways. Craig Hodgetts, writing of the Cambridge History Faculty Building, has compared Stirling's design procedures to those of the sixteenth-century anatomist Vesalius, "as first the skin, then the vessels, and finally the muscular tissue itself are magically peeled away to expose the viscera."[4] In a sense, I have found the archive to reverse this procedure, and gradually to fill out, to add the muscular tissue, the vessels, and the skin to the body of the work, adding to our understanding of his design process, of his sources, of his architectural imaginary at work, and most importantly, I believe, allowing us to tease out the thinking, even the theoretical stance of a builder-architect generally considered to be without a conscious theory.

I have made an effort to illustrate sketches and drawings that complement, rather than replicate, ones already published; where, as in many cases, the archive holds preparatory drawings for publications, especially for the two edited by the office, I have selected those that give a sense of the work that goes into their editing. Nor have I tried to give a complete representation of single projects—given the number of drawings in the archive this would have been impossible. In my running commentary with the captions I have, finally, attempted to introduce the drawings to the viewer with the impressions I felt when opening their folders for the first time, as well as noting their potential importance in revisiting Stirling's career.

All illustrations unless otherwise noted are from the James Stirling/ Michael Wilford fonds, Canadian Centre for Architecture, Montréal (illustrations 3, 4, 5, 83–87, 90, 91, 92, 199, 266, 267, 268, and 345–358: Bequest of the Stirling family).

2. James Stirling, *James Stirling: Buildings and Projects 1950–1974*, introduction by John Jacobus, layout by Léon Krier and James Stirling (London: Thames and Hudson, 1975); James Stirling, Michael Wilford and Associates, *James Stirling, Michael Wilford and Associates: Buildings and Projects, 1975–1992*, introduction by Robert Maxwell, essays by Michael Wilford and Thomas Muirhead, layout by Thomas Muirhead, James Stirling and Michael Wilford (London: Thames and Hudson, 1994); Peter Arnell and Ted Bickford, eds., *James Stirling: Buildings and Projects*, introduction by Colin Rowe (New York: Rizzoli International, 1984); Robert Maxwell, *James Stirling, Michael Wilford* (Basle: Birkhäuser, 1998);

Biographical Note and The Partnerships

James Frazer Stirling was born in Glasgow on April 22, 1924, the son of a ship's engineer and a schoolteacher. He spent his childhood in Liverpool, and in 1942 entered the Liverpool School of Art for one year before serving in World War II. He studied architecture at Liverpool University from 1946 to 1950, spending the Fall semester of 1948–49 in the United States. He graduated in 1950 and moved to London, enrolling in the School of Town Planning and Regional research from 1950–52. Between 1953 and 1956 he was a Senior Assistant with Lyons, Israel, Ellis, and Grey where he met and formed a partnership with James Gowan.

Stirling began his teaching career at the Architectural Association in London in 1955, and was a regular visiting critic at Yale University School of Architecture from 1966, where he served as the Davenport Visiting Professor of Design from 1967 to 1984. Awarded the Gold Medal of the Royal Institute of British Architects in 1980, and the Pritzker Prize in 1981, he was knighted in 1992 and died a few days later on June 25 at the age of 68.

Stirling and Gowan (1956–1963). Born in Glasgow and educated at Glasgow School of Art and Kingston School of Architecture, James Gowan had worked in the office of Powell and Moya on the project for the Festival of Britain's Skylon before moving to Lyons, Israel, Ellis, and Grey.

James Stirling and Partner (1971–1980), James Stirling, Michael Wilford and Associates (1980–1993). Michael Wilford, educated at the Kingston Technical School, the Northern Polytechnic and the Regent Street Polytechnic, had worked as Senior Assistant with Stirling and Gowan from 1960, and from 1963 to 1965 with James Stirling. From 1965 to 1971 he was Associate Partner with James Stirling (Firm) and from 1971 to 1980 was Partner in James Stirling and Partner, and subsequently in James Stirling, Michael Wilford and Associates to 1993.

Robert Maxwell, ed., *James Stirling: Writings on Architecture* (New York: Rizzoli, 1998).

3. Girouard, *Big Jim*.

4. Craig Hodgetts, ed., *Design Quarterly 100* (Minneapolis: The Walker Art Center, 1976), 12.

1

Introduction

*He is essentially a great player—even something of a gambler—
an architect cast more distinctly than most in the role of homo ludens.*

John Summerson, 1983[5]

Over the seventeen years since his untimely death, the built work of Stirling has emerged as controversial. The upkeep of his early buildings has often failed to maintain their integrity, while his projects—from the Florey Building, Queen's College Oxford, the Cambridge History Faculty Building, the rehousing at Preston and the housing at Runcorn, to No. 1 Poultry in London—have aroused scorn from traditionalists and modernists alike for transgressing both canons. His projects have been simultaneously the object of fierce admiration—the current campaign by C20 to save the Florey Building at Oxford is an example. Little or none of his public housing remains standing; on its demolition Runcorn was even compared to the American version of "failed" public housing, Pruitt-Igoe.[6] Reyner Banham, writing in 1984, stated: "Anyone will know who keeps up with the English highbrow weeklies (professional, intellectual or satirical), the only approvable attitude to James Stirling is one of sustained execration and open or veiled accusations of incompetence."[7]

It thus is a commonplace of criticism to say that historians and critics have interpreted the architecture of James Stirling in a number of widely different ways. Some have seen his work move through a series of brilliantly eclectic modern styles, from his "modernist" or "Corbusian" Thesis at Liverpool University (1950), the "Brutalist" and also "Corbusian" flats at Ham Common (1955–58, with James Gowan), through the "constructivism" of the Engineering Building at Leicester University (1959–63, with James Gowan) and the History Faculty at Cambridge (1964–67, with Michael Wilford), to the "post-" or "late" modernism of the later work. Banham cited Gowan's motto "The style for the job," Frampton entitled his essay of 1975 "Transformations in Style," Summerson spoke of him as "*homo ludens*," while Nikolaus Pevsner, less charitably, wrote of his "Expressionism."[8]

1. Portrait of James Stirling, n.d. gelatin silver print; 18.8 x 21.4 cm (7 ⅜ x 8 ⅞ in); Ray Williams, photographer; AP140.S2.SS7.D1.P6.3 © Ray Williams

5. John Summerson, "Vitruvius Ludens," *Architectural Review*, 163, no. 1033 (March 1983): 19.

6. The Editors, "Britain's Pruitt-Igoe?" *The Architects' Journal*, 189, no. 9 (1 March 1989): 5.

7. Reyner Banham, "Stirling Escapes the Hobbits," *New Society*, 4 October 1984, 15.

Others have insisted that Stirling was a steadfast modernist, freely utilizing the diverse vocabularies of the modern movement as appropriate to each commission. Others again have noted his allegiance to the tradition of British "functionalism," to regional architectures, and to vernacular and building traditions outside of architecture, as evinced in the eighteenth- and nineteenth-century Liverpool docks and celebrated in the special issue of the *Architectural Review* in 1957, six years after Stirling's graduation from Liverpool School of Architecture. Still others have proposed a fundamental break with modernism at some time in the mid-1960s, or more precisely in 1968, when the young Luxemburg architect Léon Krier joined the office. Krier, with his love of neoclassicism and distinctive drawing style, has often been seen to have steered Stirling towards a kind of "modern classicism" beginning with the stern symmetry of the Siemens Office Building (1969) and the "crescent" for the Derby Civic Centre competition (1970). Krier, who later redrew most of the earlier projects for the publication of Stirling's first volume of complete works, certainly introduced neoclassical figures and furniture, with evident inspiration from Karl-Friedrich Schinkel, into his perspectives.

Others again, like Peter Eisenman, in his canonical essay "Real and English. The Destruction of the Box. I" (1974), concluded that the design of the Leicester University Engineering Building was, precisely, iconic because it suggested that the "theoretical implications of modern architecture and the abstract implications of the abstract logic inherent in space and form, must yet again be the subject of investigation."[9] Raphael Moneo, in his own version of eight "canonical" architects, opened with a consideration of Stirling, because, as he wrote, he could not "think of another architect whose work illustrates an entire cycle of recent architectural history as eloquently as his."[10]

Finally, critics like Robert Maxwell have tried to embrace both of these last theses in one, holding that Stirling was, in Maxwell's words, a "crypto-classicist," referring at once to abstract modernism and to historical precedent through the use of fragmentation. Colin Rowe, in what remains one of the very best assessments of Stirling's architecture and its importance, concluded that he was among those who "have always thought that modern architecture was an important and never a simplistic affair."[11]

Stirling himself contributed to these diverse views through his own writings, and especially in his early essays on Le Corbusier's own shift in style from the strict modernism of the Villa Stein at Garches and the Villa Savoye, Poissy, to the postwar work at Ronchamp and the Maisons Jaoul. Le Corbusier's move represented, according to Stirling "the Crisis of Rationalism." Comparing Garches and Jaoul (which "represent the extremes of his vocabulary: the former, rational, urbane, programmatic, the latter, personal and anti-mechanistic"), he wrote: "If style is the crystallization of an attitude, then these buildings, may, on

8. Reyner Banham, "History Faculty Cambridge," *Architectural Review*, 144 (December 1968): 328; Kenneth Frampton, "Transformations in Style: The Work of James Stirling," *A+U*, 50 (February 1975): 135–38; John Summerson, "Vitruvius Ludens," *Architectural Review* (March 1983): 19–21; Nikolaus Pevsner,

"Architecture in our Time: The Anti-pioneers—II," *The Listener*, 5 February 1967, 7–9.

9. Peter Eisenman, "Real and English: Destruction of the Box. I," in *Eisenman Inside/Out: Selected Writings 1963–1988* (New Haven and London: Yale University Press, 2004), 79. This article was first published in

examination, reveal something of a philosophical change of attitude on the part of their author"; a change that in formal terms could be characterized as from the urban, cubist, Parisian, to the vernacular, Provençal farmhouse.[12] Written at the time of Stirling's own apparent shift from the Corbusian vernacular of the Flats at Ham Common to the glass and brick constructivism of Leicester and Cambridge, this indicated to his critics that Stirling was entirely self-conscious of his own stylistic moves, and perhaps concerned more with style over substance.

But Stirling also contributed to divergent interpretations of his work in another way: his well-known reticence and laconic refusal to speak in depth about influences, sources, and anything that in any way tasted of "theory." In a long and typically urbane article written for *The New Yorker* under the "Sky Line" byline in August 1989, Brendan Gill surveyed Stirling's career, and assessed the recently completed Performing Arts Center at Cornell University. Recognizing the obvious references to Italian hill towns in the composition of the Center, references that Stirling himself had shrugged off when asked, Gill concluded that Stirling's shrug was of course a veiling of his sources of inspiration, but also a silent rebuke to Gill "for a speculation too narrow to do his design principles justice." For, as Gill realized, "securely underlying his [Stirling's] pranks—his joyous exploitation of our latest technological resources—is the centuries-old language of neo-classicism": "Standing there in the shadow of the marble tempietto alongside the Center, I ought to have perceived that I was simultaneously in contemporary Ithaca, in Renaissance Tuscany, and in the Land of Stirling, where mingled traces of a couple of thousand years of architectural experiment emerge and catch the light and disappear."[13]

By far the best appreciation of Stirling's mercurial architectural temperament, however, came from John Summerson, in an essay written on the occasion of the opening of the Clore Gallery at the Tate. In the article, entitled "Vitruvius Ludens," Summerson apologized for his early dislike of the Leicester Engineering Building as "old-style functionalism grossly overdone," now seeing Stirling as the fulfillment of a prophecy he had made in 1957 to the effect that "a new generation would have to study the overtones of architecture and the geometrical discipline of space as space; to learn not only to use space but to play with space."[14] As opposed to the "dogged seriousness" that characterized the generation of the 1920s, of which the "New Brutalism" was the last gasp, this new generation would be dedicated to serious play. "I see Stirling," he wrote, "as the architect, who, more than any other in this country, or perhaps anywhere, has identified himself with this transfiguration, turned the old seriousness back to front and re-engaged it as play."[15] Stirling's play, Summerson added, would not be the "high game" of a Lutyens, or even the "jeu savant" [intellectual play] of Le Corbusier but more that of Richard Norman Shaw in his New Zealand Chambers or Lowther Lodge. If there were still traces

Oppositions, 4 (1974): 5–34; Eisenman later included the Leicester Engineering Building in his *Ten Canonical Buildings 1950–2000* (New York: Rizzoli, 2008): 154–76.

10. Raphael Moneo, *Theoretical Anxiety and Design Strategies in the Work of Eight Contemporary Architects* (Cambridge, Mass.: MIT Press, 2005), 8.

11. Colin Rowe, "James Stirling: A Highly Personal and Very Disjointed Memoir," in Arnell and Bickford, eds., *James Stirling: Buildings and Projects*, 26.

12. James Stirling, "From Garches to Jaoul. Le Corbusier as Domestic Architect in 1927 and 1953," *Architectural Review*, 118 (September 1955): 145; Maxwell, ed., *James Stirling: Writings on Architecture*, 29.

of technological functionalism or social functionalism in Stirling's work, then these were used as material for a "brilliant, arrogant play," forging an imagery expressive of a "deep functionalism." And if certain projects seemed to evoke neo-classical sources—as with Runcorn implying a debt to Gandy, Siemens to Ledoux, or Derby to the Burlington Arcade—then this was no less modern: "the Modern Movement sprang from Neo-Classical soil and to that soil it is always liable to return." But Stirling's "return" was not for Summerson a "recessional" but rather an "inspirational" act.[16]

Stirling then, resisted and resists all labeling—he rejected the appellation "New Brutalism," as much as he disliked the categorization of "postmodernism." A letter from Stirling and Gowan to the *New Statesman*, 26 July 1958, in reply to Reyner Banham's "Plucky Jims," reviewing Ham Common in the issue of 19 July, objected: "we do not consider ourselves 'new brutalist' in regard to the design of the flats at Ham Common. ('New brutalist' is a journalistic tag applied to some designers of architectural credit, in a morale-boosting attempt to sanctify a movement as 'Britain's contribution' and to cover up for the poor showing of our postwar architecture.)"[17] He subsequently contested the efforts of Banham to include him among the practitioners of New Brutalism even as he scorned the attempt of Banham's student, Charles Jencks, to put him in a postmodern niche. Indeed, the struggles revealed by and in the archive were not engaged in for the benefit of historians, but were those of an architect forging his own manner, convinced that within the discourse of architecture—a discourse that included all buildings worthy of recognition—a contemporary expression had to be teased out. His first exercises in modernist languages were learning experiences, but also attempts to work those languages for present purposes; his turn to regional and vernacular precedents was in no way nostalgic, but an understanding that their unselfconscious functionalism offered a way out of style for style's sake; his experimentation with combinations of technological and machine-age elements were entirely of the moment—not the Crystal Palace but factory sheds, not Constructivism but Cape Canaveral; his work on prefabrication and housing attempted to bring both into the spatial forms that had proved so resilient as armatures for the relation of public and private; his apparent turns to "classicism" and to the typological precedents of institutions were not literal but abstract notations of the history that these institutions brought with them into the present; his plays with colour were a not-too-subtle countering of "white architecture."

In all these shifts and more, the central unifier was his sheer ability to join and weld volumetrically, an ability aided from very early in his career by his recognition of the power of the axonometric projection, not only as representation but as a vehicle for the process of design. It is this process that the archive most clearly elucidates, as it documents the intense and difficult

13. Brendan Gill, "In the Classic Vein," *The New Yorker*, 14 August 1989, 84.

14. Summerson, "Vitruvius Ludens," 20, 19.

15. Summerson, "Vitruvius Ludens," 19.

16. Summerson, "Vitruvius Ludens," 20–21.

17. James Stirling and James Gowan, "Plucky Jims New Brutalism," letter to the *New Statesman*, 26 July 1958, 116. This in reply to Reyner Banham, "Plucky Jims," *New Statesman*, 19 July 1958, 83–84.

development of buildings that when built or drawn as projects seem both effortless and all too final. For Stirling the development of an architecture was a continuous and continuing process—even as one drawing or sketch led to another, so each building, apparently finite in itself, was simply another stage of the never-ending exploration of space and material, function and expression by which, with not a little wit and a great deal of ebullient pleasure, an "architecture" might be created.

ENTERI
ARC

NG THE
HIVE

On entering the archive at the beginning so to speak, that is, on viewing the record of Stirling's early years at architecture school in Liverpool, we are immediately struck by the variety of his school designs, and their range of programmatic and formal interest. No longer are we presented with a single perspective drawing of the Community Centre as one among many elements of the Town Centre he designed for his Thesis; nor with the simplified ascription of "Corbusianism" generally used to describe the Thesis; nor again with any real apparent dependence on the already well-developed ideas of one of his advisors, the young instructor, Colin Rowe. Rather we find an inquiring and formally sophisticated designer experimenting with a range of approaches derived from modern movement and contemporary precedents—from Bruno Taut to Marcel Breuer and Paul Rudolph as well as Le Corbusier. We are also reminded that the School of Architecture at Liverpool included a programme in Civic Design, endowed by William Lever himself in 1909, as is exhibited in Stirling's sketch schemes for Lever's Port Sunlight, and, of course, his work on the entire New Town Centre of Newton Aycliffe for the Thesis. The book he prepared for this Thesis, as well as the planning programme for the New Town, and the report by another distinguished contemporary architect, Clive Entwistle, on the planning of the centre throw light not only on the design itself, but more importantly on the emergence of Stirling's continuing preoccupation with urbanism, and especially the revision of modernist urbanism as exhibited in the doctrinaire zoning and classification schemas of the CIAM Athens Charter of 1933.

I. Stirling at School

Beaux-Arts Modern

I was left with a deep conviction of the moral rightness of the New Architecture.
James Stirling, 1965[18]

Before James Stirling went to architecture school, he went bird-watching. This we know from the carefully preserved notebook in the collection of Mary Stirling and the Stirling Foundation, compiled by Stirling and his friend G.K. Robinson between 1939 and 1942: a meticulously annotated diary of bird-watching expeditions undertaken in the Liverpool estuary, as members of the Merseyside Naturalists' Association (founded by the journalist Eric Hardy, author of a definitive work on *The Birds of the Liverpool Area*). This notebook, as Mark Girouard has remarked, contained little or no indication of a future interest in architecture; but it did evidence a meticulous habit of observation, a decidedly adventurous spirit, and an almost obsessive drive for collecting, qualities that would be very pronounced in his later career.

If bird-watching had only a peripheral relation to architecture, and his performance at school was without great academic distinction, his acceptance at the Liverpool College of Art in October 1941 marked the beginning of his practical and experimental work in the field. Working part-time in the office of a local architect during the year at the College of Art was to provide an entry into the Second Year of the School of Architecture in 1946 after four years of active service in the army.[19]

Student projects are generally a uncertain guide to the future development of an architect; caught between the dominant modes of the time and the aspirations of professors of different generations, struggling to gain expertise in design and knowledge of architecture, and equally importantly understanding the requirements of graduation, the student is hardly in a position to demonstrate entirely mature attributes (Le Corbusier himself, before his decisive move

18. James Stirling, "An Architect's Approach to Architecture," paper delivered at the Royal Institute of British Architects, 23 February 1965, *Journal of the Royal Institute of British Architects* (May 1965): 231.

19. Girouard, *Big Jim*, 13–26.

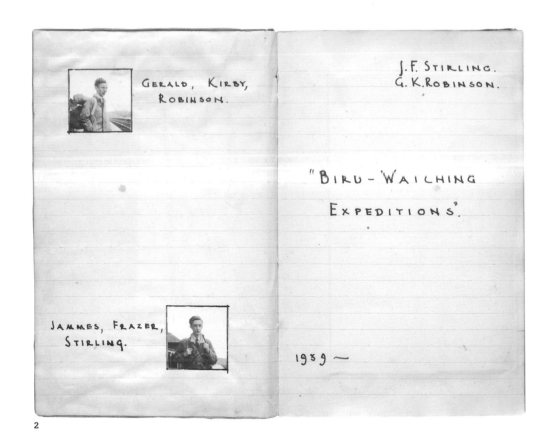

2

2. James Frazer Stirling and Gerald Kirby Robinson, "Bird-Watching Expeditions," 1939–41. Title page. Courtesy of Mary Stirling

A record of the bird-watching expeditions of Stirling and his friend Gerald Robinson as youthful members of the Merseyside Naturalists' Association. This is the only "diary" from Stirling's pre-university years, and is interesting for its meticulous observations, and evidence of Stirling's early love of land- and seascape.

to Paris, is an obvious example, where it is difficult to point to aspects of his Chaux-de-Fonds projects that survive in his post-Perret modernism). Liverpool in the 1940s was still a school in transition from its Beaux-Arts roots to a more open modernism. Founded in 1895 as The City of Liverpool School of Architecture and Applied Art, its reputation as the foremost Beaux-Arts school in England was forged under its second director, Charles Reilly; its equally strong relations to the Arts and Crafts Movement were inextricably related to the school's major donor, William Lever, whose factory and model garden village of Port Sunlight were a direct reflection of Garden City/Arts and Crafts values.

In the immediate postwar period, the school was directed by Reilly's successor, Lionel Budden, who in Stirling's words was "a liberal without opinion in the great argument…as to the validity of the modern movement," or, in the more trenchant words of his notes for his 1965 paper, "liberal, no opinion either way—quality only."[20] Then there was the place of the school in the city of Liverpool itself—the gateway to America, "the most American city in England." Stirling's experiences of the Liverpool docks—his early playground—as well as the "Mediterranean Plasticity" of the seaside architecture of Anglesea, visited in summer holidays, were, he recollected, formative, as were the early modern

20. Stirling, "An Architect's Approach to Architecture," 231.

buildings of the city, especially Peter Ellis's Oriel Chambers (1884), with its innovative glass curtain-wall in a metal frame.[21]

Mark Girouard has presented a lively view of Stirling's school years and his social and architectural relations, but what stands out is his tremendous enthusiasm for architecture, classical and modern, vernacular and designed, that is evinced from the very outset. Girouard cites Stirling's postcard from Bath, on a visit to develop measured drawings in the summer of 1947, and his excitement at "the most beautiful city I've ever seen," as he remarked on the scale of the Georgian and Regency buildings, "intimate and human," as well as—and this would become an enduring passion for Stirling in his countering of modernist "white" architecture—their colour: "lots of browns and buffs, and the Regency light blues and reds." "Modern architecture," he concluded, "can learn a lot here."[22] And colour will become a consistent preoccupation in his work, from the brightly painted interiors he envisaged for the Community Centre Thesis project, to Stirling's later equally brightly coloured exteriors and interiors.

Stirling's first year, as he recalled, was taken up with "renderings of classical orders followed by the design of an antique fountain," with a final project of a house "in the manner of C.A. Voysey"; an eclectic mix. "At Liverpool under Professor Budden, to succeed, one had to be good in many styles," Stirling affirmed as he characterized his years at Liverpool, oscillating "backwards and forwards between the antique style and the just arrived Modern Movement"— and, he might have added, moving easily among the various styles of modernism itself, themselves learned from books.[73]

Experimental Modernism

The archive, however, contains no record of school projects earlier than a single project for Stirling's Third Year—a photo-reproduction of a design for "A Fashion House," from 1947. A simple reinforced concrete structure with prefabricated panels and an L-shaped plan, it anticipates in its regularity and reduced modernism the more advanced projects of his Fourth Year, and the competition projects of 1950–51. For Stirling's Fourth Year we find the drawings of four sketch schemes, each one designed in the brief time of one week. One is a sketch scheme for "A Forest Rangers Lookout Station", designed with exuberance and wit, drawn on a single board with colour wash. The lookout, a hexagonal structure, raised on stone piers and with a pitched roof and central rubble stone fireplace and chimneystack, sits on the top of a mountain hardly bigger than itself, drawn in the blue ice cap style developed by Bruno Taut in his *Alpine Architektur* of 1917. Above hovers another form of "lookout"—a

3

3. James Frazer Stirling, photographer, Oriel Chambers, Liverpool (Peter Ellis, architect), 1950
gelatin silver print; 6.9 x 9.9 cm (2 ¾ x 3 ⅞ in); AP140.S1.SS2.D2.P1.2

Stirling mentions Oriel Chambers in his Black Notebook as the "ultimate expression" of the so-called "St Louis Waterfront" window, common in Liverpool before being adopted by Baron Le Jenny and Louis Sullivan in the United States. This is one of dozens of photographs taken by Stirling of Liverpool industrial and commercial buildings around 1950.

21. For further information on the Liverpool University School of Architecture, see Mark Crinson, *Modern Architecture and the End of Empire* (Aldershot: Ashgate Publishing, 2003), 34–36, with reference to the Department of Civic Design funded by W.H. Lever; Christopher Crouch, *Design Culture in Liverpool* (Liverpool: Liverpool University Press, 2002); Lionel

B. Budden, ed., *The Book of the Liverpool School of Architecture* (Liverpool: Liverpool University Press/ Hodder and Stoughton, 1932).

22. Girouard, *Big Jim*, 38.

helicopter, in an evident reprise of Ralph Rapson's helicopter, depicted in his aerial perspective of Case Study House number 4, published in *Arts and Architecture*, September 1945.

The second, entitled a "Community Centre for a Small Town in the Middle West USA," and signed "New York, 1948," represents one of the projects completed while Stirling was working in New York on a scholarship from the Liverpool School. This design, modernist in the style of Breuer, or perhaps more correctly of Eames, suspends a long horizontal auditorium over community

4. James Frazer Stirling, A Fashion House: photograph of plans, elevations, perspective, dated 20 November 1947, signed "JFS" gelatin silver print; 16.2 x 21.2 cm (6 ⅜ x 8 ⅜ in); AP140.S1.SS1.D11.P1.1 (detail)

This is the earliest of Stirling's school projects to be conserved in the archive. Dating from 1947, it represents his initial foray into modernism.

5. James Frazer Stirling, A Fashion House: photograph of elevations, dated 20 November 1947, signed "JFS" gelatin silver print; 16.2 x 21.2 cm (6 ⅜ x 8 ⅜ in); AP140.S1.SS1.D11.P1.2

With its regular reinforced concrete frame, precast concrete and steel infill panels, this represents the second, redrawn scheme for the Fashion House.

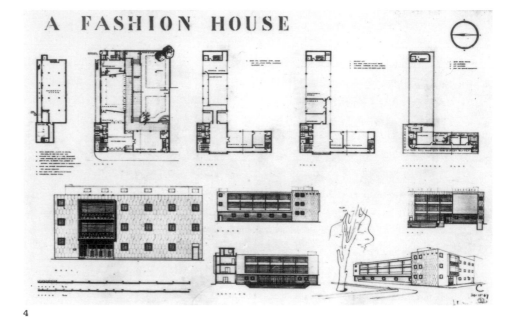

4

5

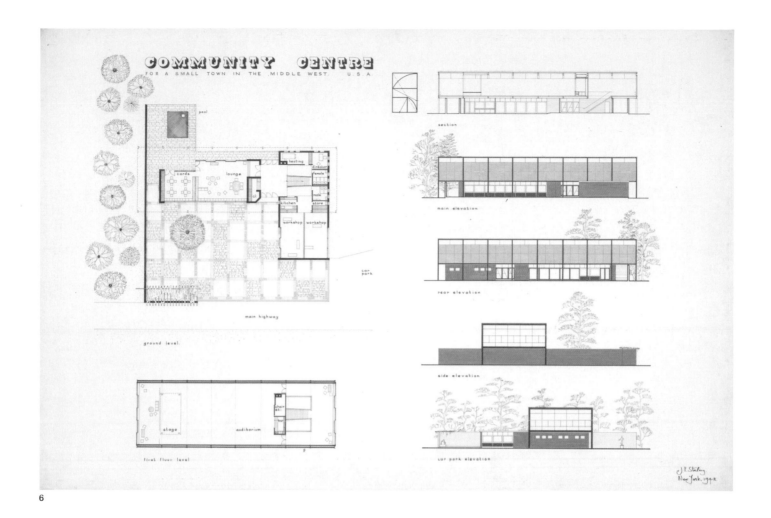

6

rooms on the ground floor. The steel frame of the first floor and its supporting structure is unarticulated vertically and horizontally—definitely not a Miesian derivation—and sits over rough stone wall enclosing the patios of the Centre. In a sign of Stirling's already developed enthusiasm for Le Corbusier the cross-section of the building is proportioned according to the "golden section." Perhaps here we can see the first influence of Rowe as he returned from the United States in the spring of 1948, to encounter the newly minted MA from the Courtauld teaching history and surrounded by the almost instant aura that accompanied his publication of "The Mathematics of the Ideal Villa" the year before—with its illustration of Ghyka's example of golden section rectangles.[24]

Another Fourth Year project, elegantly drawn in freehand, shows the plans for "A House for the Architect," together with a collaged elevation in a landscape on a single board, fitted into the box for a beautifully finished and meticulously detailed model, no doubt to be sent from New York, labeled with

6. James Frazer Stirling, Community Centre for a Small Town in the Middle West, USA: plans, section and elevations, signed: J.F. Stirling, New York, [fall] 1948 ink, graphite and gouache on cardboard; 50.9 x 76 cm (20 x 29 ⅞ in); AP140.S1.SS1.D1.P1

In New York for a term working for the firm of O'Connor and Kilham, Stirling developed this design influenced by his visits to houses by Gropius and Breuer in Massachusetts.

23. Maxwell, *James Stirling: Writings on Architecture*, 134, republication of "James Stirling: Architectural Aims and Influences," *Journal of the Royal Institute of British Architects* (September 1980).

24. Colin Rowe, "The Mathematics of the Ideal Villa: Palladio and Le Corbusier Compared," *Architectural Review*, 101, no. 603 (March 1947): 101–104.

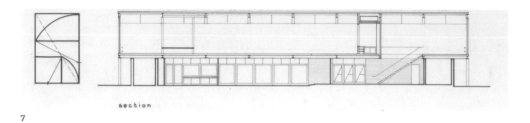

section

7

8

9

7. James Frazer Stirling, Community Centre for a Small Town in the Middle West, USA: detail of section showing "golden section" proportions of end elevation, 1948
ink, graphite and gouache on cardboard; 50.9 x 76 cm (20 x 29 ⅞ in); AP140.S1.SS1.D1.P1 (detail)

Here Stirling already shows his debt to Colin Rowe, who had arrived in Liverpool in the fall of 1948, and who, in his article "The Mathematics of the Ideal Villa" (1947), published Matila Ghyka's illustration of "golden section" taken from his highly influential book *The Geometry of Art and Life* (1946).

the instructions "Fragile. Keep Lid Uppermost." This is perhaps the one of all Stirling's early designs clearly indebted to the recent work of Marcel Breuer; indeed the project seems a deliberate exercise in the interpretation of the 1945 Tompkins House at Hewlett Harbor, Long Island, one that Stirling perhaps visited on his stay in the United States. Almost contemporary with another Breuer-influenced scheme—Harry Siedler's house for his mother, Rose, outside Sydney, built between 1949 and 1951—Stirling's house takes the form of a rectangular box, five by three bays, raised on pilotis. The resulting open plan (not a free plan in Corbusian terms), allows for the accommodation of a suite of children's rooms on the ground floor, with two bedrooms and play room; a laundry room with heating chamber; a workshop; a small bathroom; and a carport. A service hoist rises directly from the carport to the kitchen on the first floor. Above, kitchen and dining are joined by through counters, together with a gallery, study, studio and master bedroom suite, and the large central living room with rubble stone fireplace and built-in seating, leading out onto a projecting deck suspended by cables from the main structure, and overlooking a verdant landscape to the rear of the house. Framed in steel and clad in vertical wood siding, the house is entirely American in inspiration, taking its cue for services, heating and ventilating, and spatial arrangement from the "modern house" pioneered in postwar construction in the United States. Indeed, its suspended deck directly emulates a house that Stirling had seen published during his visit: Rudolph's Finney Guest Cottage in Siesta Key, Florida, of 1947, a house he mentioned in retrospect in a résumé of modern architecture in the Black Notebook in 1953–54: "American architecture," he there noted, "is natural in its planning and choice and use of materials, and logical in its structural systems."[25]

A second Fourth Year sketch scheme, worked out in plan, section, and elevation, together with a sketch model, the "Organic Chemistry Laboratories for a Northern University" (dated 17 February 1949, the Spring Term of his Fourth Year), is designed in a more "British Industrial Modern" mode, with a reinforced concrete structure and prefabricated concrete infill walls; the laboratories are contained within a four-storey slab block, raised up for entry, as well as offices and a projecting auditorium, with vertical access two-thirds along the

25. Mark Crinson, ed., *James Stirling: Early Unpublished Writings on Architecture* (London: Routledge, 2010): 36–38.

slab. The whole composition, with its sharply cut-off ends to the slab, seems to be a severely diagrammatic take on Le Corbusier's Pavillon Suisse, with an emphasis, later to be developed by Stirling, on prefabrication. Here for the first time, and in a move that would later be heralded by Reyner Banham as decisive for architectural representation, Stirling introduced the use of Zip-A-Tone, discovered during his visit to the United States, as a quick short-cut to the intensive labour of close-knit shading with ruling pen that had been marked by Paul Rudolph as the drawing style of the epoch.

Anticipating his later interest in town planning, and the scope of his Fifth Year Thesis project, was a one-week sketch programme drawn in the fall of 1949 for the redevelopment of the city centre of Port Sunlight. Port Sunlight had been built as a model garden village by W. H. Lever, founder of the Sunlight Soap industries, between 1888 and 1914, beside his new factory on the Merseyside, with housing for the families of the workers, and public and philanthropic facilities—hotel, hospital, schools, concert hall, swimming pools, church, together with educational, welfare, and recreational schemes. Inspired by William Morris and the Arts and Crafts Movement, Port Sunlight as envisaged and built was to be paradigmatic for the New Town movement, both before and after the Second World War.

Stirling's generation largely rejected what by the 1940s had become tarred with the brush of "soft" Swedish socialism—witness Stirling's famous, if apocryphal, remark, "William Morris was a Swede"—and his project for the hypothetical reconstruction of Port Sunlight's centre represents a first take on the transformation of the "Garden Suburb" model (Hampstead Garden Suburb the prime example) into a more urban and more modernist version, with echoes of CIAM Charter planning. In his scheme, Stirling completely erased the village as built to the northwest of the factory, within the site bounded by the railway and the main Chester road. A diagonal axis ran from the centre of the development to the factory gates and bus assembly shed; while a vertical axis joined the built-up areas to the southwest and southeast, cutting through the town centre. The centre itself was planned as a pedestrian precinct with village hall,

8. Matila Ghyka, "Harmonic decompositions of the Φ rectangle," from *The Geometry of Art and Life* (London: Sheed and Ward, 1946), reprinted in Colin Rowe, "Mathematics of the Ideal Villa," p. 104.

9. James Frazer Stirling, House for the Architect: model case, probably late autumn 1948 or early 1949 ink, graphite, paper, cardboard and metal fasteners; 9 x 28 x 28 cm (3 ½ x 11 x 11 in) (largest); AP140.S1.SS1.D3.P3

The carefully built box, labelled "FRAGILE KEEP LID UPPERMOST. House for the architect j.f.stirling," suggests that the model was made during Stirling's stay in New York; a note on the back of the photographic reproduction of the elevation states: "Project for House in New England USA 1949," thus completed towards the end of Stirling's trip.

10. James Frazer Stirling, House for the Architect: model, probably late autumn 1948 paper, burlap, cork, plastic, metal, thread, black ink, gouache, fibreboard; 6 x 26 x 26 cm (2 ⅜ x 10 ¼ x 10 ¼ in) AP140.S1.SS1.D3.P2

A second American project in the style of Gropius or Breuer, but also with its drawbridge-like balcony, echoing the 1947 Finney Guest Cottage, Siesta Key, Florida, by Paul Rudolph, an example later cited by Stirling in the Black Notebook as "natural in its planning and choice of materials," as opposed to European "romantic" structures like the House in Rotterdam by Bakema and Van den Broek of 1954.

10

11. James Frazer Stirling, House for the Architect, New England: plans, 1949, signed: "j.f. Stirling, Fourth Year" ink on cardboard, 25.1 x 25.5 cm (9 ⅞ x 10 in); AP140.S1.SS1.D3.P1

The plans are carefully drawn freehand with all floor textures specified. The house is conceived in true American style, with children's bedrooms, playrooms, workshop and car port on ground level, and an open-plan living, dining, kitchen space opening onto the suspended patio, master bedroom, guest room, and architect's studio overlooking the surrounding landscape.

12. James Frazer Stirling, House for the Architect, New England, USA: view of model, probably late autumn 1948 or early 1949
gelatin silver print; 8.1 x 15.9 cm (3 ⁵⁄₁₆ x 6 ¼ in); AP140.S1.SS1.D3.P4.1

Entrance elevation of architect's house from the rear, showing New England vertical wood siding and "New England" landscape to the rear.

13. James Frazer Stirling, A Forest Rangers Lookout Station: perspective, section, elevation and plans, spring 1949
ink, watercolor and graphite on paper; 56.5 x 77.5 cm (22 ¼ x 30 ½ in); AP140.S1.SS1.D4.P1

A sketch program, in the "Expressionist" style of the 1920s, one of Stirling's Fourth Year designs on his return from the United States. This is the first sign of Stirling's wit among a series of very serious efforts in modern style; not only does he adopt a "mountain style," in the manner of Bruno Taut's "alpine architecture" of the early 1920s, he perhaps sees himself flying the helicopter—a foretaste of his delight in putting himself in the picture, from the perspectives of the Olivetti Headquarters, to his equally flying image in a balloon basket above the Fiat Lingotto works, thus responding to the celebrated photo of Le Corbusier in a racing car on the Fiat works roof.

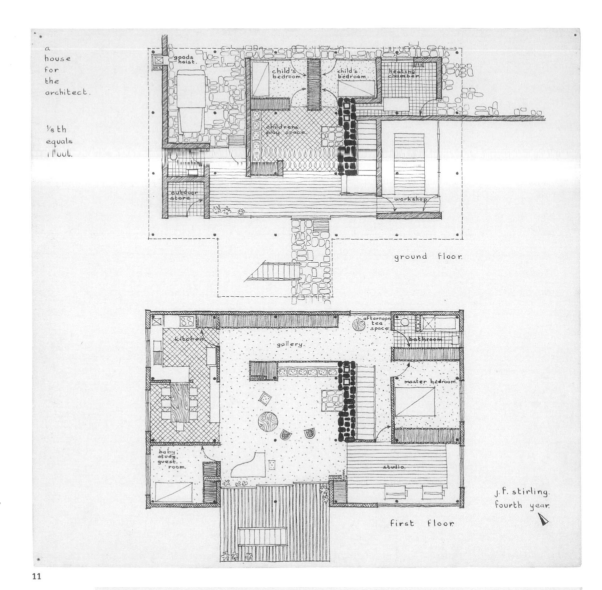

11

12

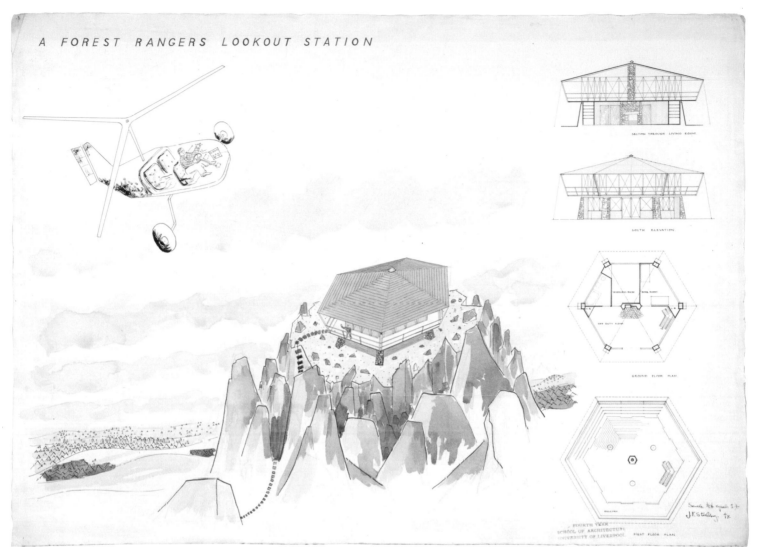

13

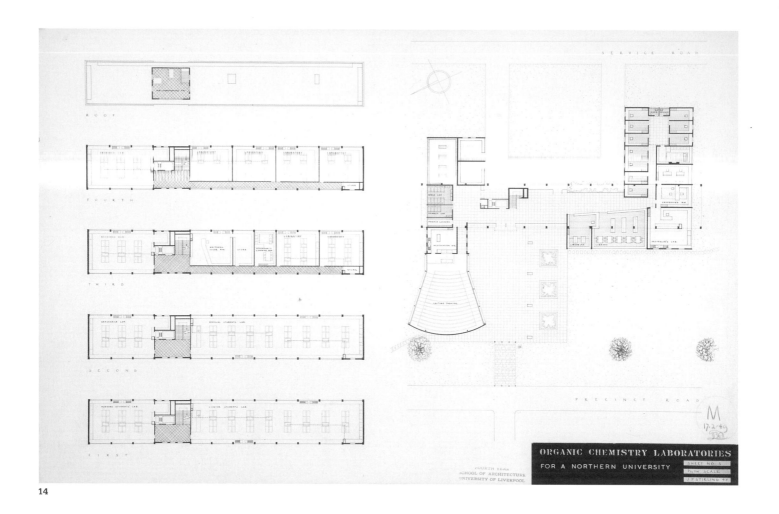

14

community centre library, church, hotel and shops clustered in low two- and
three-storey buildings, surrounded by housing. This was of two types: two-
and three-storey terrace houses, partially enclosing green space in a broken *à
redents* pattern, and six-storey flats in lozenge-shaped towers reminiscent of
Le Corbusier's Zurich and Algiers office projects. Perhaps the most interesting
aspect of this quick redesign of Garden City into a small-scale "Radiant City,"
or perhaps, better, into a small-scale version of Rotterdam, was the inclusion
of three perspectives on the margins of the board, demonstrating, in diagrammatic form, the view towards the village square from the north, the aspect of
a typical housing precinct, and the view in the centre itself from the library
towards the village hall, community centre and shopping square.

The importance of this project, despite its rapid execution, becomes
clear when compared to other city centre schemes of the period, from the
Ernö Goldfinger County of London Plan of 1942–3 with its overt debt to

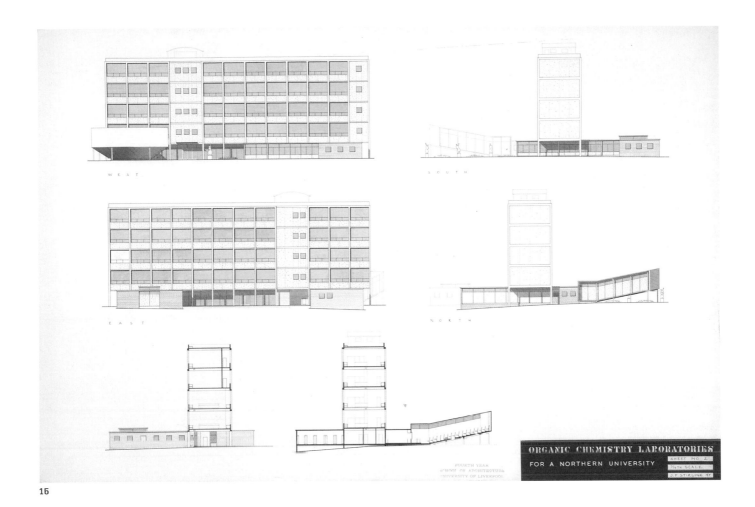

16

Le Corbusier, Walter Gropius, and Ludwig Hilberseimer, and perhaps, given his long tenure teaching planning at Liverpool, Gordon Stephenson's plan for Stevenage New Town. In these projects of the period 1940–50, the strict zoning principles of the Athens Charter separate out housing from city centre functions in distinct, and often widely spaced areas. Countering this was the sense, gathering support among the younger generation, that the "Core of the City" had to be closely integrated into the everyday life of housing and its supports: thus Ralph Tubbs developed a design for an ideal heart of the city in 1945, that mingled terrace housing, auditoria, offices, and other public institutions around a great public square built on the plan and proportions of the Piazza San Marco, Venice—later also to be a source for Stirling in his competition entry for Sheffield University.[26] Enclosure, precinct, and terrace, rather than an open field with separately zoned functions, will be a hallmark of Stirling's urban planning.

16

26. See Volker M. Welter, "From *locus genii* to the Heart of the City," in Iain Boyd Whyte, ed., *Modernism and the Spirit of the City* (London: Routledge, 2003), 51.

16. James Frazer Stirling, Organic Chemistry Laboratories for a Northern University: view of model, probably spring, 1949
gelatin silver print mounted on cardboard; 10.5 x 15.3 cm (4⅛ x 6 in); AP140.S1.SS1.D2.P1.1

One of six photographs of the model mounted on the third board of the presentation.

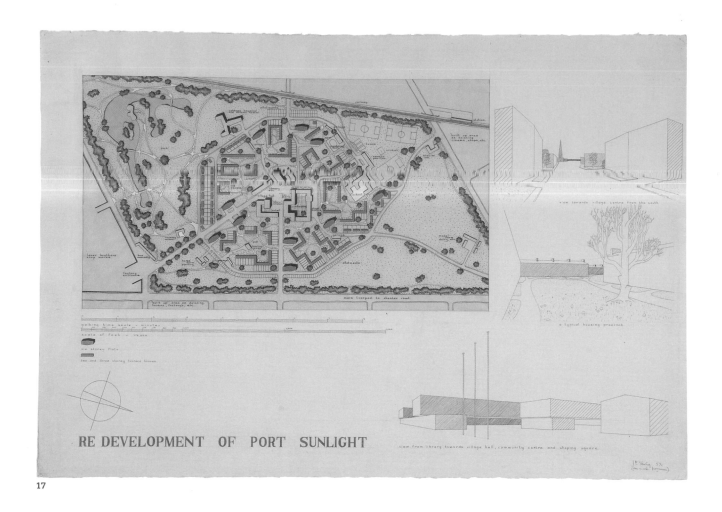

RE DEVELOPMENT OF PORT SUNLIGHT

17

17. James Frazer Stirling,
Redevelopment of Port Sunlight,
England: site plan and perspectives,
1949 or 1950, signed: "J.F. Stirling,
5yr (one week programme)"
colored pencil and ink on paper
mounted on cardboard, ink and graphite
on cardboard; 53.5 x 77.5 cm
(21 1/16 x 30 1/2 in); AP140.S1.SS1.D5.P1

A response to the many one-week
sketch design programs habitually
handed out at Liverpool, this is of great
interest for Stirling's developing interests
in urban planning. Port Sunlight was
built between 1888 and 1909 as an
ideal company town by W.H. Lever, the
soap manufacturer. The town was of
intimate interest to Liverpool School
of Architecture, as Lever was a major
donor, and the force behind its Civic
Design Programme established in 1909.
Stirling takes the opportunity to "erase"
completely the picturesque "garden
city" plan of the centre, and introduce
modern housing typologies around a
new town centre. His interests in walking
distances from residences to the centre,
and in the perspective views formed
by the new buildings would be developed
in his Thesis, designed in the same year.

Social Condensors for New Britain

My thesis (come clean)
Thesis—Corb inf.
relative free plan (maison domino)
compromised room func:
excessive circulation
accom: compressed into a box
James Stirling, 1965[27]

Although clearly entitled "Plan of Town Centre and Development of Community Centre for Newton Aycliffe C. Durham," later historians and critics have generally concentrated on the design of the Community Centre building itself and its stylistic characteristics, rather than on its context in the overall plan of the Newton Aycliffe Town Centre, all designed in some detail by Stirling. But in fact, as the wealth of evidence in the archive shows, the Thesis was a much more complicated and wide-ranging study that that of a single building. The Community Centre as a developed architectural design took its place within the plan for an entire Town Centre, the program of which was based on the published plans for a New Town at Newton Aycliffe in County Durham. The Thesis Book, bound in red cloth, that Stirling submitted with his larger-scale boards, consists of two parts: the first devoted to the "Town Centre Lay-out," and a second detailing the "Development of the Community Centre" itself. This is critical, for it establishes from the outset what had been exhibited in his sketch scheme for Port Sunlight and what was to be Stirling's ongoing interest in town planning, and the integral place of architecture in the structure of the city. It also ties his intellectual development to that of the postwar New Town movement, one that would be consistently renewed in commissions for rehousing in Preston, Runcorn's two stages, and in the competition for Lima.

Stirling visited the site on 27 August 1949, making two pen and ink drawings of trees and stones, very much in the manner of Graham Sutherland's wartime drawings, and taking a series of photographs looking from the southwest across the gently sloping fields. His program was extracted from the Planning Report for the proposed New Town prepared by the Grenfell Baines Group for the Aycliffe Development Corporation. The New Town—the oldest in the north of England, founded in 1947—was in the process of being built next to one of the largest munitions factories of the Second World War, that later became the industrial estate of the town.

The economy of the Northeast after the war was in steep decline—coal mining, steel manufacture and shipbuilding, stimulated during the war, were in the beginnings of their long-drawn-out postwar slump. Anticipating the

27. Notes for a lecture at the RIBA, 23 February 1965, later published in the *Journal of the Royal Institute of British Architects* (May 1965).

18

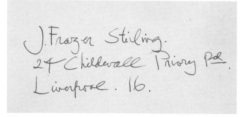

19

18. James Frazer Stirling, Plan of Town Centre and Development of Community Centre for Newton Aycliffe, Co. Durham, England (Thesis Book, cover, Liverpool School of Architecture, 1949–50) 26.1 x 21 x 2.5 cm (10 ¼ x 8 ¼ x 1 in); AP140.S1.SS1.D6.P6

This red cloth-bound book accompanies the presentation boards of Stirling's Fifth Year Thesis. It demonstrates that, far from the single building of a community centre generally thought to constitute his Fifth-Year work, the project actually encompassed the design of an entire new Town Centre, in the context of the planning for one of the first postwar New Towns, Newton Aycliffe in County Durham. Stirling analyses the region, the site, the planning report for the New Town and the proposals by planner Arthur Ling and architect Clive Entwistle for the form of the development. Stirling's interest in the place of architecture in urban design, intimated in his project for Port Sunlight, is here deepened in a way that will, expressly or by implication, inform his entire career.

19. James Frazer Stirling, signature (Thesis Book) AP140.S1.SS1.D6.P6 (detail)

Stirling, as Girouard notes, lived at his parents' home in Liverpool throughout his school career (Girouard, *Big Jim*, p. 34).

reaction of a demobilized population, the 1942 Beveridge Report had pledged to destroy poverty, homelessness, unemployment, ignorance, and disease— expectations for such rebuilding had fueled the landslide victory of the Labour Party over the Conservatives in 1945. Accordingly, in the region of Aycliffe, the huge wartime munitions factory, sited to take advantage of the flat, marshy and easily camouflaged site, was in that year turned over to the use of an industrial estate—by August 1946 nearly 6,000 workers were employed at Banda; the Bakelite plastic factory opened in July 1948. Aycliffe was thus proposed as the site of a New Town for the workers and their families in order to reduce their travel times from Darlington and surrounding towns. The first forty prefabricated aluminum houses were erected in July 1948. In the words of the Greater Aycliffe Town Council historian:

> Lord Beveridge adopted the New Town as the flagship of his new welfare state. He envisaged a "classless" town, where manager and mechanic would live next door to each other in council houses. Newton Aycliffe was to be "a paradise for housewives" with houses grouped around greens, so children could play safely away from the roads. There would be nurseries (to look after children while their mothers went shopping), a sports stadium, a park, and a "district heating system," so dirty coal fires would not be necessary. The pubs were going to be state-run, and would sell nationalised beer! The town centre was to include a luxury hotel, a college and community centre, a people's theatre, a dance hall and a cinema. There were even plans to use the Port Clarence railway to give townspeople a link to the seaside. The estimated cost of the town was £10 million; a local politician, Colonel Vickery, called it "a scandalous and unnecessary waste of public money." Lord Beveridge opened the first house on Tuesday, 9 November 1948. Its tenant was D.G. Perry, an ex-army captain. While the newspapers hailed "a dream town" and "a bold experiment," Beveridge warned the first occupants that he could only offer them a life with "no gardens, few roads, no shops and surrounded by a sea of mud."[28]

In 1949 there was little or no evidence of the future Town Centre—the Community Centre and Post Office of the New Town were temporarily to be accommodated in an adapted cow byre from November 1950, while the first primary school was housed in a block of flats until 1953; the Library was set up in one of the prefabricated houses, and the shopping centre itself was not to be completed until 1952. The field, so to speak, was therefore open for Stirling to propose a scheme without constraints from existing structures. For his design, Stirling took the overall master plan directly from the Planning Report, large extracts from which were incorporated in the Thesis Book. He also adopted the proposed rectangular site for the town centre, adjacent to sites for primary and secondary schools, park and sports arena, and surrounded by five housing areas or "wards," each with their own district centres linked by a ring road. The long

28. Greater Aycliffe Town Council, "Town History," from web site: http://greataycliffe.sedgefield.gov.uk/ccm/ navigation/about-aycliffe/town-history/ (accessed 1 July 2008).

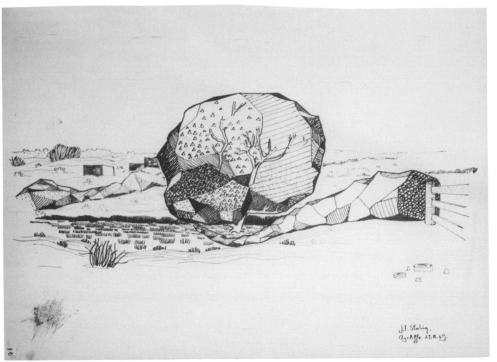

20

20. James Frazer Stirling, Town Centre and Community Centre, Newton Aycliffe, Co. Durham, England: landscape study, signed: "J.F.Stirling, Aycliffe, 27.8.49" reprographic copy; 18.6 x 25.5 cm (7 ⅜ x 10 in); AP140.S1.SS1.D6.P2.1

Visiting the proposed site of the new Town Centre in August 1949, Stirling found an undulating landscape of fields, with scattered rocks, depicted here in a style that reminds one of Graham Sutherland's landscapes of the late 1930s and 1940s—notably the *Small Boulder* of 1940. Sutherland's drawings and watercolors of wartime devastation, industrial landscapes of slag heaps and tin mines, were extremely popular in the mid-1940s. Edward Sackville-West in his Introduction to the Sutherland volume in The Penguin Modern Painters series of 1943, notes: "to see landscape like this is to rediscover the visions of childhood and of primitive man" (Edward Sackville-West, *Graham Sutherland* (Harmondsworth: Penguin Books, 1943), 11). In this sense his painting was the pictorial analog to the landscape evocations of Auden.

21. James Frazer Stirling, Town Centre and Community Centre, Newton Aycliffe, Co. Durham, England: landscape study, signed: "J.F.Stirling, Aycliffe, 27.8.49" reprographic copy; 17.9 x 25.5 cm (7 x 10 in); AP140.S1.SS1.D6.P2.2

Here the trees and rocks on the Town Centre site begin to take on architectonic forms as if the centre is, so to speak, growing organically out of the landscape.

21

22

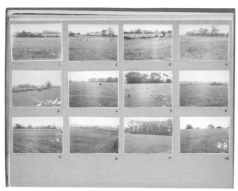

23

22. James Frazer Stirling, photographer, Town Centre, Newton Aycliffe, "General View of Site from South-West" (Thesis Book) AP140.S1.SS1.D6.P6

The Thesis Book is illustrated with Stirling's own photographs of the site, here composed as if imitating a landscape painting.

23. James Frazer Stirling, photographer, Town Centre, Newton Aycliffe, "Twelve Views of the Site" (Thesis Book) AP140.S1.SS1.D6.P6

24. James Frazer Stirling, sketch map of the Aycliffe area to show characteristics of winds from different directions (Thesis Book, p. 5) AP140.S1.SS1.D6.P6

Stirling's notion of the "track" of the four winds is delightfully geometrical— simply N.S.E.W. crossing at Newton Aycliffe in the centre.

25. James Frazer Stirling, Town Centre, Newton Aycliffe: site plan (Thesis Book, p. 14) AP140.S1.SS1.D6.P6

On the site plan, Stirling carefully noted each tree by type and height, as well as the directions of view based on the contours.

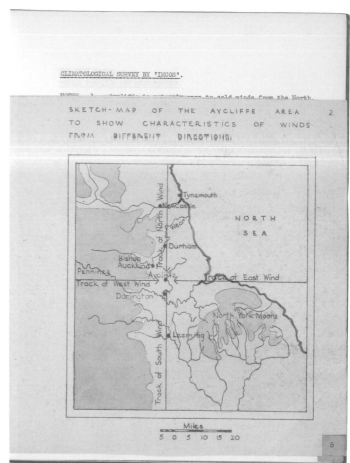

24

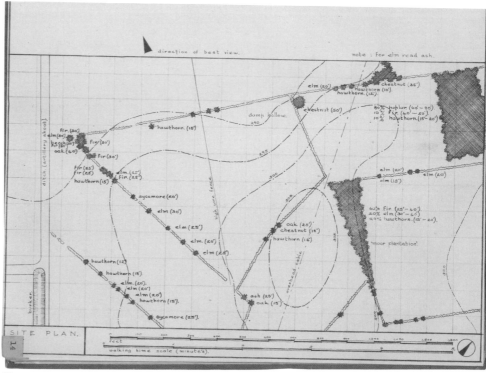

25

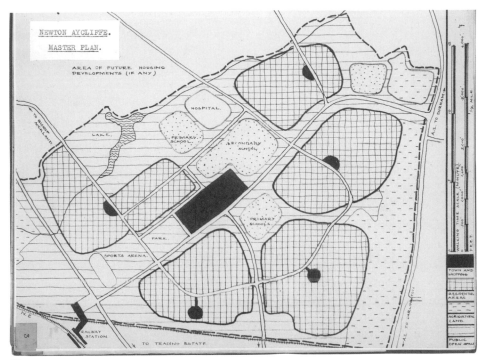

26

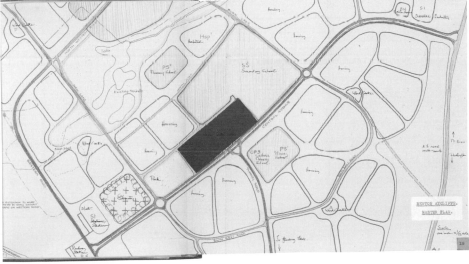

27

26. James Frazer Stirling, Newton Aycliffe Master Plan (Thesis Book, p. 3) AP140.S1.SS1.D6.P6

The Master Plan for Newton Aycliffe, as prepared by the consultants to the Development Corporation, envisaged five wards, each with five or six housing precincts around a district centre; a main spine road cuts the town in two, linking the town with the industrial estate and the Great North Road. The secondary school, infant and junior schools are sited around the the Town Centre and public park.

27. James Frazer Stirling, redesign of Newton Aycliffe Master Plan (Thesis Book, p. 19) AP140.S1.SS1.D6.P6

Stirling has marked the site for the Town Centre, slightly enlarged in red, fed by the main spine road. He has enlarged the town lake to the north-west, and indicated the sites of schools, housing and district centres.

28. James Frazer Stirling, "Stating the Problem" (Thesis Book, p. 20)
AP140.S1.SS1.D6.P6

Stirling here analyzes the site of the Town Centre "in terms of forces," considering the "sudden termination of the Trading Estate road," and the "best view ... towards the north."

29. James Frazer Stirling, "Solution" to the "Problem" (Thesis Book, p. 22)
AP140.S1.SS1.D6.P6

Rejecting the termination of the Trading Estate road, Stirling allows it to enter the site of the Centre, but not through the mid-point of the site. He stated: "There is a definite aesthetic value in being able to see multi-colored buses and automobiles passing at a safe distance."

30. James Frazer Stirling, Town Centre and Community Centre, Newton Aycliffe: first preliminary scheme for Town Centre (Thesis Book)
AP140.S1.SS1.D6.P6

In the first scheme for the town centre, the northwest/southeast access road cuts through the site, with the cinema, shops, and public facilities such as the children's crèche, and the administrative, municipal, and community services, together with the church, cinema, and dance hall to the northeast.

31. James Frazer Stirling, Town Centre and Community Centre, Newton Aycliffe: second alternative preliminary scheme for Town Centre (Thesis Book)
AP140.S1.SS1.D6.P6

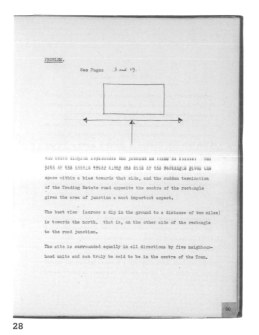

28

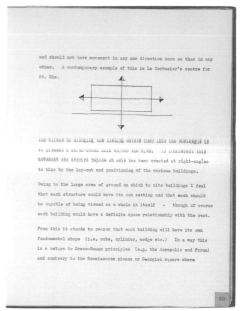

29

axis of the Town Centre was connected directly to the railway station to the southwest, and beyond this to the industrial estate. Stirling's first study was topographical as he displayed twelve photographs of the open fields that were the site of the future Town Centre; secondly, he analyzed the "climatological" conditions, drawing up a plan of the prevailing wind patterns; thirdly he developed a physical description of the site, with specific attention to tree growth and contours with views in every direction. Finally, he drew up his own colour-coded version of the Master Plan, with the road network and zoning re-elaborated from the Planning Report. The list of facilities to be accommodated in the Town Centre was taken from a list Stirling obtained from the Grenfell Baines Group (28 August 1949): Cinema, Dance Hall, Cafés and Restaurants, Public Houses, Shops, Open Market, Crèche, Private Offices, Government Offices, Municipal Offices, Banks, Post Office, Police Court, Town Hall, Concert Hall, Health Centre, Community Centre, Town Church, Car Parks, etc. These are all, except for the Health Centre and Crèche, present in his final plan for the Town Centre.

In his preliminary section, "Stating the Problem," Stirling already reveals a certain influence of Rowe, whose formal method, merging Gestalt theory and traditional Beaux-Arts compositional techniques, always began with an analysis of the "forces" impinging on a site. Stirling, taking the rectangle of the Centre, constructed a diagram that in his words "represents the problem in terms of forces," with arrows showing the imagined "pressure" on this

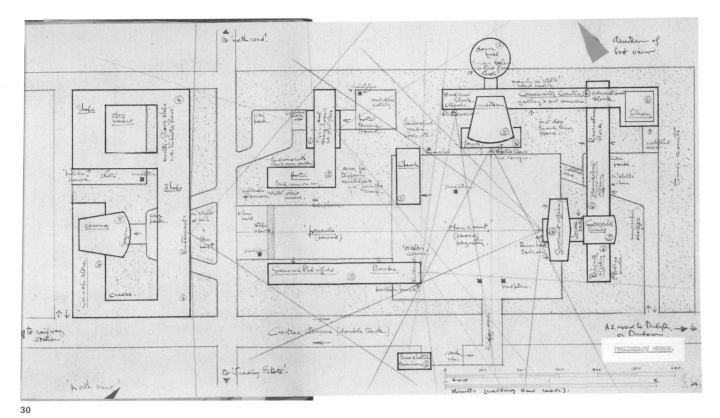

30

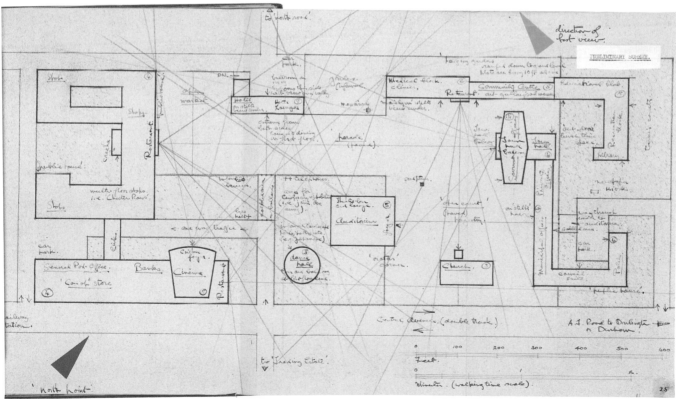

31

49

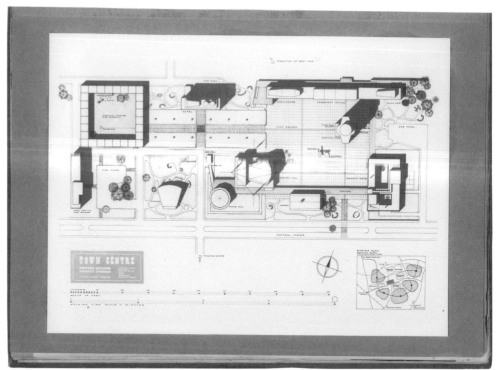

32. James Frazer Stirling, Town Centre and Community Centre, Newton Aycliffe: final plan for Town Centre (Thesis Book, p.36) AP140.S1.SS1.D6.P6

The internal road on the northwest/ southeast axis terminates at the bus hall, the town hotel, and, "for the convenience of the housewife," the shopping centre. The "buildings of leisure" (cinema, dance hall, auditorium) are at the centre of the scheme, with offices, shops and banks on the periphery (Stirling, Thesis Book, pp. 20–23).

33. Le Corbusier, the Civic Centre of St-Dié, 1944–46, from *Oeuvre complète* (1938–46), IV, 13

Key: 1 Administrative Centre. 2 Tourism and Artisinal Culture. 3 Cafés. 4 Maison commune. 5 Museum. 6 Hotel. 7 Department Stores. 8 I.S.A.I (1st stage). 9 Factories. 10 Swimming pool. 11 I.S.A.I (2nd stage). Stirling wrote: "Ideally the physical centre of the town which itself should be the town centre, should be a shape of complete repose (i.e. circle or square) and should not have movement in any one direction more so than in any other. A contemporary example of this is Le Corbusier's centre for St-Dié." (Thesis Book, pp. 21–22)

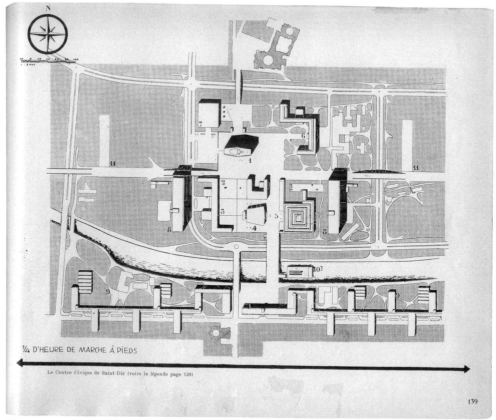

geometry by the roads passing along one side and arriving at the centre of this side of the site: this "path of the double track along one side of the rectangle," Stirling noted, "gives the space within a bias towards that side, and the sudden termination of the Trading Estate Road opposite to the centre of the rectangle gives the area of junction a most important aspect." Added to this, the most favorable view, over two miles of countryside, was to the north, away from the enclosure of the road system. This, concluded Stirling, confirmed that the site could "truly be said to be in the centre of the Town" (Thesis book, p. 20). Adjusting the Trading Estate Road so that it was brought into the Centre itself, allowing for the Bus Terminal and Hotel to be within the precinct, Stirling then announced his guiding principle of planning: "Ideally the physical centre of the town which itself should be the town centre, should be a shape of complete repose (i.e. circle or square) and should not have movement in any one direction more so than in any other" (Thesis book, p. 21). A second diagram of forces then showed the rectangle crossed by two axes at right angles. A precedent for such a diagram, he noted, would be the newly proposed city centre for the war-damaged town of St-Dié in France by Le Corbusier in 1945.

Here, and perhaps more than in the detailed architecture of the Community Centre itself, Stirling reveals his deepest debt to Le Corbusier—that of planning the relations of separate buildings to each other in a composition that forms a "centre," but one that follows the CIAM open principles of distribution as against the built-up centres of the past. Accordingly Stirling called for each building to "have its own setting" and be "capable of being viewed as a whole in itself" with respect "of course [that] each building would have a definite space relative with the rest" (Thesis book, p. 22). He concludes, in a passage that resonates with his future development as an urban architect:

> From this it stands to reason that each building will have its own fundamental shape (i.e. cube, cylinder, wedge etc.). In a way this is a return to Graeco-Roman principles (e.g. the Acropolis and Forum) and contrary to the Renaissance piazza or Georgian square where buildings of maybe entirely different functions are given very little individual treatment and are strung together to form a continuous wall around a space (Thesis book, pp. 22–23).

The tension between these two formal planning principles would dominate much of Stirling's work throughout his career—even in the Aycliffe Town Centre, the shopping was arranged around a small "town square"—but the overriding sense of the demands of each element to retain its individuality would generally prevail.

Bound into the Thesis book are two alternative schemes for the Town Centre, experimenting with varied compositions for the distribution of the functions, with specific attention paid to the quality and direction of views

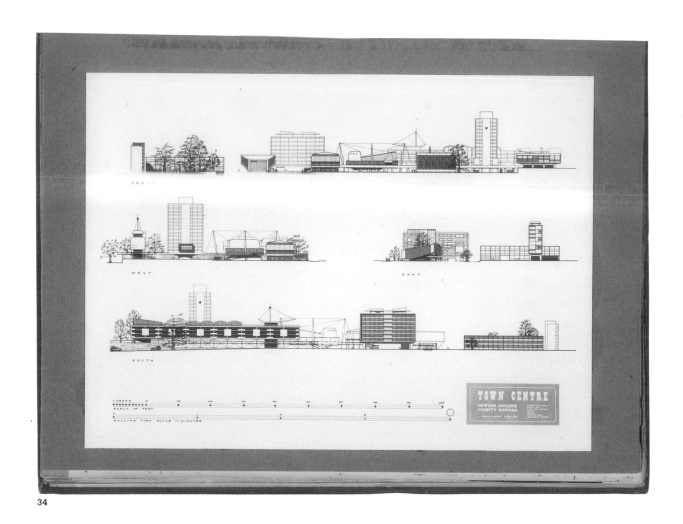

34

34. James Frazer Stirling, Town Centre and Community Centre, Newton Aycliffe: sections and elevations of Town Centre (Thesis Book, p. 37)
AP140.S1.SS1.D6.P6

from each. In the first "Preliminary Scheme," the shopping centre around an open market square is sited on the northwest corner of the plaza, with the adjoining cinema and public facilities such as a crèche to the southwest. A service road from the housing to the southeast runs through the site to the north road, providing access to parking and shopping. Moving across the site to the northeast, the hotel and General Post Office face on to the central "parade ground," which opens onto a great open court, overlooked by the office tower of the city government services and its "Mayor's Balcony," in a form reminiscent of Le Corbusier's office tower in Algiers, and bounded by the church to the northeast and the Community Centre with auditorium and circular dance hall, medical services, and municipal offices. In a second version, the shopping square holds the northwest corner of the site, with the nine-storey hotel, followed by a long articulated slab with the medical and Community Centre, the government offices and police court along the north side; the five-storey private office block and post office and car park to the southwest; the cinema, dance hall, concert hall, and church to the south; and the council offices holding the southeast corner. Free-standing, and overlooking the central civic square, is the twelve-storey Town Hall and municipal tower. Following Stirling's formal principles, the cinema and concert hall are wedge-shaped; and the dance hall is circular; the Community Centre encloses a rectangular courtyard; and the shopping precinct forms a terraced square around an open market space, while the cruciform plan Town Hall tower is a hybrid reminiscent of Le Corbusier's office towers of the 1930s and 1940s. All ground surfaces are indicated in detail, through to the design of a war memorial, and a walking-time line allows calculation of pedestrian scale.

35

35. James Frazer Stirling, Town Centre and Community Centre, Newton Aycliffe: view of model of Town Centre, 1949–50 gelatin silver print; 9.5 x 20.5 cm (3 ¾ x 8 ⅛ in); AP140.S1.SS1.D6.P9.1

36. James Frazer Stirling, Town Centre and Community Centre, Newton Aycliffe: view of model of Town Centre (Thesis Book, pp. 38–39) AP140.S1.SS1.D6.P6

36

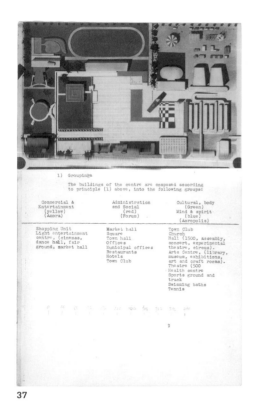

37. Clive Entwistle, Town Centre,
Newton Aycliffe: proposed plan,
June 1948
AP140.S1.SS1.D6.P8

This plan proposed to the Grenfell Baines
consulting group was carefully scaled
by Stirling and was, to a large extent,
a model for his own Thesis design.
Combining a range of modernist building
types—auditoria, offices, and an arts
centre in the form of Le Corbusier's
Museum of Unlimited Growth—it was
also a model for Stirling to critique
with his own set of type-forms.

The Planning Report for Aycliffe had been specific in its recommendations for the social life of the town, and especially for the new Town Centre. It was to be a meeting-place for the social functions of the community—political and administrative, as well as recreational—and serve the educational and consumer needs of the population. The sociologists of the Grenfell Baines Group were especially concerned with the preservation and extension of the specifically regional social ties, reinforced in the public realm by what they termed "a tradition of public assembly, procession and pageantry which survives with some strength in the politically conscious north-east region." The new centre should therefore accommodate "procession culminating in spectacle or meeting," perhaps to and from the appropriately placed Town Church; space for outdoor concerts by orchestras and bands, platforms for speeches, outdoor plays and pageants, and spaces sheltered from the rain, all planned for use during daylight and after dark. Complementing this imaginary festive community would be a series of educational facilities—arts centres, exhibition halls, library, a town club (Community Centre), and a folk museum (no doubt to instill a sense of rooted local history and customs for a newly uprooted population). This sense of municipal communality, deeply ingrained in the emerging labour sociology of the late 1930s and 1940s, even extended to the function of the hotel, a "Town Hotel" where distinguished visitors might be entertained and official functions take place.

Stirling's final design accommodates these aspirations to a remarkable degree, indicating that, as would become clear in his later housing and public projects, he took very seriously the public and community role of architecture—one that not only responded to spatial requirements, but was able to communicate and reinforce local and regional polity. The overall scheme now separates each function into a highly distinguishable and more or less autonomous form, and relies more on the grouping of elements than on their physical connections. Thus the Town Hall is furnished with a special balcony overlooking the Civic Square, "from which the Mayor could address crowds gathered in the square below," the Town Church is conceived as non-denominational, and the auditorium, with its roof suspended from "Skylon"-like pylons, is planned to serve the wider population of the region. Rowe remarked of the atmosphere at Liverpool, "there was some faint equation to be made of modern architecture with social concern," even though, in his sense of the students, "the more radical equation with Socialism did not occur."[29] But for Stirling, as evinced by his very choice of a thesis topic, and confirmed in future lectures, the accommodation of the social was fundamental to any public project. Where he was to differ from many of his more politically oriented contemporaries, was in his refusal to deny the very properties of architecture that sustained such an engaged social program, properties embedded in both vernacular and high architecture.

29. Rowe, "James Stirling," in Arnell and Bickford, eds.,
James Stirling: Buildings and Projects, 12.

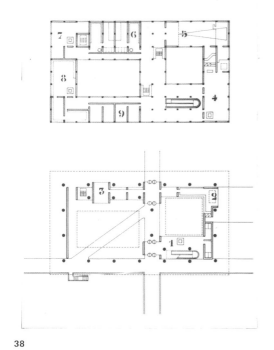

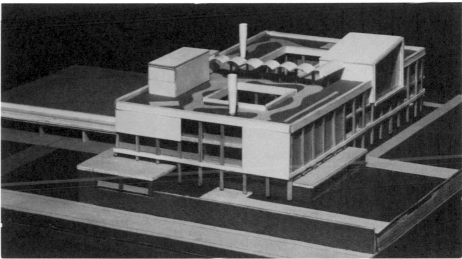

38

39

In designing his project Stirling had the advantage of a report drawn up by a distinguished modernist architect, Clive Entwistle. Entwistle had already proposed a radical scheme for the Crystal Palace site in London, published in the *Architectural Review*, and his style was that of a minimalist, Lubetkin-like and highly geometricized modern. His report to the Grenfell Group on the Aycliffe Town Centre was submitted in June 1948, two years before Stirling's own attempt.[30] It included a suggested site plan and a number of visual sketches, together with illustrations of prototype buildings. His aims, as stated in the report, were not dissimilar to those of Stirling: "to create a live, compact, efficient and splendid organism, expressing with precision the activities of the citizens in their amusement, trading, administration, and the cultivation of their bodies, minds and spirits." Architecturally, the centre was to be a composition of objects "set up in space" in "exact and moving harmony with each other," a harmony that was to be "comprehensible to the eye of a man standing and walking on the ground."[31] Entwistle went on to relate his design to the hierarchical ordering of the Greek agora and acropolis, and the Roman forum (popular references at the time to bring modernism into universal reference, as in Ralph Tubbs's own "Ideal" Town Centre), linked by a convenient circulation system, separating vehicles from pedestrians. His plans for the Aycliffe Centre

30. James Frazer Stirling, Community Centre, Newton Aycliffe: preliminary scheme, plan (Thesis Book)
AP140.S1.SS1.D6.P7.2

39. James Frazer Stirling, Community Centre, Newton Aycliffe: preliminary scheme, Model view from northeast (Thesis Book)
AP140.S1.SS1.D6.P7.4

30. Clive Entwistle, "Town Centre Aycliffe and Suggested Form of Development of N.W. Residential District," 19 June 1948. James Stirling/Michael Wilford Fonds, CCA, AP140.S1.SS1.D6.P8.

31. Entwistle, "Town Centre Aycliffe," 1.

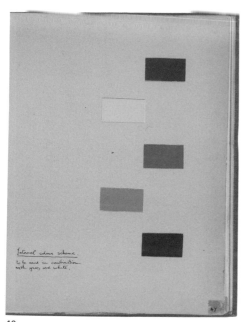

40

40. James Frazer Stirling, Community
Centre, Newton Aycliffe: internal colour
scheme to be used in combination
with grey and white (Thesis Book, p. 47)
AP140.S1.SS1.D6.P6

Stirling's life-long interest in experimenting with colour is here demonstrated
with different colors to be used, each
coded by function: school—yellow;
citizens advice bureau—yellow-brown;
workers' educational association—
brown; administration, staff—green;
public library—emerald; warden's
flat—blue; youth centre—purple;
recreation—red.

were disposed more regularly on a grid than Stirling's, but contained roughly the same functions: the commercial and entertainment functions were grouped together in the "agora"; the administration and social functions in the "forum"; and the cultural, mind, and spritual functions on the "acropolis." What seems to have been more important for Stirling, however, was Entwistle's typological sources—Le Corbusier's "Museum of Unlimited Growth" for the Arts Centre, and significantly for Stirling's concert hall, Amancio Williams's circular, dough-nut-like multi-purpose prototypical design for a "Hall for Visual Spectacle and Sound in Space," of 1945–49. More predictably, the dwelling units proposed by Entwistle followed the Unité model. Like Stirling after him, Entwistle was also concerned with the visibility of the centre's buildings, and their relationship to the housing areas outside, drawing red lines of sight between them. Stirling's plans were similarly annotated with view angles around the edges. For Entwis-tle the interpenetration of the two "space systems" of low and high buildings allowed for what he called "a veritable explosion of space," visible to someone standing in the main square.

Not surprisingly, Entwistle's report, which was retained in Stirling's archive, does not figure in the bibliography attached to the Thesis, which ranges from the most general reflections on city planning—Lewis Mumford's *The Culture of Cities*, Eliel Saarinen's *The City*, Sigfried Giedion's *Time, Space and Architecture*—to contemporary analyses of the urgent problems of central cities—José Luis Sert's *Can our Cities Survive?*, Le Corbusier's *When the Cathe-drals were White*, Frank Lloyd Wright's *When Democracy Builds*—and more pragmatic sociological and planning proposals—Ian R.M. McCallum's 1945 edited volume on *Physical Planning*,[32] Thomas Sharp's *Oxford Replanned*, Ernö Goldfinger's *County of London Plan*, and Ralph Tubbs's *Living in Cities*. Lázlo Moholy-Nagy's *The New Vision* is added for aesthetic measure. The trace of many of these studies can be found in the resulting plan.

The style of the buildings in the Town Centre (or perhaps one should say the styles) follows the conventions of British modernism—echoes of Goldfin-ger and Lubetkin, but also of Connell Ward, Lucas (a model for the Liverpool students as Rowe remembered), Maxwell Fry, and above all Owen Williams, whose Peckham Health Centre would be cited by Stirling as a source for the Community Centre design. The "Corbusian effect" is thus less evident here, save perhaps as embedded and transformed in much of British modernism in the 1930s and 1940s, and overlaid by the geometric sharpness of the plans—Lubetkin's translation of Le Corbusier's plan for the Centrosoyus Building in Moscow for his Finsbury Health Centre, with its wedge-shaped auditorium and angular plan-geometry, would be typical. If there are direct Corbusian precedents, then the plan for St-Dié already mentioned by Stirling, and more indirectly the proposal for a Cité Mondiale above Lake Geneva of 1929, would

32. Ian R.M. McCallum, ed., *Physical Planning: The Groundwork of a New Technique* (London: The Architectural Press, 1945).

have inspired the grouping of the individual buildings and the overall geometry of the plan. But, while the eclectic modern styles of the elements of the Town Centre are understandable as quickly generated in order to provide a modern tone for the whole, the procedure of identifying a "fundamental shape (i.e. cube, cylinder, wedge etc.)" for each building, articulating its character through pure geometry, would remain a leitmotif of Stirling's design approach, emerging most strongly in the apparently arbitrary shapes of the Wissenschaftszentrum pavilions and many of the later town-planning projects, notably in the compositional strategies of Canary Wharf.

Part II of the Thesis, the "Development of the Community Centre," represented the demonstration of architectural, as opposed to planning, knowledge and skill. It was thoroughly studied in program and the distribution of accommodation, in circulation, and in the detailed study of structure and building technology. As outlined by the Grenfell Group, the Community Centre was to accommodate a Medical Block with clinics, laboratories, examination and treatment rooms; a Recreation Block with swimming pool, gymnasium, games rooms, tennis courts, and meeting rooms; an Educational Block with lecture rooms, classrooms, craft rooms and a small theatre; a Library with reading room, lending library, reference room, children's room, staff room and stacks, and an Art Gallery with temporary and permanent exhibition space; and a folk museum. Stirling reported that his research into community centres over the months of August to November had led him to the conclusion that the library as proposed was too large, and that there was no need to duplicate the swimming pool of the nearby secondary school.

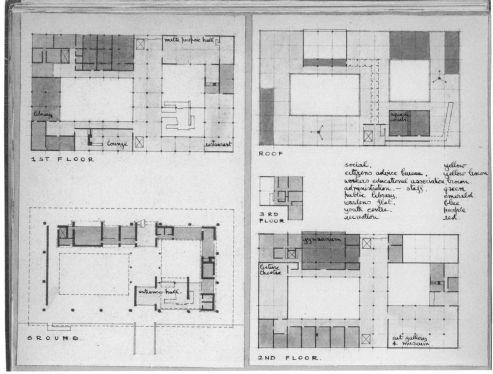

41. James Frazer Stirling, Community Centre, Newton Aycliffe; ground, first-, second-, third-floor and roof plans with colour schemes (Thesis Book) AP140.S1.SS1.D6.P6

The colours for the internal functions of the Centre plotted on the floor plans.

41

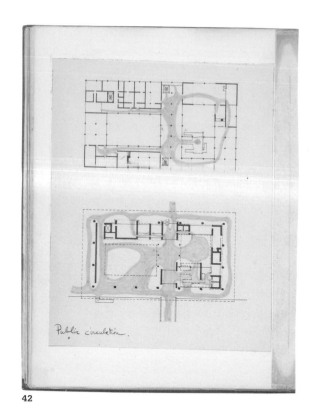

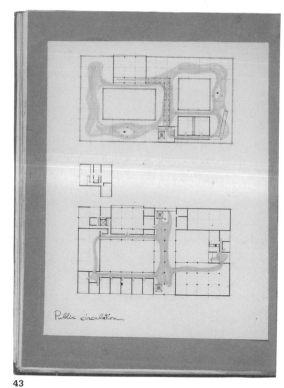

42. James Frazer Stirling, Community
Centre, Newton Aycliffe: public
circulation diagram, ground and first-
floor plans (Thesis Book)
AP140.S1.SS1.D6

Another major and continuing interest
for Stirling was the mapping of
circulation patterns through the building—
the armature that brings functions
together in the appropriate manner.

43. James Frazer Stirling, Community
Centre, Newton Aycliffe: public
circulation diagram, second floor
and roof plans (Thesis Book)
AP140.S1.SS1.D6

The problem of sustaining "community" among a displaced and urbaniz-
ing population—a "community" that sociologists were beginning to recognize
in the life of small mining villages—preoccupied planners in the immediate
postwar period. In a long extract from the Grenfell Report, itself extracted
from a study of "The People" by an official of the Regional Office of Town and
Country Planning, Stirling attests to his sense of responsibility toward the sus-
tenance of community institutions—the Chapel, the Labour Party, the Women's
Institute—and the ceremonies of the village—the whist drive, the wedding, the
funeral—and the need to embody them in an architecture at once "urban" and
"civic" and "intimate" and "domestic."

The Grenfell Group cited the example of the Cambridge Village Colleges and the Welfare Centres of the Industrial and Mineworkers' Hostels as
important precedents for the Aycliffe Community Centre, but above all they
recommended the experience of the Pioneer Health Centre at Peckham that had
been built between 1933 and 1935 by Sir Owen Williams; anticipating the need
for structural and thereby programmatic flexibility, the sponsors' foresight "had
resulted in a brilliantly successful project and building" (Thesis book, p. 44).
Not surprisingly, Stirling lists Impington Village College, Cambridgeshire, the
East Wavertree Association in Liverpool, and the Peckham Health Centre in

London together with Pease and Crocker's book, *The Peckham Experiment*, in his list of sources.[33] Of all these precedents, the Pioneer Health Centre at Peckham, established in 1925 and built to the designs of Sir Owen Williams, was the most pertinent. An urban centre, as opposed to the Impington Village College, Peckham was also one of the most successful prewar foundations; as the doctors Pease and Crocker reported in 1943, this "modern building designed as a laboratory for the study of human biology" in the context of a family health centre was "a design which invites social contact, allowing ... for the chance meeting, for formal and festive occasions as well as those for quiet familiar grouping."[34] It was a necessary haven "for these times of disintegrated social and family life in our villages, towns, and still worse, in cities." The authors write of the Centre as if it was built to construct society in all its biological and familial needs like a building—a kind of social architecture in itself. The design itself was perhaps even more redolent for Stirling. An exposed concrete structure, its three floors cantilevered on all sides and supported on wide wedge-shaped piers on the ground floor, with a central high space for a swimming pool covered with sharply pitched patent glazing, all outfitted with simple but tough technological details, it was an example of a "non-stylistic" modernism to which Stirling was always attracted.

In his discussion of the appropriate "Character" to give to the Centre, Stirling identified the problem as maintaining a sense of "domesticity" while providing a "civic aspect." For Stirling this meant a public envelope—"the external appearance of the building to harmonise with its neighbors," the Town Hall, Church, and Theatre—and a more homely interior, "with its intimate courtyards, smallness of scale and brightly colored finishes" to give it an "essentially domestic character." Colour chips are provided on the opposite page—dark red, yellow, green, ochre and purple, "to be used in combination with grey and white." Four diagrammatic floor plans are coded with these colours, showing the entrance hall, administration, the boiler room, and Youth Centre with its games room and lounge on the ground floor; the library, lounge, restaurant, multi-purpose hall and wide "bridge" between the courtyards for gatherings, on the first floor; the lecture theatre, art gallery and museum, gymnasium, and classrooms on the third floor; and a squash court, elevated gallery reached by a ramp, and terraces on the roof.

All these functions are arranged around two courtyards that are open down to the ground: a smaller "more intimate" one as an extension of the entrance hall, and a larger, more open one overlooking the civic square, and housed in a block supported by Marseilles-like pilotis that ring the rectangle of the Centre. Smaller columns support the interior floors, and the partitions are generally free of the column structure. This gives the illusion of a "free plan," and certainly the floor plates are independently sub-dividable; what it does not

33. Innnis H. Pease and Lucy H. Crocker, *The Peckham Experiment: A Study in the Living Structure of Society* (London: Allen and Unwin, 1943). The Peckham Centre was published in *Architectural Review*, 77 (May 1936): 203–16.

34. Pease and Crocker, *The Peckham Experiment*, 68–69.

do, given the strict alignment of partitions with structure, is exploit the aesthetic or spatial potentials of a Corbusian *plan libre*.

There are in the archive several photographs and a plan of Stirling's first projects for the Centre. The oldest would seem to be represented in the rough sketch model, which shows the three-storey building raised on columns regularly spaced around the perimeter. Gym and squash courts push up from the third floor to form pavilions on the roof connected by a scallop-roofed open walkway; two elongated cone-shaped smoke stacks rise above the roof. Perhaps the most interesting feature of this model is that Stirling indicated the curves of the circulation patterns on each floor in cut-out templates. What is indicated in yellow in the diagrams of the Thesis Book is here made physical as if the free flow of circulation formed a kind of three-dimensional Magritte painting. The entrances from the town and from the civic square are aligned between two courtyards, one square and one rectangular, open through the floors above. More diagrammatic and drastically simplified from the final design, this project is also more "Corbusian" in its use of an access ramp to the first floor shifted at right angles to the entrance, and another ramp from the lower level of the access road to the podium that serves as ground for the Centre and Town Centre. In what seems to be an intermediate stage plan before the final, the columns to the ground floor are suppressed, and the top two floors are supported on large, cylindrical pilotis, giving the air, if not the reality, of a "free plan."

The Thesis design itself was formally presented on seven rendered boards; one composite board; fourteen detail sheets, elevations, and sections coloured in white and light blue accents for floor plates and infill wall surfaces; and four diagrammatic plans with circulation picked out in yellow. Raised up on a stone-faced podium above the traffic circulation into the Town Centre, the Community Centre itself hovers above its entrance courtyards, supported on a combination structure of Marseilles-like pilotis and, on ground level, load-bearing walls. The first and second floors of the Centre are constructed of a monolithic concrete frame resting on a "wedge beam" that in turn transposes the loads down through the pilotis. It is this structure, of course, that has given rise to the myth of a "Corbusian" Thesis, one contradicted, as we shall see, by almost every other detail of the architecture.

It is in the sections, however, that one finds an image of the intense community life envisaged for the Centre: almost every space is filled with activity—the canteen and games room on the ground floor; on the first floor, dancing in the double-height multi-purpose room, billiards and ping-pong, the gymnasium showers, the lending library, citizens' advice bureau, and restaurant; on the second floor, the ramped lecture theatre, art gallery, classrooms, and gymnasium with its double-height roof breaking up into the third floor, which serves as a viewing gallery; squash court on the third floor. Threading vertically through

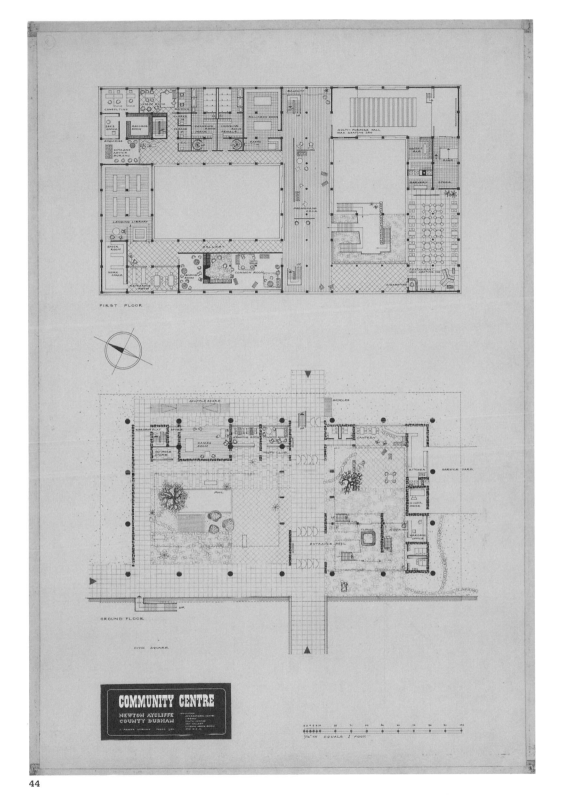

FIRST FLOOR

GROUND FLOOR

COMMUNITY CENTRE
NEWTON AYCLIFFE
COUNTY DURHAM

44. James Frazer Stirling, Community Centre, Newton Aycliffe, Thesis presentation: ground and first-floor plans pen and ink, gouache, traces of graphite with pre-printed label on paper, mounted on cardboard; 75.5 x 50.8 cm (29 ¾ x 20 in); AP140.S1.SS1.D6.P1.1

The final scheme for the Community Centre arranges the facilities around two courtyards: on the ground floor, entered from the north-west and southeast, is the warden's flat, the youth club with swimming pool, and administrative offices. Reached by a wide double stair, the first-floor "promenade deck" (another reminder of Stirling's passion for seeing buildings as "ships") gives on to the multi-purpose hall, the restaurant, lending library, citizens' advice bureau, billiard room and changing rooms for the gymnasium above.

44

45. James Frazer Stirling, Community Centre, Newton Aycliffe, Thesis presentation: second- and third-floor and roof plans
pen and ink, gouache, traces of graphite with preprinted label on paper, mounted on cardboard; 75.7 x 50.7 cm (29 ¾ x 20 in); AP140.S1.SS1.D6.P1.3

The second floor accommodates the lecture theatre, gymnasium, art library and museum, the workers' association offices, and the second floor of the warden's flat that is planned on three floors with the living quarters on the third floor. The roof is dedicated to recreation, with sun-tanning booths, tennis, squash courts, and shuffleboard courts.

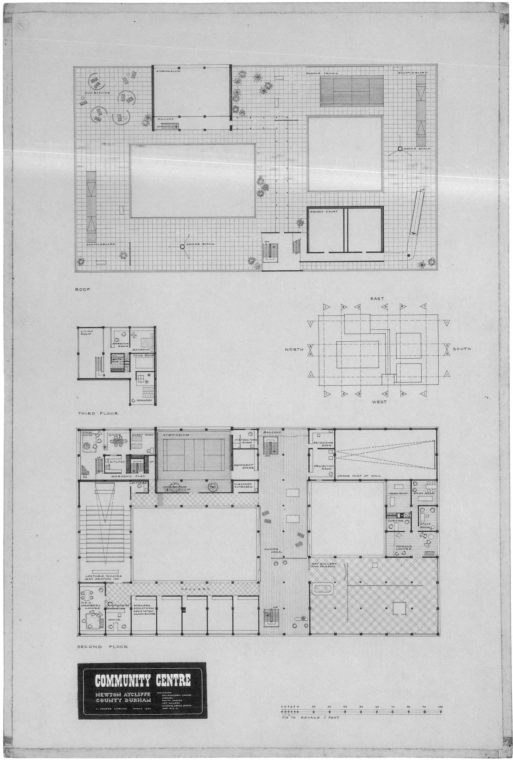

45

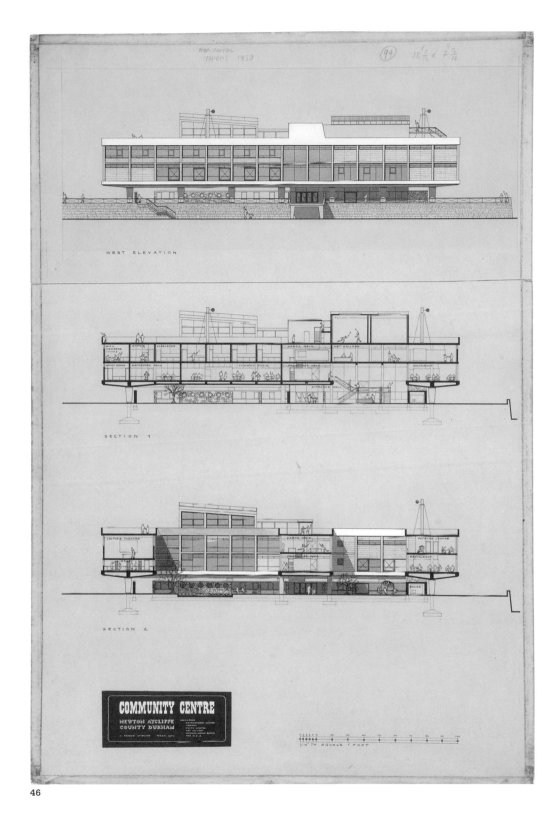

WEST ELEVATION

SECTION 1

SECTION 2

COMMUNITY CENTRE
NEWTON AYCLIFFE
COUNTY DURHAM

46. James Frazer Stirling, Community Centre, Newton Aycliffe, Thesis presentation: west elevation and sections 1 and 2
pen and ink, gouache, traces of graphite with pre-printed label on paper, mounted on cardboard; 75.7 x 50.7 cm (29 ¾ x 20 in); AP140.S1.SS1.D6.P1.2

A close look at these sections reveals how Stirling, always witty in the details, animated his spaces with active figures, dancing, playing squash, eating, reading, and so on. The smoke stack from the boiler room on the ground floor to the roof is topped with a weather vane—a motif that will reappear often in the work, notably in the centre of the courtyard of the Florey Building, Oxford.

46

47. James Frazer Stirling, Community
Centre, Newton Aycliffe, Thesis
presentation: east elevation and
sections 1 and 2
pen and ink, gouache, traces of graphite
with preprinted label on paper,
mounted on cardboard; 75.8 x 50.7 cm
(29 ⅞ x 20 in); AP140.S1.SS1.D6.P.4

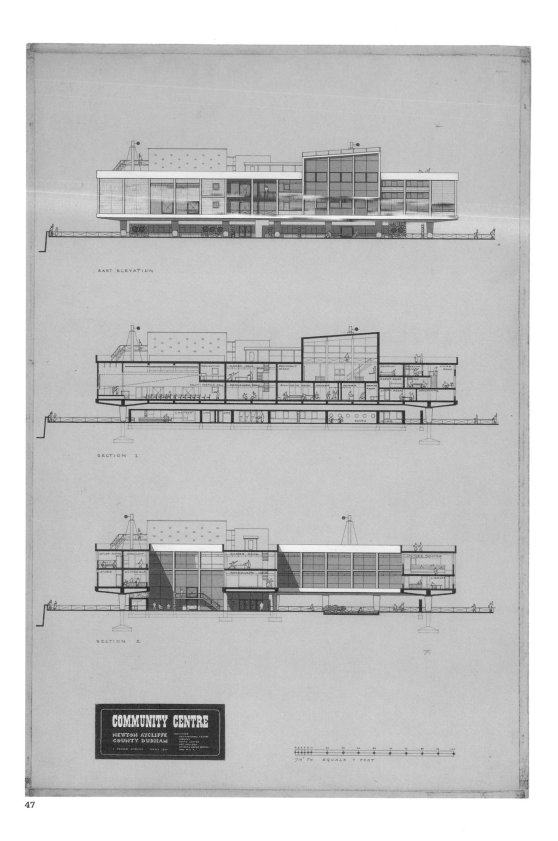

47

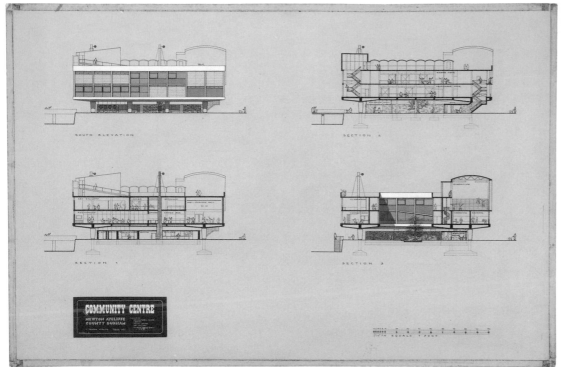

48. James Frazer Stirling, Community Centre, Newton Aycliffe, Thesis presentation: south elevation and sections 1, 2, and 3
pen and ink, gouache, traces of graphite with preprinted label on paper, mounted on cardboard; 50.7 x 76 cm (20 x 29 ⅞ in); AP140.S1.SS1.D6.P1.5

49. James Frazer Stirling, Community Centre, Newton Aycliffe, Thesis presentation: north elevation and sections 1, 2, and 3
pen and ink, gouache, traces of graphite with preprinted label on paper, mounted on cardboard; 50.8 x 75.8 cm (20 x 29 ⅞ in); AP140.S1.SS1.D6.P1.6

50. James Frazer Stirling, Community Centre, Newton Aycliffe, Thesis presentation: perspectives
pen and ink, gouache, traces of graphite with preprinted label on paper, mounted on cardboard; 76.3 x 50.7 cm (30 x 20 in); AP140.S1.SS1.D6.P1.7

The two perspectives show the horizontal block of the building raised on sturdy pilotis, reminiscent of Le Corbusier's Unité d'Habitation, Marseilles, the freestone walls of the facilities on the ground floor, and the reinforced concrete frame infilled with precast panels. As he noted in a passage later cut from the Thesis book, Stirling was against vertical buildings on pilotis, which were in his view only suitable for horizontal compositions.

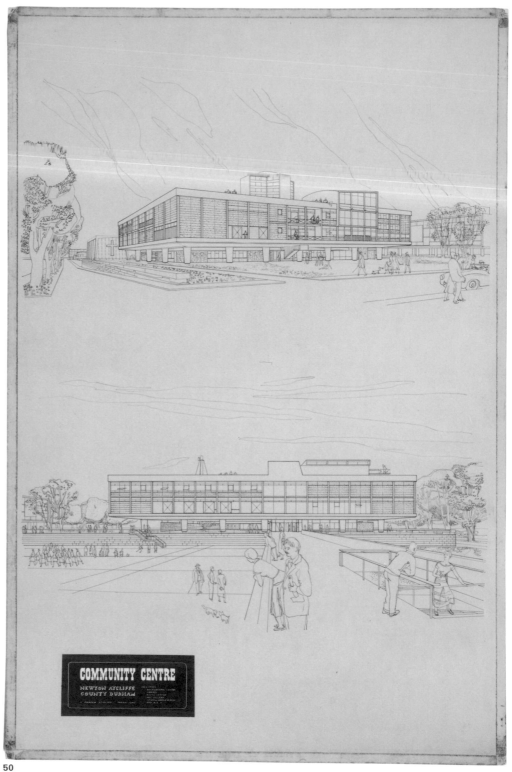

50

these levels the Warden's House forms a complete three-storey living quarters, with double-height studio living room. The figures in the section demonstrate a perfect frenzy of social life: dancing, jumping, reclining.

If style is lightly worn over geometry in the collection of buildings that make up the Town Centre, in the Community Centre, the central focus of the Thesis, it is more deeply worked and developed into a recognizable architecture. Or rather, an architecture with characteristics that would remain evident throughout Stirling's career: an apparent eclectic assemblage of elements drawn from recognizable sources, fused tightly into a coherent volumetric composition. Critics' confusion over Stirling's "style" begins here with the Community Centre, even as it was to continue later. In the light of Stirling's and Rowe's well-publicized struggle with the over-dominant precedent of Le Corbusier, and the Liverpool School's shift towards modernism in the late 1940s, the first and easiest precedent to name for the Community Centre has been consistently that of the French modernist. Stirling himself cited "LC as influence" in his lectures. John Jacobus, in his introduction to *James Stirling. Buildings and Projects 1950–1974*, dutifully followed suit: the Thesis, he wrote, is "graphically akin to Le Corbusier's work," with a façade that resembles the St-Dié factory, and with the *plan libre* "evident throughout."[35] Craig Hodgetts saw the Thesis as influenced by Le Corbusier's Unité d'habitation at Marseilles.

Rowe, whom Robert Maxwell has characterized as introducing both himself and Stirling to a broad stylistic eclecticism, was more circumspect. If for Rowe, Maxwell's thesis, which he advised at the same time, represented "Corbusian erudition … a little bit Tectonicized," Stirling's "not quite routine" Thesis was not as Corbusian as it once appeared.[36] Despite "a Corbusian affiliation (roof episodes, pilotis, ramp)," and despite Jacobus's assertion, the free plan was nowhere to be found. Instead we are here presented with an asymmetrical rendering of the unbuilt Library and Administration Building at I.I.T., raised upon a dubious transfer slab which then supports a volume owing as much to Charles Eames (at Pacific Palisades) as it does to Le Corbusier. Ostensibly this community centre is a type of distended Poissy, a disturbed memory of the Villa Savoye, but only so at top and bottom; and fundamentally, its curious middle is apt to betray rather more Los Angeles (of a certain date) than France. Rather uncharitably, indeed, Rowe was inclined to see the Thesis, with its references to Le Corbusier and Eames stripped away, as the epitome of corporate architecture—say the headquarters of "an oil outfit circa 1965–1970 in the outer suburbs of Houston." However anachronistic the comparison, one was, Rowe asserted, left with "no more than the 'successful' banalities of the 'reliable' corporate office." The project was redeemed in one particular, however: "it is in the agitated roof incident at Newton Aycliffe, far more aggressive (and even Russian) than Lubetkin would have countenanced, that the premonitions of future

35. John Jacobus, "Introduction," *James Stirling: Buildings and Projects 1950–1974*, 15.

36. Rowe, "Introduction," 19.

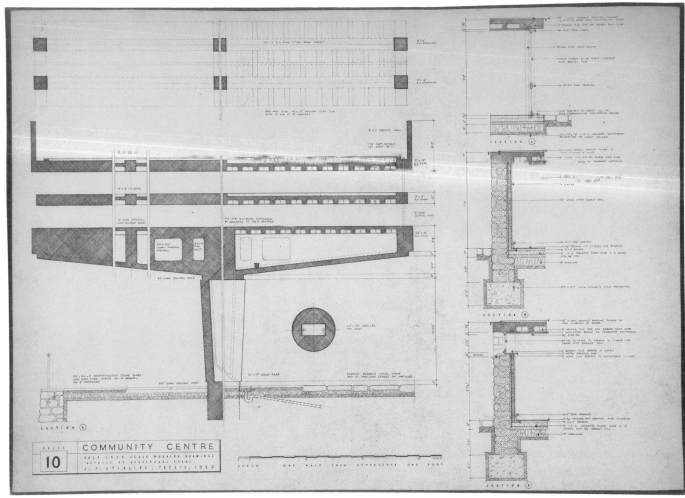

51

51. James Frazer Stirling, Community Centre, Newton Aycliffe, Thesis presentation: structural detail diazotype, mounted on cardboard; 54.6 x 76.4 cm (21 ½ x 30 ⅛ in); AP140.S1.SS1.D6.P3.6

Stirling's Thesis presentation was accompanied by a series of boards developing the scheme in working details; here the pilotis, cantilever, and foundation demonstrate Stirling's attention to construction, later to be developed in his interest in prefabrication.

development are to be deciphered."[37] Reyner Banham, when he saw it exhibited at the Architectural Association in the fall of 1953, simply tagged it "maniera Liverpudliana."

These interpretations all have some value; but on the evidence of Stirling's earlier design projects in 1948–49, it is clear that the predominant influence is more that of Eames (encountered through publications) and Breuer (visited in 1949). Even if we can trace the stone wall that encloses the Youth Centre on the ground level to the stone of the Pavillon Suisse, the more immediate reference would be to the rubble wall supporting Breuer's Tomkin's House on Long Island of 1946 in a style that J.M. Richards would characterize in 1950 as "regional organic."[38] Stirling's version with its porthole windows anticipates his own turn towards a form of regionalism.

37. Rowe, "Introduction, 19.

38. J.M. Richards, "The Next Step," *Architectural Review*, 107, no. 639 (March 1950), p. 137.

On another level, the urge to "domesticity" is countered by the obvious delight Stirling finds in the mechanistic imagery of the roof incidents—the two red-painted weather vanes that top the smoke stacks, themselves held up by tension wires, that give a semi-constructivist air to the whole composition, linking it to the suspended roof of the Auditorium. Perhaps we should not be surprised also to sense a festive tone that, as Craig Hodgetts has noted, comes (for Stirling, dangerously) close to the nearly completed Festival of Britain site—with the technological images of Skylon (Frank Newby and James Gowan) and the Dome of Discovery (Ralph Tubbs) at the service of the New Town of Aycliffe.

There would be one more hidden presence, the image of which would hover behind the Centre design, one that both authorized and rooted the horizontal block raised up on pilotis. In a fragment of text later cut out of the Thesis Book, Stirling developed an aesthetic theory for piloti buildings, under the heading "Aesthetics of Structural Form":

> The natural outcome of placing a building on stilts is to make it hover, that is if the object on the posts has direction horizontal—outwards all round.
>
> To put a box on edge (that is with greater height than breadth) on stilts is to contradict its verticality, this form should plunge into the ground like a spear. To place it on posts is against its direction. Only forms like a slab on its side, a table top, or a lying book, can be placed on posts and hover (Thesis Book, originally p. 30).

Here Stirling, in words that echo the tone of Colin Rowe, speaks to his decision to place the Community Centre on pilotis, in a similar fashion to Le Corbusier at the Pavillon Suisse and Marseilles. But more immediately, this *parti* refers to another absence from the Thesis Book: a page of source photographs, cut out later and displaced to another file, of the buildings of the Liverpool Docks; brick and iron semi-neo-classical structures raised up on pilotis, photographed by Stirling in a perspective similar to that of his own design for the Community Centre. Whether or not the "losing" of this page from the Thesis Book was deliberate, its inclusion provides a clue to the foundational character of what we might call Stirling's double allegiance: to modernism on the one hand, but also to the functional roots of modernism, themselves forged out of traditional building modes. In Stirling's case, the classical motifs of the British functional tradition allowed him to join these strands together, sustaining the thoroughly modern character of the Thesis while giving it a classical/traditional root. In any event, the photographs are evidence that Stirling was interested in regional and regional-classical architecture from the outset.

In this context, it would not be entirely possible to "strip away" the "allusions" to Stirling's sources, as Rowe would have wished. For as a whole, in its proportions and strong structural integrity; in its welding of very diverse

52

52. James Frazer Stirling, photographer, views of Liverpool industrial buildings, or buildings in construction (page detached from Thesis Book, 1950) AP140.S2.SS7.d1.P1.21

These three photographs, originally bound into the Thesis Book, are of a long, horizontal structure, no doubt in Liverpool, that, in the course of either construction or demolition, seem to raise the building up on pilotis as in the Community Centre design.

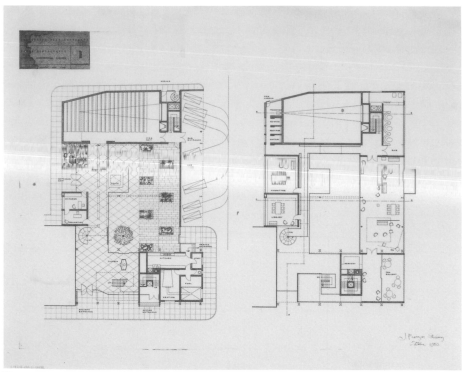

53

functions and complex spatial needs into a tightly compressed single volume,
nesting ramped, double-height, and low-height spaces into the section, with
only the roof allowing for vertical extrusions; in its vibrant understanding of
colour as identification; and above all in its use of circulation to join all the parts
together into a whole, Stirling's Community Centre not only contains the procedures and strategies of his design future, but stands on its own as a tough and
individual statement to be recognized as such by his peers and jurors. Stirling
passed with distinction.

The last Liverpool project, designed before his move to London in the
autumn of 1950, was his entry into the Liverpool Architectural Society's yearly
Honan competition, for the design of a Merseyside Film Institute. The archive
contains three of the original boards for this submission, a design that was later
to be redrawn and much elaborated for the publication of buildings and projects
in 1974.[39] Here Stirling's interest was in structure, materials, and the clear disposition of the functions, articulated in a six-storey tower block and two- and
three-storey extensions. The tower housed the typical offices, the caretaker's
flat on the roof, with roof garden; the ground floor accommodated the entry
foyer and courtyard, the large auditorium, classrooms and services. The structure was in steel, exposed in doubled vertical members outside the skin of the

39. Stirling, *Buildings and Projects 1950–1974*, p 26.

building, so that the floors seemed to hang from its frame leaving them open for flexibility; the accent of exposed steel carried through to the bridge that joined the double-height foyer to the classroom pavilion. The walls are of reinforced concrete precast panels, with the fenestration in standard steel-frame windows organized in strips as needed. The virtues of the open steel frame are clear. As Stirling notes on the drawing: "External walls of office block are removable pre-fabricated units, so that window area can be determined by the type of office and amount of light required, also to facilitate the placing of internal partitions" (Honan Sheet 3).

Architecture in Books

Our designs were eclectic, a necessary stage to the formation of a personal style. The books of Le Corbusier were thus utilized as catalogues, as had been previously the books of Alberti and Palladio in the Renaissance. Thus one's first acquaintance with Corb's buildings, and also the work of Gropius and Mies and the other masters was through the medium of the printed page.
James Stirling, 1957[40]

Throughout his time in the school Stirling was, he and his friends remembered, a voracious reader—or perhaps visual forager would be a more apt term. Le Corbusier, of course—the first two volumes of the *Oeuvre complète* and *Towards a New Architecture* but also the work of Gunnar Asplund, and the modernist round-ups by Alberto Sartoris and Alfred Roth. Perhaps the most interesting among the works listed by Stirling himself as having influenced him during these years was the large folio volume edited by Fritz Saxl and Rudolph Wittkower as a companion to the exhibition, *British Art and the Mediterranean*, published in 1948.[41] Wittkower of course had been the academic advisor of the new member of the Liverpool School of Architecture's history faculty, Colin Rowe, who had graduated in 1948 from the Courtauld before returning to Liverpool. Rowe's own Thesis had been, not incidentally, written on the subject of architecture books, an attempt through a detailed survey of architectural treatises from Alberti through the eighteenth century to piece together a supposed theoretical work by Inigo Jones from the scattered plates left at his death. Indeed the Thesis itself proposed a theory of architecture transmitted and developed through books—Palladio as a quasi-encyclopedic compendium of the Renaissance used, reused and abused for the next three, if not four, centuries. In a seminal article published in the *Architectural Review* of 1947, Rowe had gone further to imply that Palladian compositional techniques and proportional theory underlay the

40. Stirling, "Lecture Notes," c. 1957, cited by Girouard, *Big Jim*, 36.

41. Fritz Saxl and Rudolph Wittkower, *British Art and the Mediterranean* (London: Oxford University Press, 1948).

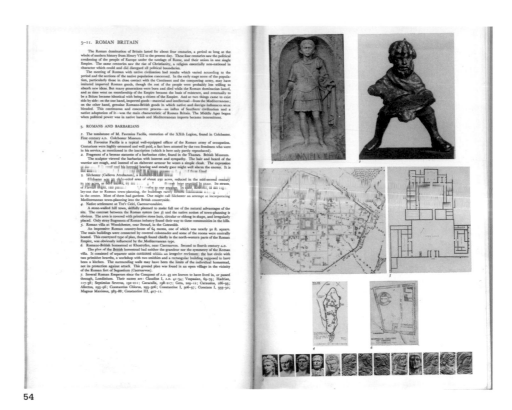

54

54. Fritz Saxl and Rudolph Wittkower, *British Art and the Mediterranean* (London: Oxford University Press, 1948)

Stirling remembered this large compendium of British and Mediterranean examples, a book no doubt suggested by Colin Rowe, who had viewed the Saxl and Wittkower exhibition at the Courtauld Institute. The passages on Roman Britain suggest that earthworks and barrows were in Stirling's mind when designing the raised embankments for Churchill College.

developed villas of Le Corbusier, and then to propose that the volumes of the *Oeuvre complète* as then published represented a similar compendium for twentieth-century modernism to that of Palladio for the Renaissance. In a second article published in 1950, Rowe had continued his comparison of late Renaissance and modern architecture with "Mannerism and Modern Architecture," which argued that the formal ambiguities and transpositions of modernism were related to similar procedures in the Mannerist period, implying that modernism was itself a "late" manner, and condemned to repeat itself endlessly.[42] It was Rowe's belief, exposed in lectures and articles for the next forty years, that there was little left for the contemporary heirs of Le Corbusier but to repeat in varied and academic combinations the already formulated language of modernism he had developed. If, for Rowe, this tendency was to come to fruition in the work of the New York Five, for Stirling, as we shall see, it represented a forceful challenge, one that he would strive to meet for the rest of his life: how to overcome the "exhaustion" of modernist language, and especially that of the so-called International Style after Le Corbusier.

In introducing his teacher Wittkower to Liverpool though the plates and notes of *British Art and the Mediterranean*, Rowe not only confirmed the "eclecticism" noted by Stirling, but implicitly established a "tradition" for the

42. Rowe, "The Mathematics of the Ideal Villa. Palladio and Le Corbusier Compared," *Architectural Review*, 101, no. 603 (March 1947): 101–104; "Mannerism and Modern Architecture," *Architectural Review*, 107, no. 641 (May 1950): 284–300. For an extended discussion of Rowe's theoretical development during the late 1940s and 1950s see my *Histories of the Immediate Present: Inventing Architectural Modernism* (Cambridge Mass.: MIT Press, 2009), 60–104.

student that allowed an entire history of architecture to be written from pre-historic times to the present, the continuing and repeated themes of which, stemming from the Greek and Roman culture of the Mediterranean, might be seen as essentially British. What the British had done with and to classical tradition was not simply a secondary, weak, spin-off, but rather a strong and idiosyncratic architecture in its own right. Side-by-side were arranged: sections through megalithic tombs from Italy and England; Sangallo and Inigo Jones; plates from the *Hypnerotomachia Poliphili* and Hawksmore's spires; the Villa Rotonda and Burlington's Chiswick villa; the Tower of the Winds and the Radcliffe Camera; and, important for Stirling's later exercises in college planning, plans of the Roman foundation of Silchester, and a "Roman British Homestead." This book of images, comparable to, but more organized than, Aby Warburg's image museum newly transported from Hamburg to London, allowed for random and interrelated comparisons: lying open on the floor as too big to shelve, it became the first among Stirling's prioritized 1980 list of source books.[43]

There was, however, another kind of architecture to be found in books, embodied in what Rowe termed the "cult of Auden" at Liverpool.[44] As Rowe remembered it, this affection for the English poet, already an expatriate in the United States, was for his early poetry: "It was the Auden of *Look Stranger* [1936] and *New Year Letter* [1940]." Allied with this was a sense that the topographies and geographies of Auden were in some way allied to those of the Liverpool students: "a taste for geology, climbing, Shropshire, the Long Mynd, Clitheroe, abandoned mills, derelict mine workings, etc."[45] This was a taste shared by many whose affections for the local, the provincial, and the material landscape were less those of a nostalgic "cult of England" than of a newly minted class of upwardly mobile (largely red-brick) university-educated graduates seeking to reconnect with their working-class roots: a taste for the rough, gritty reality of life in the provinces, together with a sense of its connections to a long-established village and town culture. Liverpool University, of course, stood a little apart from the newer red-bricks, and could claim its own civic and urban traditions. But the evident decline of the trans-Atlantic trading economy, and the partially abandoned mines, factories, and shipyards of the hinterland, created a landscape that Stirling, among others, wished to seize and take in as a cultural foundation for his work.

In a study of Auden written by Richard Hoggart,[46] a sociologist of this very uncertain class-confused condition, these tensions become clear in the landscapes evoked by Auden in the 1920s and 1930s, politicized but also alienated landscapes, as in the settings of the play, *The Dog Beneath the Skin*: "dismantled washing-floors," "ramshackle engines," "disused factories, worked out mines," "derelict ironworks on deserted coasts," "tramlines and slagheaps, pieces of

43. Girouard, *Big Jim*, 37.

44. Rowe, "Introduction," 12.

45. Rowe, "Introduction," 12.

46. Richard Hoggart, *Auden: An Introductory Essay* (London: Chatto and Windus, 1951).

55

56

machinery."[47] **Another echo of Auden may also become evident in Stirling's own compositional practices; Hoggart opens his study with a characterization of what the uninitiated reader will find in Auden:**

> He will find competence and virtuousity; carelessness, cliqueishness and obscurity; interest in people, anxiety to reform and concern over the fate of society; impersonality, clinical analysis and drum-beating; he will meet boyishness succeeding maturity, the formal laced with the idiomatic, brilliant diagnoses succeeded by the slapstick of a buffoon, controlled exposition contrasting with slipshod chatter.[48]

More especially, in the body and form of the poetics, there will be inserted "Echoes from Anglo-Saxon and Icelandic sagas ... alongside snippets from the popular press and the music-hall, odd items from scientific textbooks or from

47. Hoggart, *Auden*, 25–26.

48. Hoggart, *Auden*, 13.

musical analysis are mixed with debts to Eliot, Owen, Housman."[49] Hoggart sees Auden as one who "thinks joking a release, a protection against morbid self regard, who loves fantastic, slightly surrealistic fun ... and likes the jibe with a moral point."[50] Much the same might be said of Stirling's handling of architecture, high and low, theoretical and practical. Certainly, with many of his generation, he partook of Auden's sense that with the era of the "greats" over, what was left to the succeeding generation were shards of a former history, and the dismantling of the utopian fantasies that stimulated the first architects of the modern movement:

> It's our turn now
>   to puzzle the unborn. No world
> wears as well as it should but, mortal or not.
>   a world has still to be built
> because of that we can see from our windows,
>   that Immortal Commonwealth
> which is there regardless; it's in perfect taste
>   and it's never boring but
> it won't quite do. Among its populations
>   are masons and carpenters
> who build the most exquisite shelters and safes,
>   but no architects, any more
> than there are heretics or bounders: to take
>   umbrage at death, to construct
> a second nature of tomb and temple, lives
>   must know the meaning of If.[51]

55. Colin Rowe, "Mathematics of the Ideal Villa," *Architectural Review* (March 1947), p. 101

Colin Rowe's two articles for the *Architectural Review* in 1947 and 1950 were an important source of inspiration for the brief flowering of a Palladian revival in the early 1950s. Rowe's comparison of the Villa Malcontenta and the Villa Rotonda with the Villa Stein at Garches and the Villa Savoye at Poissy allowed for an abstract rather than a historical understanding of proportional systems and spatial organization. For Stirling they were a key to the understanding of Le Corbusier, and a spur for his own, revisionist, articles in the *Architectural Review* in 1955 and 1956.

56. Colin Rowe, "Mannerism and Modern Architecture," *Architectural Review* (May 1950)

The idea of Mannerism, introduced into art history in the early 1920s by German and Austrian historians, was applied to architecture by, among others, Colin Rowe's tutor at the Courtauld, Rudolf Wittkower. Rowe applied it directly to what he saw as an aspect of modernism interested in formal inversions, scale changes, and spatial transformations of academic formulae. Stirling, from occasional notes in his lectures, seems to have accepted that modernism was "Mannerist" in sensibility, and sometimes referred to his own work in this way.

49. Hoggart, *Auden*, 13.

50. Hoggart, *Auden*, 14.

51. W.H. Auden, "Thanksgiving for a Habitat, I. Prologue: The Birth of Architecture" [spring 1962], *Collected Poems*, ed. Edward Mendelson (New York: Random House, 1991), 687–88.

CONTEXT
THE AR

UALIZING
CHIVE

The archive materials for the period 1950 to 1954 are less voluminous than either those of Stirling's school years or those for projects after 1974. No doubt this is the result of the office move from Gloucester Place in 1986, or the pruning of documents following the publication of the first volume of work in 1974. Nevertheless, while there are fewer design development drawings, those that remain, together with the more finished renderings, demand a certain contextualization, setting them in the historical framework of contemporary architecture and its critical discourse, as well as in the continuity of Stirling's practice. Stirling's idea of "contextualism" is, of course, very different from that of "fitting in" to a context; rather it refers to the ability of an architectural expression to engage its context, animate it, and develop it out of its present state, without destroying its best historical features. "Vernacular" also takes on a different cast with Stirling, who understands architecture in a formal and volumetric sense rather than in any stylistic formula. This combination of materials, forms, and programmatic renewal that is present in his rural and urban projects, from the CIAM Village scheme to Preston, is also present in the so-called "red-brick" series of designs from Leicester through Cambridge to Oxford, but with a different context there emerges a different formal and material approach. The move from Preston to Runcorn, as a reformulation of previous difficulties with rehousing and New Town policy, joins a sense of historical fabric (Bath) to the demand for prefabrication (St Andrews, Runcorn) that is brought together in the under-studied project for Lima self-build housing. Finally, while the three German museum projects, from Düsseldorf through Cologne to Stuttgart, have been seen as breaking with earlier design strategies, the drawings in the archive demonstrate a clear continuity with his former practices—analysis of the program, separation of its elements into volumetric units, and combination of the units through circulation. The only real difference between the museums and earlier single building projects is the insertion of these elements in the existing fabric rather than their elementarist composition into autonomous buildings.

II. Modernism Redux, 1950–1954

The Conflict of Modernisms: London 1950

Let's face it. William Morris was a Swede.

James Stirling[52]

Frequently I awake in the morning and wonder how it is that I can be an architect and an Englishman at the same time, particularly a modern architect. Since the crystallization of the modern movement around about 1920, Britain has not produced one single masterpiece.

James Stirling, 1954[53]

London after the end of hostilities in 1945 was, to say the least, depressing, and the attempts of the government to jolly things up by launching the Festival of Britain in 1951 rang false to many of the architects of Stirling's generation.[54] The evocation of an industrially progressive nation settled comfortably into a rural arcadia promoted by the exhibits. However, the contrast between the "soft" modernism of the Festival Hall and the technological possibilities inherent in the otherwise useless Skylon (on the design of which Stirling's future partner James Gowan had worked with Powell and Moya), together with the increasing fashion for "Swedish modern" in both design and urban planning, were troubling to those who, returned from a brutal war and inspired by the apparent rigour of the modern pioneers—Le Corbusier and Mies—were also inclined towards a use of materials that was, so to speak, materialistic, whether or not in the political sense. Modernism, arriving late in England, and seen as "imported" (not only figuratively, but literally with the arrival of the European exiles—Lubetkin, Goldfinger, Fry, then Gropius and Breuer), was by 1945 extremely diverse, and lacked the theoretical or moral grounds of the first generation. Indeed, J.M. Richards, writing under the title "The Next Step" and admitting that "It is too soon to label and classify," proceeded to classify no

52. Remark by James Stirling cited in Reyner Banham, *The New Brutalism: Ethic or Aesthetic?* (London: The Architectural Press, 1966), 11.

53. Crinson, ed., *James Stirling: Early Unpublished Writings on Architecture*, 34.

54. By far the best account of this period in British architectural development is Nicholas Bullock, *Building the Postwar World: Modern Architecture and Reconstruction in Britain* (London: Routledge, 2002).

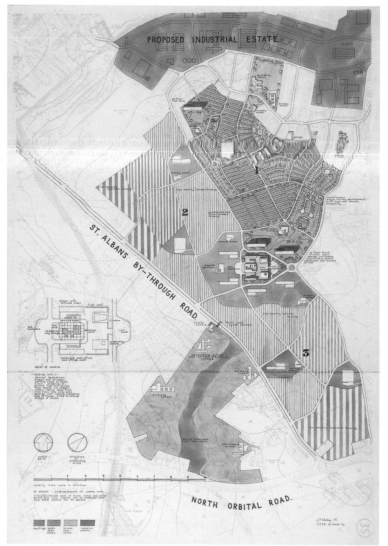

57. James Frazer Stirling,
Redevelopment of Camp Area, St Albans,
England: site plan, 1951
pen and ink, watercolor and graphite
on reprographic copy; 104.2 x 72.5 cm
(41 x 28 ½ in); AP140.S1.SS1.D8.P1

Stirling's brief experience as a
postgraduate student at the School of
Town Planning and Regional Research
in London led to two plans for the
redevelopment of St Albans, where
he experimented with housing types
that were both adopted from the
Corbusian lexicon and reworked from
the prototypes being explored
by the younger architects who later
formed the nucleus of Team X.

57

fewer than eleven varieties of modern architecture current in Britain.[55] He lists:
the "Pioneers" from Le Corbusier to Maillart; the "International Style" as exemplified by the Peckham Health Centre; "Routine Functionalism" in a 1949 project
for flats at Poplar in London; "Formalist" in the work of T.S. Tait; "Neo-Classical"
as revived by Piacentini in Rome; the "Mechanistic" approach of designers like
Buckminster Fuller; the "Machine Aesthetic" of Mies, Johnson, and the schools
of the Hertfordshire County Architect's Department; a "Diagrammatic Modern" as championed by Pietro Belluschi; the "Post-Cubist" style of Bakema; the
"Regional Organic" of Frank Lloyd Wright and Breuer, but also of Basil Spence,
as they searched for a "new regionalism"; and finally what Richards calls the

55. J.M. Richards, "The Next Step," *Architectural Review*,
107, no. 639 (March 1950): 169–78.

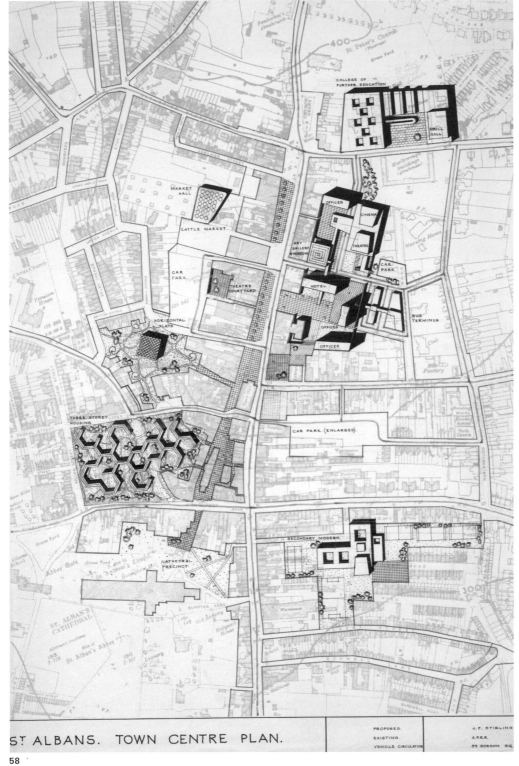

ST ALBANS. TOWN CENTRE PLAN.

PROPOSED.
EXISTING.
VEHICLE CIRCULATION

J.F. STIRLING
A.P.R.R.
34 GORDON SQ

58

58. James Frazer Stirling, Town Centre
Plan, St Albans: site plan, 1951
ink and graphite on reprographic copy;
80.2 x 54.3 cm (31 ½ x 21 ⅜ in);
AP140.S1.SS1.D9.P1

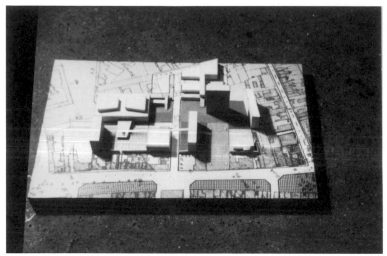

59

59. James Frazer Stirling, Town Centre Plan, St Albans: view of model, 1951 gelatin silver print; 10.6 x 15.8 cm (4 ⅛ x 6 ¼ in); AP140.S1.SS1.D9.P2

"Empirical Organic"—from Aalto and the Swedish movement to Shepherd and Partners—that sought "inspiration in the particular (site, structure and materials for example) rather than in the general." "By such and similar means," concluded Richards somewhat optimistically, "the process begins of introducing a new emotional content into the solid framework of the contemporary idiom."[56]

Resistance to what was seen as this second-hand, eclectic pseudo-modernism took many architectural forms. First there was the group within the London County Council that, taking the example of the Unité d'habitation at Marseilles, attempted to construct "community" as well as housing in high-density flats: Colin St John Wilson's housing at Roehampton was an example. Then there were those for whom Mies van der Rohe, in his uncompromising allegiance to steel construction and its aesthetic qualities, was an example of a continued modernist practice—the Smithsons' project for Hunstanton was the paradigm selected by Banham for this approach, which he named the "New Brutalism."

Stirling himself, following the path already laid out by his Thesis, first turned to the further study of town-planning, enrolling in the diploma course at the School of Town Planning and Regional Research, a course which he was not to complete, but which produced two plans for the St Albans area: one on the outskirts, proposing a neighbourhood centre and housing for a former military camp by the North Orbital Road, with a mixture of terrace housing, single family dwellings and two Unité type blocks for a thousand inhabitants each. The second plan, for a new Town Centre for the city, echoed his Thesis project, but with the addition of a spiral art gallery modeled on Le Corbusier's "Museum of Unlimited Growth." Here, breaking with the modern prototypes for slab and terrace housing, Stirling experimented with two typologies that countered the

56. J.M. Richards, "The Next Step," p. 78.

orthodox CIAM models: a "mat" project for what he called "horizontal flats" clustered together in a square chequer-board pattern, and a "net" project of three-storey housing, its continuous spine forming a hexagonal network. This mat solution was also extended to the "College of Further Education," a two-storey building punctured by a regular series of square courtyards. Both these housing types were a distinct departure from the range of possibilities considered in the meetings of CIAM, representing a first indication of the conversations among Stirling, the Smithsons, and their circle over potential new forms of urban redevelopment—diagramming terms like "cluster" and "network." The town centre plan itself was more sensitive to the existing city than many of the schemes exhibited at CIAM 8, "The Heart of the City," at Hoddesdon in 1951.

Struggling with Corb

The Paris Corbs are disappointing, one knows them so well from the books, it is a sad shock to see them in their natural habitat. My first impression is disappointment, just as when I saw Pav. Suisse five years ago.

James Stirling, 1954[57]

It was in projects designed between 1951 and 1953 that Stirling was drawn to test and implicitly to challenge the object of his first modernist affection: Le Corbusier. We have noted the very early presence of the Golden Section in the section of "The House for the Architect," and this search for the right proportional system for architecture—a question opened up for Stirling's generation by Wittkower's unexpectedly popular *Architectural Principles in the Age of Humanism* of 1949, the publication of Le Corbusier's *Modulor* in the following year, and impelled by the drive for modular standardization in the postwar school-building programs, notably in Hertfordshire—was present in the Core and Crosswall House of 1951 and in his long discussion of the *Modulor* (translated in 1951) in the Black Notebook of 1954. A single drawing in the archive shows how Stirling worked out the system of the Modulor for his own reference. The elegant Core and Crosswall house, a rectangular three-storey row house between two crosswalls with a central stair and bathroom core, was originally envisaged in brick, but in the redrawing for the "Black" volume became a structure in reinforced concrete throughout. Its façade was carefully proportioned according to square and diagonal *traces régulateurs*, and rhythmically structured in alternating short and longer bays. The Stiff Dom-ino housing prototype adopts the additive, domino-like character of Le Corbusier's original "Dom-ino" structure-type, but where Le Corbusier constructs his model as a prototype of the free plan, with columns

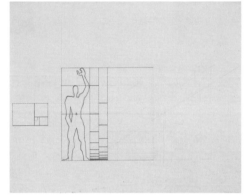

60

60. James Frazer Stirling, Diagram of Le Corbusier's "Modulor." ink and graphite on translucent paper; 39.5 x 47.3 cm (15 ½ x 18 ⅝ in); AP140.S1.SS2.D1.P1.2

An undated study reproducing the proportional system invented by Le Corbusier and published in the two volumes of *Le Modulor* between 1948 and 1955. British architects in Stirling's circle were keenly debating the merits of proportional systems, following the publication of Rudolf Wittkower's influential book *Architectural Principles in the Age of Humanism* in 1949.

57. Crinson, ed., *James Stirling: Early Unpublished Writings*, 31.

pulled back from the edge of the slab, and formulates it as a golden-section rectangle in plan, with a free-floating stair cutting up through the floor-plates, Stirling, in line with his renaming, stiffens up the type. Square in plan with fixed central stair core, the three-storey "house" is constructed as a precast reinforced concrete post-and-beam and slab system, forming a mass-produced unit which could be arranged singly or in clusters or terraces. The precast slabs are seated on the beams forming a pin-wheel around the stair in each unit. Completing this series of experimental mass-produced houses is the design for a "House in North London" of 1953, planned within two squares, slipped in order to provide for a range of additive combinations in a row or isolated.

But it was in two competitions between 1951 and 1953 that Stirling began to approach what he felt was his own manner, independent of direct Corbusian influence, or rather demonstrating the kind of independence of form-making that subsumed any influence into a larger comprehensive language. The first, a competition for Poole Technical College, entered in October 1951, almost immediately on Stirling's arrival in London, is, on the surface, a reworking of the earlier schemes for the Honan competition, with an eight-storey slab and adjoining two-storey bar, but with a distinct difference. The reinforced concrete frame is not in-filled with brick but is expressed "as 'skin' clothing the façade."[58] The windows follow an individual pattern that at first seems random, but which is "in fact an expression of the variation of room sizes and functions behind the façade." Stirling argues:

> We have become accustomed to the expression of the Georgian façade, and tend to forget that this pattern is only logical where the wall is structural (the spaces between the windows being, in fact, stanchions). To continue this tradition would be illogical. Now that

61. James Frazer Stirling, Core and Crosswall House, United Kingdom: plans, sections and elevations, 1951 graphite on paper; 21 x 29.7 cm (8 ¼ x 11 ¾ in); AP140.S2.SS1.D2.P1.1

The Core and Crosswall house was designed in response to the prevailing narrower party-wall plan, and here in accordance with Corbusian proportional systems.

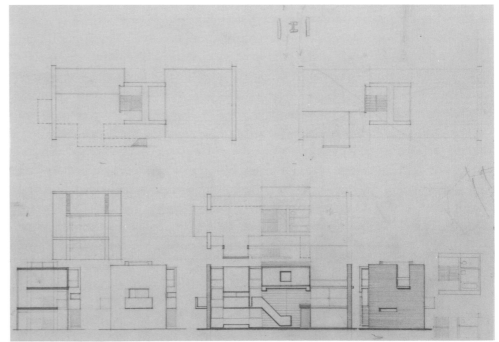

61

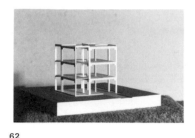

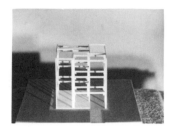

62 63 64 65

the façade is free from the dominating pattern of the frame, window sizes can be varied according to the amount of light required by the internal accommodation.[59]

With the façade free, the inside functions are expressed directly on the out-side—a maxim of the early functionalists that was largely honored in the breach in favor of horizontal strip windows or glass curtain walls.

In his competition report Stirling also hints toward a principle that would become even more pronounced in his later university work: under the heading "Character," he writes:

A definite attempt has been made to give the buildings a "technical" appearance—it being considered that the function of the college was more similar to that of a technical school than to a University (the atmosphere of the precinct and cloister) and also as distinctly different from the now over-familiar appearance of the postwar secondary modern school.[60]

Poole, he later recognized, represented a distinct shift from Corbusian prec-edents, and a "next move" that would allow him to experiment with the "traditional low-cost material" of Britain—brick. Its compact plan was also a sign of Stirling's increasing interest in circulation as what he called an "arma-ture or skeleton onto which rooms fastened."[61]

Even more "characteristic" of the nature of the given program was Stirling and Alan Cordingley's entry into the national competition for an exten-sion to Sheffield University. Critics have seized on this project as representing a fundamental beginning for Stirling, largely as a result of the exposed sec-tions of the auditoria on the façade—an anticipation, it has been felt, of the projecting auditoria of the Leicester Engineering Building. This may be so. But the real importance of the project lay in its bold site-planning gesture, and the masterly handling of differentiated volumes in three dimensions—plan, sec-tion, and elevation—irrespective of any future specific allusions, or superficial resemblance in length and roof articulation to Le Corbusier's Secretariat at Chandigarh. Once more, and this was indeed an anticipation, the building, as

62–65. James Frazer Stirling, Stiff Dom-ino Housing: views of models, 1951
gelatin silver print;
7.4 x 10.5 cm (2 ⅞ x 4 ⅛ in) /
7.4 x 9.5 cm (2 ⅞ x 3 ¾ in) /
7.4 x 10.5 cm (2 ⅞ x 4 ⅛ in) /
4.8 x 6.6 cm (1 ⅞ x 2 ⅝ in),
AP140.S2.SS1.D3.P2.1 / .P2.2 / .P2.3 / .P2.4

Another response to the Corbusian paradigm of the "Dom-ino" house of 1914; as opposed to the horizontal slab on columns that allowed for the full development of the free plan, Stirling prefers a prefabricated structural system, the framing of which allowed for vertical circulation. The result is an entirely different conception of space, from the open horizontality of Le Corbusier's "ineffable" space, to Stirling's box-like framing that accentu-ated volumetric definition.

58. James Stirling, "Poole College of Further Education: Report," Part 1, Stirling/Wilford fonds, CCA, AP140.S2.SS1.D4.P6

59. Stirling, "Poole College Report," p. 2.

60. Stirling, "Poole College Report," p.6.

61. James Stirling, "An Architect's Approach to Architecture," *Journal of the Royal Institute of British Architects* (May 1965): 231.

66

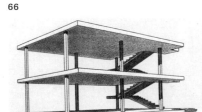

67

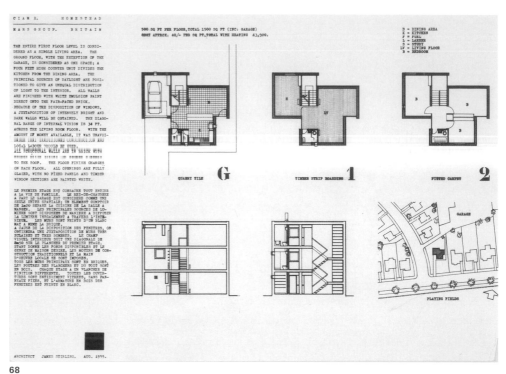

68

66. James Frazer Stirling, Stiff Dom-ino Housing: axonometric, 1951
ink, graphite and colored pencil on translucent paper; 32.7 x 29.6 cm (12 ⅞ x 11 ⅝ in) (irreg.); AP140.S2.SS1.D3.P1.1

67. Le Corbusier, Dom-ino House, 1914, Le Corbusier et Pierre Jeanneret, *Oeuvre Complète 1910–1929*, ed. W. Boesiger and O. Stonorov (Zurich: Les Editions d'Architecture, 14th ed. 1995), 23.

68. James Frazer Stirling, House in North London, Mill Hill, London: photograph of plans and sections, 1953
gelatin silver print; 16.8 x 23.5 cm (6 ⅝ x 9 ¼ in); AP140.S2.SS1.D6.P2.3

This prototype house, designed in 1953, was submitted by Stirling as a part of his contribution to CIAM 10 in 1955. As conceived it could either stand alone or be combined as terrace housing. It is a direct outcome of the Stiff Dom-ino idea, and geometrically framed within two intersecting squares in plan.

69. James Frazer Stirling, Poole College of Further Education, Poole, England: elevation and section, 1951
ink and graphite on paper; 56.1 x 76.5 cm (22 ⅛ x 30 ⅛ in); AP140.S2.SS1.D4.P3.7

In this entry to a national competition, Stirling used brick as the infill to the reinforced concrete structure, in anticipation of the later Flats at Ham Common.

69

at Poole, was considered to be a complex piece of machinery with elements joined to a circulation "spine or driving axle on to which rooms were connected like a mechanized assembly."[62] Along this spine in the main building, the Architecture School, the Arts School, the Staff Quarters and the Administration were ranged in four distinct units linked together by vertical stair cores.

It is significant that it is to this project and not to another that Stirling links a paragraph of writing describing his reactions to the three-dimensional figure–ground experiments of Luigi Moretti, published in his journal *Spazio* in 1952–53 and introduced to Stirling by his friend Sam Stevens.[63] Here the redrawing for the "Black" volume (1974), elsewhere flattening and stylistically over-unifying, takes on considerable significance. The new drawing, no doubt by Léon Krier, concentrates on two major elements of the project, abstracted and given formal authority in their own right: the roof, which is depicted in axonometric projection precisely in order to distinguish it from Le Corbusier's at Marseilles or Chandigarh as an array of mechanically distributed functional volumes disposed along the roof, and the intricate connection—like some important engine part viewed in cut axonometric from below—between ramp, lecture hall, and stair that locks together the four units of the slab. In this context the citation of Moretti gains force. As Stirling wrote,

A few years ago, Luigi Moretti illustrated in "Spazio" the plaster castings taken from inside accurate models of certain historical buildings. By treating the external surface [of] the inner constructions of a building as a three-dimensional negative or mould, he was able to obtain a solidified space.

If space can be imagined as a solid mass determined in shape and time by the proportion of a room or the function of a corridor, then an architectural solution could be perceived by the consideration of alternative ways in which the various elements of the program could be plastically assembled.

It is not assumed that every element should be expressive, but it is important that a hierarchy of the most significant volumes is recognisable in the ultimate composition. Within practical limits, room shapes are variable and the different ways of assembling accommodation, circulation, etc. may be almost infinite; nevertheless a design will start to emerge in the imagination when the relationship of space appears to have coherent organisational pattern. At this moment of coagulation, however, the cerebral exercise loses its abstract value as it is necessary for it to materialize as substance; and a successful transition from organizational pattern into structure and materials is dependent upon the author's structural vocabulary. Through its selection the method of support should assist the ideogram of the space organisation.[64]

Here Stirling takes the purely formal play of volumes created by modeling the interiors of classic buildings as solid masses, and transforms it into a precept

70

71

70. James Frazer Stirling with Alan Cordingley, competition for University of Sheffield, England: site plan, 1953 gelatin silver print; 21.7 x 16.5 cm (8 ½ x 6 ½ in); AP140.S2.SS1.D7.P3.1

This scheme, designed together with Alan Cordingley, was the first project to launch Stirling's reputation as a powerful form-giver. The overall plan stems from his already clear desire to relate to historical spaces—here the parallelogram of St Marks Square, Venice. It was exhibited at the Architectural Association where it gained the attention of a critic who was to be a life-long support, Reyner Banham.

71. Ralph Tubbs, "The Heart of the City," plan, from Ralph Tubbs, *Living in Cities* (Harmondsworth: Penguin Books, 1942), p. 36.

62. Stirling, "An Architect's Approach to Architecture," 232.

63. Luigi Moretti, "Strutture e sequenze di spazi," *Spazio*, 7 (December 1952–April 1953): 9–20.

64. Stirling, note (1953) on detached fragment in Poole archive, annotated "Sheffield," and published in his later article, "The Functional Tradition and Expression," *Perspecta* 6 (1960): 88–97, and in *James Stirling: Buildings and Projects 1950–1974*, 29.

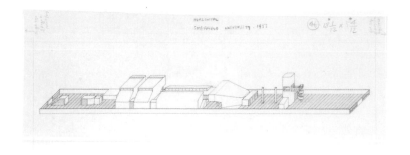

72

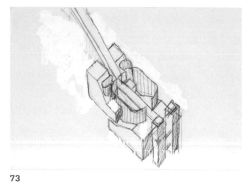

73

for the bringing together of different functions in a tightly organized circulation system through the volumetric play of their individual forms, welded so to speak into a single volume with a complex interior structure.

Perhaps we can indeed make a connection in this case with the otherwise strange exhibit Stirling and his colleagues constructed for the *This is Tomorrow* exhibition at the Whitechapel Art Gallery three years later, where the papier-maché and plaster simulation of the topologies of soap bubbles have always seemed anomalous in Stirling's formal development. In this exhibition, collaborating with artists Richard Matthews and Michael Pine, Stirling developed a theory of architecture as a total environment that would guide him throughout his career. While the large-scale model of detergent soap bubbles was perhaps more the work of his team mates, this statement was, together with his observations on Moretti, indicative of his fundamental desire for architecture to become a player in its own right as an avant-garde, three-dimensional, total environment: "Why clutter up your building with 'pieces' of sculpture when the architect can make his medium so exciting that the need for sculpture will be done away with and its very presence nullified?" In the contemporary condition, where the arts have lost vitality to architecture, the artist now becomes simply a "consultant" to the architect, parallel to the structural engineer or quantity surveyor. In keeping with the gradual dissolving of boundaries among the arts, the elements of architecture themselves will begin to fuse: "the wall at least is beginning to go. The next step will be with the volume of the building, which at present is based on structural geometry … Finally the total plastic expression (architecture, painting, sculpture) will be in the landscape with no fixed composition, but made up of people, volumes, components—in the way that trees, all different, all growing, all disrupted into each other, are brought together in an integrated clump." Here Stirling anticipates his own volumetric development: from the single unit, to the combination of units into a single building, to the assemblage of buildings into the city, to the city itself as an architectural object where public, private, inside, and outside are ambiguously

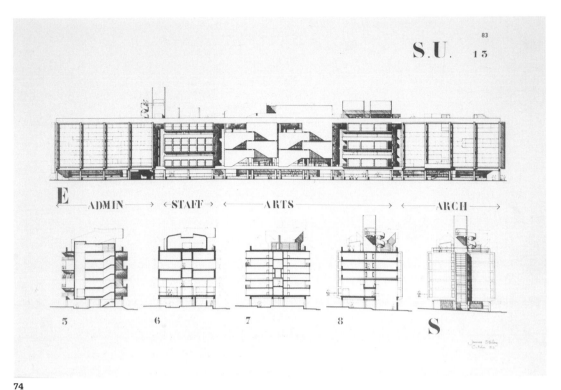

74

74. James Frazer Stirling with Alan Cordingley, University of Sheffield: photograph of elevations and sections, 1953
gelatin silver print: 23 x 34 cm (9 1/16 x 13 3/8 in); AP140.S2.SS1.D7.P4.2

The plastic forms of the auditoria, exposed in side elevation in the central module of the block, have been seen as anticipating the cantilevered lecture rooms of Stirling and Gowan's later Leicester University Engineering Building. Here they are part of a tightly articulated and spatially modulated design that reveals the different functions that make up the college: the School of Architecture, classrooms, lecture theatres, staff rooms, and college administration.

75. James Frazer Stirling with Alan Cordingley, University of Sheffield: photograph of elevations and sections, 1953
gelatin silver print; 24.9 x 29.6 cm (9 3/4 x 11 5/8 in); AP140.S2.SS1.D7.P4.6

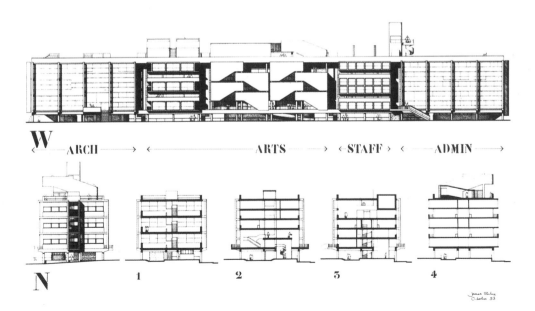

75

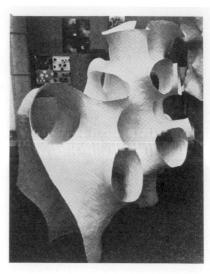

76   77   78

76. Luigi Moretti (1907–73), "Strutture e sequnze di spazi," *Spazio* 7 (December 1952–April 1953), p. 9

Moretti cast solid models of the interior spaces of canonical buildings—here Guarino Guarini's project for the church of S. Filippo Neri, Casale Monferrato (1737), compared with, bottom right, Frank Lloyd Wright's project for the Glen McCord House, 1948. Moretti refers to the "internal empty space" of architecture as a "negative matrix," the "richest seed, mirror, or symbol of the entire architectural reality" (pp. 10–11).

77. James Frazer Stirling, Michael Pine, Richard Matthews, "This is Tomorrow," catalogue of the exhibition at the Whitechapel Art Gallery, August 1956

While often discounted, and by Stirling himself, as having little to do with his developed vocabulary, this experiment in modeling the forms of detergent soap bubbles relates directly to his understanding of Moretti, as well as his sense that architecture, by itself, has fundamental sculptural qualities.

78. James Frazer Stirling, photographer, "This is tomorrow" sculpture in exhibition space gelatin silver print; 10.4 x 8.3 cm (4 ⅛ x 3 ¼ in); AP140.S2.SS7.D1.P1.18

fused.[65] Certainly it is not incidental that Stirling originally used the quotation from Moretti in the article "'The Functional Tradition' and Expression," of 1960, his most extended essay on the theory of regional vernacular in this period, as part of his argument that traditional, functional buildings accommodated their needs in directly responding, coherently composed, volumetric elements.[66]

Equally indicative of his evolving attitude towards site-planning, and away from the already commonplace modernist disposition of separate buildings on a podium, is the way in which in the Sheffield project, despite dividing the functions—Library, Arts and Architecture, Physics, Medical and Student Union—into separate buildings, they are placed on the site as if to form a grand public square (the Piazza San Marco comes to mind) as an ensemble, with the Library as a square pavilion acting as a hinge point to the northwest, and the Student Union closing the composition to the southeast. In his notes for a lecture at the Architectural Association School during the exhibition of the Sheffield competition projects, on 21 February 1954, he admitted that the site had a "Renaissance quality about it (superficial resemblance to St Mark's Venice)," but observed that "this sort of thing is not unlikely to arise, as I consider there is nothing fundamentally new about modern architecture."[67] Perhaps this sense of continuity in history reflects the increasing influence of Rowe, later to explode into the drawings for the "Roma Interrotta" exhibition, but more likely it is the combined influence of Cordingley, who would later become an architectural historian at City College in New York, and Stirling's own growing interest in expanding the references in order to expand the language. More specifically, the application of St Mark's Square to modern town-planning techniques was stimulated by the

65. Theo Crosby, ed., *This is Tomorrow*, exhibition catalogue, Whitechapel Art Gallery, London (1956).

66. James Stirling, "The 'Functional Tradition' and Expression," *Perspecta* 6 (1960): 88–97.

67. Crinson, ed., *James Stirling: Early Unpublished Writings*, 24.

example of Ralph Tubbs, the designer of the Dome of Discovery at the Festival of Britain (1948–51), whose projects for rebuilding cities' inner cores after the war were exhibited in his exhibition "Living in Cities," designed for the 1940 Council of the British Institute of Adult Education and published by Penguin Books in a popular edition in 1942.[68] In his proposal for an ideal plan for the "Heart of the City," Tubbs arranges rows of terrace housing, blocks of flats and sports and community facilities around a green in the shape of St Mark's Square beside a photograph of the piazza from the air, with the caption "Perfectly balanced but informal grouping of buildings and spaces—expression of the free spirit."[69]

From Garches to Jaoul and Ronchamp

The desire to deride the schematic basis of modern architecture and the ability to turn a design upside down and make it architecture are symptomatic of a state when the vocabulary is not being extended, and a parallel can be drawn with the Mannerist period of the Renaissance. Certainly the forms which have developed from the rationale and the initial ideology of the modern movement are being mannerized and changed into a conscious imperfectionism.

James Stirling, 1956[70]

It was in late 1953 that Stirling began to record his observations about architecture and design in a large-format account book, named by Girouard the "Black Notebook." Actually a dark blue notebook, its pages chronicle Stirling's attempts to come to grips with the inheritance of the modernist avant-garde through reading notes, rough notes for articles or lectures, records of his travels in Paris, and personal observations of contemporary practitioners. This notebook, in the possession of Mary Stirling, has recently been painstakingly transcribed and annotated by Mark Crinson and published together with other unpublished writings by Stirling; it forms an invaluable critical commentary on the projects and buildings in the CCA archive.[71]

The process of criticizing and expanding the language of modernism—expressed in the Black Notebook "resolution for 1954"—involved "exploiting the aesthetic through the structural potentialities of the various types of construction integrated into the programmatic circulation solutions."[72] Stirling called on himself to design four houses (perhaps the Core and Crosswall, Stiff Dom-ino, and North London houses fulfilled part of this resolution), and to "do a competition" that allowed for the "integration of a structural 'idea' with a spatial and circulatory complex." This of course he had already completed with Sheffield in October of 1953. But his real obsession, as revealed in these notes,

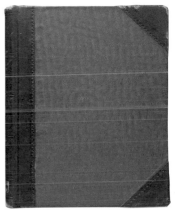

79

79. James Frazer Stirling, the Black Notebook, 1953–56. Courtesy of Mary Stirling

This invaluable notebook records Stirling's reading notes, observations on architecture in London and in Paris, and notes for articles published and unpublished, as well as many lecture notes folded into its pages. It is central to an understanding of his evolving attitudes to British modern architecture, and to Le Corbusier's move from rationalism to expressionism and vernacular style in Ronchamp and the Maisons Jaoul.

68. Ralph Tubbs, *Living in Cities* (Harmondsworth: Penguin Books, 1942) and later in his *The Englishman Builds* (Harmondsworth: Penguin Books, 1945).

69. Tubbs, *Living in Cities*, 35–36.

70. James Stirling, "Ronchamp. Le Corbusier's Chapel and the Crisis of Rationalism," *Architectural Review*, 119 (March 1956): 161.

71. Crinson, ed., *James Stirling: Early Unpublished Writings*. The so-called "Black Notebook" is transcribed on pp. 17–68.

72. Crinson, ed., *James Stirling: Early Unpublished Writings*, 23.

For a brief period in our history (sometime in the last century) we did produce appropriate technical works. ie. Crystal Palace. Iron bridges. Railway and navigation products, but with the rise in population and the development of a social conscience, so our justification in the weakened factory belt disappeared. . The belief that to have a modern Architecture it would be integrated with modern technology, still prevails ie. do turn out from year at the AA of 'intestine' ergonomic diagrams in the name of Architecture. Le Corbs recent architecture has been called, classical, academic, antiques. with justification as it is definitely anti-technological, though it is in every way progressive. , indeed it is he more than anybody who has solved the schism in our day, when the younger Architects were presented with the choice of technology. or.

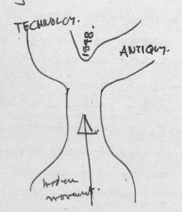

There is some 'justification in seeing the split'. as being the old 'classic or romantic' business. — To deliberately design a building which is imperfect is surely a romantic attitude. — and it is certainly a European phenomenon .— American architecture is rational in its planning and choice and use of materials and logical in its structural systems. — (with the exception of F.L.W. contrast the Rudolph house off the river with Bakema's house.). It is only to easily to apply to Europe's best architects, ie. Bakema. Moretti, Smithson. who are all conscious imperfectionists, the town schizophrenics, reflecting the general unsettled, financial and national aspects of many European countries. — see Colin Rowes theory on mannerism in

80

92

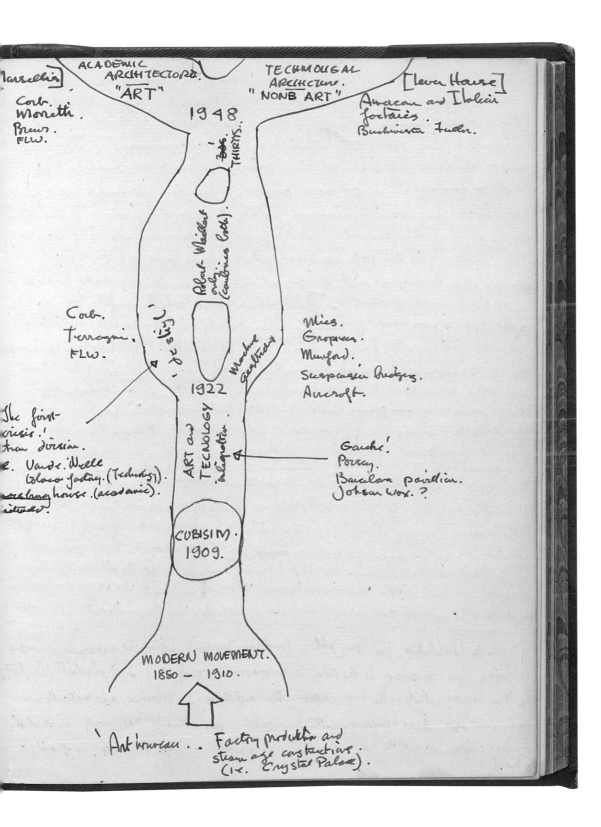

80. James Frazer Stirling, Black Notebook: diagrams of the evolution of modernism
Courtesy of Mary Stirling

In these diagrams of the modern movement envisaged as a river with islands and bifurcations flowing from 1850 to 1948, Stirling follows Banham's division of architecture between the "academic" and the "technological," a theme that will be elaborated in Banham's *Theory and Design in the First Machine Age* of 1960. Thus, "Art nouveau joined with factory production and steam age construction (i.e. Crystal Palace)" to form the modern movement between 1850 and 1910, a movement that was stopped in its flow by Cubism in 1909, after which art and technology developed until the "first crisis" and the division between academic architecture (the Rietveld House, Utrecht) and the technological (Van Nelle Factory, Rotterdam). Then the river divided between Le Corbusier, Terragni, and Wright on the one side, and Mies and Gropius on the other, inspired by suspension bridges and aircraft, with the engineer Robert Maillart combining both. By 1948 the division was complete, with the Marseilles Unité representing "academic architecture" of Corbusier, Moretti, Breuer and Wright, and Lever House standing for "technological architecture": "art" versus "non-art."

ROAD.

only view.

B
LR.

narrow

high wall

garage under 5 cars.

B
LR.

Ramp.

ROAD. highwall.

Parishouses . Maison Jaoul.

Definate art-work, — with exaggerated RW heads
and built in holes and ledges for resting birds.
By English standards the brickwork is poor, — but
it does not matter as the brickwork (loading) is not
of importance. in fact these walls could be equally
have been in rubble or mass logically (in view of the
RC vaults that spring of them) as mass concrete. I do
think Corb uses brickwork very intelligently i.e. joint
between top of walls and vault springs (shuttered RC
beams) should have been raked to prevent concrete
stains dripping down the brickwork. If the finish been
harder i.e. blue staff eng. bricks with definite joints between
wall and RC — the appearance would have been more
mechanistic and I think better. (?) — not certain.
In any case they are not- predominantly brick houses
as with all recent Corb materials (expression of) (possib
exception of core:) are overpowered by the shear dominance
of the forms. The vaults motivate (dominate) the design
far more than the not: bearing brick walls.
These houses are raised far above what we (say LCC
could possible achieve with a cross wall structure (or
partly because of the vault system. [The Doves have discovered to — not- to
make a house without a frame — can the ceiling must be of prime interest]
Externally and internally concrete is left with pronounced (exaggerated) shutter marks
— deliberately crude. and underside of vaults in brown clay tiles (apparently avoided
Brick walls backed with hollow tile and plastered internaly. The vaults make the
small box like interiors very exciting. Each house in a collection of small
rooms + a large larger Living Room. Nevertheless the internal spaces are very small
exciting — particularly the living area in relation to the vertical circulation (staircase
being part of the Living Room) — stair developed from Marseilles fire stair.
Fundamentally the SPACES are unexpected, unrelated, they are encountered sudde
as one turns a corner, or passes a slot resolving an unexpected vertical
(often route double volumes)

81

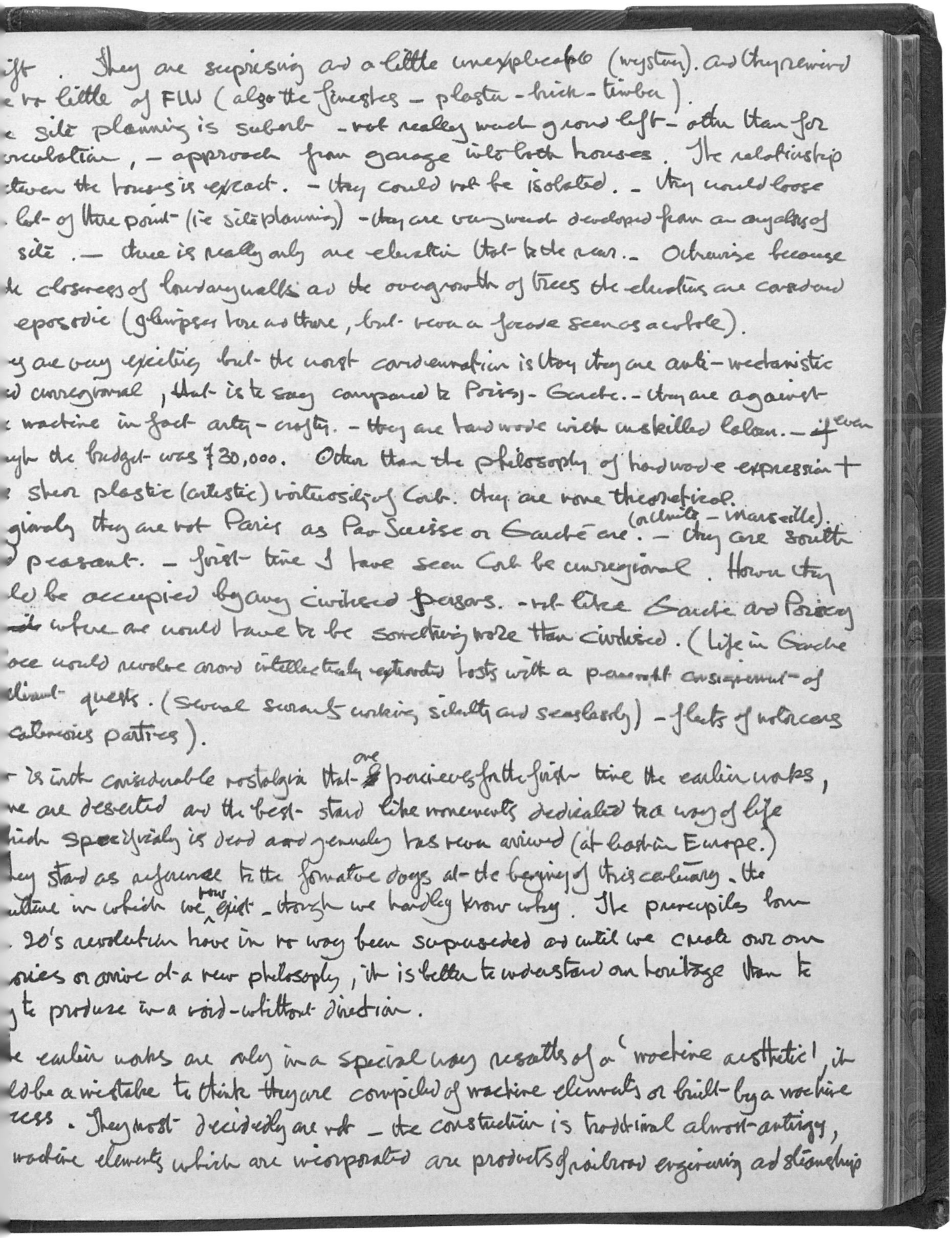

[Handwritten notebook text, left page]

...ift . They are surprising and a little unexplicable (mystery). And they remind one too little of FLW (also the fenestration – plaster – brick – timber).

The site planning is superb – not really much ground left – other than for circulation, – approach from garage into both houses. The relationship between the houses is exact. – they could not be isolated. – they would loose half of their point (ie site planning) – they are very much developed from an analysis of site. – there is really only one elevation (that to the rear). – Otherwise because of the closeness of boundary walls and the overgrowth of trees the elevations are casual and episodic (glimpses here and there, but even a facade seems acceptable).

They are very exciting but the most condemnation is they they are anti-mechanistic and unregional, that is to say compared to Poissy – Garche. – they are against the machine in fact arty – crafty. – they are handmade with unskilled labour. – if even though the budget was £30,000. Other than the philosophy of handmade expression & the sheer plastic (artistic) virtuosity of Corb. they are none theoretical. Regionally they are not Paris as Pav Suisse or Garche are (also – Marseille). – they are south peasant. – first time I have seen Corb be unregional. How are they to be occupied by any civilised persons. – not like Garche and Poissy where one would have to be something more than civilised. (Life in Garche one would revolve around intellectually orthodox hosts with a permanent consignment of cliant guests. (Several servants working silently and ceaselessly) – fleets of motorcars calourious parties).

It is with considerable nostalgia that one percieves for the first time the earlier works, are deserted and the best stand like monuments dedicated to a way of life which specifically is dead and generally has even arrived (at least in Europe.) They stand as reference to the formative days at the begining of this century. the culture in which we now exist – though we hardly know why. The principils how 20's revolution have in no way been superseded and until we create our own theories or arrive at a new philosophy, it is better to understand our heritage than to try to produce in a void – without direction.

The earlier works are only in a special way results of a 'machine aesthetic', it would be a mistake to think they are compiled of machine elements or built by a machine process. They most decidedly are not – the construction is traditional almost-antiquy, machine elements which are incorporated are products of railroad engineering and steamship

81. James Frazer Stirling, Black Notebook: plan and comments on Le Corbusier, Maisons Jaoul
Courtesy of Mary Stirling

Stirling's notes in the Black Notebook record his observations on visiting the Maisons Jaoul by Le Corbusier, still under construction in 1954. The plan sketched in the top left will be reproduced in his articles "From Garches to Jaoul," the next year. He found the brickwork poor, the finishes rough, but the site-planning superb. But despite the fact that they were "very exciting," they were unfortunately both "anti-mechanistic" and "un-regional," handmade and decidedly un-Parisian as "from the south and peasant." They were also "non-theoretical." Most endearing, however, was his note, reminiscent of an earlier passion: "exaggerated RW [rain water] heads and built in holes and ledges for resting birds."

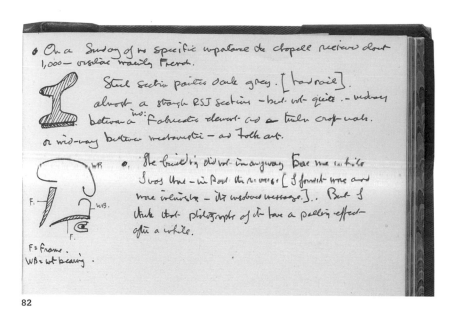

82

82. James Frazer Stirling, Black Notebook: detail of steel handrail and structural plan, Notrè Dame-du-Haut, Ronchamp, France (Le Corbusier, architect), detail

Stirling visited Ronchamp in 1955, preparatory to writing his article on the church. For him it represented the "crisis of rationalism" at its height, expressing the rejection of the technological and the triumph of pure expressive form. The section of the handrail, however, was, according to Stirling "midway between a fabricated element and truly craft work, or midway between mechanistic and folk art." He was critical of the way in which the walls were indistinguishably load-bearing or framed.

was the lack of a truly great English architect to follow "Mackintosh, Archer, Hawksmoor, Vanbrugh and perhaps Soane," and to produce even a single masterpiece to compete with the masters of Europe, Scandinavia and the United States. Stirling, in a delightful image of the evolution of the modern movement as a river, diagrammed the insistent division in modernism since the nineteenth century, one that, as Banham had already indicated, culminated in the great divide between the academic and the mechanistic streams.[73] This was the root of his disappointment with Le Corbusier, who rather than achieving the promise of unifying the functional and the formal, the non-academic and the academic, the technological and the non-technological, had, with the Jaoul Houses, and more so with Ronchamp, opted for the non-technological.

1954 was indeed crucial to Stirling's attempts to formulate an attitude to architecture that would respond to his growing sense of modernism's exhaustion, to the radically new needs demonstrated by the social and cultural emergence of a postwar Britain, and strongly counter, if not replace entirely, the Corbusian model. His visit to France in 1954, where he sought out as many Corbusian buildings as he could find, and to Ronchamp the following year confirmed him in his feeling, not only that the era of high modernism was definitively past, but also that the alternative posed by Le Corbusier at the Maisons Jaoul and Ronchamp were lacking in authority for present conditions. The photographs in the archive dating from Stirling's visit to France in September 1954, and again in the next year, document this, his first real encounter with Corbusian architecture—the villas in and around Paris, and Ronchamp.[74] For Stirling, modernist rationalism had obviously come to a crisis point, and in his two seminal

73. Crinson, ed., *James Stirling: Early Unpublished Writings*, 39.

74. On his return to London, Stirling engaged in a discussion with Colin St John Wilson and Peter Smithson on the topic of Ronchamp, 15 October 1955.

83

84

85

86

87

83. James Frazer Stirling, photographer, view of the Unité d'habitation, Marseilles, France (Le Corbusier and André Wogenscky, architects), 1955
gelatin silver print; 10.2 x 7.7 cm (4 x 3 in); AP140.S1.SS2.D2.P4.2

84. James Frazer Stirling, photographer, view of Notre-Dame-du-Haut, Ronchamp (Le Corbusier, architect), 1955
gelatin silver print; 6.6 x 10 cm (2 ⅝ x 3 ¹⁵/₁₆ in); AP140.S1.SS2.D2.P4.3

05. James Frazer Stirling, photographer, view of the Pavillon Suisse, Cité Universitaire, Paris (Le Corbusier and Pierre Jeanneret, architects), 1954
gelatin silver print; 9.9 x 6.8 cm (3 ⅞ x 2 ⅝ in); AP140.S1.SS2.D2.P4.4

86. James Frazer Stirling, photographer, view of the Villa Savoye, Poissy, France (Le Corbusier and Pierre Jeanneret, architects), 1954
gelatin silver print; 6.7 x 9.8 cm (2 ⅝ x 3 ⅞ in); AP140.S1.SS2.D2.P4.6

87. James Frazer Stirling, photographer, view of the Villa Stein, Garches, France (Le Corbusier and Pierre Jeanneret, architects), 1954
reproduced from black and white negative; negative: 2.4 x 3.7 cm (1 x 1 ½ in); AP140.S1.SS2.D2.P4.178.1

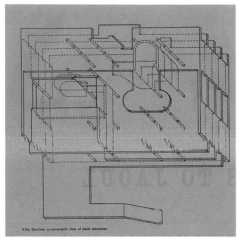

88

89

88. James Frazer Stirling, "Villa Stein, Garches, axonometric view of basic structure," diagram from "Garches to Jaoul," *Architectural Review* (September 1955), p. 146

Stirling's axonometric of the Garches villa's "basic structure" differs considerably from Rowe's analysis; instead of seeing the building as a sequence of vertical layers of space Stirling understands it as a three-dimensional structure, horizontally layered floor by floor.

89. James Frazer Stirling, photographer, Colin Rowe and David Crowe at the Maison de Verre, Paris (Pierre Chareau, architect), 1959
reproduced from colour transparency; 3.5 x 3.5 cm (1 ⅜ x 1 ⅜ in); AP140.S1.SS2.D2.P5.2

Colin Rowe (on the right) and David Crowe (centre) wait to gain entry into the Maison de Verre—a revelation to Stirling for its total absorption of the technological into design.

essays recounting the French visits for the *Architectural Review* in 1955 and 1956, he was quick to point this out. In "Garches to Jaoul" he was struck by the shift in Le Corbusier from a utopian evocation of a new way of life (Garches) to a more everyday sense of comfort and present accommodation (Jaoul).[75] While he appreciated the "regional" qualities of Jaoul, as they stemmed from traditions that Le Corbusier had encountered in India, he felt that they were entirely non-regional in the context of Paris, built as they were by Arab labourers with low-tech materials, and equally important, being "non-theoretical."[76] In "Ronchamp" the next year he found himself in awe of the plastic form of the church but troubled by what he felt was its lack of structural and spatial rigour in favor of pure expression. Later, in 1959, together with Colin Rowe and David Crowe, he visited other canonical buildings of the modern movement—notably Pierre Chareau's Maison de Verre (1928–31), which seemed to have the technology at least right. He concluded:

> Aware that progress has let him down (or not caught up with him) Corb is now producing architecture which is a development of the local native tradition, local craftsmanship allied to his mastery of form and space plus his sheer virtuosity in plastic expression (expressionism).[77]

The result of this abdication was to leave architects without foundations save for "the beauty of FORM," which led to the "beaux-arts shoe shop modern" of postwar architecture. Nevertheless, in a ringing assertion of his mature position, Stirling wrote: "The principles born in the 20s revolution have in no way been superseded and until we create our own theories or arrive at a new philosophy, it is better to understand our heritage than to try to produce in a void without direction."[78]

75. For a comprehensive treatment of these two articles and Stirling's complicated relationship to Le Corbusier in general see Crinson, ed., *James Stirling: Early Unpublished Writings*, 108–39: "'L'Architecte anglais' Stirling and Le Corbusier."

76. Crinson, ed., *James Stirling: Early Unpublished Writings*, 53.

77. Crinson, ed., *James Stirling: Early Unpublished Writings*, 53.

78. Crinson, ed., *James Stirling: Early Unpublished Writings*, 53–54.

III. The Crisis of Rationalism

This is an age of multi-aesthetic styles, and each problem appears to have its appropriate aesthetic, in contrast with the twenties, when much of the strength of the movement lay in the naïve conviction that all buildings could be designed in "international style."

James Stirling, 1958[79]

Towards a New Vernacular

The method of design to a modern mind can only be understood in the scientific, or in the engineer's sense, as a definite analysis of possibilities—not as a vague poetic dealing with poetic matters, with derivative ideas of what looks domestic, or looks farmlike, or looks ecclesiastical—the dealing with a multitude of flavours—that is what architects have been doing in the last hundred years. They have been trying to deal with a set of flavours— things that look like but that were not the things themselves. Old farmhouses and cottages are things themselves—cottages and farmhouses

W.R. Lethaby, 1922[80]

The English house—in general considered a rural house, whether an aristocratic mansion or a cottage—had attracted a great deal of scholarly and nostalgic journalistic attention in the late 1930s, increasing in intensity after the war. For it was widely recognized as a disappearing species. The efforts of the non-governmental organization of the National Trust under the benign ministrations of James Lees-Milne had succeeded in saving a large number of small and great estates from destruction; but small towns and villages were undergoing rapid transformations both in population and economic development; villages were depopulated, suburbs were encroaching on formerly rural land, the landscape was being littered with the detritus of technological civilization—the special issue of *The Architectural Review* in June 1955, entitled

79. James Stirling, "A Personal View of the Present Situation," *Architectural Design* (June 1958), reprinted in Maxwell, ed., *James Stirling: Writings on Architecture*, 61.

80. W.R. Lethaby, *Form in Civilization* (1922), cited by Stirling in "Regionalism and Modern Architecture," *Architect's Year Book*, 8 (London: Eleck, 1957), 65.

90

91

92

90. James Frazer Stirling, photographer, view of kilns, United Kingdom, 1950s–1970s
gelatin silver print; 6.9 x 9.9 cm (2 ¾ x 3 ⅞ in); AP140.S1.SS2.D2.P3.6

The following is a selection of prints from dozens of negatives that record Stirling's interest in vernacular architecture from the 1950s on. Stirling was rarely photographed without a camera around his neck, and while his first bird-watching camera was partially destroyed by water damage, he continued to purchase better and better cameras. The guarantee for his new Contaflex Super by Zeiss Icon is preserved in the archive and dated 10 December 1959. With its Tessar 2.8 lens it was regarded as the most advanced compact camera on the market.

91. James Frazer Stirling, photographer, view of farm buildings, United Kingdom, 1950s–1970s
gelatin silver print; 6.9 x 9.9 cm (2 ¾ x 3 ⅞ in); AP140.S1.SS2.D2.P3.7

92. James Frazer Stirling, photographer, view of oast houses, United Kingdom, 1950s–1970s
gelatin silver print; 6.9 x 9.9 cm (2 ¾ x 3 ⅞ in); AP140.S1.SS2.D2.P3.8

"Outrage" and illustrated by dramatic photographs and drawings by Gordon Cullen of the deteriorated environment of "Subtopia," underlined this concern. As Sydney Jones wrote in his comprehensive survey of village architecture, *English Village Houses*, first published in 1936, "old houses and cottages in the villages are diminishing rapidly. A heritage of unique value is in danger of being destroyed."[81] The middle class was discovering the possibilities of second homes in the country, and a series of books advising on restoration and traditions of construction were issued by the Architectural Press and Batsford. A planner like Thomas Sharp, imbued with the organic premises of Patrick Geddes, was seriously concerned with the implications of uncontrolled development, publishing his *Design in Town and Village* with contributions by William Holford and Frederick Gibberd in 1953.[82]

It is in this context that we have to understand Stirling's first essays in regional vernacular. For while he was often caustically to dismiss the strictures of "LAs" or Local Authorities, as they more often than not blocked his building permits, he was, nevertheless, deeply concerned with the question—not of vernacular "style" but of a regional manner that, tied to site and program, would bring about a new kind of modernism. Between 1954 and 1959 Stirling would slowly develop his own, idiosyncratic, regional vernacular, while at the same time elaborating its theory in seminal articles. His two articles of 1957 and 1960, resuming this period of reflection and work, are extended critical and theoretical meditations on the problems and paradoxes of "regionalism," the "vernacular," and the "functional tradition." The archive holds dozens of Stirling's photographs from this period as he looks more closely at buildings that had always attracted his attention, and armed with the newly introduced Zeiss-Ikon Contaflex Super, which he bought in 1959, Stirling photographed the Liverpool docks, oast houses, barns, castles, and the strongly functional defenses and sea walls of the war.

But his approach was also worked out in lectures—at the Architectural Association where he became a tutor and encouraged many of his students to experiment with regional forms, and after 1960 at Yale. The archive holds many

81. Sydney R. Jones, *English Village Houses* (London: Batsford, 1936; 2nd edn., 1947), 12.

82. Thomas Sharp, ed., *Design in Town and Village* (Ministry of Housing and Local Government, London: HMSO, 1953) with chapters by Thomas Sharp, "The English Village," Frederick Gibberd, "The Design of residential Areas," and W.G. Holford, "Design in City Centres."

of the notes for these talks that supplement his published essays and designs with trenchant, off-the-cuff remarks and interesting comments on the slides he showed. Here, too, we might once more detect the influence of that early enthusiasm for the writings of W.H. Auden, as the poet wrote of the "landscapes" of early industrial England: those "relics of old mines," "tramways overgrown with grass," and the "derelict lead-smelting mill," that, in voluntary exile in the United States, were integral to the geology and experiences of his boyhood in the North of England.[83]

Both of Stirling's articles on regionalism are explicit responses to *The Architectural Review*'s special issue on "The Functional Tradition," of July 1957; they are also critical assessments of the various "regionalisms" that had emerged since the war. He identifies two movements that have seen architects turn towards the historical past, as opposed to a modern future. The first was the tendency inspired by Wittkower and Rowe and taken up fleetingly by the Smithsons in England and Johnson in the United States: "neo-Palladianism," with its interest in the academic and classical roots of modernism and in new "humanist" proportional systems such as the Modulor. This sensibility seems to Stirling to be on the wane. The second, and in reaction to this, was the "re-assessment of indigenous and usually anonymous building and a revaluation of the experience embodied in the use of traditional methods and materials."[84] In this latter movement, Stirling signals a shift away from what he saw at Jaoul—"the plastique of folk and anonymous architecture initially stimulated by Mediterranean building"—towards an interest in British examples: "Martello towers, oast-houses, brick-kilns ... warehouses"; those works where "the outside ... is an efficient expression of their function."[85] Together with this new regionalism, a tendency which Stirling obviously finds attractive, there is a renewed interest in early modern British architecture—Voysey and Mackintosh—again a theme that Stirling has been developing in his understanding that "the Continental innovations of the 'twenties and early 'thirties are incapable of development." Returning to these twin roots of British modern functionalism will, Stirling hopes, serve to restart the process.

Interestingly enough, Stirling associates this new sensibility with that engendered in what his friend, the jazz player and critic George Melly, termed "The New Movement," in literature, with its interest in the revival of folk art at all levels, from the heights of the intellectual Third Programme of the BBC to the music of Elvis Presley. Coinciding with Stirling's own predispositions against academicism, the New Movement, as Melly described it, was "anti-intellectual, anti-posh, and anti-official-minded."[86] For Sirling's generation, as Stirling himself wrote, "the metropolitanism of Sartre and Moravia is being replaced on the one hand by 'Lucky Jim' provincialism and, on the other, the 'mythismus' of Dylan Thomas and Bert Brecht."[87]

83. W.H.Auden, "New Year Letter [1 January 1940]," *Collected Poems*, 228.

84. Stirling, "Regionalism and Modern Architecture," 62.

85. Stirling, "Regionalism and Modern Architecture," 65.

86. George Melly in *Intimate Review* (1956), cited in Stirling, "Regionalism and Modern Architecture," 65.

87. Stirling, "Regionalism and Modern Architecture," 65–69.

The *Architectural Review* published in July 1957 a special number called "The Functional Tradition"; this illustrated many anonymously designed buildings in England of a regional type, such as farmhouses, barns, warehouses, mills, etc. This selection was perhaps a little narrow, faintly Georgian, and too nearly confined to early industrialism. It could have included fortifications, village housing, and early office building. Sibyl Moholy-Nagy has also published a book illustrating similar buildings in America.

The merit of this type of building as seen by an architect today is that they are usually composed of direct and undecorated volumes evolved from building usage and particularly from the functions of their major elements. They adapt to a wide variety of materials and locality and their structural support is sensibly derived from the organization of the building. Though dating back to medieval times, they are peculiarly modern, suggestive of the early ideas of Functionalism, but probably less of the machine aesthetic, which was primarily a style concern. Le Corbusier has always been aware of the uncompromising appearance of this type of building, and as the theoretical impetus of the modern movement has diminished, their influence upon him has become apparent, particularly in his later work. (1, 2)

The flats of Ham Common (4) were probably influenced by de Stijl and the Jaoul houses, but at the same time we were fascinated by the quality of vernacular brick buildings such as the Liverpool warehouses, (3) and in general by the great virtuosity of English nineteenth-century brick technology. (7) The design of a small house in the country (6) was probably affected by the roof complexes of traditional farm buildings, (5) and the pyramidal massing results from giving the living-room a double height space with a sloping ceiling, and by placing a studio/bedroom on the upper level. The roofs are simple lean-to's spanning between walls.

On both sides of the Atlantic the current dilemma of modern architecture seems to be that top architects are absorbed in becoming either stylists or structural exhibitionists and as the "Functional Tradition" indicates, there is an alternative architectural expression to that of style or structure. This is by the direct expression of the actual accommodation volumes in relation to each element determining the plastic composition of the building. ("The section is the elevation" — Le Corbusier) The architectural quality of a solution will of course depend upon the particular organization of the accommodation, circulation, services, etc., and vernacular buildings usually have

89

93

93. James Frazer Stirling, "The Functional Tradition and Expression," *Perspecta* 6 (1960), pp. 88–89

This, together with his article on "Regionalism and Modern Architecture," 1957, was Stirling's most developed statement on the need for modernism to be revised in the light of a functional tradition inherent in regional and vernacular architecture.

In the background of this shift in cultural emphasis hovered the still powerful presence of T.S. Eliot, whose essays "The Function of Criticism" (1923) and "The Social Function of Poetry" (1943) remained the touchstones of modernist "high" criticism and its social relations. Against Eliot's mandarin version of culture, "The Movement" in poetry, plays, and film was dedicated to a questioning of the commonplaces of a class-based modernist literature through the examination of working-class and popular sources, and a sharp critique of social attitudes. The character of Dixon in Kingsley Amis's first novel *Lucky Jim* (1954) is typical as he stumbles through his first job at a provincial university in the North, in a series of episodes that satirize the pompousness of academic life; that his downfall occurs as he delivers a lecture on "Merrie England," and his eventual triumph through the winning of the daughter of his rich patron epitomize the drive towards class-blind anti-pretension typical of "The Movement."

But while there are obvious aspects of Stirling's own attitudes towards institutions and academic authority—later to be evinced in his tussles with Oxbridge dons—he is reluctant to relinquish the strengths that he attributes to the "programmatic" architecture of the modern movement, by which he means an architecture dedicated to a logic and a formal consistency that combined "a common synthesis of the recent past and a definite attitude towards the future." Against the implicit nostalgia and reactionary anti-modernism of the attitude, "Stonehenge is more significant than the architecture of Sir Christopher Wren," Stirling desired another form of synthesis that did not, as his final citation from an article by John Wain (another member of The Movement) claimed, empty the baby "away with the bathwater."[88]

The illustrations to Stirling's article "Regionalism" provide a clue to his emerging response to the trend, one in which he is increasingly playing a major part. First are his own photographs of early warehouses, storehouses, and office buildings in Liverpool, together with shots of a Martello tower on the South coast, a Staffordshire tile kiln and an oast house and farmhouse in Kent, contrasted with a picturesque view of "Mediterranean Plastique" in Ibiza and the locally regional modernism of Aalto at Paimio and Säynätsalo. More importantly, Stirling includes the recent work of his students at the Architectural Association: a spiral bird observatory built in stone-wall construction by Janet Kaye; a house in the South of England with pitched tile roofs by Kit Evans, and a forestry village in Scotland with its clustered houses and pitched roofs, a Thesis project by Peter Ahrends. Finally, he includes one of his own designs, that for a house at Woolton Park (1954–55), near Liverpool, in plan, section, and model. This house, evidently the inspiration for Kit Evans's later design, consists of two pitched-roof sections, one with a double-height living and dining room, the other with two bedrooms and a carport.

Here he found a way to integrate the common rural signs of pitched roof and landscape profile with the internal needs of the occupants.[89] Indeed the profile of the roofs is uncannily similar to that of a rural roofscape illustrated side by side with that of a model of Woolton in the article "'The Functional Tradition' and Expression," with Stirling's remark that Woolton was no doubt influenced by such examples, as well as providing the necessary double-height living space for the clients.[90]

In this experiment with regional vernacular, Stirling was, as he noted in a lecture given at Yale University in 1960, concerned to "look around for a way to continue the development and also extend the limited vocabulary of modern arch[itecture]." Indeed he qualified a wholesale acceptance of regionalism, one that might be understood as "looking backward over one's shoulder" and a "rejection of modernity," by dividing the architect's task into two. The one dealing with "timeless architectural problems such as the design of the house and places of worship," that are "valid by this method of regional observation," and the other, "uniquely modern" problems such as the "industrial plant," that should be designed in a more "radical" and "even science fiction way."[91]

88. John Wain in *The London Magazine* (1956), cited in Stirling, "Regionalism and Modern Architecture," 69.

89. James Stirling, "House near Liverpool," *Architectural Design*, 26 (July 1956): 241.

90. Stirling, "Regionalism and Modern Architecture," 89–90.

91. James Stirling, lecture notes for the talk "The Functional Tradition and Expression," Stirling/Wilford fonds, CCA, AP140.S2.SS4.D7.P5.2.1-4. The lecture was later published as "The 'Functional Tradition' and Expression," *Perspecta 6* (1960): 88–97

Farmhouse to Village

Respect for tradition is an excellent thing, provided that the tradition respected is a genuine living tradition. A true tradition is subject to growth and development.
Thomas Sharp, 1926[92]

The call for entries to the tenth meeting of CIAM, to be held in Dubrovnik in 1956, was based on the theme assayed at the previous meeting of CIAM at Aix-on-Provence in July 1953, "Habitat," where a group of younger members including Jacob Bakema, Aldo van Eyck, and Georges Candilis, with the Smithsons, Bill Howell, and John Voelcker from England's MARS group, had sought to substitute a "Charter of Habitat" for the original Charter of Athens (1933). Organized into grids, under the titles of "Hierarchy of Association" and "Urban Re-Identification Grid," their new categories, replacing the old "dwelling," "work," "transportation," and "recreation," emphasized the connections between house, street, district, and city, dramatically illustrated by photographs of young children at play. At the preliminary meeting for CIAM held at Doorn in 1954, the Smithsons produced their declaration on "Habitat," which was presented as the Doorn Manifesto, based on a reconsideration of Patrick Geddes's "Valley Section," itself taken from the work of the sociologist Frédéric le Play, together with five of their designs under five categories: "Isolated" ("Bates' Burrows Lea Farm," originally designed between 1953 and 1955); "Hamlet" ("Galleon Cottages," in the Dales hamlet of Bainbridge, North Riding, Yorkshire, 1954); "Village" ("Fold Houses for Village Infill," in the Dales village of West Burton, North Riding, Yorkshire, 1955); "Town" ("Close Houses"), and "City" ("Terraced Crescent Houses," London, 1955).[93] Bill Howell prepared an entry based on his scheme for a competition for old people's houses, John Voelcker submitted a project that linked village houses along a bedroom spine, and Stirling's tackled the problem of village development.[94]

Stirling, who was the only member of the group not to attend—and indeed not invited as a result of the Smithsons' opposition—engaged the problem with great seriousness. His scheme was based on the plan of what Thomas Sharp, in his timely book, *The Anatomy of the Village* (1946), had called the "Roadside Village," among other types such as the "Squared Village," the "Seaside Village," and the "Planned Village." Taking the roadside village of West Wycombe, together with its plan taken directly out of Sharp's set of elegant drawings, Stirling paraphrased Sharp in his typed explanation to the two boards submitted to Doorn: "The form of the English village has not changed in the last 400 years and has hardly been affected by the Industrial Revolution," and he proposed a system of party-wall structures with pitched lean-to roofs built out of local materials by unskilled labour. It was a system, he wrote, that would provide "order with infinite variety," that could be adapted to flat or sloping ground and,

---

92. Thomas Sharp, *The Anatomy of the Village* (1926) (Harmondsworth: Penguin Books, 1946), 5.

93. See Alison and Peter Smithson, *The Charged Void: Architecture* (New York: Monacelli Press, 2001), 130–39.

94. W.G. Howell, "Village Housing," *The Architects' Journal*, 126, no. 3264 (19 September 1957): 428–36. Howell is reviewing the rebuilt village of Rushbrooke in Suffolk by Richard Llewelyn Davies and John Weeks, designed for agricultural workers on the private estate of Rushbrooke. He compares these houses—"the first scheme ... which breaks right outside the established

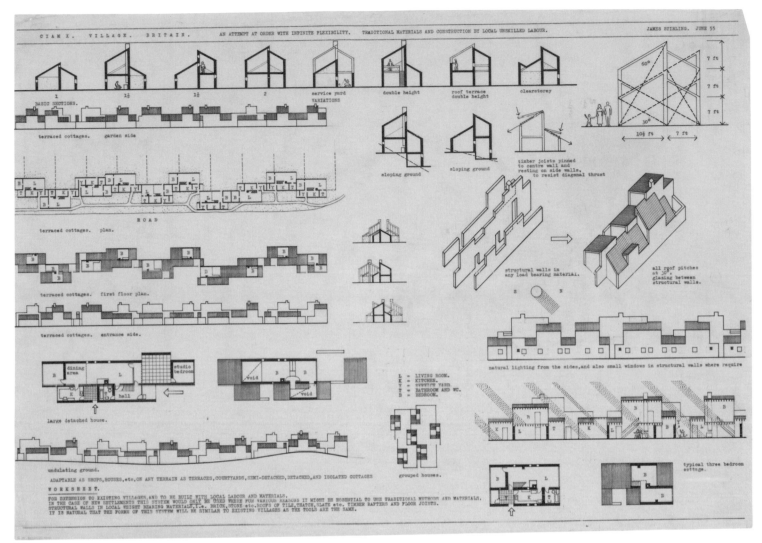

94. James Frazer Stirling, Village Housing for CIAM 10: plans, sections, elevations, details and axonometrics, 1955
ink on paper; 47.2 x 66.4 cm
(18 ⅝ x 26 ⅛ in); AP140.S2.SS1.D9.P1.2

Demonstrating interest in prefabrication, and the need for architects to provide templates for self-built dwellings—later realized at PREVI—Stirling designed these houses to be built "in traditional materials [brick, stone, tile, thatch, slate, timber] and [for] construction by local unskilled labour." The scheme was to be applied "for extension of existing villages," and was adaptable to flat and undulating sites. Prototypes included terraced rows, clusters, and individual detached houses. Stirling thought that "it is natural that the forms of this system will be similar to existing villages" because the "tools" he prescribed would be the same. It was, he concluded "an attempt at order with infinite flexibility."

The Crisis of Rationalism

95

95. Thomas Sharp, High Street, West Wycombe, Buckinghamshire, from *The Anatomy of the Village* (Harmondsworth: Penguin Books, 1946), pp. 8–9

The threat to the British village, from suburban development, the flight to the cities, and more importantly from ill-conceived building and planning in the villages themselves, was noted long before the Second World War. The planner/architect Thomas Sharp published widely on the subject, and investigated the plan-types, visual structures, and potential design criteria for responsible development. He was seen by Stirling's generation as a counter to Gordon Cullen from the *Architectural Review*, whose response was primarily small-scale and visual rather then systematic and rational. Stirling was unique in taking Sharp's description of West Wycombe as a program for his village housing project for CIAM 10.

96. James Frazer Stirling, Village Housing for CIAM 10: combinatorial plans, 1955
diazotype; 50.8 x 66.9 cm
(20 x 26 5/16 in); AP140.S2.SS1.D9.P2.1

Stirling demonstrates the flexibility of his housing prototypes by showing terraced cottages on flat and irregular ground, and grouped houses around courts, always preserving open country at the village edge.

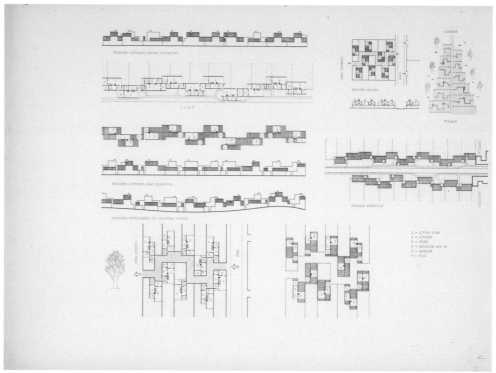

96

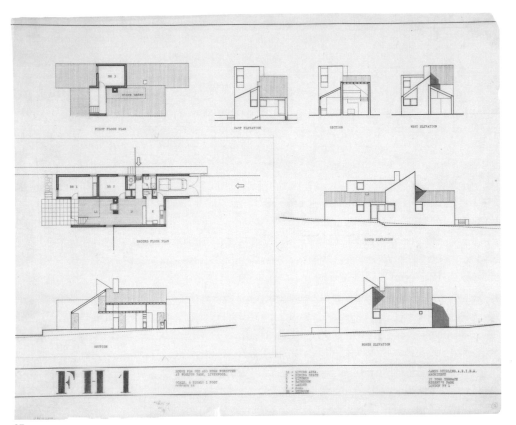

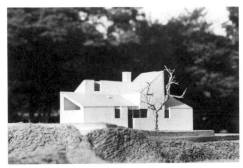

97. James Frazer Stirling, Woolton House, Liverpool, England: plans, sections and elevations, 1955
ink, transfer type and traces of coloured pencil and graphite on paper;
54.4 x 66.2 cm (21 ⅜ x 26 ¹⁄₁₆ in);
AP140.S2.SS1.D8.P1.1

Designed as a regional-vernacular building, with pitched roofs and embedded in a sloping site, construction was abandoned, according to Stirling, because of the unstable garbage fill beneath the foundations.

98. James Frazer Stirling, Woolton House, Liverpool: sketch, 1955
ink on paper, 19.2 x 27.4 cm
(7 ½ x 10 ¾ in); AP140.S2.SS1.D8.P2.3

A perspective drawing of the Woolton project as if it was a rural farm building—photographs of which Stirling published in "The Functional Tradition and Expression."

99. James Frazer Stirling, photographer and architect, Woolton House, Liverpool: view of model, 1955
gelatin silver print; 12.6 x 18.4 cm
(5 x 7 ¼ in); AP140.S2.SS1.D8.P3.1

in a series of different arrangements, used as linear extensions to an existing roadside village, or, at right angles to the main road, develop small clusters in depth. One- to four-bedroom cottages were planned according to the general two-segment Woolton house, with their pitched roofs carefully angled to bring in light—perhaps following the Corbusian precedent of the Maisons Murondins of 1940, but with greater attention to the notion of standardization, if not mass production, that would be a preoccupation of Stirling's in many of his housing schemes from Runcorn to Lima.[95] In accordance with the program of CIAM 10, Stirling also submitted a board with the design of his House in North London described as a typical "Suburban" house.

Equally important, demonstrated on two large boards, was the maturity of Stirling's graphic approach, unique among the presentations, with its clear plans, elevations, and sections demonstrating the additive and compositional strategies of the units, as well as the axonometric diagrams that showed the load-bearing wall construction, in sequence, from parallel walls, timber roof members and final cottages. Here, ten years before the fully developed axonometrics of the Leicester University Engineering Building and Cambridge University History Faculty Building, Stirling hints at what will be his very personal vision, not only of representation, but also of the design process itself, carefully built up element by element in a form that shows structure, use, and space in a single iteration.

Village to Worktown

Home may be private, but the front door opens out of the living-room on to the street, and when you go down the one step or use it as a seat on a warm evening you become part of the life of the neighbourhood. To a visitor they are understandably depressing, these massed proletarian areas; street after regular street of shoddily uniform houses intersected by a dark pattern of ginnels and snicket (alley-ways) and courts; mean squalid and in a permanent half-fog ... But to the insider, these are small worlds, each as homogeneous as a village.
Richard Hoggart, 1957[96]

I dare say, this building looks a bit Victorian.
James Stirling, 1965[97]

The long-drawn out battle over the proper forms for new housing and rehousing developments that were a constant preoccupation of sociologists and reformers in the postwar years, was essentially a battle over the nature of a neighbourhood.[98] The grand designs of the modern movement, and especially those urban

imagery of postwar rural housing"—with the four projects presented by the English group at CIAM; see "Village Housing, Rushbrooke," *Architectural Review*, 121, no. 727 (August 1957): 98–102; John Voelcker, "Farm Buildings," *Architectural Review*, 127, no. 761 (September 1960): 180–89.

95. James Stirling, "Village Housing for CIAM X," typed explanation in Stirling/Wilford Archive at the CCA, reproduced in *James Stirling: Buildings and Projects 1950–1974*, 36.

96. Richard Hoggart, *The Uses of Literacy: Aspects of Working Class Life* (London: Chatto and Windus, 1957): 37–38.

diagrams of CIAM and its followers, were already the object of critique by the younger generation raised in an era of heightened sociological (and anthropological) understanding of the working classes and their districts, and less prone to demolish indiscriminately. Without necessarily abandoning the preconceptions over densities and certainly without forsaking the modernist project as they saw it, architects like the Smithsons attempted to reconstruct the social relations of housing through ideas of cluster and network, most directly demonstrated by their schemes for Golden Lane (1952) and Robin Hood Gardens (1966). Later, other architects, like Leslie Martin and Patrick Hodgkinson, were less enamored of the "high slab with streets in the air" schemes, and proposed low-rise high-density alternatives, four and five stories stepped back over inner courtyards for play and security. Somewhere in between, and at a scale of an existing neighbourhood, were infill projects of "rehousing," developed to maintain community life and its structures without the displacement of a local population.

Through the firm of Lyons, Israel and Ellis, where he had worked from 1953, and now in partnership with James Gowan, Stirling received the commission for a rehousing development in the Avenham district of Preston, Lancashire; as determined by John Turner and Sons Ltd., the local contractor that had control of the work through the Borough Council, the low-rise terrace housing was to be designed by Stirling, the old-people's housing by Gowan, and the tower flats retained by Lyons, Israel, and Ellis with Alan Colquhoun.

This project, designed and built between 1957 and 1961, has been the object of a unique and comprehensive analysis by Mark Crinson.[99] In his article Crinson surveys the attitudes toward working-class housing and rehousing in 1950s Britain in the context of Stirling's turn toward regionalism, and the sociology of street-life that was emerging among postwar social scientists—the "rediscovery," so to speak, of the vitality of working-class communities, and the paradoxical problem of a modernist housing strategy that failed to recognize the role of the street and the neighbourhood in this vitality. Paradoxical, because the need for new and modernized environments and services had, in this vision of working-class life, to be balanced against the potentially regressive move of locking communities into their own past. Stirling's industrial brick terraces with their blunt outlines and formal reference to the "backs" of Victorian terraces—the outdoor toilets and sheds that were seen as symbolic of slum life at its worst—were immediately criticized by supporters and critics alike: supporters feeling that the social ideals of the modern movement were betrayed by this obvious allusion to a "bad" history; and critics who might have been satisfied with a "Swedish" solution, finding Stirling's formal rigour at odds with the varieties of social life it sheltered. On the one hand, modernists felt that the move signaled a romantic nostalgia that paternalized the working class; on the other even lovers of Victorian architecture like Nikolaus Pevsner felt that progress was being reversed.

97. Stirling, "An Architect's Approach to Architecture," 233.

98. See also P. Addison, *Now the War is Over: A Social History of Britain, 1945–51* (London: Pimlico, 1995); Lewis Mumford, "East End Urbanity" (1953), in *The Highway and the City* (London: Secker S Warburg, 1953); N. Tiratsoo, *Reconstruction, Affluence. and Labour Politics,* *1945–1960* (London: Routledge, 1990); P. Dunleavy, *The Politics of Mass Housing in Britain, 1945–75* (Oxford: Oxford University Press, 1981); J.M. Richards, "Failure of the New Towns," *Architectural Review*, 114 (1953): 29–32; Gordon Cullen, "Prairie Planning in the New Towns," *Architectural Review*, 114 (1953): 33–36; Arthur Korn, *History Builds the Town* (London: Lund Humphries, 1953);

100

101

100. James Frazer Stirling, photographer, street in Avenham, Preston, England, 1957–61
gelatin silver print; 12 x 10.6 cm
(4 ¾ x 4 ⅛ in); AP140.S2.SS7.D1.P1.122

101. James Frazer Stirling, photographer, backs of houses in Avenham, Preston, Lancashire, 1957–61
reproduced from black and white negative; 5.4 x 5.6 cm (2 ⅛ x 2 ³⁄₁₆ in); AP140.S1.SS2.D2.P3.10

Reyner Banham, Stirling's friend, had the difficult task of defending the project while admitting all these objections.[100] His article in the *New Statesman*, February 1962 was entitled "Coronation Street, Hoggartsborough," referring to the popular television series "Coronation Street," set in and around a pub in a Manchester working-class district, that had premiered in December of 1961, and to the book by the critic Richard Hoggart, *The Uses of Literacy*, published in 1957. From Banham's point of view, Coronation Street represented the false claim that "working-class virtues were the product of physical propinquity," and what he called "Hoggartry" was merely a sentimental nostalgia for a world already passed away. Housing for the working class was, Banham warned, poised between two uneasy poles—"socialist formalism" and "working-class scene painting." Certainly the "street" as a focus of sociability could be retained in a modernist guise—he cited Denys Lasdun's cluster-block solution at Claredale and Jack Lyn and Ivor Smith's housing at Park Hill, Sheffield. But the evident vernacular/regional aesthetics of Preston would (and perhaps he implicitly meant *should*), Banham averred, raise the question: "if this isn't socialist (or any other kind of) formalism comparable to the 'William Morris Revival' sponsored in the early Fifties by the party group in the LCC Architect's Department"? And, despite the fact that Banham admits that "these cottages, considered purely in the abstract are a joy to look at," and that the architects had "taken over a vernacular language of local warehouse-builders' usages" in such a way that "everything fits together with an unforced logic," he was nevertheless perturbed by the unspoken intentions of the architecture: dangerously close to one "that forces the working-class into the role of picturesque peasantry, a foreground frieze of Roger Mayne Figures armed with Nigel Henderson bassinets, bicycles and Yogi Bear masks."[101] Here Banham was referring, not so charitably, to Nigel Henderson, a fellow member of the Independent Group, and Roger Mayne, both documentary street photographers whose work in the East End of London had served to support the new sociology of the street. His conclusion was clear, even if couched as a question: Stirling and Gowan had produced a "visual setting" for the present state of working-class culture—but did this not "leave a developing working class lumbered with an unsuitable functional environment 20 affluent years from now?"[102]

The popular press was less ambiguous: on the awarding of the Good Housing Competition prize to the Preston rehousing in 1963, the correspondent of the *Daily Mail* asked, "Frankly, do you think this is WORTH A PRIZE?" For many, this development simply represented a "nostalgia for the slums," the last gasp of "the kitchen sink school of architecture" that believed in "bolts and bricks," where the public were looking for "something pretty and cosy." It was perhaps with a certain defiant pride that Stirling clipped the article and carefully preserved it in the archive.[103]

F.E. Gibberd, *Town Design* (London: Architectural Press, 1953); Tom Harrison, *Britain Revisited* (London: Gollancz, 1961); Michael Young and Peter Willmott, *Family and Kinship in East London* (London: Routledge and Kegan Paul, 1957).

99. Mark Crinson, "The Uses of Nostalgia. Stirling and Gowan's Preston Housing," *Journal of the Society of Architectural Historians*, 65, no. 2 (June 2006): 216–31.

100. Reyner Banham, "Coronation Street, Hoggartsborough," *New Statesman*, 9 February 1962, 200–201.

102

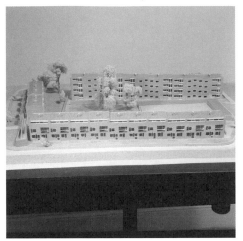

103

That nothing now remains of the terrace houses at Preston, re-roofed in pitched style in the 1970s and torn down in 1999, might well lead us to agree with Banham's prescient commentary, but a closer examination of the representations and statements by Stirling and Gowan might also lead to a different conclusion. Certainly Stirling opened himself up to the charge of nostalgia—quoting Somerset Maughan's memory of Charlie Chaplin revisiting his South London childhood habitats as exhibiting the actor's "nostalgia of the slums," and publishing a reproduction of L.S. Lowry's painting of a factory town. But in all his other statements, nostalgia is strictly resisted; rather he finds himself agreeing with the sociologists of worker life, that something not-yet-dead has been killed by the wholesale demolition of slum-clearance programs, and the isolated blocks in a park favored by post-CIAM development. Already in 1954 Stirling had criticized the point blocks of the London County Council housing estates as "intellectually completely meaningless,"[104] and following the completion of Preston had emphasized in a lecture delivered to the California Council of the AIA at a conference dedicated to the analysis of the problems of suburban sprawl, in 1963: "TOWERS NO GOOD ... 'new slums,'" referring to the tower blocks by Lyons, Israel and Ellis on the Preston site. Against what he called in the same lecture "French barracks," Stirling advocated a low-rise terrace solution that would continue to nurture working-class cultural vitality through propinquity:

> The character of a society is formed to a very great extent by the buildings it inhabits, and we have tried here to maintain the vital spirit ("Saturday Night and Sunday Morning") of the alley, yard, and street houses that the new development is replacing, and from which its occupiers have recently moved.[105]

102–103. Stirling and Gowan, rehousing redevelopment, Avenham, Preston: views of a presentation model, 1957–1961 reproduced from black and white negative; 5.8 x 5.6 cm (5 5/16 x 2 3/16 in); AP140.S2.SS1.D18.P15.1.2 / P15.2.1

This scheme for rehousing for the neighbourhood of Avenham shows three-storey terraces with one-bedroom apartments on ground level, and maisonettes above entered from a raised walkway.

101. Reyner Banham, "Coronation Street," 201.

102. Reyner Banham, "Coronation Street," 201.

103. Shirley Conran, "Frankly, do you think this is WORTH A PRIZE?" *Daily Mail*, 18 October 1963.

104. Crinson, ed., *James Stirling: Early Unpublished Writings*," 41.

105. James Stirling and James Gowan, "Rehousing at Preston," *The Architects' Journal*, 1, no. 221 (8 June 1961): 845.

Novels like *Saturday Night and Sunday Morning* (1958), Alan Sillitoe's tale of working-class life in a northern town (later turned into a film directed by Karel Reisz, with Albert Finney and Shirley Anne Field, 1960), and his *The Loneliness of the Long Distance Runner* (1959), far from celebrating the life of the pubs and factories, streets and alleys of postwar industrial towns, were stories less of disillusion than rebellion, moods mirrored in John Osborne's play *Look Back in Anger* (1956) and John Braine's novel *Room at the Top* (1957). This last was also noted by Stirling, together with Joan Littlewood's production of Shelagh Delaney's *A Taste of Honey* (1958), an equally desperate depiction of life in industrial northwestern England. Yet despite his admission that "the 19th century industrial town is justly condemned," Stirling insisted on the existence of "a neighbourliness and a community vitality which are quite absent in

104. Shirley Conran, "Frankly, Do You Think This Is Worth a Prize?" *Daily Mail* newspaper, 18 October 1963
AP140.S2.SS1.D18.P11.1

This will not be the last time that Stirling's housing faces criticism in the press—this time for apparently looking too much like the housing it replaced.

104

the standard solution—the suburban dilution of the garden city." Garden City developments were, for Stirling, "an anachronism, evoking a villa system of living inappropriate to an industrial mass community."[106]

Here he takes his cue not from "kitchen sink" literature or film, whose scenes no doubt evoked images of his own childhood, but from contemporary sociology, and especially from the publications of the surveys of the group known as Mass Observation, a social research organization founded in 1937 by the anthropologist Tom Harrisson, the poet Charles Madge, and film-maker Humphrey Jennings, concerned to understand the cultures of the working class through direct observation. Harrisson's project in "Worktown" (the town of Bolton, Lancashire) was renewed after the war, and published in his book, *Britain Revisited*,[107] with the object of recording the changes that had occurred since the late 1930s. As Harrisson wrote in 1961, "it is difficult to remember (now) how in those far-off days, nearly everybody who was not born into the working-class regarded them as almost a race apart," an attitude that explained both the shock and the excitement of the middle-class "discovery" of working-class life after the war, as well as the discomfort of those, like Hoggart, and perhaps Stirling himself, as they were propelled by education into another world, in which they belonged by talent, but not by birth.[108]

Harrisson, on returning to "Worktown" in 1960, observed that indeed "some things had visibly changed," but what struck him most forcefully was that "Others had visibly *unchanged*—including many that anyone reading newspapers and listening to the radio from abroad would expect to have changed almost beyond recognition."[109] It was this statement that attracted Stirling as he made the argument for retaining some of the forms if not the original substance of worktown's street and alley life. "Recently it has been noted," he wrote, "('Britain Revisited,' T. Harrisson, Mass-observation) that the most remarkable aspect of worktown over the last two decades is its great unchange, particularly in the habits and character of its people—despite greater affluence."[110] Perhaps too Stirling was interested in Bolton as the birthplace of Lord Leverhulme, benefactor of Liverpool University and builder of Port Sunlight. Beneath this sense of a vital community surviving the depredations of the emerging consumer society and increasing suburbanization, was perhaps a lingering and more modest version of the grand utopianism of the modern movement that he had declared lost in the transition from Garches to Jaoul, from the villa to the domestic house; an architecture that assumed as its purpose the retention of social values, while at the same time "incorporating the essential improvements in space, light and convenience," might "perpetuate a familiar and vital environment."[111]

Accordingly, Stirling strived to invent what we might call a "realist regionalism," with brick details taken from the "idiom" of the cotton mills: "functional brick detailing; bull-nosed sills, splayed set-backs, and brick-on-edge

106. Stirling and Gowan, "Rehousing at Preston," 84

107. Tom Harrisson, *Britain Revisited* (London: Victor Gollancz, 1961).

108. Harrisson, *Britain Revisited*, 26.

109. Harrisson, *Britain Revisited*, 28.

110. Stirling and Gowan, "Rehousing at Preston," *Architects' Journal*, 221 (8 June 1961): 845.

111. Stirling and Gowan, "Rehousing at Preston," 845.

105

106

copings," all constructed out of local red engineering brick in order to "reiterate the thin, brittle surface quality of the outsides of the mills."[112] Instead of repeating the street pattern of the old "by-law" town, however, Stirling privileged the public areas—the terraces grouped around a central communal space with playground and a grassed-over pyramid built out of the rubble of demolition, and the houses accessed by ramps and galleries that encouraged social interrelations.

Perhaps the strongest indications of his thinking at Preston, however, were the numerous photographs he took of the completed development. As if in competition with the photographers of East End life, Nigel Henderson and Roger Mayne (and certainly with the Smithsons), Stirling took shots of children playing, running up and down the access ramps, sitting with their legs dangling over the brick walls, as if the entire complex was overrun by children. The only adults to be seen are two mothers with their strollers and shopping, and an elderly woman standing in front of Gowan's old people's houses and flats. Enlarged and mounted on boards for exhibition, these photos claimed ownership of a special kind of social purpose for architecture: not one of utopian isolation, nor one of windy and empty streets-in-the-air, but rather one of direct relationship with conditions on the ground, so to speak, social conditions that might be held in precarious balance with the intrusive effects of "piped radio and television," all the while improving the hygienic and health standards of the dwelling.

In an article written some fourteen years after the completion of the Preston housing, Nicholas Taylor, perhaps echoing J.M. Richards's piece on "The Failure of the New Towns," published in the *Architectural Review* in 1953,[113] traced what

112. Stirling and Gowan, "Rehousing at Preston," 845.

113. Richards, "Failure of the New Towns," 29–32.

107

he called "The Failure of 'Housing,'" accompanied by a series of deeply disturbing photographs by Marilyn Stafford and others edited by Cedric Price and Brian Richards depicting the completed housing estates in use. The results, wrote the editors, were "collectively frightening," despite the fact that most developments had received Ministry awards for "Good Design in Housing."[114]

Preston was among them, and the photographs are not at all inviting: indeed the commentators speak of the "humiliation" of an environment that combines "visual bedlam and environmental pathos;" admittedly the total development was the result of an indifferent block plan designed by the Borough Engineer, and the combination of high-rise tower blocks and low rise housing from four different architectural firms, built by a local contractor. But the critique is nevertheless reserved for Stirling and Gowan's project. While lauding the aspirations of "two brilliant architects" who "turned their backs on arid functionalism" in an attempt to re-create "the best qualities of the local Victorian environment," the editors pointed out that the original Victorian vernacular housing possessed walled private yards for all the activities of children's play, adults' hobbies, storage, rubbish disposal, washing lines and even a bit of gardening." The replacement, however, was set back too far from the road to accommodate anything more than a patch of grass, and the "access deck" turned out to be no more than "an exposed gallery of the minimal width and maximum exposure to the elements." The architects, they concluded, "have not done what they set out to do."[115]

Yet for Stirling and Gowan, as for many postwar architects, the issue was one of joining a sense (visual and functional) of the vernacular with an attempt to construct a modern alternative to the nineteenth-century slum. The

105–107. Stirling and Gowan, James Frazer Stirling, photographer (presumed), views of housing redevelopment at Avenham, Preston, 1959 or after gelatin silver print;
19.8 x 19.9 cm (7 ³/₁₆ x 7 ³/₁₆ in) /
19.3 x 19.3 cm (7 ⅝ x 7 ⅝ in) /
15.5 x 15.2 cm (6 ¾ x 6 in);
AP140 S2 SS1 D18 P3.13 / .P3.8 / .P3.14

These mounted photographs form part of a series of twenty-eight boards presenting the completed re-housing at Preston, with numerous images of children populating the ramps, walls, terraces, and streets, as if to rival the contemporary photographs by Nigel Henderson of London's East End that had been used by the Smithsons to animate their perspectives of the Golden Lane scheme.

114. Nicholas Taylor, "The Failure of Housing," *Architectural Review*, 142, no. 849 (May 1965): 29.

115. Taylor, "The Failure of Housing," 345–346.

contradiction lay in the stubborn resistance of modernist housing typologies to that essential component of traditional urban life, the street and its adjoining facilities. The gradations that pertained to a homogeneous row-house development, from the public (the neighbourhood, the block, the street) and the semi-public (the front door, the back yards and sheds and garden plots) to the private (albeit deprived of essential amenities), were inevitably destroyed in an assemblage of autonomous elements arranged in imitation of streets and squares, but controlled by by-law setbacks that did not allow for back yards, and access "galleries" that stood in for the street but without the density of public occupation. Turned away from the street, the inner "green" courts emulated the ideal of modern movement open space, but were without defined function. The result was an arrangement of modern pieces in a simulation of vernacular planning, where the amorphous ground around high-rise blocks was replicated by amorphous ground around bits of row housing.

Here the by-law legislation against slum development, a trickle-down space-planning technique derived from the health codes of the 1930s and 1940s, entirely negated any reconceptualization of the traditional environment, while the postwar idealization of the gallery-street as a mechanism for preserving modern planning techniques, whether "in the air" or on two or three storeys, worked against the functioning of the traditional community spaces. In subsequent housing projects, in the two stages of Runcorn and the competition for Lima, Stirling would attempt to address these contradictions by adopting entirely modern construction techniques joined to planning principles with a more distinguished heritage than that of the Victorian tenement street, but with similar contradictory results.

Definitely Not "New Brutalism"

The "new brutalism," a term which we used to regard on the one hand as a narrow interpretation of one aspect of architecture, specifically the use of materials and components "as found"—an already established attitude; and on the other hand, as a well-intentioned but over patriotic attempt to elevate English architecture to an international status.
James Stirling and James Gowan, 1959[116]

When Reyner Banham wrote his seminal article on "The New Brutalism" in 1955 he was deeply ambiguous about the use of descriptive art-historical labels that all too easily became "applied" or simply "decorative," while at the same time attempting to demonstrate that the phrase "The New Brutalism" held more content than most as referring to the ethic as well as the style of Britain's "first

116. James Stirling and James Gowan, "Afterthoughts on the Flats at Ham Common," *Architecture and Building* (May 1959): 167.

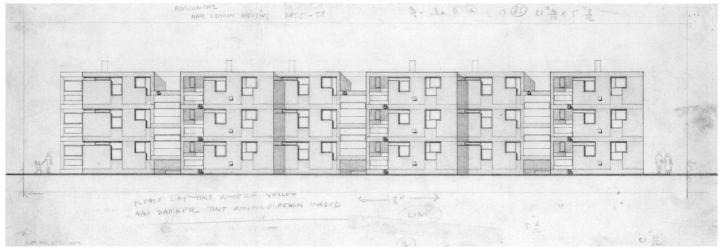

108

native art-movement since the New Art History arrived" with the forced exile of the Pevsners and the Wittkowers in the late 1930s.[117] Yet for all his enthusiasm and detailed exposition of what the movement represented and implied, he had only two major examples in architecture to play with: Alison and Peter Smithson's recently completed school at Hunstanton, and their competition entries for the Golden Lane and Sheffield housing developments, and one non-British example, Louis Kahn's Yale University Art Gallery. By the time he published his book on the movement ten years later, however, he had gathered a host of other buildings under this umbrella, again noting that few architects themselves were prepared to adopt the appellation.

As we have noted, Stirling and Gowan were among the first to reject the term "The New Brutalism" as applied by Banham in his review of the Flats at Ham Common. Despite this, it was these flats that figured in Banham's book as paradigmatic exemplars of what he meant by the term. Admitting that the firm of Stirling and Gowan had "repudiated it both in spoken and printed statements," he concluded that this was less an ideological opposition than an opportunistic one—their fear of "frightening off clients"—and that in the event Stirling's major role in introducing the Maisons Jaoul to Britain made it "impossible for critics and historians to avoid calling them [the Flats at Ham Common] Brutalist."[118] For Banham, indeed, the entire movement was bracketed between Hunstanton and Ham Common at the beginning and Stirling and Gowan's Engineering Building for Leicester University at the end—the last photograph in the book. Leicester was, Banham stated, even "nearer to Brutalism" than the Smithsons' Economist Building, "in the emotional sense of a rough, tough building, and in the dramatic space-play of its sectional

108. Stirling and Gowan, Ham Common Flats, Richmond, London, 1956–63: elevation, 1955–58
graphite and coloured pencil on tracing paper; 20.9 x 59.7 cm (8 ¼ x 23 ½ in); AP140.S2.SS1.D10.P2.1

A three-storey terrace and two two-storey pavilions set in the garden of a Georgian House overlooking Ham Common.

117. Reyner Banham, "The New Brutalism," *Architectural Review*, 118 (December 1955): 354–61, reprinted in *A Critic Writes: Essays by Reyner Banham*, selected by Mary Banham, Paul Barker, Sutherland Lyall, and Cedric Price (Berkeley: University of California Press, 1996), 7–15.

118. Reyner Banham, *The New Brutalism: Ethic or Aesthetic?* (London: The Architectural Press, 1965), 87.

organization," carrying "still something of the aggressive informality of the mood of the middle fifties."[119]

While it was Banham's genius to be able to turn a term in such a way as to imply an entire movement, the reality was that Stirling's work was never that close to the manner that Banham had originally articulated according to the example of the Smithsons' early buildings. "Basic structure," "honest use of materials," and "formal legibility of plan," together with a lack of eloquence and absolute consistency, an "abstemiousness" in the under designing of the details—in all a "ruthless logic"—were the attributes of Hunstanton.[120]

In this context, it is easy to understand Stirling's resistance to the epithet "Brutalist." Firstly, the Flats at Ham Common were less a stylistic imitation of the Maisons Jaoul than a critique. In his article "Garches to Jaoul," Stirling found Le Corbusier's houses "primitive in character ... out of tune with their Parisian environment," their brickwork "by English standards ... poor."[121] Perhaps equally important, his critique of both Garches and Jaoul was primarily formal, contrasting their spatial organization and surface qualities, between the "point structure" and "free plan" of Garches and the load-bearing brick cross-walls and "cellular" planning of Jaoul, the "explosion in terms of cubist space" of the one and the "small boxes" inside the other, the one an exercise in the "machine aesthetic," the other making "no advance on medieval building." His comparison was between a villa built as "a monument, not to an age which is dead, but to a way of life which has not generally arrived," and houses which "are almost cosy ... built by and intended for the status quo."[122] If there was an "ethic" implied here it was one that recognized the inevitable transition from a grand utopian design to the more pragmatic circumstances of postwar life.

In both, however, Stirling insisted on the "sheer plastic virtuosity" of Le Corbusier's composition, and it is this sense of volumetric spatiality that carries over into the Flats at Ham Common, and the entire sequence of "red brick" buildings that follow: the House in the Chilterns (1956); the students' residences for Churchill College (1958); the School Assembly Hall, Camberwell (1958); the housing for Selwyn College Cambridge (1959); the Leicester University Engineering Building (1959); the Children's Home, Putney (1960); the Old People's Home, Blackheath (1960); the Cambridge University History Faculty Building (1964); and the Florey Building for Queen's College, Oxford (1966). In all of these buildings and projects, brick and glass are manipulated in a manner that evokes the regional vernaculars of the British nineteenth century, with continuing reference to the paradigmatic structures of the modern movement, from de Stijl and Constructivism to Purism, and with a volumetric virtuosity that transcends all implications and effects of eclecticism.

Kenneth Frampton, in his assessment of Stirling's "transformations in style," starts from the premise that the "cardinal points of departure" of

119. Banham, *The New Brutalism*, 134.

120. Reyner Banham, "The New Brutalism," in *A Critic Writes*, 10–11.

121. Stirling, "From Garches to Jaoul," 146.

122. Stirling, "From Garches to Jaoul," 151.

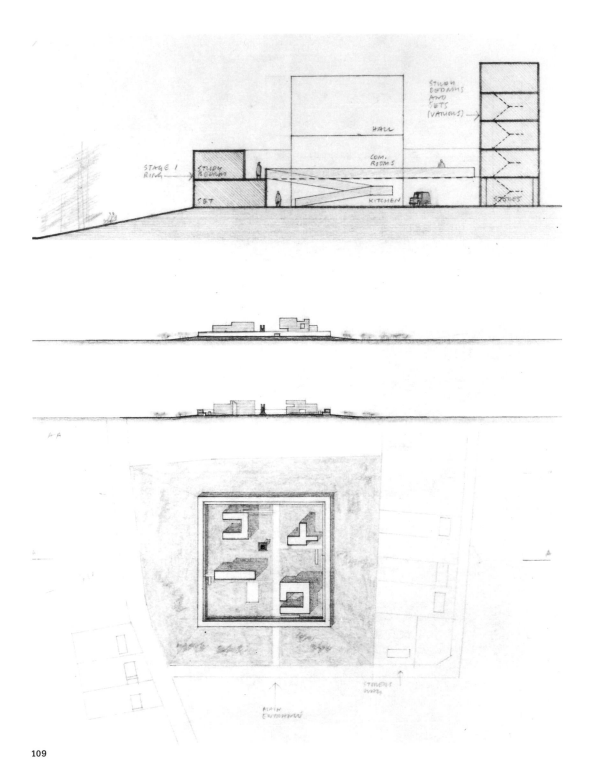

109. Stirling and Gowan, limited competition for Churchill College, Cambridge, England: first scheme gelatin silver print; 20.6 x 15.6 cm (8 ⅛ x 6 ⅛ in); AP140.S2.SS1.D19.P3.1

This first scheme for Churchill College, probably developed for the first stage of the competition, already contains the idea of the enclosed court with individual buildings within, raised on an earthwork in the flat landscape of the Cambridge fens.

109

The Crisis of Rationalism

110

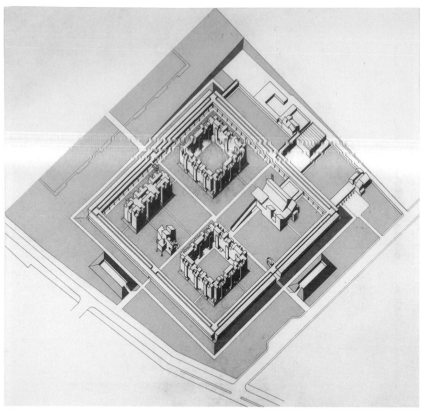

110. Stirling and Gowan, Churchill
College: Report and Outline
Specification, 1958
33 x 22 x 0.5 cm (13 x 8 ⅝ x ⁵⁄₁₈ in);
AP140.S2.SS1.D19.P11.1

Stirling and Gowan's Report on their
scheme went to great lengths to justify
the scale of their court by comparison
with other Cambridge courts, here a
plan comparison with Downing College.
Colin Rowe in his 1959 article on the
competition results remarked on what
he saw as an "epidemic of claustrophilia"
that "infected" the submitted designs.
("The Blenheim of the Welfare State",
The Cambridge Review (31 October 1959)

111. Stirling and Gowan, Churchill
College, Cambridge: axonometric,
1958 or after
gelatin silver print with colored transfer
film mounted on masonite panel;
81.7 x 84.6 cm (32 ³⁄₁₆ x 33 ⁵⁄₁₆ in);
AP140.S2.SS1.D19.P2

112. Stirling and Gowan, Churchill
College, Cambridge: axonometric of
the library, 1958
ink on paper; 50.1 x 40.6 cm
(19 ¾ x 16 in); AP140.S2.SS1.D19.P1.1

This axonometric, probably prepared for
publication in the "Black" volume nevertheless demonstrates the way in which
the early work was already conceived in
these three-dimensional terms.

111

112

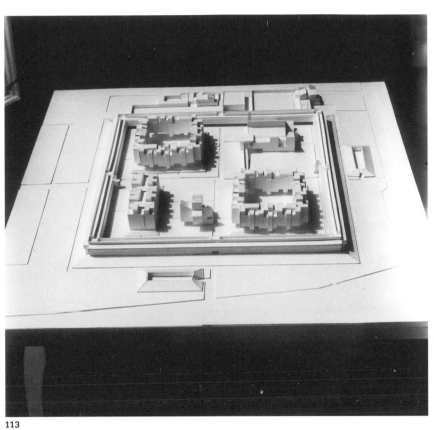

113

113. Stirling and Gowan, Churchill College, Cambridge: view of model, 1958 gelatin silver print; 10.9 x 10.6 cm (4 ¼ x 4 ⅛ in); AP140.S2.SS1.D19.P4.10

114. Stirling and Gowan, School Assembly Hall, Brunswick Park Primary School, Camberwell, London: axonometric, 1958–61 ink, coloured pencil and graphite on paper; 49.1 x 67 cm (19 ⅜ x 26 ⅜ in); AP140.S2.SS1.D21.P2.2

Unsuccessful at Churchill College, Stirling and Gowan nevertheless succeeded in retaining some of the primary features of their design in microcosm in this school building raised up on a steep berm and composed with geometrical precision.

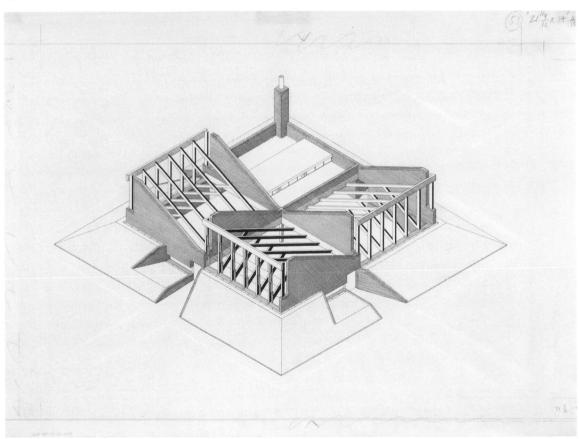

114

Stirling's work are the dialectics between "*high art* versus *low art* and *high tech* versus *low tech*" as represented in the "distinct aspects of a native 19th century 'vernacular.'"[123] This dialectic began to emerge strongly in the late 1950s, when the notations of regional style that pervaded the earlier domestic projects began to emerge side by side with more conventional references to the historical traditions of high architecture and experiments in reformulating the languages of the early avant-gardes for the present.

Thus, the competition project for Churchill College at once pays homage to the long history of fortifications, with its square court set on a geometrically pure bank of earth—Girouard notes that Gowan had photographed the castle walls at Restormel in Cornwall (a reference that is echoed in the vertical castellated residential blocks)—and to the architecture of Cambridge colleges; the great court itself is directly contrasted by the architects in scale and in form with that of Downing College, and the smaller student housing courts with Pembroke. Rowe, in his note to the republication of his review article of the competition, "The Blenheim of the Welfare State," even hazarded that Stirling had been influenced by the description of the arcaded plaza of the Mexican town of Chiapas de Corzo.[124]

Here, however, historical references stop, and are translated into a strict geometry of ideal city proportions: square great court with four pavilions set within it. An early scheme, preserved in the archive, diagrams the plans of these pavilions—residential blocks, library, and dining halls, but with a sectional development that differs from the final submission. Where the final plan designed the perimeter student residences to form a colonnaded cloister arcade on the ground level, the earlier solution reversed this, with a walkway on the second floor connecting to bridges and ramps that linked common rooms, halls and the five-storey residence buildings on this upper level. In this drawing, but not included in the final scheme, one can just make out a witty allusion to the college's founder: a two-storey-high monument figuring Churchill's characteristic two-finger victory sign; were this to have survived the design process it would have nicely countered the enormous obelisk in the project by Sir Hugh Casson—a monument, as Colin Rowe noted, that would have enraged purists but with the passage of time would have joined the wind-swept fenland site of Churchill College to other spires of the old city.

But the *tour de force* of the project was the smallest pavilion of all, containing the library. This was a little jewel of volumetric complexity developed from a simple Greek-cross plan, one arm taken up with the stairs to the second-storey reading room and stacks; another with administration, and the two remaining with the book stacks. These last were lit from the top by raked skylights in the roof trusses. The total composition is a fully transitional object, joined on the one hand to the series of ideal "House Studies" drawn by Stirling and Gowan three years before, and on the other looking forward to the elementarist forms and

123. Frampton, "Transformations in Style: The Work of James Stirling," 135.

124. Colin Rowe, *As I was Saying: Recollections and Miscellaneous Essays*, ed. Alexander Caragonne, 3 vols. (Cambridge, Mass.: MIT Press, 1960), 1: 43.

angular glass constructions of Leicester and the Cambridge History Faculty. A miniature version of this unbuilt project *was* realized, however, in the School Assembly Hall at Camberwell in 1958, where a square plan, also set on sloping berms, was bisected into four, containing a kitchen and the hall, each with steeply monopitched roofs, and a flat-roofed service wing, the whole faced in white brick.

Their grand square great court for a free-standing and isolated Churchill College having been refused, Stirling and Gowan adopted an opposite strategy when planning an extension to Selwyn College, this time in the gardens of the existing courtyard structure. Rather than replicating what Colin Rowe had called, in the context of the Churchill College competition, the "claustrophilia" that seemed to attack all who took on Cambridge college development, the architects produced a scheme in three gently curved segments that established itself as a "new garden-wall building reminiscent of Jefferson's plan for the University of Virginia."[125] Again raised up on a grass-covered mound, these four-storey apartment blocks were entirely glazed towards the interior with a faceted façade facing onto the gardens, with service towers and rear wall in brick.

And Certainly Not "New Historicism"

Let me ask this question to start with: is one entitled to speak of Neo-Expressionism today? My answer is "yes."
Nikolaus Pevsner, 1967[126]

Six years after he had delivered his celebrated warning to the RIBA that a "new historicism" was swiftly taking over the purity of Modern Movement language, Pevsner visited the Leicester University Engineering Building, then already four years old. In his BBC Third Programme account of this visit to the building, he took, he said, "a good look at it," noting the exposed concrete of the projecting auditoria and the "blue engineering-bricks" of the cladding. Linking the building to Paul Rudolph's Art and Architecture Building at Yale and Eero Saarinen's TWA Terminal at Idlewild (Kennedy) Airport, he summed them up in one word: Expressionism, concluding that "We cannot, in the long run, live our day-to-day lives in the midst of explosions."[127] If we ignore the fact that his "good look" mistook red for blue bricks, and detected exposed concrete where none existed, Pevsner's observations stand as the lament of a die-hard "modernist" in the Gropius tradition, concerned at the impropriety of "self-indulgent" and "self-expressive" architecture where decorum called for simplicity and low-key functionality—what he felt was the increasing tendency of architects to transform buildings built for anonymous clients into monuments to themselves.

125. Stirling, *Buildings and Projects 1950–1974*, 85.

126. Nikolaus Pevsner, "Architecture in our Time: the Anti-pioneers—II," *The Listener*, 5 January 1967, 7.

127. Pevsner, "Architecture in our Time," 7, 9.

115. Stirling and Gowan, student apartments for Selwyn College, Cambridge, England: bird's-eye axonometric, 1959 ink and traces of graphite on paper; 29.6 x 20.8 cm (11 ⅝ x 8 ³/₁₆ in); AP140.S2.SS1.D22.P1

Abandoning the strict "classicism" of their Churchill College scheme, Stirling and Gowan conceived of the new housing for Selwyn College as a linked chain of glass fronted pavilions, delicately threaded through the gardens as a transparent and mobile boundary. Perhaps this project, and others that follow, at once look to the tradition of British greenhouses and to the more avant-garde traditions of Bruno Taut's "Glass Chain" in Germany (1919–20) and to the Russian Constructivists after 1918.

116–118. Stirling and Gowan, Selwyn College, Cambridge: views of model, 1959 gelatin silver print; 11.1 x 14.7 cm (4 ⅜ x 5 ³/₁₆ in) / 13.6 x 9.3 cm (5 ⅜ x 3 ¹¹/₁₆ in) / 12.1 x 20.1 cm (4 ¾ x 7 ¹⁵/₁₆ in); AP140.S2.SS1.D22.P3.2 / P3.1 / P3.3

The model shows the glass front and the castellated, solid rear of the housing, a theme that reappears in the Florey Building at Oxford.

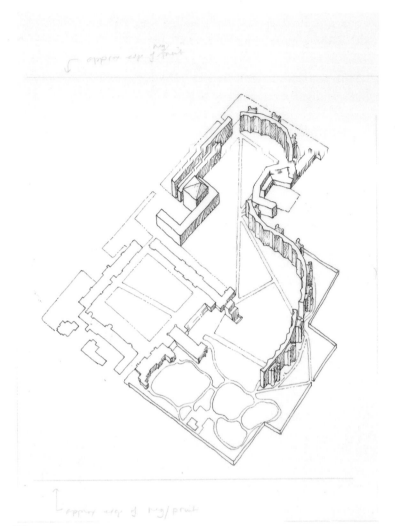

115

116

117

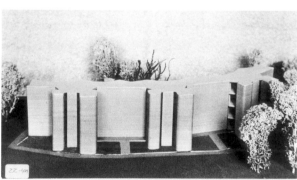

118

Banham, by contrast, saw the building as "world-class," "one of the very few" that Britain had produced since the war. Yes, it suggested its antecedents in the Werkbund, or in Futurism, and "in some obtuse way of its own regained a good deal of the bloody-minded élan and sheer zing of the pioneer Modernism of the early Twenties," but its originality transcended these echoes, and it stood on its own "as a natural machine-age architecture."[128] Built out of the cheapest industrial materials, mostly left "as found," its relaxed and unpretentious composition simply manifested "the style for the job," as Banham quoted Gowan.

In the event, discussions over the "style" or "styles" of Stirling and Gowan's work at Ham Common or Leicester obscure the fact that all the elements of a mature architectural manner were already formed: from the regionalist sensibility came the "fortification" podiums and their ramps, the contrasting use of glass, steel and brick, the reflection of vernacular forms; from the arsenal of modern architecture came the "constructivist" display of functional components, most notably the stacked lecture halls in the façade of Sheffield and the projecting and winding stairs in the library of Churchill College. More importantly, these elements—formed as it were as "found"—already possessed a three-dimensional compositional technique: that of the binding together of the whole through a process of volumetric experiment. As Gowan later noted, this technique had been a part of the partners' "conversations through drawing" from the beginning, and had been explored through the "House Studios" of 1956, and elaborated in the House at Woolton, the House in the Chilterns, and in the interiors of Ham Common. This formal "welding together" of preconceived elements would become a hallmark of Stirling's developed design strategies for the rest of his career.

The topic of the partnership has necessarily evoked the critically vexed question of the "contribution" of each partner to the process—a question that was to be exacerbated by the evidently irritable relations between the partners after the break-up. But while certain art-historical approaches might trace back such contributions from a study of the later work of each partner—certain critics have noted the verticality of Gowan's later houses, and Gowan himself has clarified the design process through interviews—with respect to the overall analysis of the work such speculation is largely irrelevant. Perhaps the most salient of Gowan's reminiscences of that moment is that the two partners "learned from each other," and that the discussion was conducted through drawing rather than cerebral speculation. The image depicted by Michael Wilford, the partners seated on either side of him as he passed notes and drawings from one to the other, is on the one hand an amusing insight into a non-verbal relationship, but on the other testifies to a way of working that will become Stirling's own, as he increasingly relies on the repeated iteration of a design in drawn form in order to clarify the ideas embedded in the scheme.

128. Reyner Banham, "The Style for the Job,"
New Statesman, 14 February 1964, 261.

IV: Typology Redivivus

Machines for Learning

Stirling follows in the mainstream of the 20th-century "pioneer" tradition which at its best has concerned itself with the formation of new types for the accommodation of socially unprecedented solutions—with the creation of that which El Lissitzky chose to call the new "social condensers."

Kenneth Frampton, 1968[129]

With the critique of the International Style and the CIAM programs of the 1940s, the generation of Team X sought to revivify the modernist search for typological expression, first in housing, as Colin St John Wilson experimented with the Unité block for the London County Council, and with the Smithsons' projects for Golden Lane, and then in the forms of social institutions such as schools and community centres as exemplified by the Smithsons at Hunstanton, and Stirling from the outset with his Thesis Project for Newton Aycliffe, both employing already developed languages from, respectively, Mies and Breuer. The brilliance of Leicester was to weld the functional and the architectural traditions together in an apparently seamless way. The functional tradition is there—with patent glazing and engineering brick—but Melnikov is also there (had he perhaps already been there too in Sheffield's auditoria?), as is the verticality of Sant'Elia's Futurism. Both these early modernisms had been recently rediscovered by the historians, notably Futurism by Reyner Banham and Constructivism by Vittorio de Feo, and both were readily assimilated into the iconographic analysis of Leicester.

The success of Leicester, however, derives not so much from the assembly of recognizable historical elements, but more from the fundamental redefinition of modernist typology this assembly represented. For despite Stirling's rather perfunctory remarks on circulation and accommodation, it was these concerns, joined to the demand for volumetric expression, that developed in the projects

129. Kenneth Frampton "Stirling's Buildings," *Architectural Forum*, 129, no. 4 (1968): 44.

after Churchill College a functional expression of use, that drew on both the functional tradition and the early modern architectural tradition. The functional tradition as it responded to the new building needs of nineteenth-century industrial culture had, with the help of engineers and architects, established a range of new building types with their own characteristic forms—prisons, railway stations, factories, warehouses, hospitals. The architectural tradition had gradually developed its own responses to these needs as, for example, it divided the railway station into two parts—the architectural entrance and the functional shed, at the same time as it developed answers to the higher cultural functions of museums, libraries, theatres, and the like. These also often incorporated elements of the functional tradition—as in Henri Labrouste's Bibliothèque Sainte-Geneviève, Paris, where the interior reading room is constructed out of iron and glass with a stone exterior, faced with stone panels incised with the names of great authors. The relations between these two strains of tradition were mediated by a double reliance on the functional diagram and the use of technology on the one hand, and on available classical prototypes on the other. The modern movements were equally preoccupied with functional typology, with the difference that the combination of abstraction in form and industrialization in technology allowed for a unification of the two traditions, but with various emphases according to aesthetic or political interests. Le Corbusier was more concerned to connect with the academic and classical tradition, taking his concept of unity from the holistic axonometrics of Auguste Choisy that tied all history together in a common representation of plan, section and elevation. The Futurists and Constructivists were in different ways convinced of the power of architecture to forge new social relationships in a technological era. Thus Le Corbusier would develop the type of the modern villa out of a pseudo-Palladian prototype, and the type of the collective dwelling out of the communitarian programs of the early nineteenth century—the Unité out of the Phalanstery. The Constructivists, intent on inventing new social condensers for the new socialist society, were less dependent on precedent and assembled the elements of the program in expressive combinations—thus Constantin Melnikov's workers' clubs.[130]

Stirling himself was clear that the diagram of Leicester was a self-conscious attempt to establish a "type form" for university laboratories. In a previously unpublished lecture given at Royaumont to the Team X meeting in September 1972, and with the memory of Churchill College still fresh, he spoke of the difference between a traditional university, with living, dining, and learning in a single building surrounding a courtyard, and the new university, where learning was separated from living, and accommodated in highly specialized buildings.[131] For this, as he elaborated in the ensuing discussion, he had in mind the prototype of the factory, where the administration building and entrance at the front and the machine sheds behind were traditionally separated.

130. Examples of Russian Constructivist architecture were eagerly studied in the late 1950s and early 1960s. See Berthold Lubetkin, "Soviet Architecture. Notes on Development from 1917 to 1932," *Architectural Association Journal* (May 1956): 260–64; "Soviet Architecture. Notes on Development from 1937 to 1955," *Architectural Association Journal* (October 1956): 85–89; Vittorio de Feo, *U.R.S.S. architettura 1917–1936* (Rome: Editori Riuniti, 1963).

131. Crinson, ed., *James Stirling: Early Unpublished Writings*, 85–100.

119. Stirling and Gowan, Leicester University Engineering Building, Leicester, England: axonometric, 1959–63
graphite and colored pencil on paper; 33.6 x 75.8 cm (13 ¼ x 29 ¹³/₁₆ in); AP140.S2.SS1.D23.P1.2

The archive contains few if any preliminary sketches or design development drawings for Leicester. This celebrated axonometric, however, does reflect the interest of the office in the crystalline effects of intersecting glass facets and the cascading ribbons of glass that join the solid vertical elements of the stair and laboratory towers.

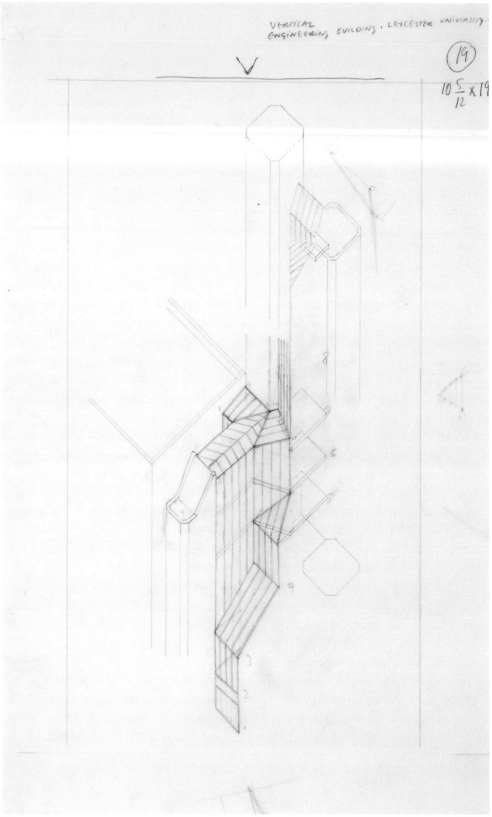

119

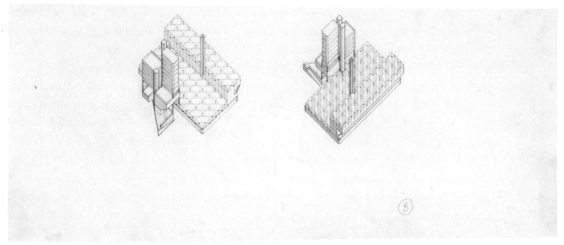

120

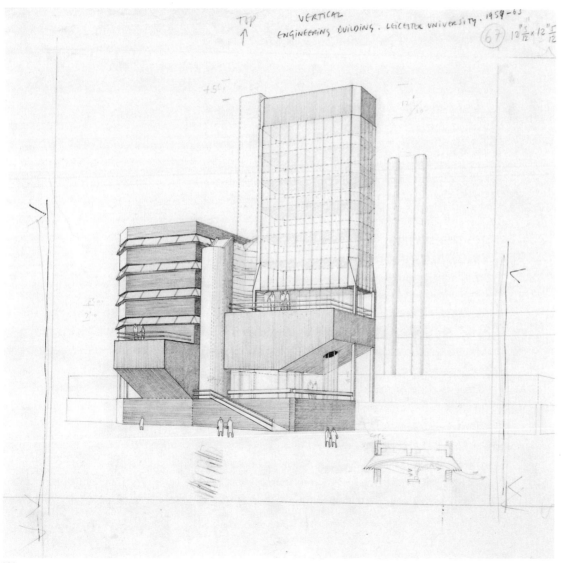

121

120. Stirling and Gowan, Leicester University Engineering Building: axonometric, 1959–63
graphite on paper; 33.6 x 75.8 cm (13 ¼ x 29 ¹³⁄₁₆ in) (unfolded); AP140.S2.SS1.D23.P1.3

These are the equally celebrated set-up drawings for the axonometric projections of Leicester, the form that became a hallmark of Stirling's representational technique, and also of his implicit approach to design. He was referred to as "Isometric Stirling," in a review of the 1974 RIBA exhibition of his drawings in *Design*, 304 (May 1974), pp. 66–69.

121. Stirling and Gowan, Leicester University Engineering Building: perspective, 1959–63
graphite on paper; 25.8 x 25.7 cm (10 ³⁄₁₆ x 10 ⅛ in); AP140.S2.SS1.D23.P1.1

The typological argument was in fact crucial for Stirling, who was faced with the question raised at Royaumont by Amancio Guedes: was Leicester indeed a prototype, or was it simply an "immensely personal," "very formal" building, that, as Peter Smithson avowed, was designed first in "an artistic way" and only afterwards justified in functional terms? For the Royaumont audience, charged with investigating the Smithsons' ideas of "building group concepts," urban infra-structure, and infill, where the one-off design was rejected in favor of the building being seen as a "fragment" among many others, Leicester seemed all too traditional, a brilliant design by a single personality. (Crinson notes that in his lecture Stirling failed to acknowledge the role of Gowan in the partnership.) Equally startling, no doubt, was the apparently radical shift in expression from Preston (perhaps the project that the Smithsons had hoped would be presented) to Leicester.[132]

It was Kenneth Frampton, a more enthusiastic critic than Peter Smithson, who, in his treatment of Leicester, the Cambridge History Faculty Building, and the student housing for St Andrews University, saw them as exemplary types, expressing their distinct natures as institutions. Thus at Cambridge, as he noted, where the other entries to the limited competition for the commission saw the library "as a semi-self-contained prism, linked to office and seminar space housed in a free-standing slab," Stirling had realized a fusion of the two, "into a composite geometric model," as a result of "the architect's conception of the building as a particular 'type,'" a concern that Frampton saw as central to the recent work.[133] That Stirling had also employed references to the language of the Soviet avant-garde made it easy for Frampton, the historian of Constructivism, to draw the obvious comparison.

Leicester, Cambridge, Oxford, and to an even greater extent, St Andrews, Olivetti, Dorman Long, and Siemens, were in this ascription "machines." Their diagrams, like those of many similar *machines à guérir* ("Curing machines") from the hospital movement of the late eighteenth century, *machines à punir* ("punishment machines") from the prison movement of the early nineteenth century, or *machines à habiter* ("dwelling machines") from the housing movements of the twentieth, were fundamentally simple: Leicester with its horizontal machine shed and vertical administration and research tower; Cambridge with its L-shaped administration and office tower wrapping a semi-pentagon with fanning stacks for central control; the Florey Building with its contemporary version of a cloister and courtyard, and its wrapping of stepped-back apartments; St Andrews with its precast unit fingers from a central entry; Dorman Long with, as Frampton observed, its vertical version of the Florey Building, its glazed administration block stepped back; the Olivetti Training Centre with its central entry and wings; Siemens with its stern rows of cylindrical towers, and culminating in the project for the Olivetti Headquarters, Milton Keynes, with its

132. Crinson, ed. *James Stirling Early Unpublished Writings*, 95, 100.

133. Kenneth Frampton, "Stirling's Building," *Architectural Forum*, 129 (1968): 44.

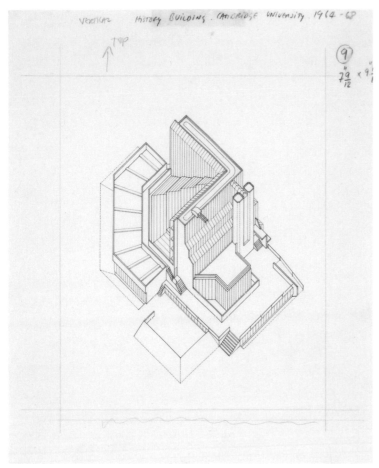

122

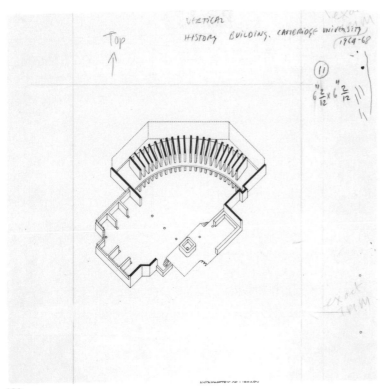

123

122. James Stirling (Firm), History Faculty Building, University of Cambridge, England: axonometric, 1963–67
ink on paper; 34.2 x 27.8 cm (13 ½ x 11 in); AP140.S2.SS1.D26.P3.1

The cluster of axonometrics that surrounded the presentation for Leicester, Cambridge, St Andrews, and Dorman Long led Charles Jencks to assemble them on a single page of his *Modern Movements in Architecture* (1973), comparing them to an analytical drawing of a Mariner spacecraft: "A whole aesthetic and a way of life comes from the logic and articulation possible with such a method" (p. 267). His thesis adviser and mentor Reyner Banham was less convinced, however: the comparison was misleading, he stated, in two ways. Firstly the method of composition of building and spacecraft was radically different (the spacecraft was a collection of modules joined by struts, the building a complete totality) and secondly because the drawing of the Mariner was a perspective not an axonometric (Banham, Introduction, *James Stirling* (exhibition catalogue, RIBA, Heinz Gallery, London, 1974).

123. James Stirling (Firm), History Faculty Building, Cambridge: cutaway axonometric of library and radial book-stacks, 1963–67
ink on paper; 25.8 x 25.7 cm (10 ³⁄₁₆ x 10 ⅛ in); AP140.S2.SS1.D26.P3.2

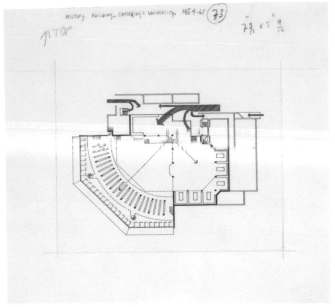

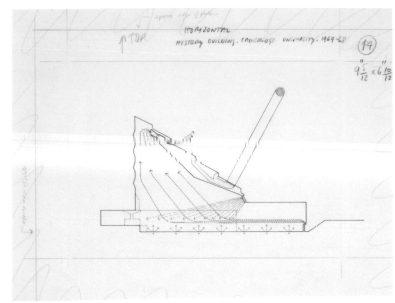

124

125

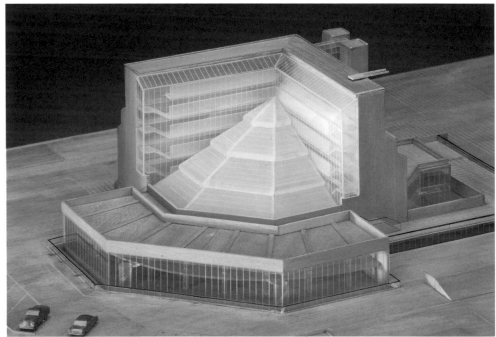

126

124. James Stirling (Firm), History Faculty Building, Cambridge: plan, 1963–67
ink on paper; 24.5 x 26.4 cm (9 ⅝ x 10 ⅜ in); AP140.S2.SS1.D26.P4.1

This plan shows the lines of sight from the control desk to the radial stacks, emphasizing the "panoptical" nature of the plan.

125. James Stirling (Firm), History Faculty Building, Cambridge: diagram of interior environment controls, 1963–67
ink on paper; 25.8 x 33.8 cm (10 ³⁄₁₆ x 13 ⁵⁄₁₆ in); AP140.S2.SS1.D26.P2.2

In the light of the many criticisms of the environmental conditions created by the glass-roofed reading room, this diagram at least demonstrates that the firm was entirely conscious of potential ventilation conditions during the design phase.

126. James Stirling (Firm), History Faculty Building, Cambridge: presentation model in site model, 1963
wood, plastic, graphite and metal; 57 x 67 x 15 cm (22 ⁷⁄₁₆ x 26 ⅜ x 5 ⅞ in) (largest); AP140.S2.SS1.D26.P30

This presentation model of the Cambridge History Faculty Building was used, detached from its site and suspended above eye level at the Museum of Modern Art, New York's exhibition of Stirling's "Three Buildings" in 1969 so that the visitor could stand beneath it and look up directly into the glass-roofed space.

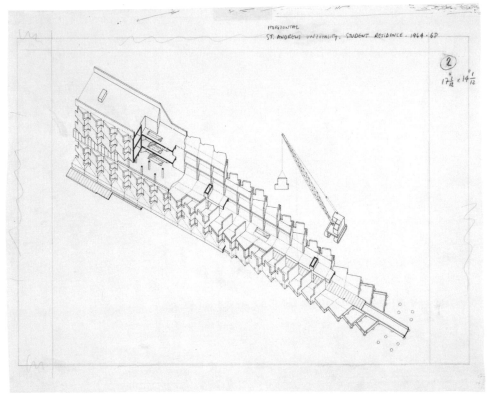

127

127. James Stirling (Firm), Students'
Residence, University of St Andrews,
Scotland: axonometric, 1963–68
ink on paper; 44.5 x 54.7 cm
(17 ½ x 21 ½ in); AP140.S2.SS1.D28.P4.2

Stirling, replying to Banham's
Introduction to his drawing show in 1974,
noted that "Drawings (axos [onometric])
of assemblage type buildings (i.e. St
Andrews, Runcorn) always show incomplete buildings but make explicit the
assemblage process. Therefore an image
of assemblage and not a building entity"
(*James Stirling*, exhibition catalogue,
RIBA, Heinz Gallery, p. 16).

128. James Stirling (Firm), Students'
Residence, University of St Andrews:
site perspective, 1963–68
ink on paper; 21.9 x 32.5 cm
(8 ⅝ x 12 ¾); AP140.S2.SS1.D28.P5.2

The fingers of Stirling's residences
set into the landscape and pointing
towards the sea.

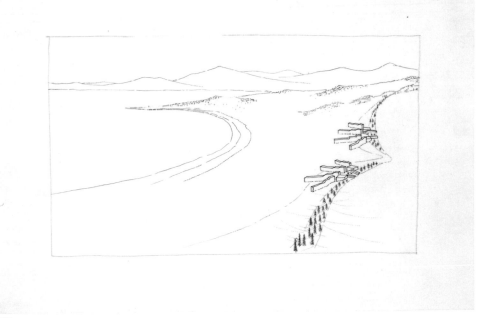

128

129. James Stirling (Firm), Students' Residence, University of St Andrews: bird's-eye view, 1963–68 watercolor and graphite on reprographic copy and gelatin silver print mounted on cardboard; 28.4 x 33.6 cm (11 ⅛ x 13 ¼ in); AP140.S2.SS1.D28.P6

A photo-collage of the model of the two built wings together with the unbuilt housing in the landscape.

130. James Stirling (Firm), Florey Building, The Queen's College, Oxford, England: site plan, 1966–71 ink on paper; 41.7 x 73.5 cm (16 ⅜ x 28 ¹⁵⁄₁₆ in), AP140.S2.SS1.D31.P6.22

In this figure-ground plan of the Oxford colleges, Stirling shows the Florey student residence as taking part in the sequence of courts along the High Street and across the river.

129

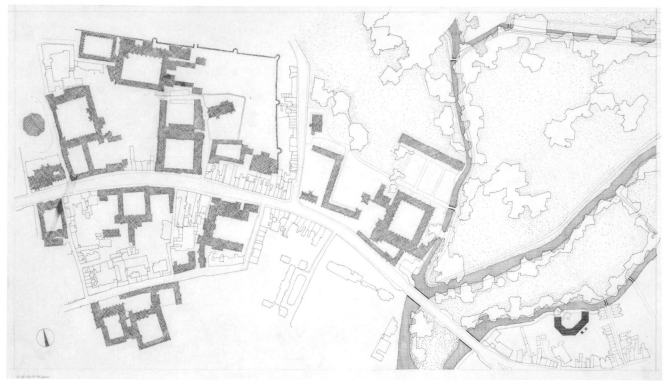

130

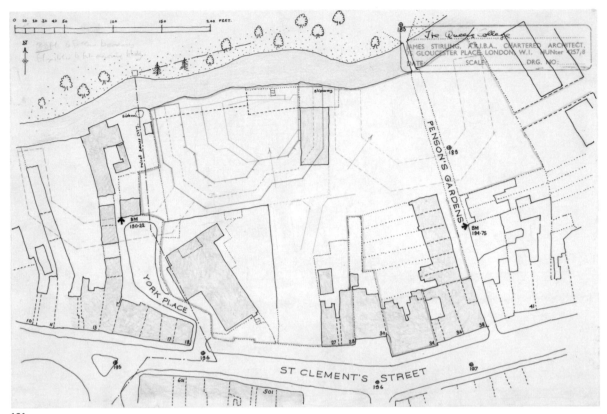

131

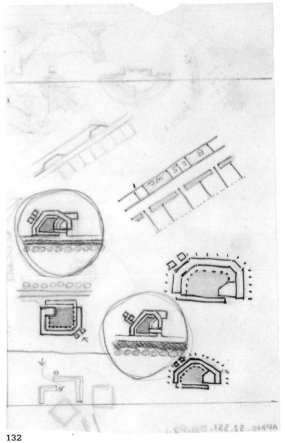

132

131. James Stirling (Firm), Florey
Building, The Queen's College, Oxford:
site plan, 1966–71
ink, graphite and colored pencil on
paper; 25.3 x 37.1 cm (10 x 14 ⅝ in);
AP140.S2.SS1.D31.P1.3

132. James Stirling (Firm), Florey
Building, The Queen's College, Oxford:
sketches, 1966–71
ink, graphite and colored pencil on
paper; 16.3 x 10.4 cm (6 ⅜ x 4 ⅛ in);
AP140.S2.SS1.D31.P2.1

Stirling was well known for his interventions in red "biro" pen that accepted,
noted, or rejected a particular drawing
or project.

133

133. James Stirling (Firm), Florey Building, The Queen's College, Oxford: sketches, 1966–71
ink, graphite and coloured pencil on paper; 25.3 x 33.1 cm (10 x 13 in); AP140.S2.SS1.D31.P2.13

This became the set-up for the published "wide-angle" perspective of the court seen from the river.

134. James Stirling (Firm), Florey Building, The Queen's College, Oxford: plans, elevation and perspective, 1966–71
ink, graphite and coloured pencil on paper; 21.9 x 16.8 cm (8 ⅝ x 6 ⅝ in); AP140.S2.SS1.D31.P2.14

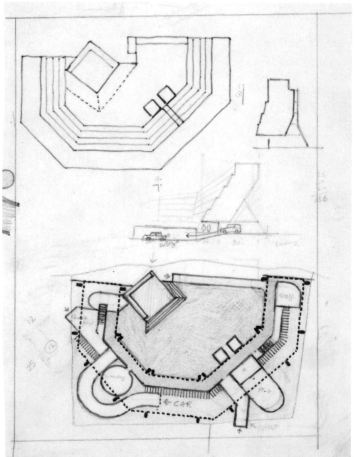

134

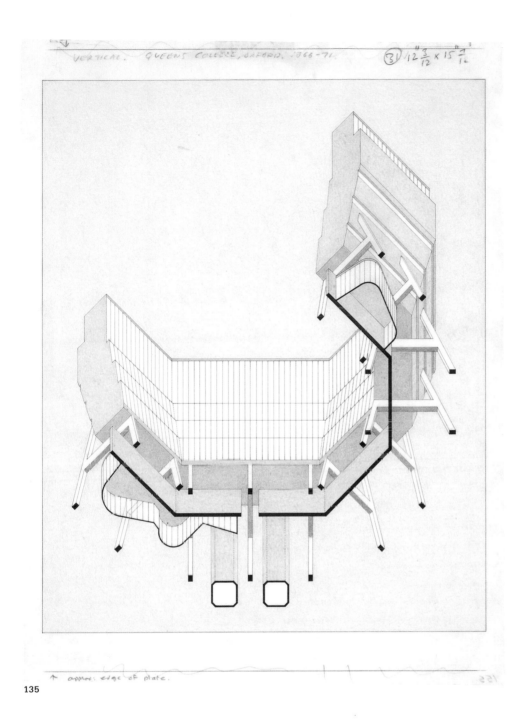

135

136

135. James Stirling (Firm), Florey Building, The Queen's College, Oxford: axonometric, 1966–71 ink, graphite, and coloured crayon on tracing paper; 44.7 x 33.6 cm (17 ⅝ x 13 ¼ in) (irreg.); AP140.S2.SS1.D31.P5.2

Perhaps the most celebrated of Stirling's "worm's-eye views," this original drawing was exhibited in the RIBA exhibition of 1974 complete with its original mat.

136. James Stirling (Firm), Florey Building, The Queen's College, Oxford: elevation for kitchen ventilator, 1966–71 watercolour and coloured pencil on reprographic copy; 23.8 x 21.6 cm (9 ⅜ x 8 ½ in); AP140.S2.SS1.D31.P4.2

This ventilator looks back to the original weathervane and chimney depicted on the roof of the Community Centre for Newton Aycliffe. Throughout Stirling's career he rarely forgot an unbuilt scheme or detail motif and consistently worked to bring them into new contexts and built projects.

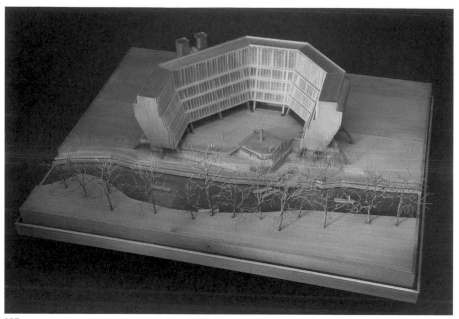

137

137. James Stirling (Firm), Florey Building, The Queen's College, Oxford: presentation model, 1966–71 wood, cork, plastic and metal; 38 x 49 x 15 cm (15 x 19 ¼ x 5 ⅞ in); AP140.S2.SS1.D31.P16

extended "Leicester" typology of vertical office wing attached to a horizontal workshop and warehouse. On these grounds, some critics have hazarded, Stirling was, far from radically shifting the architectural debate over functionalism, indeed more traditionally modern than many modern functionalists.

Indeed, Stirling seems to delight in developing his "types" out of the more functional modern traditions—the non-architectural vernacular types. Thus in Leicester, the building "like" a machine (the vertical tower) stands alongside the building "produced" by machine (the laboratory block) in order to evoke the early factory. In the Cambridge library, the reading room is conceived like a Panopticon, the vertical offices as mass-produced service spaces. In the Siemens competition entry, the building has, as it were, almost entirely become a machine, with a distinct resemblance to gasometers stranded in the landscape. Here, however, there emerged a problem that both Stirling and his critics sensed—the question of appropriate expression that haunted his early essays on the vernacular. While not "Expressionist," in the terms launched by Pevsner, the attempt to make these originally vernacular types fully expressive in contemporary *architectural* terms led to an individualization of the works, and hence to their apparent non-reproducibility.[134]

134. See: Kenneth Frampton, "Leicester University Engineering Laboratory," *Architectural Design*, 34 (February 1964): 61–89; Reyner Banham, "The Style for the Job," *New Statesman*, 14 February 1964, 261, Reyner Banham, "The Word in Britain: 'Character,'" *Architectural Forum* (August–September 1964): 118–25; Kenneth Frampton, "Stirling's Building," *Architectural Forum*, 129,

no. 4 (1968): 44–46; John Jacobus, "Engineering Building, Leicester," *Architectural Review*, 135, no. 806 (April 1964): 252–80.

Formal Critique/Functional Tradition

Leicester is a commentary on the Le Corbusier/Rowe conception of the vertical plane, and ultimately an assault on any modernist conception of plane. This attack on modernist sensibilities also brings us face-to-face with Leicester as a critique of Constructivism, the direct constructivist references in Leicester being more difficult to refute.

Peter Eisenman, 1974[135]

Between 1957 and 1963 there emerged in Britain three alternative modes of architectural analysis represented by three major essays: John Summerson's polemical essay "The Case for a Theory of Modern Architecture," published in the RIBA *Journal* in 1957; Reyner Banham's 1960 *Theory and Design in the First Machine Age;* and Peter Eisenman's "Towards an Understanding of Form in Architecture," which took aim directly at the first two.[136] For Summerson the only "source of unity" for modern architectural theory was to be found in the program; from Banham it was to be found in the use of the appropriate technologies for the second industrial age; and for Eisenman, only the formal structure of the artifact could justify its existence. One road led to a kind of neo-functionalism driven by biology and scientific research; one led to the technology of a Buckminster Fuller-like universe; and the other to a world of formal moves that critically framed those of previous modern movements and classical architectures. For Eisenman, both a renewed functionalism and a dominant technologism were inadequate criteria for a universal critique of "any architecture."[137] Rather, the interplay of what he called "generic form," thought of in a Platonic sense, as a definable entity with its own inherent laws, and "specific form"—"the actual physical configuration realized as a result of a specific intent and function"—would produce the complex dialectic through which a building would control its relations to function, technology, and structure.[138]

When, just over ten years later, Eisenman turned his attention to Leicester in a now canonical essay, "Real and English," he was taking on a design that quite evidently had not been conceived in his own formal terms, but that, in fact, directly challenged the very aspects of modern movement formal composition out of which they had been derived. Indeed Eisenman admits that his analysis was not intended to represent the way in which Stirling himself conceived of the building, or even to represent the way in which it exists, but solely to "present an alternative interpretation, a way of seeing this building within another conceptual framework."[139] The result of this brilliant, if long-drawn-out, exercise in formal analysis was paradoxically (or more likely intentionally) to demonstrate precisely how this building existed, and to establish beyond doubt its fundamentally radical position within the history of modern architecture. For Eisenman, basing his argument on Rowe's discussion of the Corbusian

135. Peter Eisenman, "Real and English. The Destruction of the Box. I," in *Inside Out: Selected Writings 1963–1968* (New Haven: Yale University Press, 2004), 69. This essay was originally published in *Oppositions*, 4 (1974): 5–34.

136. John Summerson, "The Case for a Theory of Modern Architecture," *Journal of the Royal Institute of British Architects* (June 1957): 307–10; Reyner Banham, *Theory and Design in the First Machine Age* (London: The Architectural Press, 1960); Peter Eisenman "Towards an Understanding of Form in Architecture," *Architectural Design* (October 1963): 457–78.

137. Eisenman, *Inside Out*, 3.

precedent of the Dom-ino system, realized in its consummate example at Garches, Leicester, far from developing the principles of Le Corbusier's dialectic between the horizontal layers of the floor-plates and the vertical planes that define occupied space, precisely inverts them. For Stirling, Eisenman proposes, space is more a solid than a void, and the vertical planes are no longer the "paper-thin surfaces" of Garches or the Salvation Army Building (the "Cité de refuge"), but imply an architecture that is mass-like, and volumetric: "all potential planes are cut, chamfered or splayed to imply depth in volume."[140]

Together with this commentary—explicit or implicit—on Le Corbusier, Eisenman finds that Leicester also implies a critique of the more obvious motifs deployed, those of Constructivism. In Eisenman's view, the formal constituents of Constructivist architecture are exhibited by solid volumes assembled in order to create "dynamic visual configurations," volumes that are treated as passive space-containers rather than revealing any tension (as with Le Corbusier) between surface and depth, all composed in an additive, articulated mode. Leicester, by contrast, while taking the compositional techniques of Constructivism, treats its volumes—notably the projecting lecture theatres that recall Melnikov's Rusakov Club in Moscow—as enclosed by thin, tile-clad surfaces rather than as monolithic solids. Finally, Leicester reverses the additive compositional mode of Constructivism in order to privilege a discussion between additive and subtractive forces, emphasized by the oscillating play of apparently solid, but literally transparent glass.

In this revealing analysis, couched primarily in terms that see Stirling denying both the principles and the procedures of the modernism he seems to be quoting, Eisenman definitively establishes Stirling as neither a Corbusian copyist nor a Constructivist eclectic, and lays the basis for understanding him as equally distinct from the incipient historicism identified by Pevsner and the emerging postmodernism to which he would soon be linked by Jencks. And while purely formal analysis will never be able fully to pin down the techniques and vocabularies of Stirling, it nevertheless sets up a paradigm that will be useful for analyzing the later, even more radical departures from orthodox modernism.

In the last analysis, Leicester, Cambridge and Oxford might tantalize critics with allusions to historical precedents, but as Banham found at Leicester they are not buildings that can be taken apart—they resist, as he wrote, "the kind of historical style-sporting that passes for criticism in architectural circles." If, as Banham knew well, Stirling gained great pleasure "out of embarrassing critics by challenging them to name the influences," it was also the case that he knew "recent architectural history so well" as to be "long past cribbing."[141]

138. Eisenman, *Inside Out*, 5.

139. Eisenman, *Inside Out*, 63.

140. Eisenman, *Inside Out*, 69.

141. Banham, "The Word in Britain: 'Character,'" 124.

Techne in Arcadia

"Techne in Arcadia" was the title of Peter Buchanan's essay reviewing Stirling's entry for the competition for the agro-biochemical research centre for Bayer AG, Monheim, in 1978. Stirling himself speaks of the project as intended "to create an arcadian landscape similar to that of an 18th century *schloss* set in picturesque surroundings." Yet Stirling had been interested in this special kind of contrast from early in his career, a contrast between the architectural "machine" and its landscaped setting. Thus, the early scheme for Selwyn College student housing, with its rippling, faceted glass façade, raised on a grass berm and facing towards the Fellows' Garden, and the equally machine-like building for The Queen's College, Oxford, on the banks of a branch of the Isis and overlooking the sweep of meadows beyond, both revel in the contrast between a factory aesthetic and a verdant site.

There was, however, a less arcadian side to Stirling's understanding of building in the landscape than in the Bayer competition; rather it followed the alternative to the picturesque landscape tradition, that of the special kind of landscape formed by the abandoned industrial sites of Auden's "New Year Letter" (1940), the "relics of old mines," the "tramways overgrown with grass," the "derelict lead-smelting mill" (*Collected Poems*, 228), landscapes evoking the dark sublime of decay. The photo-collage of the 1965 Dorman Long project in the archive is exemplary of this form, set, as Stirling noted, in "a landscape of slag heaps, cooling towers and steelworks," its pristine steel structure and

138. James Stirling (Firm), Siemens AG Headquarters, Munich, Germany: aerial perspective, 1969–70 ink on paper; 58.2 x 101.4 cm (22 5/16 x 39 15/16 in); AP140.32.331.D37.P3.1

This was one of two projects documented as conceived in conjunction with Léon Krier, who worked in the Stirling office from 1968 to 1970. While the firm had always employed perspective views, this drawing set the tone for the multiple perspectives that were drawn by Krier or under his supervision for the "Black" volume of 1974, and became a hallmark of the office together with the axonometric view

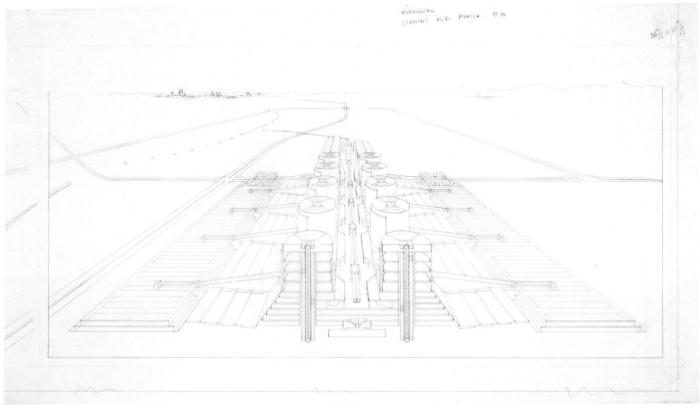

138

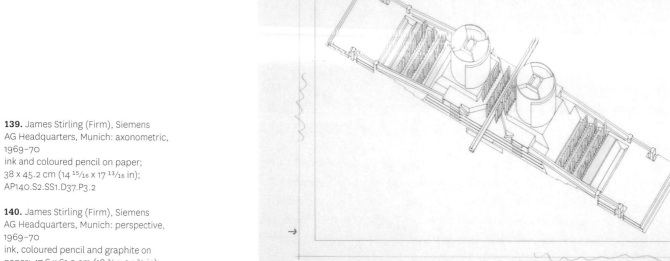

139. James Stirling (Firm), Siemens
AG Headquarters, Munich: axonometric,
1969–70
ink and coloured pencil on paper;
38 x 45.2 cm (14 ¹⁵⁄₁₆ x 17 ¹³⁄₁₆ in);
AP140.S2.SS1.D37.P3.2

140. James Stirling (Firm), Siemens
AG Headquarters, Munich: perspective,
1969–70
ink, coloured pencil and graphite on
paper; 47.6 x 61.9 cm (18 ¾ x 24 ⅜ in);
AP140.S2.SS1.D37.P3.4

139

140

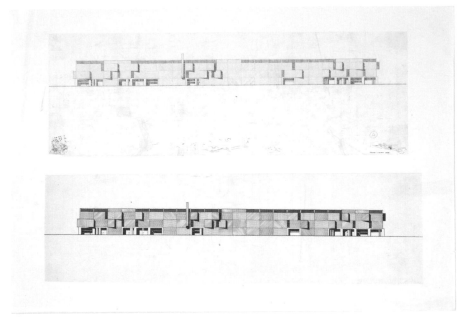

141

continuous linear section allowing for growth along a travelator line.[142] The structural system, with its exposed steel girder framework, was not only a support but also an advertisement for Dorman Long, an outgrowth of the "Steel Mill Cladding" project of 1958.

Designed in 1965 only two years before the formation of British Steel, the project was doomed to failure. But the similarities between the headquarters building and the "Madeley Transfer" building proposed by Cedric Price in the same year for his Potteries Thinkbelt scheme are too many to overlook. The Madeley Transfer was one of three "transfer" stations in a project Price developed on the basis of the rail connections between three North Staffordshire pottery towns, in an attempt to utilize an already existing rail network transformed into a mobile educational system. As with Dorman Long, the Madeley Transfer is a linear extruded section, served by rail, with service towers at intervals, and a gantry crane for loading and unloading.

The ultimate "machine in the garden" was the project for Siemens AG in Munich (1969), designed with Léon Krier. Indeed, the entire complex was designed as a real machine—a huge "main-frame" complex for a computer manufacturer accomplished with its ten huge cylindrical office and laboratory towers each surrounded by a computerized revolving screen programmed to the sunlight and time of day. Frampton aptly characterized "the quiet elegance" of its cybernetic technique. "In Siemens," he wrote, "as in the projects for Dorman Long, the metaphors are patently industrial—the 'flat-scape' megastructures of

142. *James Stirling: Buildings and Projects 1950–1974*, 109.

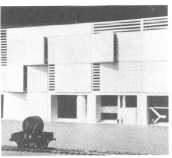

142

141. Stirling and Gowan, Steel Mill Cladding, Wales: elevations, after 1958 colour reprographic copy; 61 × 89.1 cm (24 × 35 ⅛ in); AP140.S2.SS1.D20.P1

Stirling's early interest in prefabricated buildings systems was here evinced in a project for sheet-steel cladding panels for an already engineer-designed steel mill.

142. Stirling and Gowan, Steel Mill Cladding, Wales: partial view of model, 1958 gelatin silver print; 7.8 × 8.1 cm (3 ⅛ × 3 ³⁄₁₆ in); AP140.S2.SS1.D20.P2.1

143

143. James Stirling (Firm), Dorman Long
Headquarters, Middlesbrough, England:
aerial view, 1965–67
graphite drawing mounted on gelatin
silver print; 19.8 x 24.4 cm
(7 ¾ x 9 ⅝ in); AP140.S2.SS1.D29.P1.2

Dorman Long was absorbed by British
Steel in 1967 and the project was
abandoned. Designed as an extruded
section, segmented at intervals for
vertical circulation, with offices above
and increasingly wide spaces below
for offices, and ground-level laboratories. Stirling envisaged the building as
extensible to at least eight segments
served by a travelator.

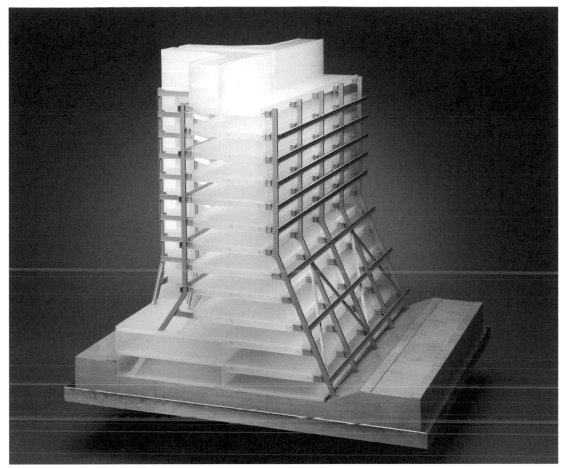

144

144. James Stirling (Firm), Dorman Long Headquarters, Middlesbrough: presentation model, 1965–67 wood, plastic, and metal; 58 x 60 x 59 cm (22 ⅞ x 23 ⅝ x 23 ¼ in) (largest); AP140.S2.SS1.D29.P17

The external steel structure was, as Stirling noted, a literal advertisement for the steel company.

145. Cedric Price, architect, Axonometric of the Madeley transfer area for the Potteries Thinkbelt, 1964 diazotype; 60.1 x 84.8 cm (23 ⅝ x 33 ⅜ in); DR1995:0216:279 Cedric Price fonds

Cedric Price designed this "Transfer Building," for his projected "Potteries Thinkbelt" university; while there is no direct evidence that Stirling knew this scheme while planning the Dorman Long Headquarters, the idea of a linear, extensible section served by mechanical pedestrian transportation was clearly "in the air" at the time. Certainly, Price's collaborator on the project, the engineer Frank Newby of Frank Samuely and Partners, was close to Stirling and had worked with him on many previous projects.

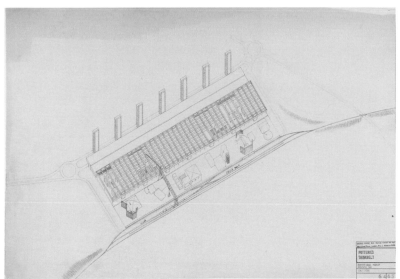

145

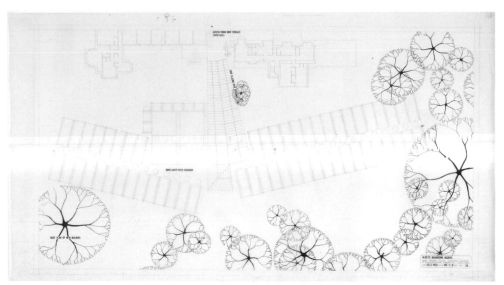

146

146. James Stirling (Firm), Olivetti Training School, Haslemere, England: site plan, 1969–77
ink and graphite on translucent paper; 64.7 x 115.7 cm (25 ½ x 45 ⁹/₁₆ in); AP140.S2.SS1.D36.P24.17

"This picture of what looks like a falling Messerschmidt is in fact on the site where a Messerschmidt was shot down in the Battle of Britain … but of course the form of the building has absolutely nothing to do with that fact." Stirling, Hornbostel Lecture at Carnegie-Mellon University, spring 1974. [Stirling/Wilford fonds, AP140.S2.SS4.D7.P1]

147. James Stirling (Firm), Olivetti Training School, Haslemere: axonometric, 1969–77
coloured pencil and colour sample on reprographic copy; 29.8 x 21.6 cm (11 ¾ x 8 ½ in); AP140.S2.SS1.D36.P35

One of the colour studies for the GRP (glass-reinforced polyester) panels of the Training School; Stirling originally specified violet and lime green; when this was rejected he tried silver and yellow. This was followed by seventeen other colour schemes before the final scheme of white and "mushroom" was approved.

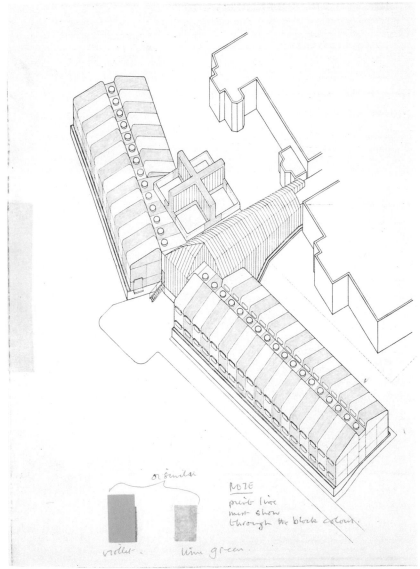

147

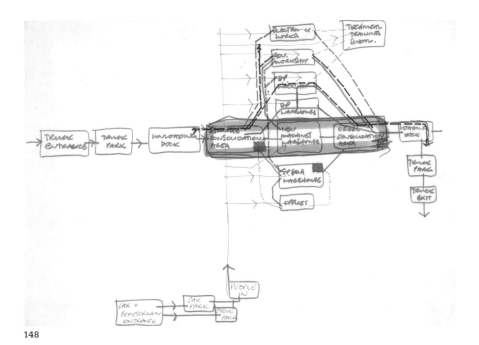

148

the blast furnace and the oil refinery," "'plug-in' structures, set as free-standing objects in the open 'motopia' landscape of the 20th century."[143]

The Olivetti Training School at Haslemere (1969–72), however, was built, and postured as an eighteenth-century pavilion, or glass house in the gardens of an existing country house. Here Stirling substituted for the traditional patent glazing, his favorite for Leicester and Cambridge, a pre-fabricated glass-reinforced polyester panel system, which in section seemed to emulate a temporary tent structure. The two wings of this plastic "tent" were then joined to the main house by a glass arcade with ramps joining the different levels of the two structures. The project for the British Olivetti Headquarters (1971), its long curved office block and galleria concourse sweeping along the lakeside in Milton Keynes, backed by horizontal workshops and warehouses above parking, reprises Leicester but now in an idyllic setting.

The theme was taken up again over fifteen years later in the Headquarters for Braun AG, Melsungen (1986–92) where the curved four-storey office block is raised up on giant tapered pilotis—reminiscent of those that supported Stirling's Thesis project. In Stirling's words, this factory and office complex represented a perfect welding of "functionalism" and "historic association": "It recalls the man-made objects in the landscape of the Roman *campagna*: viaducts, bridges, canals, and embankments."[144] It was as if the lessons of "Roma Interrotta" had been reverse-engineered so as to create the Gianicolo in the "rolling hills" northeast of Frankfurt.

148. James Stirling and Partner, British Olivetti Headquarters, Milton Keynes, England: schematic plan, 1970–74 ink on paper; 20.9 x 29.6 cm (8 ¼ x 11 ⅝ in); AP140.S2.SS1.D40.P26.1

The functional requirements organized in sequence and spatial arrangement.

143. Kenneth Frampton, "Transformations in Style," 137.

144. *James Stirling, Michael Wilford and Associates: Buildings and Projects 1975–1992,* 169.

149. James Stirling and Partner, British Olivetti Headquarters, Milton Keynes: sections, plans and axonometric, 1970–74
ink on paper; 29.7 x 21.1 cm
(11 11/16 x 8 5/16 in);
AP140.S2.SS1.D40.P26.2

150. James Stirling and Partner, British Olivetti Headquarters, Milton Keynes: section and plans, 1970–74
ink and graphite on paper;
29.7 x 20.9 cm (11 ¾ x 8 ¼ in);
AP140.S2.SS1.D40.P26.13

151. James Stirling and Partner, British Olivetti Headquarters, Milton Keynes: conceptual sketches, 1970–74
ink and traces of graphite on paper;
21 x 29.9 cm (8 ¼ x 11 ¾ in);
AP140.S2.SS1.D40.P26.15

152. James Stirling and Partner, British Olivetti Headquarters, Milton Keynes: plans, 1970–74
ink and graphite on paper;
15.3 x 25.4 cm (6 x 11 ¾ in);
AP140.S2.SS1.D40.P26.16

Experimenting with the free form of the entry lobby, conference room and restaurant.

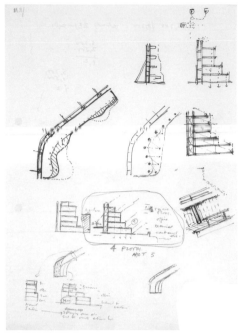

149

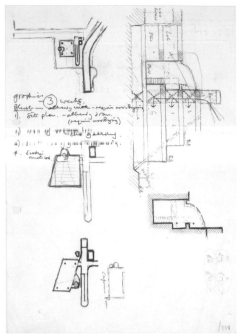

150

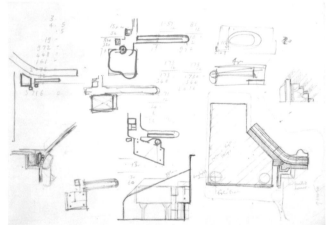

151

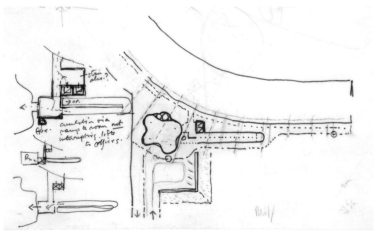

152

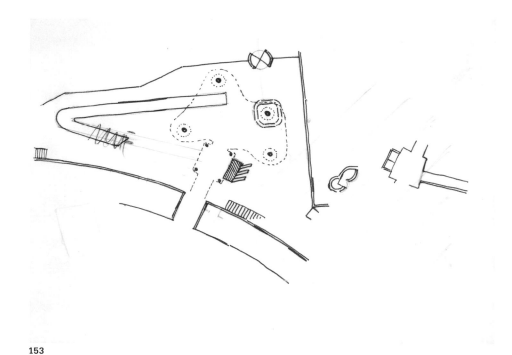

153

153. James Stirling and Partner,
British Olivetti Headquarters,
Milton Keynes: plan, 1970–74
ink, graphite and coloured pencil on
paper; 20.7 x 29.7 cm (8 ⅛ x 11 ¾ in);
AP140.S2.SS1.D40.P28.4

Planning the ramp to the conference
room and restaurant.

154. James Stirling and Partner,
British Olivetti Headquarters,
Milton Keynes: axonometric, 1970–74
graphite on paper; 23.4 x 22.1 cm
(9 ¼ x 8 ¾ in); AP140.S2.SS1.D40.P28.6

The penultimate solution to the conference room and restaurant pavilion.

155. James Stirling and Partner, British
Olivetti Headquarters, Milton Keynes:
cutaway axonometric, 1970–74
ink. coloured pencil and traces of
graphite on paper; 60.3 x 67 cm
(23 ¾ x 26 ⅜ in); AP140.S2.SS1.D40.P23.9

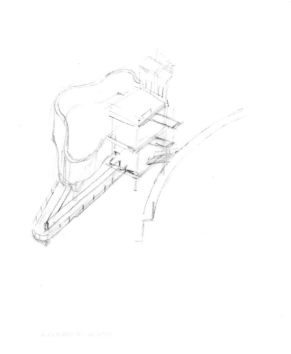

154

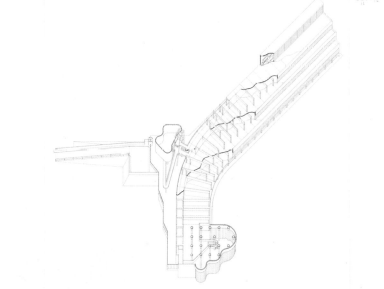

155

Typology Redivivus

156. James Stirling and Partner, British Olivetti Headquarters, Milton Keynes: interior perspective, 1970–74 ink, colored pencil and graphite on paper; 41.6 x 55.1 cm (16 ⅜ x 21 ¾ in); AP140.S2.SS1.D40.P23.7

In this perspective by Léon Krier, the older Stirling seated in his favourite Hope chair faces his young assistant Brian Riches, who stands beside a bust of Krier, who surveys the Olivetti lobby like a ghost from the classical past.

157. James Stirling and Partner, British Olivetti Headquarters, Milton Keynes: presentation model, 1970–74 wood, cork, plant material, clear plastic and painted plastic; model: 88 x 89 x 12 cm (34 ⅝ x 35 x 4 ¾ in); AP140.S2.SS1.D40.P24

157

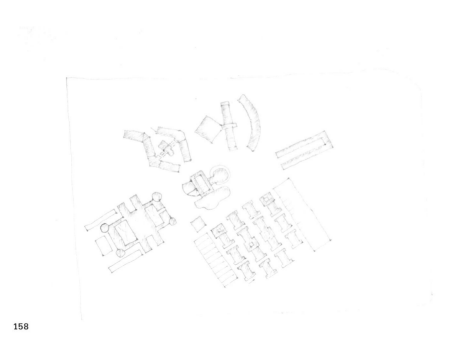

158

Stirling searches for a unifying theme to
bring together the research laboratory
complexes—trying the idea of a picturesque garden, a formal square, and
a walled precinct in quick succession.

159

160

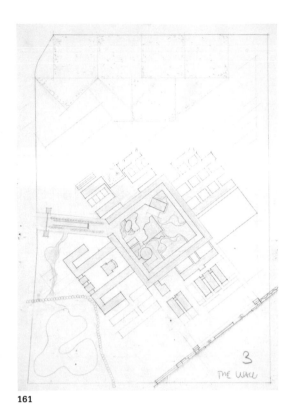

161

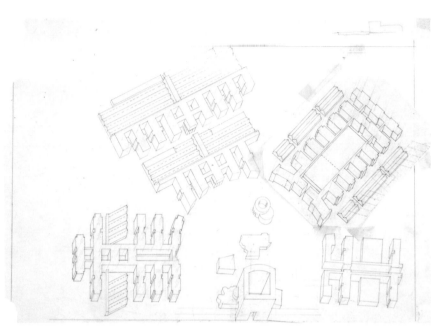

162

161. James Stirling and Partner, Bayer AG Research Centre, Monheim: alternative site plan, 3, "The Wall," 1977–78 graphite, coloured pencil on tracing paper; 41.7 x 29.9 cm (16 ⁷⁄₁₆ x 11 ¾ in); AP140.S2.SS1.D54.P3.13

The grand semicircular park emerges as a primary theme, leading to the radial positioning of the research laboratories, in a strict neo-classical format.

162. James Stirling and Partner, Bayer AG Research Centre, Monheim: development of site plan, 1977–78 graphite on tracing paper, tracing paper attached to paper, attached with tape; 29.9 x 42.5 cm (11 ¾ x 16 ¾ in) (irreg.); AP140.S2.SS1.D54.P3.6

163. James Stirling and Partner, Bayer AG Research Centre, Monheim: development of site plan, 1977–78 graphite, pen and ink, coloured pencil on tracing paper; 29.8 x 41.6 cm (11 ¾ x 16 ⅜ in); AP140.S2.SS1.D54.P3.4

The resemblance of this radial scheme to that of Claude-Nicolas Ledoux's plan for the Saltworks at Arc-et-Senans in France (1774–78) has often been noted. Stirling elaborates on the theme with the tall U-shaped administration tower, replacing Ledoux's temple-like Director's House with a fortified castle keep.

163

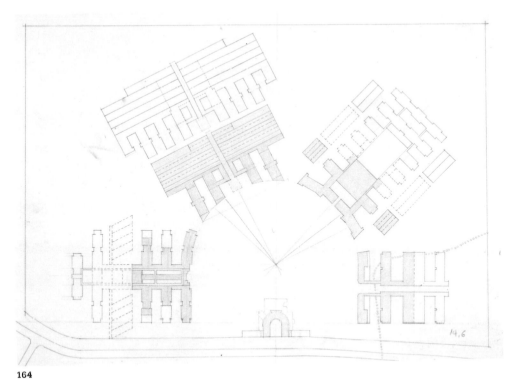

164

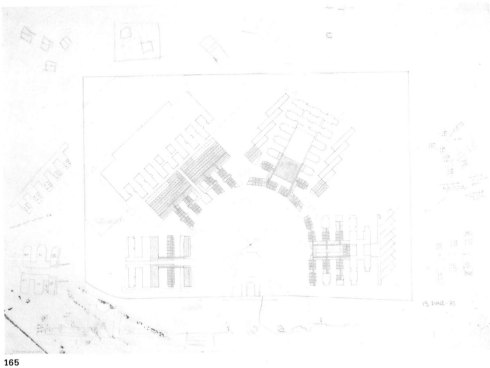

165

164. James Stirling and Partner,
Bayer AG Research Centre, Monheim:
development of site plan, 1977–78
graphite, coloured pencil on tracing
paper; 30.2 x 41.7 cm (11 ⅞ x 16 ⅜ in);
AP140.S2.SS1.D54.P3.8

165. James Stirling and Partner,
Bayer AG Research Centre, Monheim:
development of site plan, 1977–78
graphite, coloured pencil on tracing
paper; 41.9 x 59.3 cm (16 ½ x 23 ⅜ in);
AP140.S2.SS1.D54.P3.7

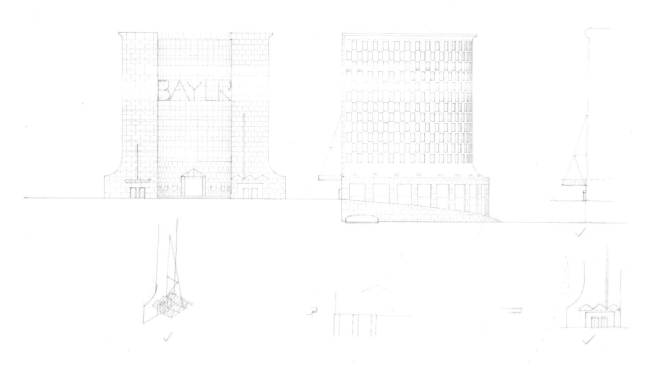

166

166. James Stirling and Partner,
Bayer AG Research Centre, Monheim:
central administration building,
elevations, 1977–78
graphite, pen and ink, coloured pencil
on tracing paper; sheet: 29.9 x 41.8 cm
(11 ¾ x 16 ½ in); AP140.S2.SS1.D54.P3.5

167. James Stirling and Partner,
Bayer AG Research Centre, Monheim:
view of a presentation model, 1978
gelatin silver print; 16.3 x 24.7 cm
(6 ⅜ x 9 ¾ in); John Donat, photographer;
AP140.S2.SS1.D54.P9.2
© John Donat Photography

167

V: New Town Revisionism

Worktown to New Town

There are various aspects to consider: town silhouette, landscape design, relationships to buildings, both in plan and height, enclosures space, buildings within space, choice and control of materials, etc. The purpose of putting forward a three-dimensional design policy at this stage is to encourage amongst all those who make a partial contribution by way of a building or detailed layout of a larger group an awareness of the importance of their contribution to the whole design ... It is so easy in the process of urgent programming for the opportunity to create a total design such as was seized, for instance, in the case of Bath, to be lost in a series of piecemeal contributions which, however satisfactory in their individual expression, do not give the sense of continuity which should differentiate a new town from the erratic smaller scale site developments or redevelopments in an existing town.

Arthur Ling, 1967[145]

Stirling's Thesis was sited at the centre of one of the first New Towns authorized after the war by the New Towns Act of 1947; his rehousing at Preston formulated a response to the call for a "modern" vernacular in terms that, for him at least, resisted nostalgia and provided an answer to the criticisms of New Town and public housing development that seemed to detach their inhabitants from familiar contexts; his last foray into urban housing was to be set in the context of the Labour government's bid to construct a series of Mark II and III New Towns with the wisdom inherited from the Mark I developments, and was planned as a part of the development of Runcorn New Town (1964–1981).[146] **As John Dawson and David Kirby summarize the development:**

> Britain's Mark I New Towns (designated between 1946 and 1950) were intended to become economically and socially self-contained and balanced communities. In proposals for Mark II and Mark III New Towns both concepts have been abandoned as planners have

145. Arthur Ling Associates, *Runcorn new town: master plan / prepared for the Runcorn Development Corporation* (Runcorn, Cheshire: Runcorn Development Corporation, 1967), section 14.1, "The Form and Character of the Town," posted on http://www.rudi.net/ books/3339 (accessed 27 August 2010).

146. The New Towns Act of 1946 called for New Towns to be established, in the words of the Cheshire Record Office, "as self-contained, balanced communities for work and living" by means of "a Development Corporation for each designated town." The Runcorn Development Corporation was set up in April 1964; the draft Master Plan by Arthur Ling and Associates

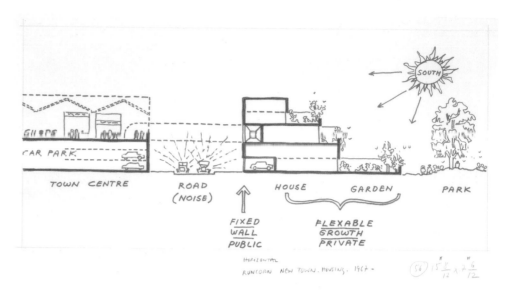

168. James Stirling and Partner, Southgate Housing, Phases I and IA, Runcorn, England: section, 1967–76 ink on paper; 24.5 x 41.8 cm (9 ⅝ x 16 ⁷⁄₁₆ in); AP140.S2.SS1.D33.P5.9

Stirling adopted the stepped-back, low-rise section pioneered by Leslie Martin and Patrick Hodgkinson at Caius College, Cambridge.

questioned the practicability of self-containment. As a consequence new towns are now seen as part of a regional or metropolitan planning concept.[147]

Planned as an "overspill" New Town fourteen miles from Liverpool's Lime Street station, Runcorn New Town was intended for a population of 45,000 rising to 100,000 by the year 2000. Runcorn itself is an old port town sixteen miles west of Liverpool on the River Mersey, prosperous in the nineteenth century for its soap, tanning, chemical, and shipbuilding industries. The New Town, midway between Liverpool and Manchester, was situated around the old village of Halton, with its ruined castle on a hill. Its location was chosen according to the latest theories of traffic circulation developed in Colin Buchanan's report "Traffic in Towns," and it was planned by Arthur Ling, formerly of the MARS Group and the London County Council, between 1964 and 1967. Served by an expressway in a figure eight, a dedicated busway for public transport to the centre with stops a five- to seven-minute walk from the housing, it was designed to obviate the flaws of the Mark I New Towns, mixing high-density "urban" housing with bungalows and their accompanying play areas, served by shops and social facilities. The shopping centre itself, Halton Lea, mixed shopping, education and social facilities, and in contrast to the older New Towns like Newton Ayclife, was fully built out and functioning before the housing was occupied. Ling's brief to the architects was explicit as to the "form and character of the town," seeing it as a "total design such as was seized, for instance, in the case of Bath," and with its "genius loci" residing in the "old places of the designated area,"

was published in January 1966 and approved by the Minister of Housing and Local Government in August 1968. The Corporation was dissolved in April 1981, after the construction of 10,500 housing units and 90,000 square metres of office and commercial space. See: Cheshire Record Office, Warrington and Runcorn Development Corporation:http://archive. cheshire.gov.uk/dserve/dserve.exe?dsqIni=Dserve. ini&dsqApp=Archive&dsqCmd=Show.tcl&dsqDb= Catalog&dsqPos-0&dsqSearch=(AltRcfNo='NTW') and "Runcorn New Town," http://www2.halton.gov. uk/yourcouncil/townsandvillages/runcornnewtown/ (accessed 27 August 2010).

such as the village and castle of Halton. Its construction, was, stated the report, "a unique opportunity to design a total environment." "Continuity," Ling concluded, was of the essence.[148]

Stirling's office began their design for the first stage in the sector called "Southgate" in 1967, and included flats, maisonettes and terrace houses in a five-storey structure; the second stage, consisting of two- and three-storey terrace houses, was finished in 1977, and used a lighter prefabricated system with prefabricated glass and polyester panels on timber framing, and local heating delivered from a roof-level network. The instructions to the architect from the Development Corporation were for about 1,500 dwellings with pedestrian access to the town centre. The first stage incorporated a second-storey public walkway that entered the centre's shopping and entertainment level.

Stirling was therefore committed to two major conditions that had been tentatively tried out, one at Preston, the other at St Andrews: the first was the idea of a truly urban structure for the overall plan, necessary, he wrote in the case of Runcorn, "as a variation to the suburban (less dense) housing being built as the majority type."[149] The second, a consistent interest from the beginning of his career with the Stiff Dom-ino project, was the development of a standardized, prefabricated system that would at the same time reduce the costs of mass housing and provide a distinctive architectural character to the project.

Squaring Bath

In the case of Runcorn, however, the notion of "urban" was less "regional" or "vernacular" than it was to be based on historical precedent. Eagerly taking up the brief's mention of Bath in Arthur Ling's planning report, and remembering his early visits to the city, Stirling analyzed the qualities and scales of a series of eighteenth-century urban squares in Bath, London, and Edinburgh, and explored them in some thirty-three variations for the given site. The result was a combination of history, modernism, and the critique of modernism that had been growing since the 1950s. As he noted, the height of the terraces "relative to the size of a typical urban square (300 ft by 300 ft) is of similar proportion to eighteenth-century squares." Where, however, in a Georgian square "all terraces front onto the square with public roads intervening between terrace and the garden square on each of its four sides," the arrangement at Runcorn broke the enclosure of the square into two L-shaped terraces, two with fronts facing the square and two with their backs to it. Such a plan allowed for consistent orientation of living spaces to the south and west, and visual access both to the garden square and to neighboring squares.[150] Here Stirling ingeniously transformed a

147. John Dawson and David Kirby, "Outshopping from a British New Town: the Case of Cwmbran," *GeoJournal*, 1, no. 4 (July 1977): 57. For a comprehensive review of the results of New Town planning see Barry Cullingworth, ed., *British Planning: 50 Years of Urban and Regional Policy* (London and New Brunswick: The Athlone Press, 1999)

148. Arthur Ling and Associates, Master Plan for Runcorn, Chapter 14, "The Form and Character of the Town": http://www.rudi.net/books/3339 (accessed 27 August 2010).

149. James Stirling, "Housing, Runcorn New Town, Architect's Statement," *Architectural Review*, 160, no. 957 (November 1976): 288–89.

169. James Stirling and Partner,
Southgate Housing, Phases I and IA,
Runcorn: site plan, 1967–76
ink on paper; 38.5 x 53.9 cm
(15 ⅛ x 20 ⅞ in); AP140.S2.SS1.D33.P5.5

170. James Stirling and Partner,
Southgate Housing, Phases I and IA,
Runcorn: plan, 1967–76
ink on paper; 44.9 x 44.8 cm
(17 ⅝ x 17 ⅝ in); AP140.S2.SS1.D33.P5.3

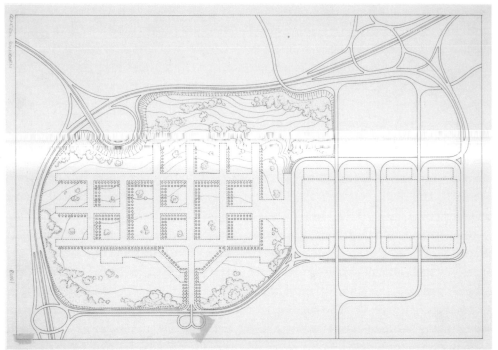

169

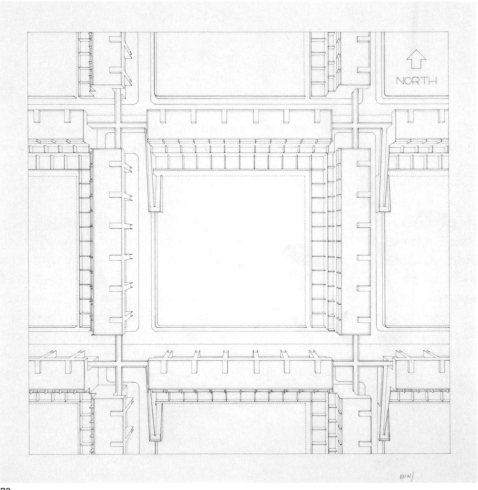

170

historic urban typology through the intervention of modern movement criteria—light and air, protected open spaces, separation of pedestrian and vehicular movement and, of course, mass-produced units.

In formal terms, this strategy was informed by the underlying grid of the complex. This grid was reminiscent of the models for low-rise, high-density housing developed by Leslie Martin and Lionel March in Cambridge—experiments that almost simultaneously had found their built expression in the partially realized prototype of Caius College by Leslie Martin and Colin St John Wilson. In these university housing units, the "academic courtyard" implied a continuous grid of such courts looking in onto themselves and stepped back over their service spaces. Such approaches, developing out of Team X's critique of modernist tower blocks, are present in the network schemes of Candilis, Josic, and Woods in Berlin. In Runcorn, this grid was modified by a typological rationalism comparable to, for example, the relentless "scientific" rationalism pioneered by Alexander Klein in his typological diagrams for a "Functionalist House for Frictionless Living" (1928), a rationalism that seem echoed in Stirling's diagrams for alternative layouts.[151] The grid and rationalist typology were then informed by the historical typology of the city square, thus welding a version of 1920s rationalism to 1970s proto-historicism, a condition that resulted in the "square" being assembled out of already functionally defined and closed "elements," rather than the enclosed volume characteristic of eighteenth-century squares.

Machine-Made City

Stirling had been seriously concerned with the technologies of mass production from the outset. In an essay entitled "Packaged Deal and Prefabrication," published in *Design Magazine* in 1959, he surveyed the contemporary field of "packaged deal housing," distinguishing among three systems of production, delivery, and construction: the packaged superstructure, where the variation in plan form and accessories allowed for the expression of individuality by the owner ("the hipped oriel window, coronation porch, etc."), the packaging of internal services (kitchen and bathroom assemblies, heating systems, etc.), and the totally prefabricated assembly.[152] As precedents, Stirling mentioned the American "Techbuilt" houses by Carl Koch, Wates' Dormy houses, and what he felt was the most successful, Buckminster Fuller's Dymaxion House of 1946, which included a moderate flexibility, efficiency, and speed of erection.

More interesting in terms of his own predilection for what Charles Jencks and Nathan Silver would, much later, name "adhocism," he appreciated the approach of Charles Eames, selecting different components from trade catalogs

150. Stirling, "Housing, Runcorn New Town, Architect's Statement," 288–89.

151. The Russian architect Alexander Klein (1879–1961) developed his studies of the functional house in Berlin in the 1920s; his diagram plans were published as "Illustrations of German Efficiency Studies," in

Architectural Record (March 1929), p. 299, diagrams taken from *Die Baugilde* (29 November 1927).

152. James Stirling, "Packaged Deal and Prefabrication," in Maxwell, ed., *James Stirling: Writings on Architecture*, 66.

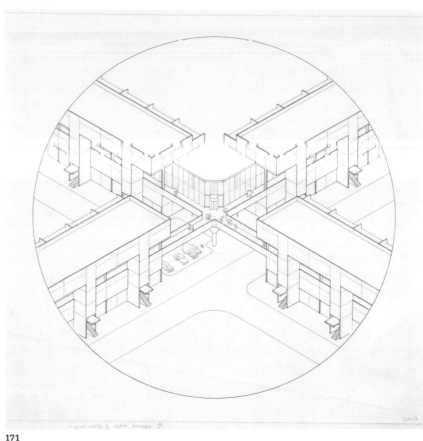

171

171. James Stirling and Partner,
Southgate Housing, Phases I and IA,
Runcorn: axonometric, 1967–76
ink on paper; 41.8 x 41.6 cm
(16 ⁷⁄₁₆ x 16 ⅜ in); AP140.S2.SS1.D33.P5.10

172. James Stirling and Partner,
Southgate Housing, Phases I and IA,
Runcorn: perspective, 1967–76
ink, graphite and colored pencil on
paper; 51.7 x 47.7 cm (20 ⅜ x 18 ¾ in);
AP140.S2.SS1.D33.P5.22

of marine and aircraft fittings and factory building systems; such a process of "sifting through catalogs, price tagging and collecting information," would require considerable organization; but it would also, Stirling the architect concluded, "require an artist to select the parts and compose the building."[153]

But, already in 1959, Stirling was aware of two fundamental objections to prefabrication. The first was the word itself, "nasty," with its "overtones of the war, standardization, working-class and temporary building," associated with the "prefabs" erected in blitzed areas. The second objection was linked to this: the lack of flexibility in the expression of the house, "the embodiment of its owner's individuality," and personal tastes. As if anticipating his future struggles with prefabricated housing, he concluded: "Any designer or manufacturer involved in prefabricated housing in this country must be prepared to take into account and resolve a conflicting set of requirements, ranging from the style implications of production methods to the uncertain and sometimes irrational preferences of the consumer and the class he represents."[154]

153. Maxwell, *James Stirling: Writings on Architecture*,
68; see Charles Jencks and Nathan Silver, *Adhocism:
The Case for Improvisation* (New York: Doubleday, 1972).

154. Maxwell, *James Stirling: Writings on
Architecture*, 70.

VERTICAL
RUNCORN NEW TOWN. HOUSING. 1967–
69 $14\frac{7}{12} \times 15\frac{11}{12}$

173. James Stirling and Partner,
Southgate Housing, Phases I and IA,
Runcorn: perspective, Léon Krier,
draftsman, 1967–76
ink on paper; 20.9 x 29.8 cm
(8 ¼ x 11 ¾ in); AP140.S2.SS1.D33.P5.1

Krier returned this sketch to Stirling
on the 11 July 1972; he explained that,
while he had drawn it in the process
of developing the perspectives of
Runcorn, he had not shown it in case
he was asked to draw another.

174. Runcorn New Town, Southgate
Housing Photos reproduced from
a colour transparency; 10 x 12.5 cm
(3 ¹⁵/₁₆ x 4 ¹⁵/₁₆ in); Richard Einzig,
photographer; AP140.S2.SS1.D33.P22.17
© Richard Einzig

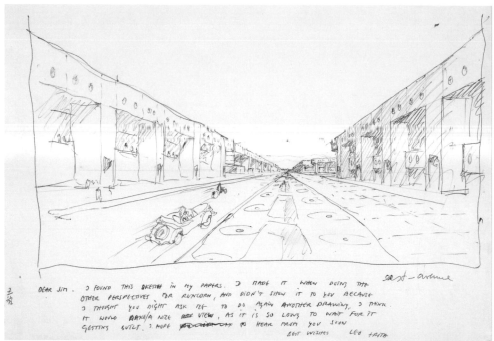

173

174

162

Britain's Pruitt-Igoe?

Since the abrupt decision of the development corporation to demolish the entire Runcorn site in February 1989, there has been a continuous debate over what *The Architects' Journal* questioned might have been "Britain's Pruitt-Igoe," referring to the demolition of Yamasaki's housing complex in Saint-Louis, a demolition generally seen to have hastened the "death" of modernist solutions to the housing problem.[155] Certainly there were major failures in the management of the housing—appalling lack of maintenance, enormous difficulties in the heating and cooling of the units leading to mold-covered walls, financial strains, the shifting nature of the inhabitants. Certainly, too, the non-traditional form of the housing was a barrier to its acceptance by many residents. But as Brian Hatton asked in his balanced assessment, "The Future in Ruins,"[156] "was it a failure of architecture, or technical specification, or management which did for Southgate? Or was it some mixture of all three, compounded by the kind of economic depression that was never supposed to happen in a New Town?"[157]

Stirling himself responded by pointing out that "the very specific and comprehensive requirements, drawn up by local government officials," had left little room for manoeuvre by architects, determining "almost every aspect of the housing," from overall costs, density, prefabricated techniques, over-deck access, district heating systems, floor-to-ceiling heights and room sizes, to garages and refuse and storage bins. Further, he reminded the critics of his scheme, Runcorn was part of a generalized "social vision" that believed in industrialized housing, and was intent on innovating with high-density, low-rise developments in the light of past experience of high-rise structures.[158] In the end, Hatton concluded that the demolition was the combined result of a gross failure in management, regional economic collapse, and the "irreconcilable goals," social and economic, involved in building an isolated "vehicular cul-de-sac" where each housing community was separated from the next by earthen barriers that, as Stirling himself had remarked, produced "the disturbing effect of being able to drive through the New Town hardly seeing it."[159] This "kind of proletarian Los Angeles," he argued, could never have become a city in itself, never reached the appropriate density, and was never supported, either as an autonomous unit or as a dormitory town.[160] But while Hatton claims that its failure was a result of "the short-sightedness and lack of rationality in a purchase dominated building industry without a strong national housing policy," there is no doubt that any such policy as it was developed after 1945 suffered from Labour's defeat, and the election of Margaret Thatcher's government, which substituted for the New Town Development Corporation a "Commission for New Towns," a name which, as Hatton noted,

155. The Editors, "Britain's Pruitt-Igoe?" *The Architects' Journal*, 189, no. 9 (March 1989): 3.

156. Brian Hatton, "The Future in Ruins," *Blueprint* (September 1990): 46–50.

157. Hatton, "The Future in Ruins," 46.

158. Stirling, *Building Design*, 926 (March 1989): 3.

159. Stirling, "Housing, Runcorn New Town, Architect's Statement," 287.

160. Hatton, "The Future in Ruins," 46.

"is just ... for the government's auctioneers/estate agents," allowing New Town land to be sold to the highest bidder. Perhaps the "Failure of Housing," as "The Failure of the New Towns," was, in the end, less of an architectural than a political/economic phenomenon.

Self-Build Vernacular

The international competition launched by the government of Peru for an experimental housing project in Lima in conjunction with the United Nations Development Program in 1969, the Proyecto Experimental de Vivienda or PREVI, afforded Stirling another opportunity to explore the relationships of pre-fabrication and housing, on a scale and with a brief that was directly joined to a serious attempt by a government to improve the lives of its poorest citizens. The competition's organizers selected thirteen Peruvian architects and thirteen international architects; these last represented the gamut of post-Team X professionals, including Atelier 5 from Switzerland, Candilis, Josic, Woods from France, Aldo van Eyck from Holland, Charles Correa from India, Christopher Alexander from the United States, Maki and Kikutaki from Japan, and Stirling himself. The jury included Sir Leslie Martin, Carl Koch from the United States, and José Antonio Coderch from Spain. The project was directed by Peter Land, a British architect working for the United Nations with several years of experience in Peru.

The various entries provide a veritable catalogue of the range of architectural responses to what was seen in the late 1960s as the most urgent of architecture's social roles: the provision of low-cost housing, especially for the populations of the *barrios* and *favelas* of Latin America. Peter Land had studied at the Architectural Association and at Yale, and had organized a two-year interdisciplinary graduate program in urban and regional planning for Yale at the National University of Engineering in Lima between 1960 and 1964. Working with the Peruvian Government and the Organization of American States, and developing a strong personal relationship with Fernando Belaunde Terry, elected President in 1964, Land proposed the international competition for a low-rise, high-density demonstration neighbourhood. PREVI was the resulting pilot project. Land's idea, as he recalled twenty years later, was a project that would "embrace the rich urban planning traditions of Peru with the patio house, and demonstrate improved new designs for the neighbourhood, houses, clustering and building technology" in a form that was neither suburban low-rise, low-density, nor high-rise.[161] The brief he developed outlined four major principles for the neighbourhood and its housing. Firstly, that "the houses could be

161. See Peter Land and Stephen White, "Previ Twenty Years After," *Architecture+Design* (March–April 1994): 53–59, and "PREVI/Lima Low Cost Housing Project," *Architectural Design*, 40, no. 4 (April 1970): 187–205. In what is now the best summary of the planning, construction and afterlife of the Pevi development, Elisa Maria Cisneros Celero's Master's Thesis for the Catalan Polytechnic University, *Vivienda, barrio y sociedad. Estudio de tres barrios: Cano Roto, PREVI, La Malagueira* (2008), the contributions of each architect to the planning of the quarter, and their different projects for housing, are analyzed in a comparison between the development of Cano Roto outside Madrid, with its mixture of tower blocks and terraced houses

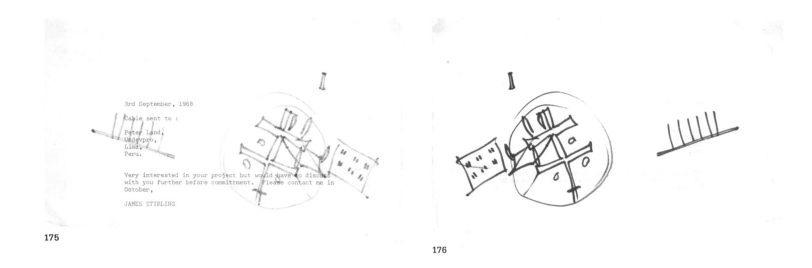

built in stages over time, by expanding horizontally or vertically; secondly that each house should have a small private garden; thirdly that open space should adjoin the private gardens; and fourthly that vehicular streets should be minimized, with landscaped walk streets for access to houses. He insisted that each architect be associated with an engineer in order that the construction of the housing would be studied innovatively.[162]

Stirling's entry was developed after he had visited the site in March 1969, having experienced what he recounted as "the energy and inventiveness of even the most poverty-stricken people taking fate into their own hands when they establish these settlements in areas of dead landscape, often in the face of massive police action."[163] In the plans for his sector Stirling was able to realize to the fullest possible extent that special combination of prefabrication set out in the early project for the Stiff Dom-ino House, and the notion of a one-storey, expandable house developed by Stirling and Gowan in 1957.[164] In addition, the appellation "patio," while responding closely to Land's program, was perhaps a sly response to his rivals the Smithsons and to their "Patio and Pavilion" of 1956. Stirling developed an additive plan within a square, that would grow in four stages around a central patio in order to accommodate three to eight inhabitants. Each house was then clustered in a group of four, and in turn five of these clusters were grouped around a central communal space, and these grouped to form neighborhoods separated by linear parks with schools and communal facilities. Here Stirling brought together his own precedents in a communal reformulation of the MARS plan for London, but on a smaller, more intimate scale.

The precast concrete walls and columns, erected in a government "first build," would establish the framework for each of the four-house units—a kind

175–6. James Stirling (Firm), telegram replying to Peter Land's invitation to participate in the PREVI (Proyecto Experimental de Vivienda) competition for low-cost housing, Lima, Peru. "Very interested in your project but would have to discuss it with you further before commitment. Please contact me in October," with sketch on verso of possible layout of housing for PREVI competition, 3 September 1968. Behind is the telegram of invitation. 30 August 1968.
typescript with ink sketch on verso; 14.1 x 12 cm (5 9/16 x 8 1/4 in); AP140.S2.SS1.D35.P6.2 recto and verso

from 1959, the development of La Malagueira near Evora in Portugal designed by Alvaro Siza in 1979, and the PREVI project. See, for a complete report on PREVI forty years after Fernando Garcia-Huidobro, Diego Torres Torriti, and Nicolás Tugas, El tiempo construye! Time Builds! (The Experimental Housing Project (PREVI) Lima: Genesis and outcome) (Barcelona: Gustavo Gili, 2008).

162. Land and White, "Previ Twenty Years After," 55.

163. James Stirling: Buildings and Projects 1950–1974, 138.

164. James Stirling and James Gowan, "A House which Grows," House and Garden (April 1957): 67–71.

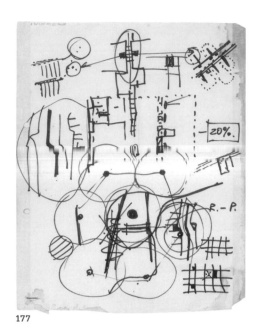

177

177. James Stirling (Firm), sketch of possible layouts for housing for PREVI competition, Lima, on verso of telegram sent by Peter Land inviting Stirling to take part in competition, 30 August 1968. ink on paper; 26.9 x 21.6 cm (10 ⁹⁄₁₆ x 8 ½ in); AP140.S2.SS1.D35.P6.3

178. James Stirling (Firm), PREVI competition, Lima: site plan for Second Phase with Stirling's site highlighted, 1968–76 ink on diazotype; 41.4 x 59.1 cm (16 ¼ x 23 ¼ in); AP140.S2.SS1.D35.P6.1

Attachment to a letter from Peter Land to James Stirling, 2 November 1970, outlining the beginning of the second phase of the project. Stirling's site is marked in red.

179–182. James Stirling (Firm), PREVI competition, Lima: sketch plans for the Second Phase, 1968–76 ink and graphite on paper; 25 x 30.9 cm (9 ⅞ x 12 ⅛ in) / 27.6 x 25 cm (10 ⅞ x 9 ⅞ in) / 30.4 x 25.2 cm (12 x 9 ⅞ in) / 24.5 x 28.2 cm (9 ⅝ x 11 ⅛ in); AP140.S2.SS1.D35.P6.4 / .P6.5 / .P6.6 / .P6.7

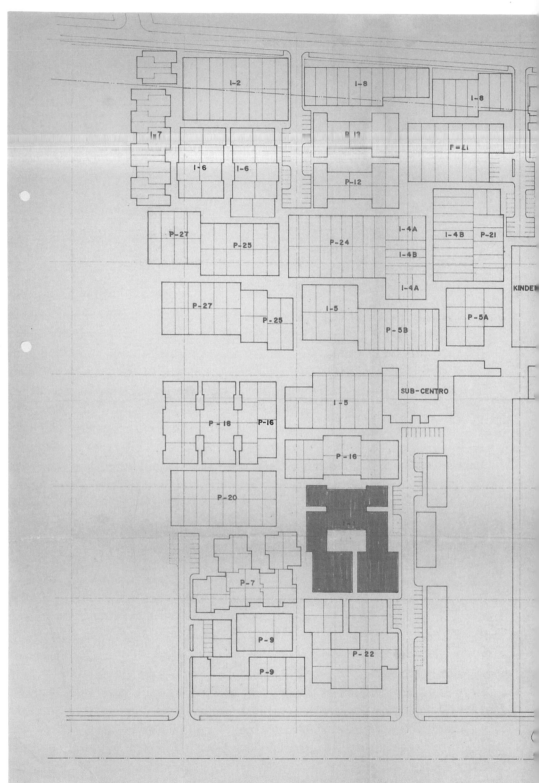

178

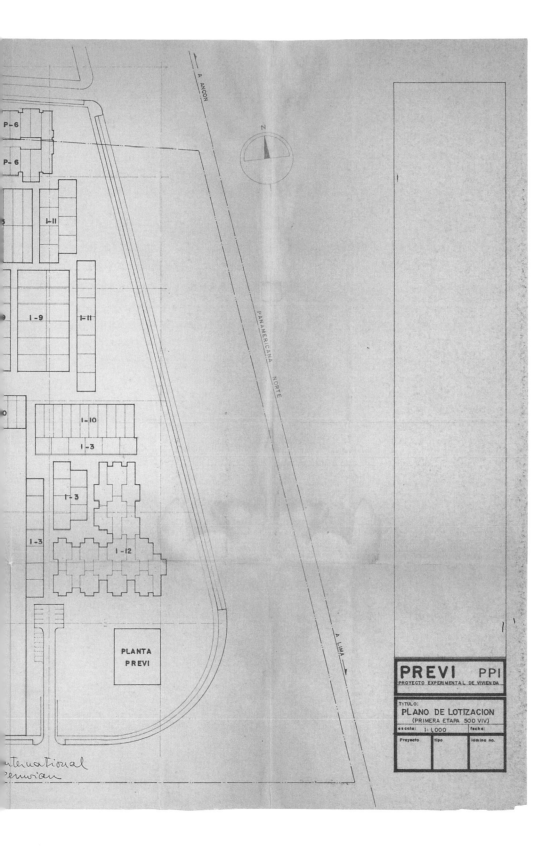

PREVI PPI

PROYECTO EXPERIMENTAL DE VIVIENDA

TITULO:
PLANO DE LOTIZACION
(PRIMERA ETAPA 500 VIV)

escala: 1:1,000   fecha:

Proyecto   tipo   lámina no.

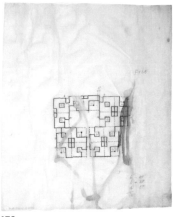

179

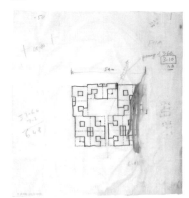

180

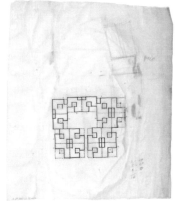

181

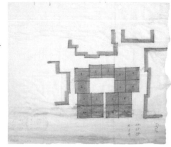

182

of "climbing frame," as Stirling called it—which later could be built in and up according to the needs of each family. In a departure from his usual aesthetic control, Stirling presented four axonometrics showing the gradual build-out of the structure, with a range of stylistic motifs, some from his own Runcorn and Olivetti panels, others indigenous to Peru. He wrote: "the pride and sense of ownership achieved through self-building, will be retained and the inventiveness and variety of neighbourhood which this produces (in Peru) is essential for a dynamic community."[165] The result, twelve dwellings inserted into the pilot project together with those of the other twenty-five selected architects, was perhaps the most lively and "popular" of his public housing projects, and still serves today as a model of community development. Surely Stirling would be pleased to know that one of his patio units has now been transformed by the Zamora family into a small two-storey villa with a central pediment—one might name the house "Palladio in PREVI." Another of his units has been built up into a four-storey-high school.[166] In a report on the development of the PREVI housing complex published in 2003, the Stirling units were praised: "James Stirling interpreted the future behaviour of the families with a certain amount of accuracy and their houses even resisted a building system different to the one foreseen; Stirling's houses were the most requested and those that display PREVI's finest qualities of occupancy."[167]

183

183. PREVI competition Lima: aerial view of a portion of the site, 1976
From *Time Builds*.

184. James Stirling (Firm) and unknown builders, Patio House, PREVI, Lima, as built and as imagined completed in two storys, from *James Stirling, Michael Wilford and Associates: Buildings and Projects, 1975–1992* (London: Thames & Hudson, 1994)
gelatin silver prints; 21.1 x 16.3 cm (8 ¼ x 6 ⁷/₁₆ in);
AP140.S2.SS1.D35.P8.3 / P8.4

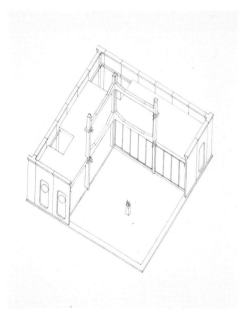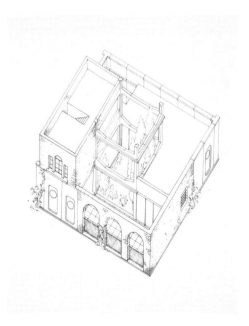

184

165. *James Stirling: Buildings and Projects 1950–1974*, 142.

166. Other transformations are the kindergarten in Atelier 5's unit, and a food market in Maki, Kurokawa, and Kikutake's houses.

167. Garcia-Huidobro et al., *Time Builds!*, 128.

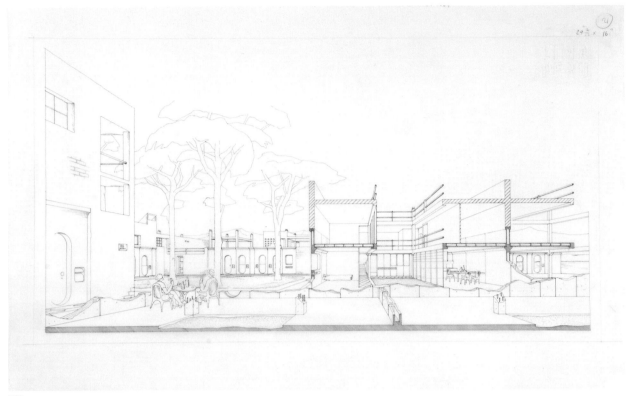

185

186

187

188

185. James Stirling (Firm), PREVI competition, Lima: perspective, 1968–76 ink on paper; 53 x 82.1 cm (20 ⅞ x 32 ⅜ in), AP140.S2.SS1.D35.P11.1

186–188. James Stirling (Firm) and the Zamora family, PREVI house, Lima, built out 1976–2004, from Fernando Garcia-Huidobro, Diego Torres Torriti, and Nicolás Tugas, *El tiempo construye! Time Builds! (The Experimental Housing Project (PREVI) Lima: Genesis and Outcome)* (Barcelona: Gustavo Gili, 208)

189. Stirling and Gowan, Expandable House, England: view of model, 1957 gelatin silver print; 19.6 x 25.1 cm (7 ¾ x 9 ⅞ in); AP140.S2.SS1.D15.P1.7

Stirling's scheme for PREVI seems to have been an amalgam of two earlier unbuilt projects: the Stiff Dom-ino House and the Expandable House for *House and Garden*, April 1957.

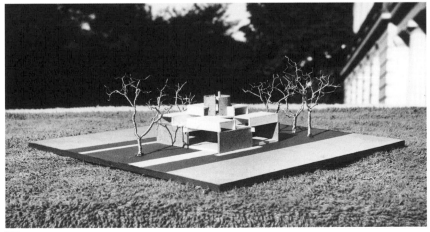

189

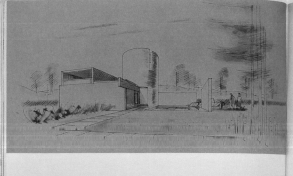

A HOUSE WHICH GROWS

For young-marrieds

whose ambition

outruns their bank balance,

building in stages

can be the answer

James Stirling and

James Gowan A/ARIBA

suggest a quadrant house

convertible for all stages

of family life

The house which grows with the family has often been attempted, usually by adding rooms and wings to an existing house. Historically the problem did not arise; houses were simply built to the anticipated maximum requirements. Today, because building is expensive, and servants almost unobtainable, dwellings are much smaller. These minimum houses, however, do not allow for the growth and change which form the pattern of family life.

The semi-detached of suburbia (in style diluted from the large Edwardian country house) is the national panacea for all housing problems, but in relation to today's need for flexibility, it is quite obsolete. Normally, it is too large for a newly-married couple; it is too small when the family has grown up; it is once more too large when the children have left home and the parents have it to themselves again (with the inconvenience of stairs and an upper floor).

The problem, then, is to build a house which can be added to in stages, which will appear an architectural entity at each step, and which is capable of contraction and an accumulation of empty rooms. This is an idea for such a house.

The quadrant house is designed around a two storey central area which forms the services hub of the house. Inside this core is a spiral stair to the first floor—initially a study, bedroom or store, ultimately an upstairs bathroom and store. To this hub is added, first, the basic requirement for a newly-married couple or single person—a large multi-purpose room. All structural walls, including the cylindrical wall of the core, are built at this first stage, so that it will be unnecessary to recall bricklayers when the later additions are made. The building of these walls in fact confines the future structural work to the addition merely of three identical roofing units, as and when the infilling of the three remaining quadrangles takes place. Two upper bedrooms are constructed at the third stage. At the fourth and completed stage of expansion, the house can accommodate three or four children as well as their parents.

After this, it can be contracted at will by conversion. As the children grow up and leave home in an ordinary house, rooms become empty and disused. Here it is intended that, by moving two partition walls, the vacated space becomes available for sub-letting—first as one room with its own entrance, kitchen and bathroom, and eventually as a three-bedroom dwelling. By the time all the children have left home and the parents have retired, the sub-letting of three-quarters of the house could provide a welcome private income. If these portions of the house were re-let to married children, the house could be handed on from generation to generation in the manner of the great houses of the past, but without the wastage of space and uneconomical services which were their problems.

The idea behind this house points a national problem which, ideally, should be solved through mass production. Such an undertaking on a national scale could incorporate advanced technological methods. However, for the individual client and at a low cost, use has to be made of traditional methods and materials. Nevertheless, with this quadrant house, where each quarter is structurally identical, a considerable amount of pre-fabrication, particularly of the roof, would be possible. The average house is constructed to last 60 years (though invariably occupied indefinitely regardless of deterioration). The solution offered by the quadrant house would remain valid until the present social pattern changes and might have to stand for 200 years. This aspect influenced the construction and choice of materials (the details are on page 124). Complete, it would cost around £4,850. This figure and those given for each stage are only approximate as they would be affected by site locality and current prices.

Opposite: Views of the house at its first and fourth stage

67

190

First stage

Second stage

Third stage

Fourth stage

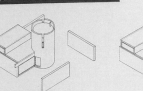 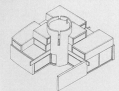

For a single person or newly-married couple: there is a multipurpose room with a service core. A spiral staircase leads to a room for storage, sleeping or study. All load-bearing walls are built and form a walled garden. Gas boiler and first stage underfloor heating are installed. Cost £1,800.

For a married couple with or without children: the second quarter has been developed as a bedroom and garage. The service equipment in the core comprises, as before (moving clockwise from the living-room door), w.c., boiler, linen cupboard, cooker, sink, shower and store. Cost £300.

For family occupation: the kitchen in the core becomes a utility room—a washing machine replacing the cooker. There is a new kitchen separated from the dining-room by a counter unit, and a back door has been added. The first floor has been expanded (below, right). Cost £1,300.

For the family at its largest: the house reaches its limit of expansion. The sitting-room increases in size and there are two large bedrooms on the ground floor. At each stage additional underfloor heating is installed and partition walls are simply used again in new positions. Cost £950.

First conversion

Second conversion

Third conversion

First floor

When the children grow up and begin to leave home, the unused space becomes a self-contained room for sub-letting with kitchen and bathrooms in the core (as in the first stage) and its own entrance. Cost of altering partitions for this and the other subsequent conversions would be negligible.

As the needs of the original owners become less, more of the house can be sub-let and the new family can take over the process of expansion so that the house becomes a pair of semi-detached dwellings. The first floor remains with the original family and the garage can be used by either.

All the children have left home and the parents' needs in retirement are again very simple. The growing family takes over the first floor and another quarter of the ground floor. The fourth conversion comes when the house returns to one-family occupation as in the fourth stage.

At the third stage the spare room (for storage, sleeping or study) of the first stage is turned into a bathroom and clothes cupboard, and two small bedrooms for children are added. This upper floor remains with the original family until the third conversion. For details of the core, see over.

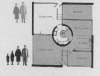 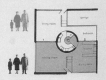

68

67

191

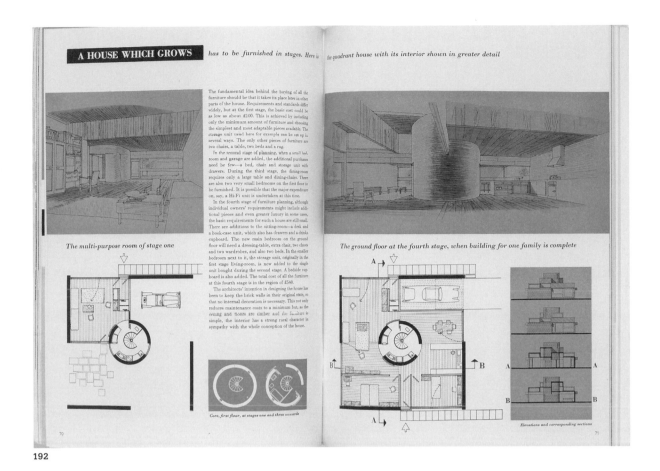

192

190–192. Stirling and Gowan, Expandable House, from "A House which Grows," *House and Garden*, April 1957

VI: Context and Association

This contextual-associational method of planning is somehow akin to the historic process, albeit instant, whereby built form is directly influenced by the visual context and is a confirmation of, and a complement to, that which exists.
James Stirling, 1979[168]

Connections to Tradition

I realize that an interaction between the design for a new building with associations of the past is a dangerous tightrope to walk, with compromise and sentimentality on either side.
James Stirling, 1974[169]

Towards the end of 1974, Stirling addressed the International Congress of Architecture, held at Persepolis in Iran. A wide range of contemporary architects were invited, including Buckminster Fuller and Paolo Soleri, the older generation of CIAM, Josep Lluís Sert, Kenzo Tange, Georges Candilis, and the younger members of Team X, Jacob Bakema, and Aldo van Eyck, together with architects from the developing countries—Balkrishna Doshi and Hassan Fathy. As reported in the *Architectural Review*, much of the discussion centred on problems of architecture and planning in the industrializing countries; but Stirling chose to answer another question: "to what extent should/can modern architecture be influenced/affected by the buildings of the past?"[170] Rejecting Wright's "truth to materials" philosophy (a dictum he had rejected on seeing the brickwork of Palladio's columns beneath the peeling stucco), Stirling chose to reverse the terms of the day's theme, "Materials and Methods of Expression," into "Methods of Expression and Materials."[171] For Stirling "the shapes of a building should indicate—perhaps display—the usage and way of life of its occupants." Here he expands the commonplace of modern functionalism to embrace, although not

168. James Stirling, "Nolli, Sector IV. Revisions to the Nolli Plan of Rome," *Architectural Design*, 49, nos. 3–4 (1979): 42.

169. James Stirling, "Stirling Connexions," *Architectural Review*, 157 (May 1975): 273–76.

170. The Editors, "Introduction," to "Stirling Connexions," 273.

171. Stirling, "Stirling Connexions," 275.

in a deterministic way, the "forms and shapes which the everyday public can *associate* with and be *familiar* with," from the single elements of stairs, rooms, and entrances, to the overall pattern of the whole. Thus the Florey Building offered to the "normal man and not only its architect" a set of recognizable forms—courtyard, entrance gate, towers, cloisters—as well as "a central object replacing the traditional fountain or statue of the college founder." The public would not then be "*dissociated* from their cultural past." This aspect of cultural *association* working to prevent dissociation was, Stirling hazarded, the very "art" of architecture, the putting together of the "functional-symbolic" elements of a building.[172]

Here Stirling took aim at purely technological determinism—the "banality of space frames, tents, domes, and bubble covering everything"; the expression of functional-symbolic forms and familiar elements should dominate over the secondary expression of structure. Indeed, every technique of building from the past and present should be open to the architect—from earthworks to plastics—according to appropriateness and availability, and the economic and climatic conditions of different countries. In this sense, the "boring, banal and barren and usually derivative and unharmonious" ninety percent of modern architecture was deeply lacking, especially when "placed in older cities." In a revealing and increasingly typical observation, Stirling called for "some humour in modern architecture," urging architects to mine "the rich vein in serious puritanical modern that can be satirised and commented upon."[173]

Accordingly, not for the first time in a lecture, but for the first time in a published lecture, Stirling offered (in a Wölfflinian style inherited from Rowe) a set of comparative examples, relating a building from the past to one of his own projects. His Corbusian phase—the Core and Crosswall House—is paired with the Maison Cook; his vernacular phase—the house at Woolton—with a Cotswold barn; Preston is shown side by side with Queen's Docks, Liverpool, and the earthworks of the Brunswick Park School compared to the thirteenth-century fortifications of Restormel Castle. More surprisingly, the tower of Leicester is compared to the steeple of Christ Church, Spitalfields. Refusing analogies to Cape Canaveral (a source he had already admitted), the roof of the Cambridge History Faculty Building is brought closer to home with the Liver Street Station roof in Liverpool. In keeping with his sense of the immediacy of the distant past, the prefabricated panels of the St Andrews student residences are seen together with a close-up of Inca stonework. Churchill College is predictably paired with Blenheim Palace, while the Florey Building's court and cloisters are compared to those of Trinity College, Cambridge, and its stair towers to those of Trinity Gate. The more technological Olivetti Training Centre at Haslemere is placed beside the Olivetti "Divisumma" calculator as if to imply that the building of 1969 had influenced the design of the machine in 1973. Perhaps the greatest

172. Stirling, "Stirling Connexions," 275.

173. Stirling, "Stirling Connexions," 275–76.

stretch, but the most poetic of these comparisons, is that between the Siemens project and a de Chirico perspective, *Melancholy and Mystery of a Street.*

Equally interesting, and important for the next phase of his work, are Stirling's comparisons for his urban projects. Runcorn's arcades are paralleled with a view of Bedford Square, London; Derby's Civic Centre, with its preserved Georgian façade, is shown with the ruined fragment of Mowbray Folly, and St Andrews University Arts Centre is graced with that ultimate homage to Rowe, the Villa Giulia courtyard. It was not surprising that this composition was the first of Stirling's works that Rowe genuinely professed to admire.

The crisis of modernism was now revealed to be one of expression—functional and symbolic—and one that was especially problematic in existing cities. While single buildings might stand on their own for single concepts appropriate to their use—colleges, laboratories, libraries—complexes of buildings, and uses inserted into everyday life, were more susceptible to the demands of association, of connectivity and continuity with a lived past and a living present. And if modernism was wanting in humor, Stirling would wish to introduce his own—commenting on modernism's puritanism from the point of view of an architect, but at the same time provoking a social response that would see the building not as a deadly serious "high architectural" monument, but as a genuinely popular and affectionate commentary on its context.

The Architecture of the City

Between the late 1960s and the early 1970s, interest in the architectural character and formal structure of cities began to spread from purely historical and theoretical studies to the design programs of schools and the profession at large. Spurred by the publication and translation of Aldo Rossi's *L'architettura della città* (1966) and Giorgio Grassi's *La costruzione logica dell'architettura* (1967), and supported by schools of architecture such as La Cambre in Brussels, the sense of urban structure as made up of discreet and semi-discreet elements of architecture, from houses and institutions to galleria and arcades, led to the study of whole typological families. At first this "tendency" was confined to the study of individual building-types, reconstituting their form either "critically," responding to the influential series of studies by Michel Foucault and his architectural followers in France, or in order to reformulate "meaning" and "expression" for a contemporary society, all the while retaining a sense of the historical evolution of the type in semi-abstract references.

Such was the rationalism exhibited in the international section of the Milan Triennale of 1973, curated by Aldo Rossi.[174] Rossi's introduction to the

174. Aldo Rossi, ed., with Franco Raggi, Massimo Scolari, Rosaldo Bonicalzi, Gianni Braghieri, Daniele Vitale, *Architettura Razionale*, XV Triennale di Milano, Sezione Internationale di Architettura (Milan: Franco Angeli, 1973).

publication listed his sources for a revived sense of modern rationalism, a grouping of 1920s architects that conspicuously omitted Le Corbusier, Wright, Aalto, and Mies van der Rohe. For Rossi, the Russian avant-gardists—Leonidov and Ginzburg—were joined in their "materialist" vision to J.J.P. Oud, Bruno Taut, Ludwig Hilberseimer, Hans Schmidt and, of course, Adolf Loos. Giuseppe Terragni and Piero Bottoni were the only Italian architects admitted to this canon, which was updated by the addition of Ernesto Rogers, Rossi's editor at *Casabella*. The exhibition itself assembled a very heterogeneous group including the New York Five, accompanied by an excerpt from Colin Rowe's and Kenneth Frampton's contributions to the publication *Five Architects* (1972);[175] Leslie Martin in Cambridge, Giuseppe and Alberto Samona, Carlo Aymonino, Giorgio Grassi, and Adolfo Natalini of Superstudio, in Italy; Oswald Ungers and Ludwig Leo in Germany; and a group of younger rationalists led by Robert and Léon Krier from Luxembourg via Stuttgart. Such a broad definition of a tendency was bound to founder on individual and national differences, and while Rossi, together with Grassi, Gianni Braghieri, and Massimo Scolari, would work consistently within the tenets of the neo-rationalism outlined by Rossi, the Kriers, and especially Léon in tandem with Maurice Culot at La Cambre, were less concerned with individual typologies than with the fabric of the city itself, a fabric torn apart and emptied by the redevelopment programs of the 1960s, programs that seemed to adhere to a vulgarized version of CIAM modernism. It was this modernism that, for Léon Krier, became the arch-enemy, leading him quickly to self-censure his own early projects.

But sandwiched in between Rossi's introduction and the US projects were two projects by Krier—a design for the restoration and extension of the baroque

175. *Five Architects: Eisenman, Graves, Gwathmey, Hejduk, Meier* (New York: Willenborn, 1972).

193. James Stirling (Firm), Derby Civic Centre, England: existing site plan, 1970 ink on paper; 33.4 x 38.1 cm (13 ⅛ x 15 in); AP140.S2.SS1.D38.P6.7

The competition project for Derby Civic Centre was the second of the two schemes developed together with Léon Krier. It was selected by Aldo Rossi for publication in the catalogue of the Architettura razionale exhibition for the Milan Triennale in 1973, and in a reduced form selected by Krier for republication in *Rational Architecture* (1978), where it is credited as by James Stirling and Léon Krier.

194. James Stirling (Firm), Derby Civic Centre: site plan with proposed ring road and pedestrian centre, 1970 ink, coloured pencil and graphite on paper; 33.4 x 37.9 cm (13 ⅛ x 14 ¹⁵/₁₆ in); AP140.S2.SS1.D38.P6.6

Stirling's entry was described by the jurors as "brilliantly conceived," but it did not receive a prize. Stirling wished to re-establish the market square as the central focus of the town: "to create for Derby a public space with as great a significance as has the Piazza del Campo to Siena, the Royal Crescent to Bath, or the Rockefeller Plaza to New York" ("Black" volume, 164) The two figure-ground plans of Derby, showing the centre before and after in the intervention of the "arena" proposed by Stirling and Krier, register the effect of Rowe and Koetter's "Collage City" article of three years earlier.

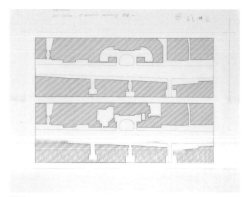

195

195. James Stirling (Firm), Arts Centre, University of St Andrews, Scotland: figure-ground studies, 1971–74 ink and colored pencil on paper; 40.7 x 50.4 cm (16 x 19 $^{13}/_{16}$ in); AP140.S2.SS1.D41.P10.1

These studies show the existing state (bottom) and the proposed solution (top).

abbey of Willibord, Echternach in Luxemburg (1970), and a housing project for Lewishamstrasse, Berlin (1971)—and one project by Stirling, developed in collaboration with Krier: the Civic Centre for Derby (1971). The common theme running through these three projects is a respect for the total urban fabric, exhibited in the Derby scheme in figure-ground plans and in the Echternach project by Krier's soon-to-be signature aerial perspective of the city and monastery, showing a continuous and rehabilitated roofscape. Joining together the parts of each project is another signature of the emerging urban rationalist movement: galleries or arcades, one of the urban elements privileged in neo-rationalism from the outset. Together, all three schemes respect the integrity of the urban block—rapidly to become another of the leitmotifs of the movement for the "reconstruction of the city"—and envisage a city made up, not of discontinuous monuments in modern space, but of continuous fabric opened out from time to time for public squares and pedestrian routes. "Architecture" was here absorbed into the structure of the city and porous to urban social life. Krier will later "X" out his own housing for Berlin—ambiguously related to the Stirling–Krier project for the Siemens AG computer research and administrative centre in Munich from two years earlier. The mechanistic vision of the cylindrical towers, with apartments in the Berlin project, and research laboratories in Siemens, did not fit well with his quick retreat into traditionalist nostalgia after the mid-1970s.

The Derby project, and its role as marking as an apparent shift in Stirling's attitude towards urban design, has been seen as the product of Krier's arrival in the office beginning in July 1968 and lasting two years until December 1970, when he returned to Germany, before returning in 1973 to work on the redrawing and editing of the *Works 1950–1974* (the "Black" volume). Krier, according to his own account, was the driving force behind both Derby and Siemens, and he is credited as such in the "Black" volume—but not in later publications of the firm's work. Krier has also been credited with the introduction of a new style of drawing—the spare, thin-line axonometrics from above and below that unify the "Black" volume—and a new taste for the neo-classical, with symmetrical compositions and classical references in drawings that were populated by late eighteenth-century people and furniture; the most celebrated example of course is the depiction of Stirling seated in one of his favorite neo-classical chairs in the middle of the Olivetti Headquarters arcade.

And yet there is, in fact, no aspect of Derby that cannot be traced to earlier moments in Stirling's career. The influence of Rowe on the figure-ground plan is evident, and Stirling's omnivorous delight in neo-classical architecture from Friedrich Gilly to Schinkel was notable from very early on. Certainly there are no precedents lacking for the arcades—the use of patent glazing in Leicester and Cambridge, the garden façade of the Florey Building, the "arcades" of Haslemere and Milton Keynes, not to mention the urban arcades of Reston and Runcorn.

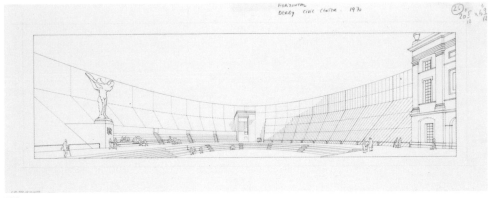

196

197

The most elegant of all, the twin symmetrical curved galleries joining the main building to its wings at St Andrews Arts Centre (1971), was, despite its small size, the most satisfying of all these urban galleries. Finally, not even the introduction of single-line axonometrics can be attributed solely to Krier—they had become a prevalent house-style since Leicester. Perhaps, then, it would be more accurate to say that Krier's influence helped crystallize this house-style, and systematically formulate its special qualities—the perspectival isometrics such as the redrawn roofscape of Sheffield, the mole's-eye axonometric views that give the drawings of the Florey Building and the German museums their special character.

Certainly the incorporation of the rescued façade of the old neo-classical Assembly Hall slanted against the glass of the arcade in Derby, and the symmetrical semicircle of the arcade to either side of the eighteenth-century house of St Katherine's at St Andrews indicate a respect for the classical tradition; but more important, as is indicated by the even grander arcade in the design for the Olivetti Headquarters Building at Milton Keynes, is the consolidation of a generalized utilization of patent glazing into an element that, in the city, constructs a pedestrian joint in a recognizable type-form, and, outside the city, in Olivetti and Siemens, provides an urban referent in an otherwise suburban context.

When, in 1978, *Rational Architecture* was issued in an entirely renewed edition, it was edited not by Rossi but by Léon Krier and Maurice Culot, and published in Brussels, with an introduction by Robert Delevoy, a critic and art historian, and director of the Ecole Supérieure de L'architecture et des Arts Visuels at La Cambre. Krier and Culot radically restructured the book in order to diminish the earlier emphasis on individual building projects, and to emphasize the main theme of "The Reconstruction of the City," and the European city in particular. This was no "revival of the Rationalism of the 1920s," wrote Krier, but a "re-creation of the public realm" by means of a return to the principles of an architecture that defined a place for a public realm of culture and political

196. James Stirling (Firm), Derby Civic Centre: perspective, 1970
ink on paper; 22.3 x 56.7 cm;
(8 ¾ x 22 ⁵/₁₆ in); AP140.S2.SS1.D38.P6.5

197. James Stirling (Firm), Derby Civic Centre: interior perspective, Léon Krier, draftsman, 1970
ink and graphite on paper,
47.8 x 28.5 cm (18 ⅞ x 11 ¼ in);
AP140.S2.SS1.D38.P6.1

Krier's perspective of the arcade proposed for Derby alludes to the grand arcades of the Regency period—hence the fancy dress of the *flâneurs* of Derby.

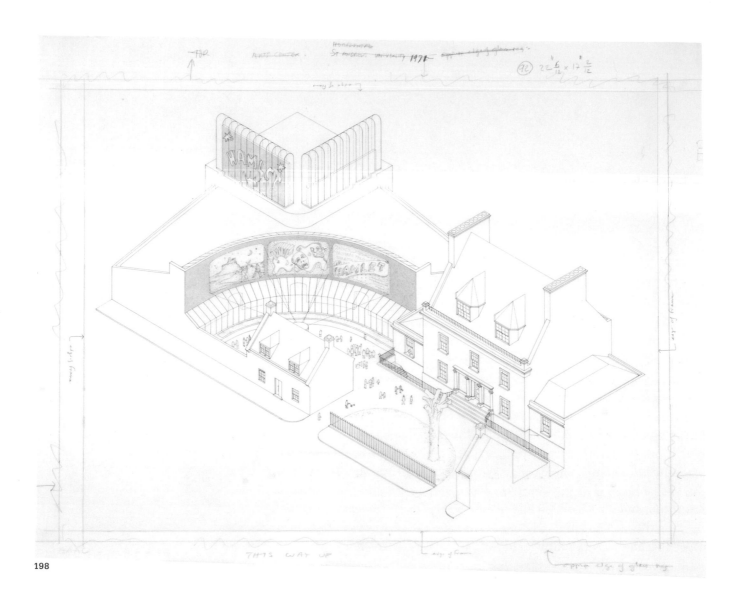

198

198. James Stirling and Partner,
Arts Centre, University of St Andrews:
axonometric, 1971–74
ink, coloured pencil and graphite on
paper; 53 x 66.42 cm (20 ⅞ x 26 ¹⁄₁₆ in);
AP140.S2.SS1.D41.P10.3

Of this project, the historian Manfredo
Tafuri noted, having compared it to the
glass arcades proposed by Ebeneezer
Howard for his ideal Garden City model
of 1898: "The Civic Centre in Derby is in
fact an urban 'heart.' It is, however, part
of a real city and not a utopian model"
Manfredo Tafuri, "Architecture dans
le boudoir," *Oppositions* 3 (1974): 37–62.

responsibility. The New York Five were explicitly omitted and Stirling's Derby
and St Andrews were included, but in reduced scale.[176]

For what had become clear by 1978 was the great divide that separated
the generation of Stirling from that of Krier. The one a modernist at heart with
a love of an architecture in play, and an endless capacity to invent and rein-
vent the languages of modernism; the other a deep antagonist of modernism
and its urban effects. The extent and nature of this divide was dramatically
displayed, in the same year, in the generational rifts that marked the widely
different approaches to the revisions to the Nolli plan of Rome in the exhibition
"Roma Interrotta."

176. Léon Krier et al., eds., *Rational Architecture/
Architecture Rationnelle. The Reconstruction of the
European City/Le reconstruction de la ville européenne*
(Brussels: Editions Archives d'Architecture Moderne,
1978). For review of the exhibition created by Léon Krier
in London, see Alan Colquhoun, "Rational Architecture,"
Architectural Design 45, no. 6 (June 1975): 365–70.

In the event, Stirling's contribution towards a "reconstruction of the city" was neither couched in terms of a proto-Rossi structuralism, nor in terms that echoed the formal devices of a Krier or a Rowe. Urban architecture, for Stirling, was not a composite of static, ahistorical types, nor a fixed and ultimately imaginary "return" to a tradition that had never quite existed the way it was reconceived, but an energized play and interplay of forms that opened new institutional and social potentials in modern, technological society, with a *sense* of the past rather than its literal repetition. His conception of a city was at once more architectonic, three-dimensional and volumetric than that of "Collage City," a concept which privileged the two-dimensional figure-ground, and it was less bound to historical allusion. In this context, the three projects for museums in Germany are exemplary moments in the development of Stirling's mature urbanism, and still offer today a sense of urban form that has only rarely been tested.

The City as Museum [177]

In Stirling's projects and buildings from the late 1950s on we have identified the persistent exploration of two dominant themes of modernism: that of *typicality*, the rational construction of buildings for collective and individual social tasks, and that of *tradition*, or history, and the need to respond to existing contexts and ideas of the past. Joining these concerns is his equally consistent respect for the more recent tradition of the modern. In other terms, we might characterize this apparently contradictory set of strongly held beliefs as a more direct opposition between the static nature of typology and the dynamic, changing process of history: of, in other words, *type* against *time*.

This conflict had emerged, paradoxically enough, in the late eighteenth century, the moment of historical self-consciousness of the Enlightenment. What the twentieth century understood as the relativist historicism of the nineteenth century—the belief in difference, change, culturally shifting values, and transformations seen as the law of history itself—was born out of the belief that beneath all things lay a single, unchanging natural law. And yet this project to reduce and regulate all social and natural things according to the same ordered grids, tables, classifications, structures, and taxonomies was, in turn, increasingly challenged by a sense of the relativity of all cultural phenomena.

Nowhere was this conflict demonstrated so clearly as in a type that was centrally concerned with the didactic exposition of history—the museum. In the early nineteenth-century museum the question of housing the *Zeitgeist* gave rise to two alternative models, each of which presented a single axis, a

199

199. James Frazer Stirling, photographer, view of the Salvation Army Building, Paris (Le Corbusier, architect), 1954
gelatin silver print; 6.7 x 10 cm (2 ⅝ x 3 ¹⁵⁄₁₆ in); AP140.S1.SS2.D2.P4.1

Visited in 1954, this was, according to Stirling's notes in the Black Notebook, the "least disappointing" of Le Corbusier's Paris buildings, and "the most urban," in the way it prepared for entry into the dormitory slab by a sequence of pavilions: a cubic gate, a bridge, a cylindrical foyer with a curved reception desk leading to the bank of stairs and elevators. Conceived by Le Corbusier as a kind of urban "still life" standing in front of the slab's facade, this composition, disaggregated, became an inspiration for Stirling in the three museum projects for Germany.

177. For my former views on this subject, now revised through study of the archive, see Anthony Vidler, "Reconstructing Modernism. The Architecture of James Stirling," *Skyline* (November 1981): 16–19; "Losing Face: Notes on the Modern Museum," *Assemblage*, 9 (1989): 40–57.

unitary solution for the accommodation and representation of time in a typical manner. The first was simply to unfold the time-line of history in space, in a route that could be followed by the visitor. Thus Alexandre Lenoir, in one of the first museums to display architectural and sculptural history, the Musée des monuments français in Paris, constructed between 1795 and 1810, deployed a sequence of rooms, one per century, through which a visitor might walk as if literally strolling through the past. Each room was further decorated in the style of the period of the exhibits it displayed. Within such a time machine the public might meditate on its past, recapturing by an elaborate *mise-en-scène* the feeling and sensibility of different periods and cultures, but cumulatively so to speak, progressing, with the centuries towards the present. Private citizens emulated these spaces of reverie in their apartments, *à la chinoise, à l'indien, à la gothique*.

The second, exemplified in the Altes Museum, Berlin, of Karl Friedrich Schinkel (1823–30), was to construct a new building type suitable for the exhibition of a number of kinds of historical artifacts in differing combinations and chronologies. This required a more neutral structure than Lenoir's fixed route, while at the same time still having to represent its essentially "historical" nature. The solution was a building that allowed for several routes and exhibition plans, while utilizing architecture and its own historical motifs to refer to the past. Schinkel, as is well known, combined three architectural types in one: the basic plan was that of the Baroque palace, referring to the Royal residence across the square, in which the chronological sequence of periods and styles could be arranged in sequence. Inserted at its centre was a "Pantheon," emblem of idealized and aestheticized memory, for the exhibition of sculptures that seemed to transcend time. And for the entrance, in a socially and politically evocative move, Schinkel adopted not a temple (used elsewhere for museums in London and Munich) but a stoa, the open colonnade of Greek secular democracy, in order to represent the museum as belonging to the citizenry of Berlin.

Consciously or not, Stirling, in his three projects for museums in Germany, reformulated these traditional "forms" of historical representation—not, like so much postmodern work, against the typifying, rationalizing mode of the modern movement, but rather as the logical extension of the modernist preoccupations that had been embedded in his work from the beginning. Rather than directly imitating the typologies of the museum, as it developed from Lenoir and Schinkel, through to Le Corbusier's "Mundaneum," Stirling reconstructed the type on a number of levels in order to overcome what, by the 1950s, had already become the commonplace and exhausted conventions of a late modern movement.

In Stirling's museum projects the nineteenth-century idea of type, repeated in abstract form in the twentieth, and by Stirling in his earlier work at Leicester

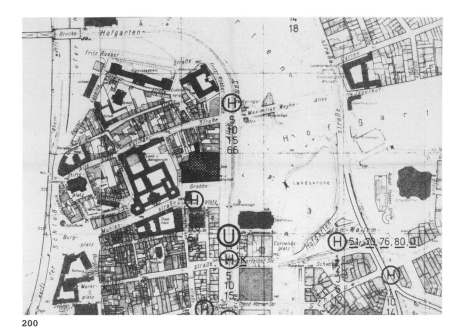

200

201

200. James Stirling and Partner, Nordrhein-Westfalen Museum, Düsseldorf, Germany: site plan, 1975 reprographic copy; 59.8 x 84.1 cm (23 9/16 x 33 1/8 in); AP140.S2.SS1.D43.P1.5

The competition brief for the Nordrhein-Westfalen Museum and redesign of the Grabbeplatz stated: "It is intended that an urban square be created on Grabbeplatz in connection with the existing buildings. The design of this square should on the one hand take into account the possibility of connection to the Old Town and on the other hand integrate the important existing buildings of the surrounding environment."

201. James Stirling and Partner, Nordrhein-Westfalen Museum, Düsseldorf: site plans, 1975 reprographic copy; 72.6 x 59.8 cm (28 5/8 x 23 1/2 in); AP140.S2.SS1.D43.P1.1

202. James Stirling and Partner,
Nordrhein-Westfalen Museum,
Düsseldorf: sketches, 1975
ink on reprographic copy; 29.6 x 21 cm
(11 ⅝ x 8 ¼ in); AP140.S2.SS1.D43.P3.1

In these preliminary sketches, the cube,
the cylinder, and the curved link, all
extracted from the entry sequence to
the Salvation Army Building, and seen as
a dominant figure to be inserted into the
existing city fabric. The sketches were
afterward renumbered in a sequence
from 1–9.

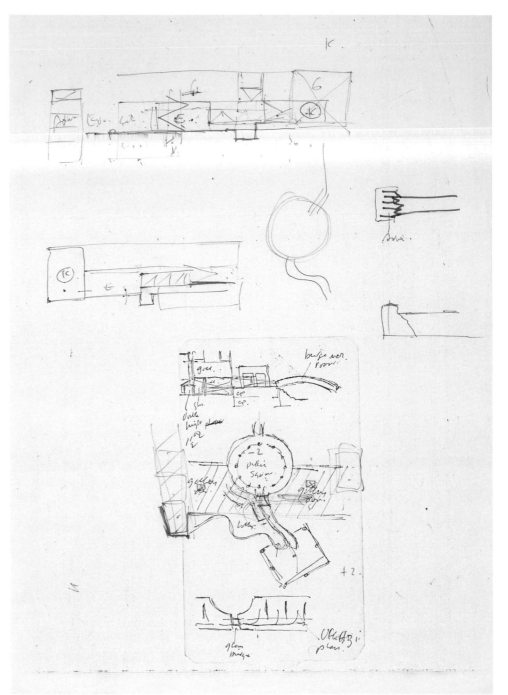

202

and Cambridge, as a synthetic structure resolving social, institutional and technical needs all at once within a single pristine envelope, was now exploded by the need to express increasingly complex functions by differentiating the architectural elements that it comprised. This compositional and expressive technique was, as we have noted, developed as early as the house studies of 1956, and, in the museum projects of Düsseldorf, Cologne, and Stuttgart, became a method of avoiding the overt references to historical precedent evident in the Arts Centre, St Andrews, and Derby Civic Centre. The traditional museum as represented by Schinkel's Altes Museum was fragmented into a combination of elemental volumes connected by circulation routes, embedded in the urban context. The museum as an object was elided, and, with figure and ground oscillating, the compositions reach through the city fabric to repair, stitch up, and recombine what is left over after the incursions of war and modern redevelopment.

In 1954, on his second visit to Paris, Stirling confessed that he was disappointed with the majority of Le Corbusier buildings, seen for the first time in context, and not through the idealized form of the drawings and photographs in the *Oeuvre complète*. One exception was the Salvation Army Building, however, that he noted for its array of primary forms—the cube of the entry pavilion, and the bridge to the cylinder of the foyer, tied together with the long curve of the reception desk—standing in front of the tall, thin slab of dormitories: "These elements which I have always considered sculptural thereby have a definite reason and as sculpture they are not the same as the Marseilles roof—they are much more akin to machine parts and less to Roman tombs and antiquity—note the way the drum is recessed into the ground. The whole of the entrance is very clear functional town planning and has a real space-time kick." He concluded: "The whole of the entrance business is a terrific drama and excavation of a ROUTE. The toughest Corb I've seen yet—masterly town planning."[178]

Whether or not construed as a direct reference, but the more likely given Stirling's memory for formal motifs, the cube, the cylinder, and the curved reception counter, now transformed into a formal connection, return as thoroughly urban elements, introduced as a way of de-monumentalizing the institution of the museum in the three projects designed between 1975 and 1977. From the competition projects for Cologne and Düsseldorf, to the built Staatsgalerie at Stuttgart, Stirling is concerned at once to relate the modern museum to its past as a monument and to absorb it into the fabric of the city. Here "contextualization" does not mean the camouflage of historical styles or the imitation of what already exists in the surrounding sites; rather it looks to a form of abstraction among the architectural elements, and their relations in space, tied together by pedestrian circulation to signify a historical typology, while pointing to its re-permutation as a contemporary urban installation.

178. Crinson, ed., *James Stirling: Early Unpublished Works*, 48.

Thus, if we find historical allusion in this work, it is the allusion of the plan: the dismembered fragments of the *Salvation Army Building*, together with the rotunda of the Altes Museum, or that of Gunnar Asplund's Stockholm City Library, recomposed into a chain of spaces, each one an abstract emblem of past institutional architecture, each one a part of a concatenation that might be extended indefinitely as part of a regenerated city. "Collage," yes, but one that formulates quite consciously the belief in the power of the new, the unexpected, the yet unformulated, as a strategy. Here we might distinguish between architectural propositions that imply references to and *about* history and those that merely quote history as a sign of itself. Stirling's formal skill was, in this context, directed to composing and reformulating half-recognized or obsolete types into new ones, joining a lightly worn quotation, or applied motif, to a strong discipline of the plan and its three-dimensional figure. So while he inevitably partook in the heightened sense of context and urbanity emerging after the late 1960s, his solutions were for all intents and purposes still modern, contained *in nuce* within the complex entry system of the Salvation Army Building.

Stirling himself pointed to the strong relations between his developing thought in design and that of Colin Rowe; we only have to note the appearance of Stirling's essay on Garches and Jaoul in 1955, five years after Rowe's own "Mannerism and Modern Architecture," to chart the beginnings of this quasi-competitive relationship, first cemented in the School of Architecture at Liverpool and continued with Stirling's writing on Ronchamp. Each had different aims, it was true, but both were inquiring into the fate of modernist utopia. A similar connection might be made between the emergence of the "Collage City" paradigm, in Colin Rowe and Fred Koetter's article of 1975 in

203–204. James Stirling and Partner, Nordrhein-Westfalen Museum, Düsseldorf: sketches, "1,"1975 ink on paper; 12.5 x 5.6 cm (4 ¹⁵/₁₆ x 2 ³/₁₆ in); AP140.S2.SS1.D43.P3.7 recto and verso

The scheme for Düsseldorf is then worked out on Stirling's flight to Chandigarh—on the back of his embarkation card for Nepal Airways …

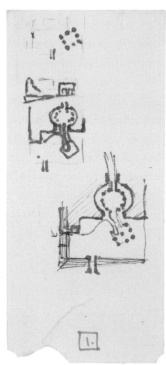

203

204

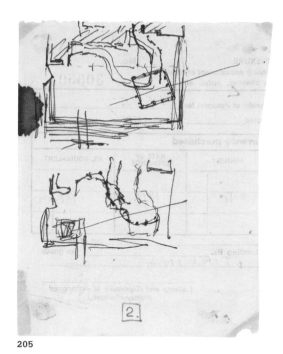

205

206

206

the *Architectural Review*, and the new sense of temporality and context in Stirling's museums.[179]

But the often uneasy relationship between the two should not be immediately equated with influence. For *Collage City*, in its post-historical guise, is permeated with a sense of defeat; or, rather, in the face of the assumed debacle of modern urbanism, it celebrates, if nothing else, a new-found freedom for historical allusion on every scale. *Collage City* ends with an appeal to the "great moments of the past"; a sense of the "eternal values" of architecture hardly commensurate with the invention of new solutions to different and identifiably new problems that permeated modernism, and that still marks Stirling's projects. While *Collage City* proposes a nostalgic utopia based loosely on the anti-utopian philosophy of Karl Popper—a counter to what the authors see as the horrifying effects of "totalitarian" progressive utopias—Stirling pursues the new combination, the invention of solutions characteristic of his typological imagination. In this respect there is no difference between the sensibility present in the Cambridge History Faculty Building, that most unitary of type forms, and the dispersed, sprawling miniature cities of Stuttgart or Dusseldorf. Both are in the end inventions, empirically formulated and constructed with a combinatorial skill reminiscent of a Vanbrugh, Soane or Schinkel, rather than a Burlington, Chambers, or Barry—a kind of Picturesque, radical, mannerist classicism rather than an academic neo-classicism.

179. Colin Rowe and Fred Koetter, "Collage City," *Architectural Review*, 157 (August 1975): 65–91. This article later became the basis for the book of the same name: Colin Rowe and Fred Koetter, *Collage City* (Cambridge, Mass.: MIT Press, 1978).

205–206. James Stirling and Partner, Nordrhein-Westfalen Museum, Düsseldorf: sketches, "2,"1975 ink on paper; 13.5 x 10.8 cm (5 5/16 x 4 ¼ in); AP140.S2.SS1.D43.P3.8 recto and verso

… on the back of his currency exchange receipt …

207–208. James Stirling and Partner, Nordrhein-Westfalen Museum, Düsseldorf: sketches, "3", 1975 ink and graphite on paper; 21.9 x 13.7 cm (8 ⅝ x 5 ⅜ in); AP140.S2.SS1.D43.P3.4 recto and verso

… on the back of his Pan Am ticket …

209–210. James Stirling and Partner, Nordrhein-Westfalen Museum, Düsseldorf: sketches, "5", 1975 ink and graphite on paper; 14.3 x 7.8 cm (5 ⅝ x 3 ¹⁄₁₆ in); AP140.S2.SS1.D43.P3.5 recto and verso

… and on the reverse of his boarding pass.

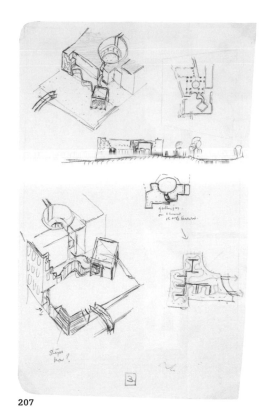

207

208

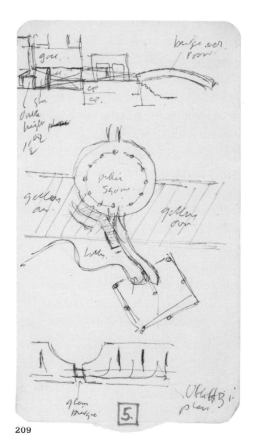

209

210

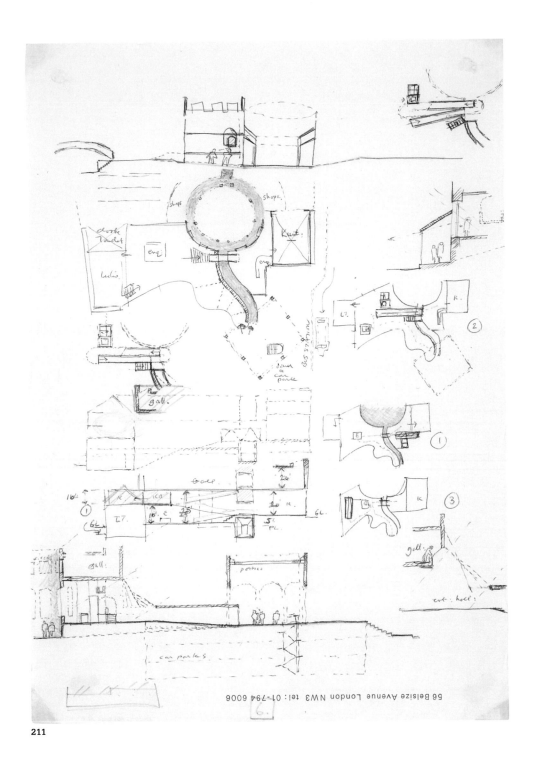

211

211. James Stirling and Partner,
Nordrhein-Westfalen Museum,
Düsseldorf: sketches, "6", 1975
ink and graphite on paper; 29.8 x 21 cm
(11 ¾ x 8 ¼ in); AP140.S2.SS1.D43.P3.3

Returning to London, Stirling elaborates
the scheme developed in the air.

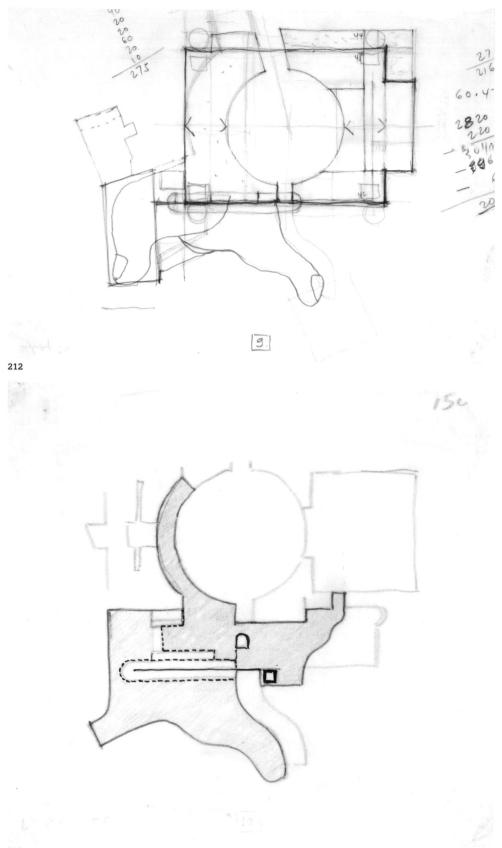

212. James Stirling and Partner,
Nordrhein-Westfalen Museum,
Düsseldorf: plan, "9," 1975
graphite and ink on paper; 21 x 29 cm
(8 ¼ x 11 ⅜ in); AP140.S2.SS1.D43.P3.11

Perhaps the discussion over the form
of the entry lobby to the museum,
beneath the raised cubical portico, took
the form of comparing it to thumb and
fingers stretched to reach out to the
city square—at least Stirling's red biro
seems to trace the outline of a hand.

213. James Stirling and Partner,
Nordrhein-Westfalen Museum,
Düsseldorf: plan "11," 1975
graphite, coloured pencil and ink on
paper; 19.7 x 20.7 cm (7 ¾ x 8 ⅛ in);
AP140.S2.SS1.D43.P3.9

212

213

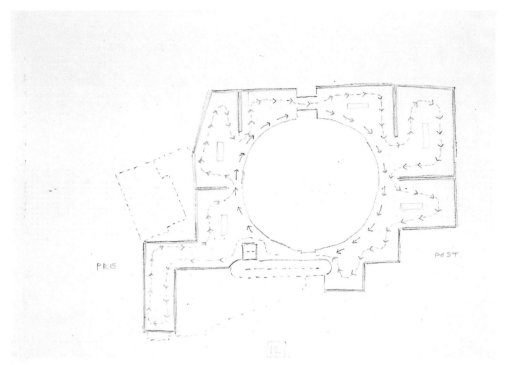

214

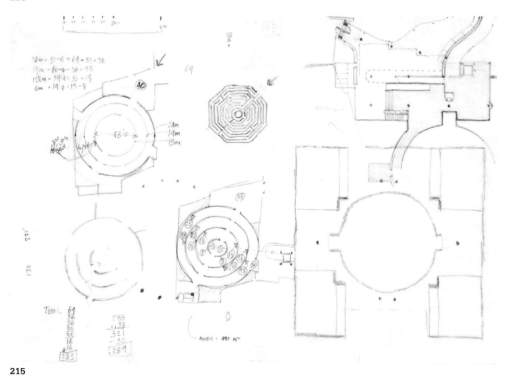

215

214. James Stirling and Partner, Nordrhein-Westfalen Museum, Düsseldorf: circulation plan,"12," 1975 graphite and coloured pencil on paper; 21 x 29.6 cm (8 ¼ x 11 ⅝ in); AP140.S2.SS1.D43.P3.13

Stirling's meticulous attention to circulation was often marked on plans with hundreds of tiny red arrows.

215. James Stirling and Partner, Nordrhein-Westfalen Museum, Düsseldorf. plans, "15," 1975 graphite, coloured pencil and ink on paper; 20.8 x 29.4 cm (8 ⁵/₁₆ x 11 ⅝ in); AP140.S2.SS1.D43.P3.15

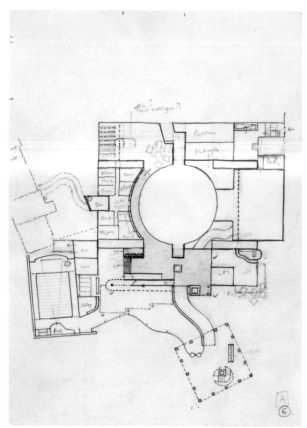

216

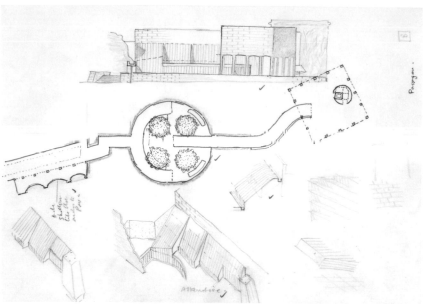

217

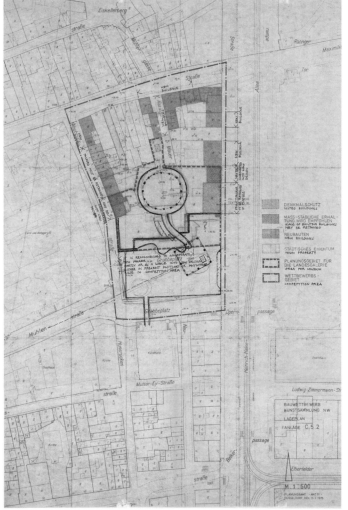

218

216. James Stirling and Partner,
Nordrhein-Westfalen Museum,
Düsseldorf: plan, 1975
ink and graphite on paper;
29.5 x 20.9 cm (11 ⅝ x 8 ¼ in);
AP140.S2.SS1.D43.P4.9

217. James Stirling and Partner,
Nordrhein-Westfalen Museum, Düsseldorf: plan, elevation and sketches, 1975
ink, graphite and coloured pencil on
paper; 20.9 x 29.5 cm (8 ¼ x 11 ⅝ in);
AP140.S2.SS1.D43.P4.1

A public walk leads from the entry
pavilion to the museum, to the garden
within the open cylindrical courtyard,
and out to the city again.

218. James Stirling and Partner,
Nordrhein-Westfalen Museum,
Düsseldorf: site plan, 1975
ink and graphite on diazotype;
90.4 x 60.5 cm (35 ⁹⁄₁₆ x 23 ¹³⁄₁₆ in);
AP140.S2.SS1.D43.P4.23

Stirling's scheme is inserted delicately
into the fabric of the existing context,
retaining the outer walls of the block, and
developing a raised plaza, with routes that
lead through and around the museum.

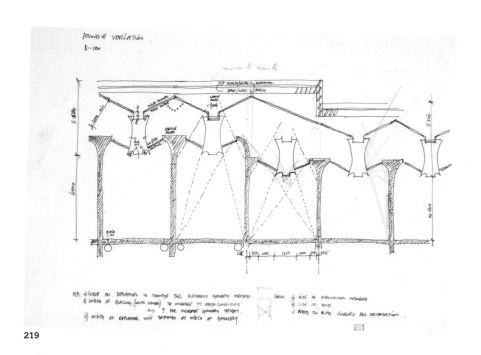

219. James Stirling and Partner, Nordrhein-Westfalen Museum, Düsseldorf: section through skylights 1975
ink and graphite on paper;
21 x 29.6 cm (8 ¼ x 11 ⅝ in);
AP140.S2.SS1.D43.P4.16

As in his future museum projects, Stirling experiments with reflected top-lighting for the museum galleries, reminiscent of the designs by John Soane for the Dulwich Picture Gallery (1817).

220. James Stirling and Partner, Nordrhein-Westfalen Museum, Düsseldorf: axonometric, 1975
graphite and coloured pencil on paper;
20.9 x 29.5 cm (8 ¼ x 11 ⅝ in);
AP140.S2.SS1.D43.P4.5

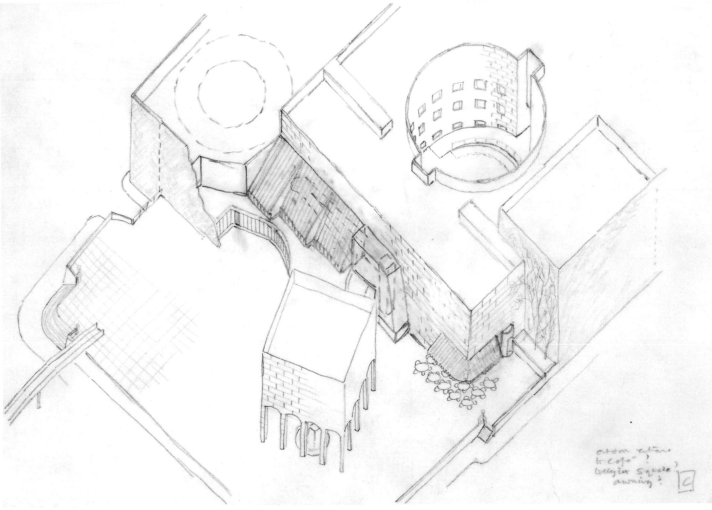

Context and Association

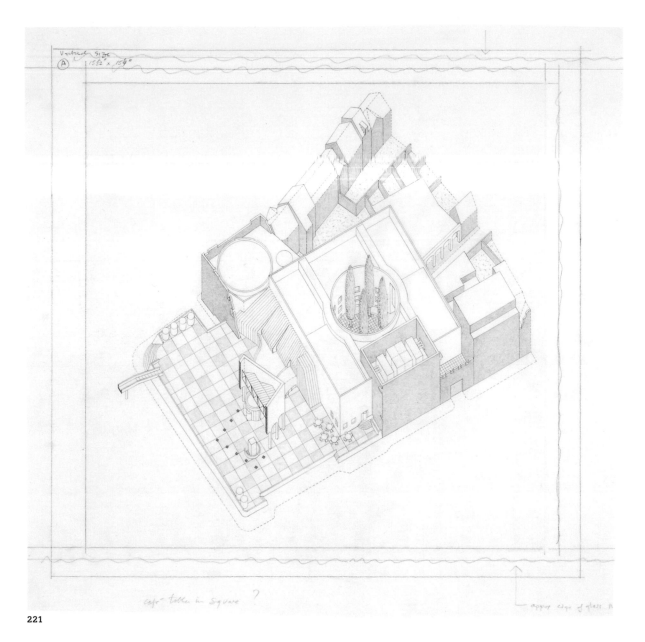

221

221. James Stirling and Partner,
Nordrhein-Westfalen Museum,
Düsseldorf: axonometric, 1975
graphite and coloured pencil on paper;
48.9 x 49.6 cm (19 ¼ x 19 ½ in);
AP140.S2.SS1.D43.P6.12

222. James Stirling and Partner,
Nordrhein-Westfalen Museum,
Düsseldorf: up axonometric, 1975
ink and coloured pencil on paper;
40.3 x 33.8 cm (15 ⅞ x 13 ⁵/₁₆ in);
AP140.S2.SS1.D43.P6.7

Developing the "worm's-eye view"
technique, Stirling uses it to pick
out the distinctive public elements
of the project—the cubic entry
pavilion and the open cylinder at
the heart of the museum.

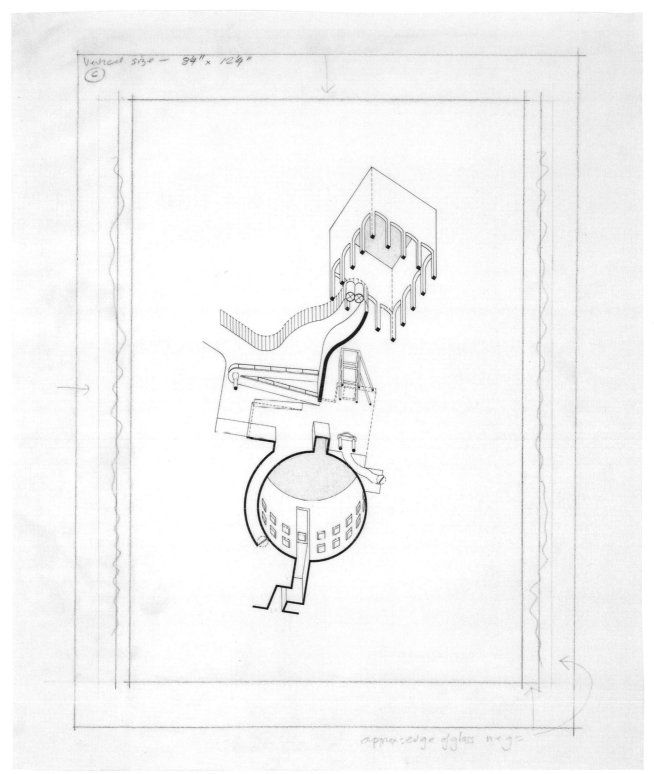

Vertical size — 84" x 12'9"

ⓒ

approx edge of glass neg=

222

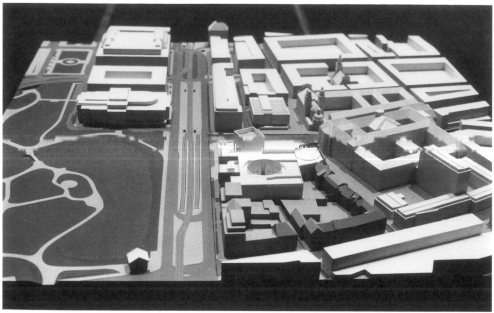

223. James Stirling and Partner, Nordrhein-Westfalen Museum, Düsseldorf: view of model set within competition model, 1975
gelatin silver print; 13.6 x 20.4 cm
(5 ³⁄₈ x 8 ¹⁄₁₆ in); AP140.S2.SS1.D43.P7.11

223

224. James Stirling and Partner, Nordrhein-Westfalen Museum, Düsseldorf: competition model, 1975
painted cardboard and painted and varnished wood; 16 x 37.5 x 48 cm
(6 ⁵⁄₁₆ x 14 ³⁄₄ x 18 ⁷⁄₈ in);
AP140.S2.SS1.D43.P43.14

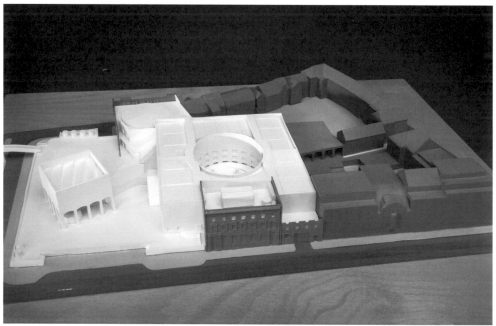

224

225

225. Competition Brief for the
Wallraf-Richartz-Museum, Cologne,
Germany: cover showing site
between the railway tracks and the
cathedral, 1975
offset lithograph and lithographs;
29.7 x 42.3 x 1.6 cm (11 ¾ x 16 ⅝ x ⅝ in);
AP140.S2.SS1.D44.P10.1

A competition for the development of
the area between the cathedral and
the Rhine: the brief stated: "the whole
area between the river and the
historical old town should be formed
into a recreational and green zone."

226. James Stirling and Partner,
Wallraf-Richartz-Museum, Cologne:
conceptual sketches, 1975
graphite and ink on paper; 21 x 8.6 cm
(8 ¼ x 3 ⅜ in); AP140.S2.SS1.D44.P2

Preliminary sketch of site and
design strategies on the back of an
announcement of a Palladio exhibition
in Paris. The top sketch (1) shows the
two entry pavilions flanking the entry to
the cathedral plaza at the Rhine bridge;
the second (2) shows the possible
underground parking alongside of the
railway tracks; the third (3) shows
the service level, and the fourth (4) the
underground building and the ramp
to the plaza level.

227. James Stirling and Partner,
Wallraf-Richartz-Museum, Cologne:
plan, 1975
graphite on paper; 41.2 x 27.7 cm
(16 ¼ x 10 ⅞ in); AP140.S2.SS1.D44.P3.1

Sketch axonometric of the route from
the circular courtyard beneath the
auditorium in the gateway pavilion,
through the foyer of the museum to the
sunken sculpture court that mimics
the plan of the cathedral in negative—
a reversal of the Moretti technique of
casting volumes in solid form. Here
is an intimation of the strategy used at
the Wissenschaftszentrum, of taking
diagrammatic forms of historic types
as compositional elements—here
including the "ziggurat" form of the
electrical substation..

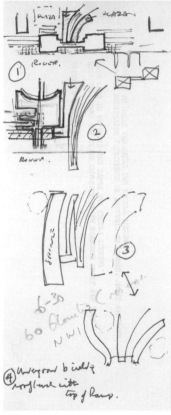

226

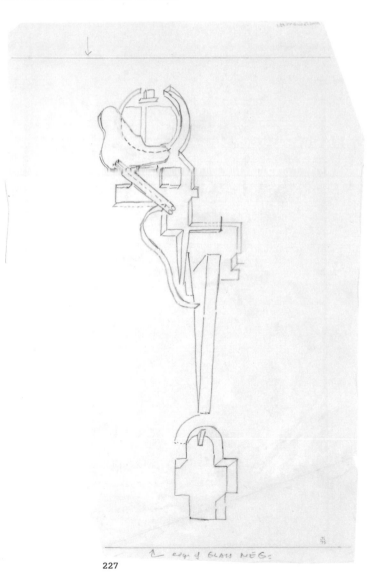

227

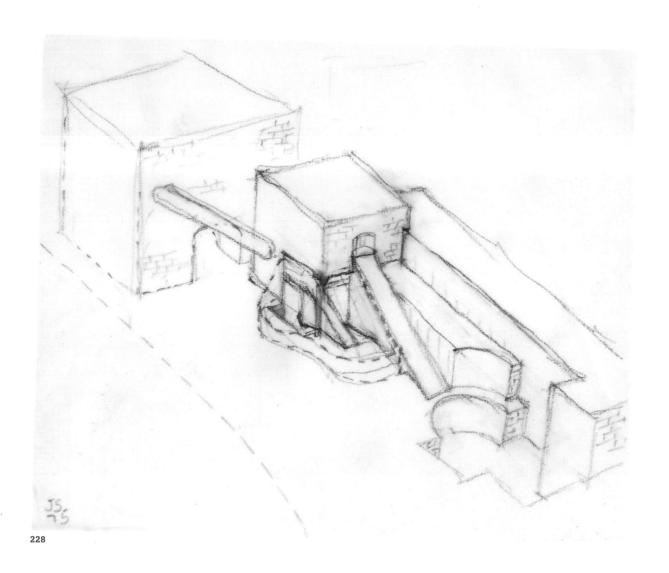

228

228. James Stirling and Partner,
Wallraf-Richartz-Museum, Cologne:
sketch perspective, signed "JS-75," 1975
graphite on paper; 11 x 13.1 cm
(4 ⅜ x 5 ⅛ in); AP140.S2.SS1.D44.P3.2

Stirling, in this drawing, elaborates on
the three-dimensional volumes that
compose the route from the river to
the cathedral, with emphasis on their
character as stone-built solids.

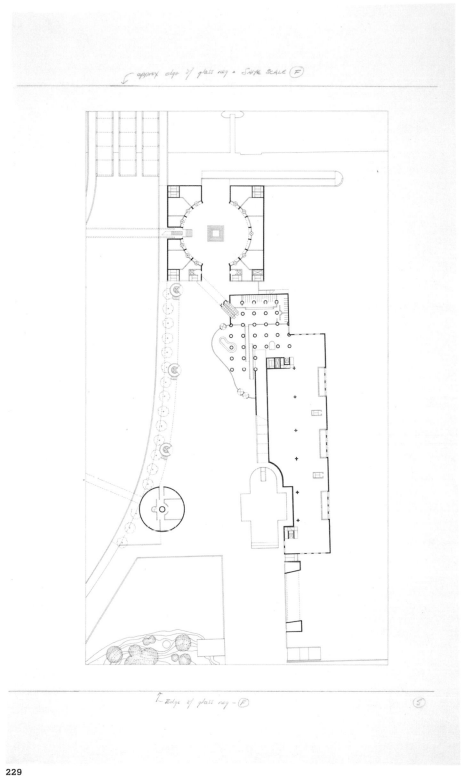

229

229. James Stirling and Partner,
Wallraf-Richartz-Museum, Cologne:
plan, 1975
ink on paper; 75.6 x 43.4 cm
(29 ¾ x 17 ⅞ in); AP140.S2.SS1.D44.P4.10

Plan of the pedestrian route through the
cathedral plaza. The circular courtyard
beneath the auditorium in the gateway
pavilion repeats that in the Düsseldorf
competition, and anticipates that developed for the Staatsgalerie, Stuttgart.

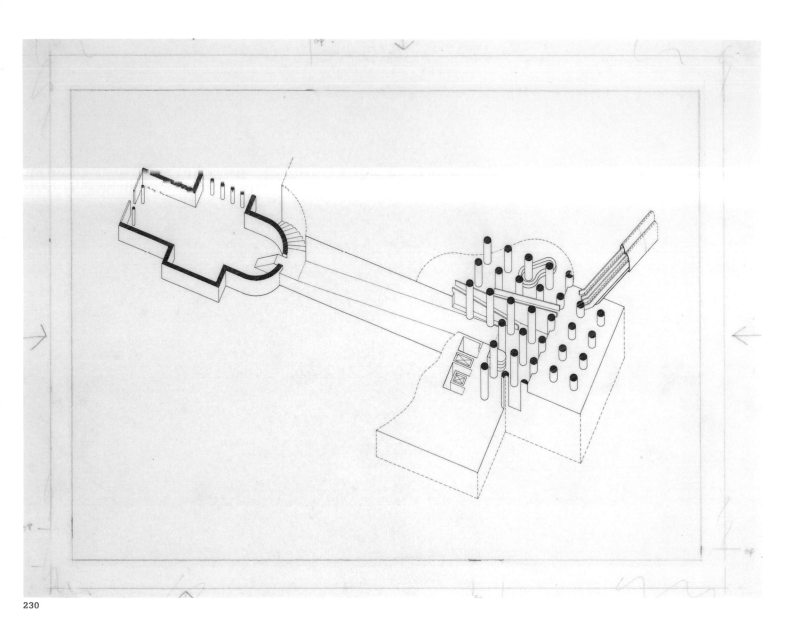

230

230. James Stirling and Partner,
Wallraf-Richartz-Museum, Cologne:
cutaway axonometric, 1975
ink on paper; 27.5 x 36.5 cm
(10 ⅞ x 14 ⅜ in); AP140.S2.SS1.D44.P4.28

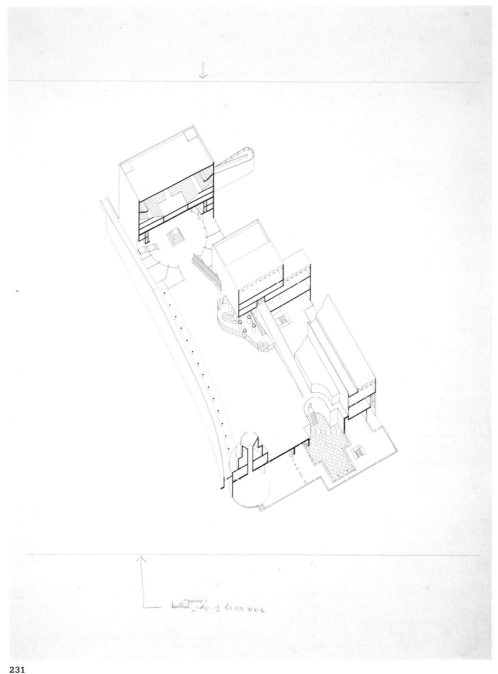

231. James Stirling and Partner,
Wallraf-Richartz-Museum, Cologne:
axonometric, 1975
ink on paper; 76.7 x 55 cm
(30 ³/₁₆ x 21 ⁵/₈ in);
AP140.S2.SS1.D44.P4.30

231

232. James Stirling and Partner,
Wallraf-Richartz-Museum,
Cologne: site plan, 1975
reprographic copy; 34.2 x 34 cm
(13 ½ x 13 ⅜ in); AP140.S2.SS1.D44.P5.1

233. James Stirling and Partner,
Wallraf-Richartz-Museum, Cologne:
longitudinal section, 1975
ink on sepia diazotype on plastic film;
62.3 x 116.6 cm (24 ½ x 45 ⅞ in);
AP140.S2.SS1.D44.P5.39

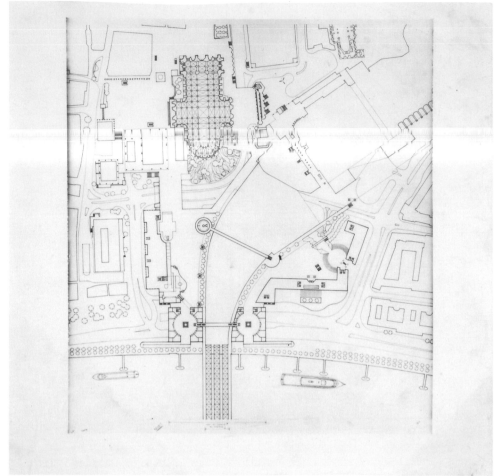

232

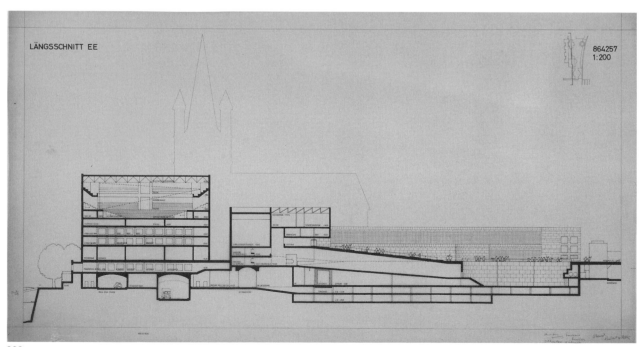

233

234

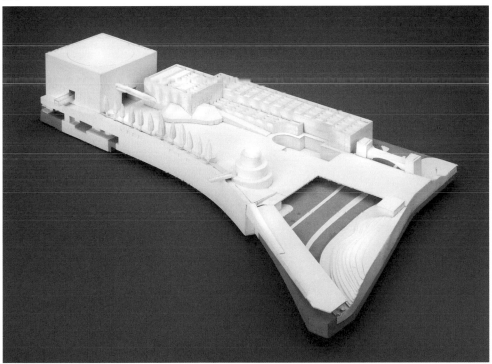

235

234. James Stirling and Partner, Wallraf-Richartz-Museum, Cologne: view of model set within competition site model, 1975 gelatin silver print; 10.2 x 15.3 cm (4 x 6 in); AP140.S2.SS1.D44.P9.2

235. James Stirling and Partner, Wallraf-Richartz-Museum, Cologne: competition model, 1975 wood, paper, plastic and paint; 10.5 x 51.5 x 33 cm (4 ⅛ x 20 ¼ x 13 in); AP140.S2.SS1.D44.P11

236. James Stirling, Michael Wilford, and Associates, Staatsgalerie, Stuttgart, Germany: conceptual sketch, 1977–84 graphite on reprographic copy; 20.3 x 32.8 cm (8 x 12 ⅞ in); AP140.S2.SS1.D52.P1.14

This was a limited competition for the new Staatsgalerie adjoining the old neo-classical Staatsgalerie. The result of this competition gave rise to considerable controversy from German architects committed to the continuation of technological and stylistic "modernism." Among them were the engineer Frei Otto and Professor Benisch, the third-placed in the competition (and earlier the winner of the first competition in 1974), who claimed that Stirling's project was formalistic, Palladian, and even quasi-fascist. In response, Alan Colquhoun in his review of the completed building (1984) called it a "democratic monument." This sketch on the basis of a diagrammatic site plan proposes a first scheme, the "piano" scheme, that established the new addition as entirely separate from, and added to, the old museum.

237. James Stirling, Michael Wilford, and Associates, Staatsgalerie, Stuttgart: conceptual sketches, 1977–84 ink and graphite on paper; 20.9 x 14.8 cm (8 ¼ x 5 ³/₁₆ in) AP140.S2.SS1.D52.P1.3.2

In this early sketch, Stirling explores the potential routes through the site down the hillside to the multi-lane Konrad-Adenauer Strasse, and the opera house.

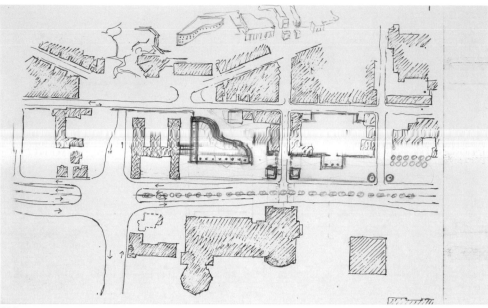

236

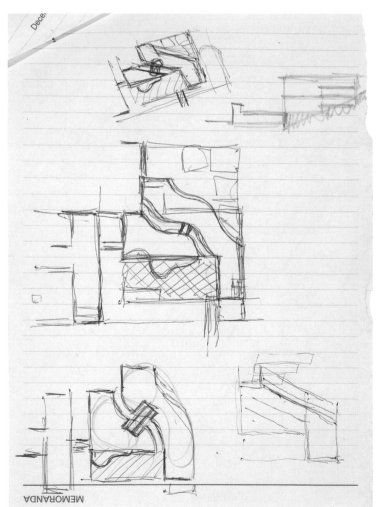

237

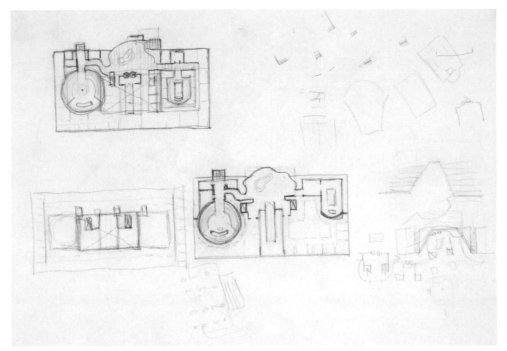

238

238. James Stirling, Michael Wilford, and Associates, Staatsgalerie, Stuttgart: sketches, 1977–84
graphite on paper; 21 x 29.7 cm (8 ¼ x 11 ¾ in); AP140.S2.SS1.D52.P1.10

This is one of the earliest pages of sketches to introduce the rotunda (auditorium) and the cube (gallery) on either side of a free-form entry.

239. James Stirling, Michael Wilford, and Associates, Staatsgalerie, Stuttgart: plans, section, and perspectives, 1977–84
ink on paper; 20.9 x 29.5 cm (8 ¼ x 11 ⅝ in); AP140.S2.SS1.D52.P1.12

Reprising the *parti* for Düsseldorf, the rotunda is now inserted in the cube as a separate pavilion; elevations and another plan to the right-hand side indicate that the slope was inspiring "Priene" like solutions with ramps to the top of the site.

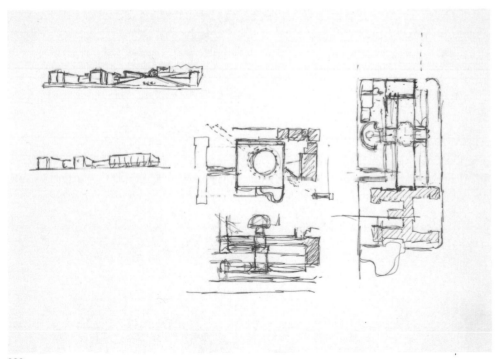

239

240. James Stirling, Michael Wilford, and Associates, Staatsgalerie, Stuttgart: conceptual sketches, 1977–84
reprographic copy; 20.9 x 29.7 cm
(8 ¼ x 11 ¾ in); AP140.S2.SS1.D52.P1.13

Here the stepped section of the site is joined to a rotunda and ramp, within a U-shaped gallery building,

241. James Stirling, Michael Wilford, and Associates, Staatsgalerie, Stuttgart: sketches, 1977–84
graphite on paper; 20.9 x 29.6 cm
(8 ¼ x 11 ⅝ in); AP140.S2.SS1.D52.P1.22

Here the open rotunda, with obvious traces of Schinkel's Altes Museum, Berlin, with arcaded galleria, the passage from the top of the site to the bottom, the free-form entry, and the ramp from the entry podium are all in place in a centralized scheme.

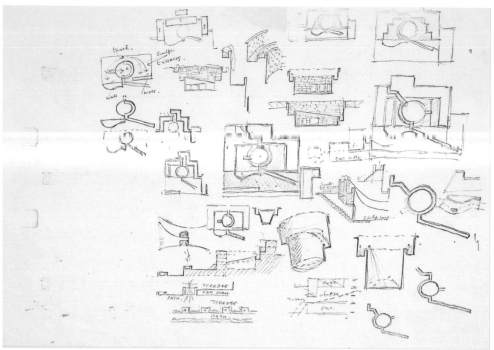

240

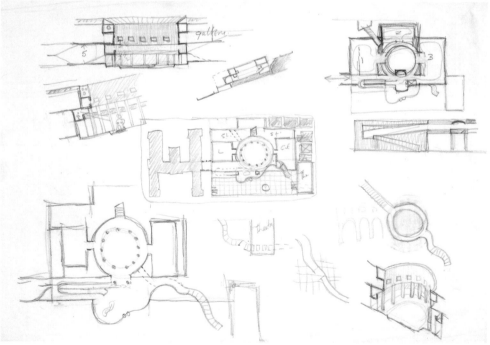

241

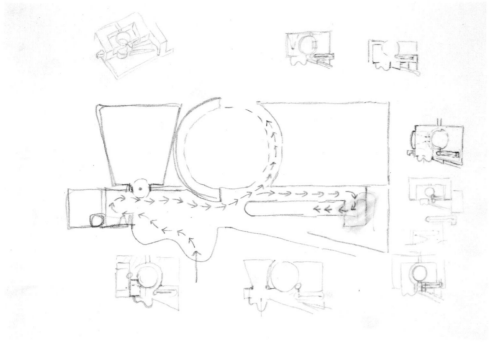

242

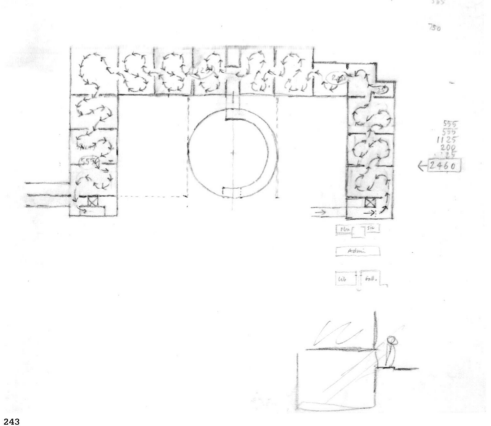

243

242. James Stirling, Michael Wilford, and Associates, Staatsgalerie, Stuttgart: circulation plan and sketches, 1977–84 graphite and coloured pencil on paper; 20.8 x 29.4 cm (8 ⁵/₁₆ x 11 ⁵/₈ in); AP140.S2.SS1.D52.P2.7

Stirling traces the circulation from the entry to the auditorium, the rotunda, and the garage below.

243. James Stirling, Michael Wilford, and Associates, Staatsgalerie, Stuttgart: circulation plan, 1977–84 graphite on paper; 25.9 x 29.8 cm (10 ³/₁₆ x 11 ³/₄ in); AP140.S2.SS1.D52.P2.11

In this witty drawing the perambulations of a visitor through the enfilade of gallery spaces are traced with care; this traditional arrangement of galleries was much criticized at the time as too controlling for contemporary installation.

244. James Stirling, Michael Wilford, and Associates, Staatsgalerie, Stuttgart: sketch, 1977–84
graphite and colored pencil on paper; 9.3 x 13.6 cm (3 ⅝ x 5 ⅜ in) (irreg.); AP140.S2.SS1.D52.P4.25

Volumetric study of the ramp and stair from the entrance lobby. In this, as in many of Stirling's designs, movement is treated as a sculptural event within the larger whole.

245. James Stirling, Michael Wilford, and Associates, Staatsgalerie, Stuttgart: sectional elevation, 1977–84
ink on paper; 29.7 x 41.6 cm (11 ¾ x 16 ⅜ in); AP140.S2.SS1.D52.P4.73

The "historical" rotunda undergoes many iterations in an attempt to summarize the history of architecture as a kind of sculptural panorama—Romanesque and Gothic arches, Egyptian doorways, classical orders are all tested.

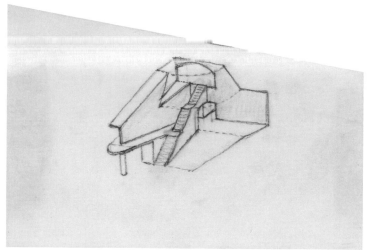

244

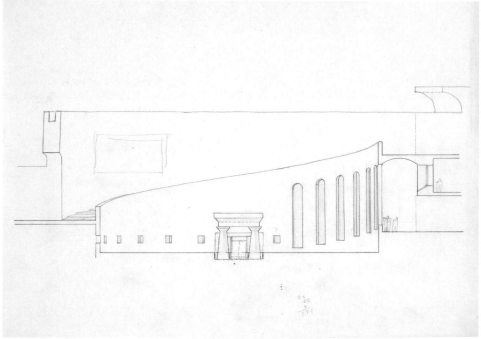

245

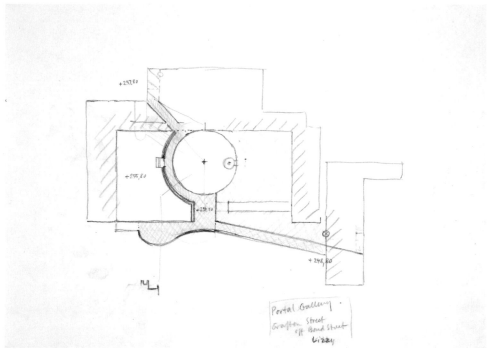

246

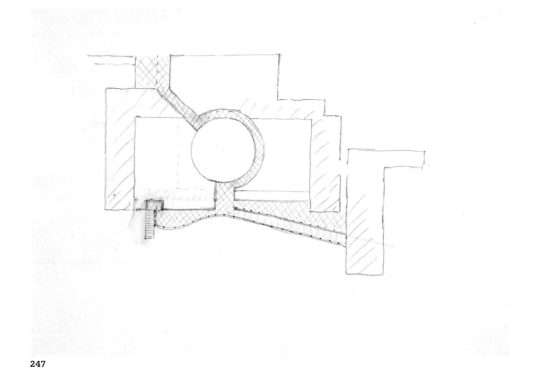

247

246. James Stirling, Michael Wilford, and Associates, Staatsgalerie, Stuttgart: plan, 1977–84
graphite and coloured pencil on paper; 29.7 x 41.6 cm (11 ¾ x 16 ⅜ in); AP140.S2.SS1.D52.P121.54

A number of sketches investigated the position of the ramp down the site—outside the rotunda on one side, or, as in the next figure, outside on the other side?

247. James Stirling, Michael Wilford, and Associates, Staatsgalerie, Stuttgart: plan, 1977–84
graphite and coloured pencil on paper; 29.7 x 41.6 cm (11 ¾ x 16 ⅜ in); AP140.S2.SS1.D52.P121.55

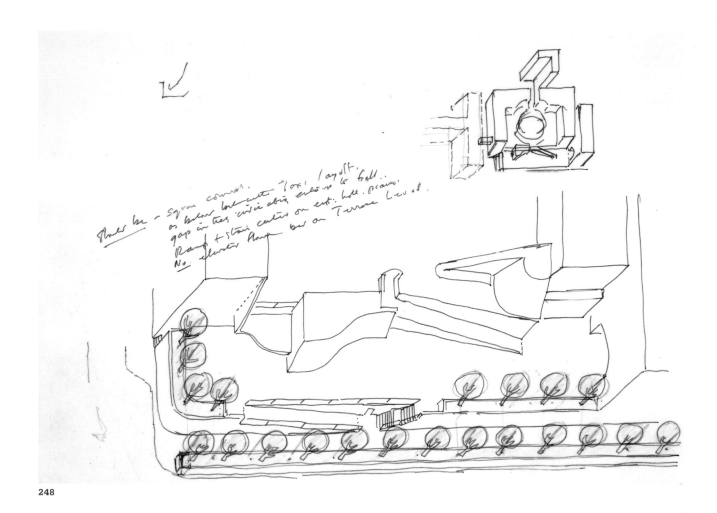

248

248. James Stirling, Michael Wilford, and Associates, Staatsgalerie, Stuttgart: axonometrics, 1977–84
ink, graphite and colored pencil on paper; 20.9 x 29.6 cm (8 ¼ x 11 ⅝ in); AP140.S2.SS1.D52.P122.25

One of many studies for the front "non-façade" of the museum, exploring the relationship between the ramp and the tree-lined street.

249. James Stirling, Michael Wilford, and Associates, Staatsgalerie, Stuttgart: axonometric, 1977–84
graphite and colored pencil on paper; 20.9 x 29.5 cm (8 ¼ 11 ⅝ in); AP140.S2.SS1.D52.P122.68

Cut-away axonometric of rotunda, entry cylinder, ramps, and stairs, emphasizing the volumetric nature of the elements on the entry podium.

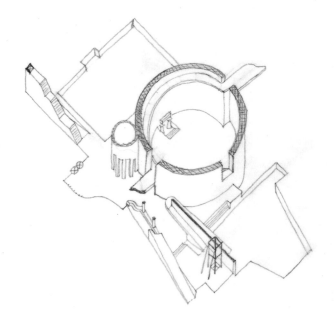

249

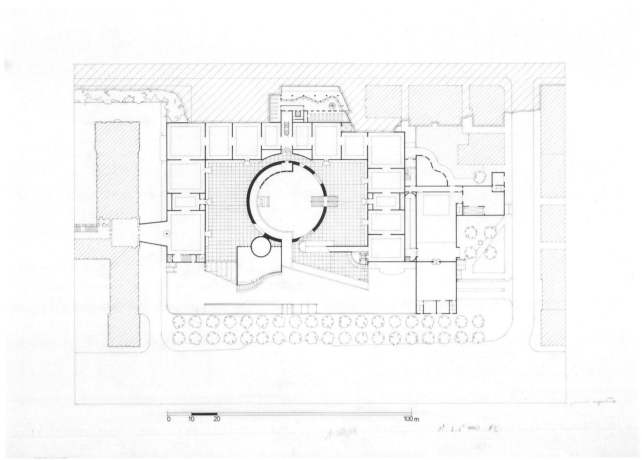

250

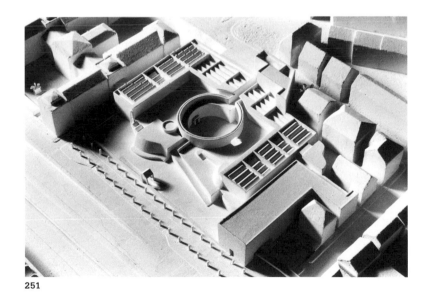

251

250. James Stirling, Michael Wilford, and Associates, Staatsgalerie, Stuttgart: plan, 1977–84
ink and coloured pencil on paper;
50.7 x 70.8 cm (20 x 27 ⅞ in);
AP140.S2.SS1.D52.P125

Rendered plan at gallery level, with outdoor sculpture terraces.

251. James Stirling, Michael Wilford, and Associates, Staatsgalerie, Stuttgart: photograph
of competition model, 1977–84
gelatin silver print; 16.7 x 24.6 cm
(6 ⁹⁄₁₆ x 9 ¹¹/16 in);
John Donat, photographer
AP140.S2.SS1.D52.P64.4
© John Donat Photography

Perhaps Not "Collage City"

It is easier to design the cities of the future than those of the past. Rome is an interrupted city because it has stopped being imagined and begun to be (poorly) planned. In Rome the issue is more about time than about space. The tides of centuries have passed and left behind on the sand the relics of remote shipwrecks; and, like all relics they are surrounded by an immediate and boundless space, the sea and the beach. It is a city that was initially inhabited by remains, then by ruins, and today, by rubbish ... fortunately Rome has never been afraid of a shambles. It is a city of Providence, and Providence patches up shambles. The beauty of Rome exists in its being a messed-up city patched up a countless number of times. Could we pretend that Providence was followed by utopia, a mother and daughter detesting each other? Utopia has never set foot in Rome, much less so than in Las Vegas.
Giulio Carlo Argan, 1978[180]

The exhibition "Rome Interrupted," or "Roma Interrotta," held in the cavernous ruins of the Mercati Traianei (Trajan Markets) in May and June of 1978, was the brainchild, among others, of the Roman architect Piero Sartoga and the American Michael Graves, and supported by the art historian and Mayor of Rome, Giulio Carlo Argan. The matrix set for the invitation to twelve Italian and international architects to imagine a kind of "Roman Utopia" was that of the 1748 plan of the city drawn by Giovanni Battista Nolli, originally published in twelve sections. Each architect was assigned a "Sector," and invented a reformulation of the urban plan of 1748 as it might be ideally proposed in 1978. Assembled together, side by side with the Nolli plan, the result was a kind of imaginary Rome, according to the particular approaches to urban design represented among the contributors.

As was to be expected in an exhibition with so open a brief, the new planned sectors varied widely according to the commitment of the authors: some, like Robert Krier, were frankly dismissive—"to me, the idea of the organizers in Rome to redraw and interpret the Nolli plan seemed rather absurd right from the beginning."[181] Others, like Robert Venturi and John Rauch, simply superimposed their own favorite city, in this case Las Vegas, as a billboard image on the map; others tended to caricature their own signatures—Michael Graves, for example, superimposing a huge broken keystone on the map. Krier simply imposed his hugely monumental project for a communal social centre, its multi-storey columns of housing supporting a vast roof over an open square. Many others took the call extremely seriously, at the same time inventing narrative strategies in one form or another in order to give a frame of reference to their work. Piero Sartogo invented a story out of Fourier in order to give life to his utopian deconstruction of the Vatican and its reformulation into a twentieth-century Phalanstery. Antoine Grumbach fantasized an underworld of Rome along the lines of

180. Giulio Carlo Argan, "Roma Interrotta," *Architectural Design*, 49, nos. 3–4 (1979), Profile 20, *Roma Interrotta*, guest editor Michael Graves (London: Architectural Design, 1979), 37.

181. Robert Krier, "Nolli: Sector X," "Roma Interrotta," Profile 20, p. 97.

252

252. James Stirling and Partner, "Roma Interrotta" exhibition, Rome: page layout for publication, 1977–79
graphite on paper; 24.7 x 24.6 cm (9 ¾ x 9 ¹¹⁄₁₆ in); AP140.S2.SS3.D7.P2.11

The exhibition "Roma Interrotta" was organized by the City of Rome under the auspices of the Mayor, the art historian Giulio Carlo Argan, in the form of "revisions" by twelve invited architects to the twelve sections of Giovanni Battista Nolli's 1748 Plan of Rome.

the drawings of Jean-Jacques Lequeu—ruins built upon ruins. Others were consistent in their application of their particular formalisms to their sites. The most elegant of them was Costantino Dardi's careful morphological analysis of Nolli's own "analysis of the urban structure … [that] breaks down all materials (networks and morphologies of built form such as monuments, palaces, courtyards, churches, gardens, villas, monasteries, and public gardens)."[182] Dardi's insertion of interwoven patterns of water, pavement, and greenery brought together three-dimensional geometry and historical analysis to form a "a modern urbanisation founded on networks and layouts … a concrete and real experiment on a portion of the ideal city," a project that in a real sense consummated Rossi's rationalism in a truly urban structure.[183] Aldo Rossi himself, resisting "any hypothetical alternative pattern for the city's growth," on the grounds that the development of Rome had been, as the competition brief suggested, "interrupted," took the opportunity of "restoring" the Roman baths of Antoninus as a newly eroticized centre of urban pleasures—the kind of counter-institutional institution fantasized by many following the institutional critiques of Michel Foucault.[184]

The most serious of all, however, because integrally related to his emerging project of Collage City, was that of Colin Rowe. Given Nolli's "Sector" VIII,

182. Costatino Dardi, "Nolli: Sector II," "Roma Interrotta,"
Profile 20, p. 34.

183. Dardi, "Nolli: Sector II," 34.

184. Aldo Rossi, "Nolli: Sector XI," "Roma Interrotta,"
Profile 20, p. 88.

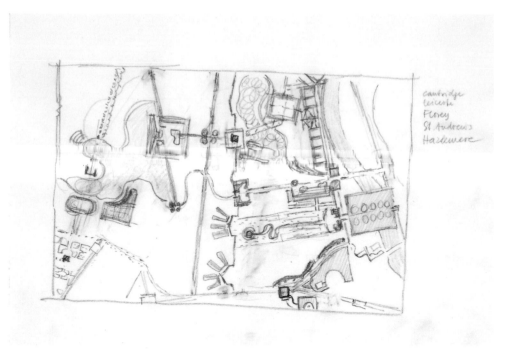

253

253. James Stirling and Partner, "Roma Interrotta": conceptual sketch, 1977–79 graphite and coloured pencil on paper; 20.8 x 29.6 cm (8 ⁵⁄₁₆ x 11 ⁵⁄₈ in); AP140.S2.SS3.D7.P2.38

his team, including Peter Carl, Judith Di Maio, and Steven Peterson, carefully studied the original state of the landscape around the Circus Maximus, "an arid and deserted region of ancient remains, unkempt vineyards, malarial *villine* and battered monastic foundations," and its successive transformations in the eighteenth, nineteenth, and twentieth centuries, proposing a dense urban fabric interrupted by restored monuments and reclaimed villas and churches. The proposal, in essence, was a first and major demonstration of the principles of Collage City, that had been outlined three years before in the long article that preceded the publication of the book of the same name.[185] This was emphasized in the *Architectural Design* publication of "Roma Interrotta" by Steven Peterson's didactic essay on "Urban Design Tactics," with its formulation of figural "space: the medium of urbanism" interlocked with "urban elements."[186] Rowe was explicit in his understanding of the role of the competition as "an oblique criticism of late 19th-century and, particularly, present-day urban strategies," with their "terrible lessons, best forgotten"; and the remedy was "to constitute a fragment of the city which could appear as no more than a 'natural' extension of the 'old' Rome of the Campus Martius, a city of discrete set pieces and interactive local incidents, a city which represents a coalition of intentions rather than the singular presence of any immediately apparent all-coordinating ideas."[187]

185. Colin Rowe and Fred Koetter, "Collage City," *Architectural Review*, 157 (August 1975): 65–91.

186. Steven Peterson, "Urban Design Tactics," *"Roma Interrotta,"* Profile 20, pp. 76–82.

187. Colin Rowe and team, "Nolli: Sector VIII," *"Roma Interrotta,"* Profile 20, p. 75.

254

254. James Stirling and Partner,
"Roma Interrotta": site plan, 1977–79
ink on paper; 41.6 x 29.7 cm
(16 3/8 x 11 3/4 in), AP140.S2.SS3.D7.P2.40a

As a whole, the "new" Nolli map, whether ironically or substantively, represented a gamut of urban design ideologies, each tied to their authors, and exhibiting, in retrospect, a vivid picture of a moment when, modern movement urbanism having been effectively challenged, the turn towards contextualism had yet to be fully identified in the later ossifications of "Collage City," "Collision City," "Pop-City," or the "New Urbanism." These differences were as apparent in the texts accompanying the plans as in the plans themselves, as they represented a range of political, social, and formal positions from the utopian to the formalist.

Amid this gamut of responses, that of Stirling stood out for its refusal to enter into any kind of utopian urbanism and in the distance it took from the other entries. And, despite Stirling's own reference to Rowe's "Collage City" model, his approach was anything but collagist, and owed as little to Rowe as it did to Krier. Indeed, if an analogue might be found it would still be that of Rossi, with his belief in articulated typologies. For Stirling made the decision to populate his largely unpopulated (at the time of Nolli) Gianicolo, much of which lay outside the walls, with a range of his own built and unbuilt projects, not as a simple catalogue or advertisement, but rather in order to demonstrate a principle: that of the appropriateness of *context* and *association*, "either to the circumstances of 1748, or to JS projects at the time they were designed—sometimes to both. Projects are disposed in prototypical ways, with wall buildings

255. James Stirling and Partner, "Roma Interrotta": final drawing, 1977–79
ink on reprographic copy; 88.5 x 139 cm
(34 ⅞ x 54 ¾ in); AP140.S2.SS3.D7.P4

related to, or reinforcing the Gianicolo and Aurelian walls. Sometimes topography has influenced the choice, with hill buildings on the Gianicolo slope and water-edge buildings along the Tiber."[188]

Accordingly, a selection was made of existing buildings that were "essential to preserve/integrate/intensify," and these considerations were joined to "contextual, associational, topographical, prototypical, typological, symbological, iconographical and archeological" considerations in order to create what Stirling envisaged as a new kind of environment—one "with a similar density to that evolved via history."[189] It was as if the juxtaposing of Stirling's projects and Nolli's Rome had collapsed historical time so as to bring Rome into the modern era but with a sensitivity to its own internal laws of growth and form.

Thus Stirling selected some thirty out of fifty projects designed since the 1950s. The matrix of the plan was a proposed new autostrada, named the "Vacuum Strada" as it vacuumed cars from the centre of Rome; its toll gates

188. Stirling and team, "Nolli: Sector IV. Revisions to the Nolli Plan of Rome," "Roma Interrotta," Profile 20, p. 42.

189. Stirling, "Revisions of the Nolli Plan of Rome," p. 42.

and station were formed by the museum project for Cologne, with the Oratorio replacing Cologne Cathedral and its axis focused on a Villa Lante "improved" by the addition of the St Andrews Arts Centre, connecting by a winding path to the St Andrews dormitories; the Tiber was bridged over with a version of the Siemens project, bringing together both sides of the river, as, Stirling remarked, should have happened to the Thames at the Festival of Britain; the Gianicolo was flanked by Runcorn housing; near to the St Andrews dormitories, Churchill College incorporated the old convent of the Onofrio, and a walled compound was provided for the early project for Basil Mavolean's three houses in London. The New York West Side study was restored as a new Porto Leonino ferry and shipping terminal on the Tiber; a new university campus assembled Leicester, Cambridge, and Sheffield on the grounds of the Villa Corsini, with the Florey Building backing onto the river. The Villa Farnesina was given Olivetti's Haslemere pavilion; Selwyn College housing paralleled the Aurelian Wall. Inside the wall, Trastevere was developed with the Meineke Strasse housing and the Marburg Bank, and its new neighbourhood centre bore a striking resemblance to Derby Civic Centre. There was a new museum of architecture—with Bramante's Tempietto as its main feature, restored to its original intended garden setting as described by Serlio; an adminstrative centre on the Via Aurelia, modeled on that designed for Florence, became the new administrative hub of Rome. Around a park and lake, similar to that of Stourhead, a number of pavilions were distributed—the Stiff Dom-ino project, the Expandable House, the Model Village for CIAM, while Olivetti's Milton Keynes headquarters became a "Castle" along the water; an island in centre was occupied by the Isle of Wight House. A rural housing commune in the form of Lima's PREVI development completed the roster. Stirling's text then read like a stroll through the Gianicolo, an architectural promenade through the ideal city of his projects, almost like a mapped version of John Soane's oeuvre painted as an ensemble by Gandy.

More serious, however, and belying the obviously ironic tone of the description, was Stirling's almost angry critique of the previous decades of urban renewal and experiment. He wrote of the recent realization of the New Towns' "devastating effect" on the old towns from which they were supposed to relieve the pressure; he reflected on Runcorn's supposedly rational planning—the implantation of sewers, services, and infrastructure, that in turn dictated the layout of roads, and thus the disposition of buildings, with the resulting "abject environment." He railed against the postwar destruction of the magnificent nineteenth-century cities—Liverpool, Glasgow, Newcastle—in the name of progress, only to be replaced with a lethal combination of urban motorways and modern commercial architecture, what he called "block modern": "Thus cities have lost their identity and townspeople are numbed with loss of memory while their children grow up in kitschplace and junkland."[190]

190. Stirling, "Revisions of the Nolli Plan of Rome," p. 42.

A New Contextualism

Stirling, in 1978, was already deeply conscious of the sense of cultural and social loss implicated in total redevelopment. In notes to his description of his Nolli project, he cited his report to the client for the Strasse Hotel Meineke, Berlin, as an attempt "to repair the street from post-war damage done to it by modern architecture and commercialism … and restore it to a pleasant mixed residential character," and "to use the established language of the street (i.e. types of windows, entrance doors, gables, balconies etc.) and the traditional materials of the old buildings (i.e. masonry, rendering etc.). The new building includes architectural elements of veneer (blind façade), portico (house form), gateway (garage entry), hinge corner transition …"[191] Already developed in the postwar period in typical fashion—a multi-storey garage and a corner gas station, the Meineke Strasse project had attempted to tie together the various and disparate parts of the street façade, and the corner with Lietzenburger Strasse, with a linear building containing apartments and small shops. The general effect was that of a repaired modernism, with continuous horizontal bands of metal windows, but the massing was broken up in scale, as in a traditional terrace, with entrances and access towers.

This scheme, for which the Berlin office prepared dozens of alternative designs, many highly colored and with diverse three-dimensional patterns, was the first of a series of many "contextual" designs, as Stirling named them; projects that were concerned less with the insertion of institutional "non-monumentality" into an existing urban fabric than following from the project for Derby Civic Centre, knitting together an already decimated fabric. There followed the design for the Dresdner Bank in Marburg (1977), which took careful account of an existing old mill building and the public passages into the old city; a study of the Müller Pier in Rotterdam (1977), with its nine-storey terrace housing forming an amphitheatrical space at the centre of the pier; plans for eleven town houses for the Upper East Side of Manhattan (1978), and culminating in the extraordinary and witty building for the School of Architecture at Rice University, Houston (1978–81).

All of these schemes were studied with particular attention to the rhythms, variations, and material colorations of their façades—the Manhattan town houses in particular echoing the curved bay fronts of the traditional brownstone row houses but, except in the case of Rice, never abandoning a trace of modernist detailing. In Rice, however, all pretext as to variations on the modern was abandoned, in the face of Ralph Adams Cram's dictates as to the style appropriate to a Texan campus. Here the apparently "Spanish" style of the exterior, fusing with the existing building to which the extension of the school was added, is in direct contrast to the interior, which seems for all intents and

191. James Stirling, "Architect's Report, Hotel Meineke Strasse, Berlin," cited in "Revisions to the Nolli Map of Rome," p. 46.

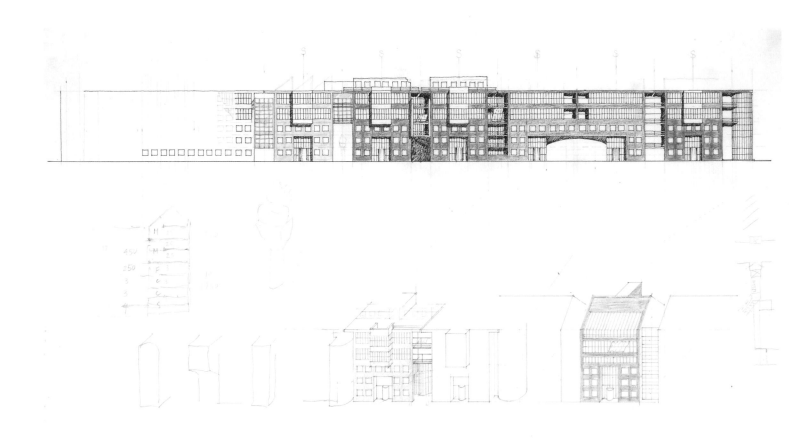

256

256. James Stirling and Partner, Hotel, Meineke Strasse, Berlin: axonometric and elevation, 1976 graphite, coloured pencil and ink on paper; 29.7 x 41.6 cm (11 11/16 x 16 3/8 in); AP140.S2.SS1.D45.P3.26

This project involved restoring a corner lost to a filling station and a multi-level parking garage.

purposes to be a modernist insert, sculpturally envisaged as a composition in itself. This "wrapping", however much it refers to its campus context, is, as one might expect, also subtly mannered—the modeling of the façade with its horizontal and vertical cuts, the off-centre round window at the end of the entry wing, and the central column dividing the entrance itself all attest to the inventiveness of the Stirling office when faced with ostensibly fixed parameters. Perhaps, as Peter Papademitriou noted, Cram's 1909 prescription was seen to allow a certain flexibility to contemporary interpretations: "Round arched style based on the Southern development during the 11th and 12th centuries, of the architectures of the Byzantine and Carolingian epochs. It will bear some

257

257. James Stirling and Partner,
Dresdner Bank, Marburg, Germany:
elevation, 1977
graphite on paper; 21 x 29.8 cm
(8 ¼ x 11 ¾ in); AP140.S2.SS1.D49.P2.9

This project for the Dresdner Bank
included a pedestrian pathway through
an arcade, with access to the bank and
stairs to the old city.

258. James Stirling and Partner,
Dresdner Bank, Marburg:
plan, section and details, 1977
coloured pencil and graphite on
reprographic copy; 29.7 x 21 cm
(11 ¹¹⁄₁₆ x 8 ¼ in); AP140.S2.SS1.D49.P2.15

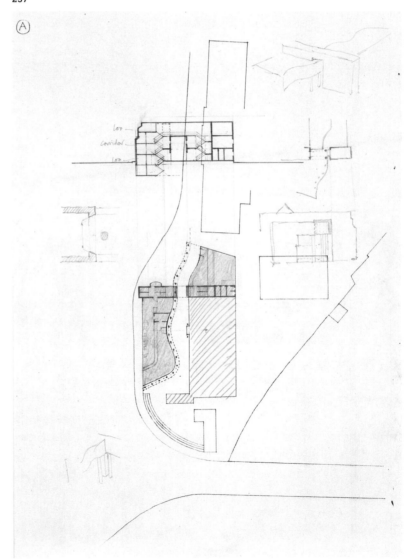

258

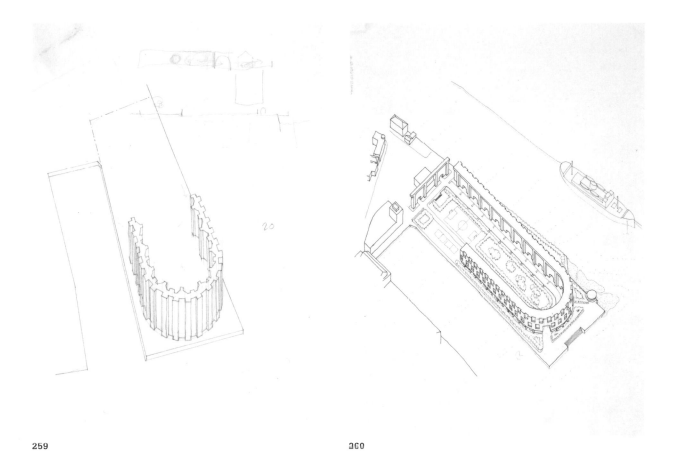

relationship to the early medieval work of Italy, Southern France and Northern Spain together with lines borrowed from the East and also from the Spanish missions of the neighbourhood," all interpreted to provide "a modern quality that will mark it as distinctly American."[192]

At Rice, the two modes of Stirling, contextual and volumetric, are brought together, the one wrapping the other, with great ease; the more so in that the modernist insert is locked into the outer shell by the two conical skylights—a Stirling trademark—that pierce the roof, and the circulation pattern from outside to inside. The elegant axonometrics of the "bridge" connecting the two wings of the school, and spanning the jury room and exhibition space, are perhaps the clearest representations of a design philosophy that began with a citation from the Italian architect Luigi Moretti in the 1950s.

259. James Stirling and Partner, Housing, Müller Pier, Rotterdam, The Netherlands: axonometric, 1977 graphite on paper; 29.5 x 20.9 cm (11 ⅞ x 8 ¼ in); AP140.S2.SS1.D50.P2.6

This was a project for new housing on the Müller Pier in the harbour district, including 800 dwelling units with views to the garden inside and the harbour outside, a community centre, shops, and recreation facilities. In this preliminary scheme, what seems to be a linked chain of apartments loosely based on the earlier residences for Selwyn College, Cambridge, would have produced the effect of a rippling glazed screen from the waterfront.

260. James Stirling and Partner, Housing, Müller Pier, Rotterdam: axonometric, 1977 ink and traces of graphite on paper; 29.8 x 20.9 cm (11 ¾ x 8 ¼ in); AP140.S2.SS1.D50.P2.12

The final scheme is more muted and classical in its amphitheatrical enclosure of a green courtyard within, and open views of the harbour to the outside, perhaps drawing on the precedent of Amsterdam social housing from the 1920s.

192. Ralph Adams Cram, cited by Peter Papademetriou, "Stirling in Another Context," *Progressive Architecture* (December 1981): 60.

261. James Stirling, Michael Wilford, and Associates, School of Architecture Addition, Rice University, Houston, Texas: elevation studies, 1979–81 graphite and colored pencil on paper; 41.8 x 29.9 cm (16 ½ x 11 ¾ in); AP140.S2.SS1.D56.P8.4

These studies form a small portion of the drawings concerned with the outer appearance of a building that was called on to fit into the stylistic dicta outlined by the original architect of the campus, Ralph Adams Cram.

262. James Stirling, Michael Wilford, and Associates, School of Architecture Addition, Rice University, Houston: axonometric sketches, 1979–81 graphite on translucent paper; 30 x 20.9 cm (11 ¹³⁄₁₆ x 8 ¼ in); AP140.S2.SS1.D56.P10.53

Internally, however, the design was free to develop the architectural school's program in a contemporary mode. In a brilliant stroke, Stirling and Wilford decided to model the interior as an entirely modernist "insertion" as if one building, as a three-dimensional (modern) volume, was encompassed by an historicist shell. Of course, as many critics pointed out, the firm hardly followed Cram's guidelines to the letter, introducing witty plays on conventional details. Here in this preliminary exploration, the interior is envisaged as a solid volume cut out for the large-scale rooms.

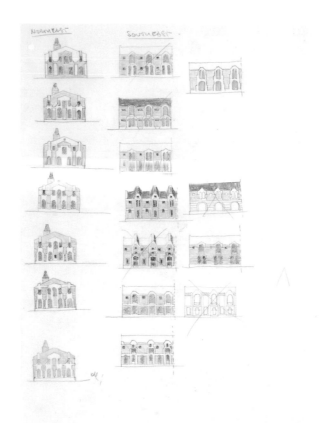

261

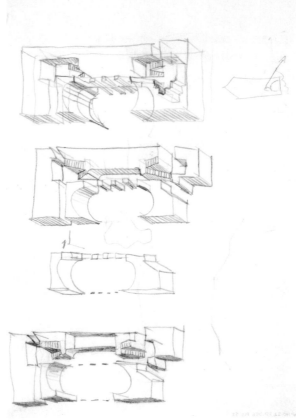

262

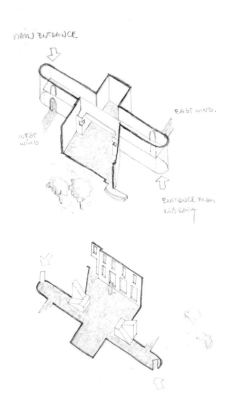

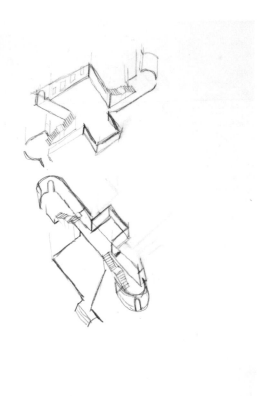

263

264

265

263–264. James Stirling, Michael Wilford, and Associates, School of Architecture Addition, Rice University, Houston: axonometric sketches, 1979–81 graphite on translucent paper; 29.9 x 21 cm (11 ¾ x 8 ¼ in); AP140.S2.SS1.D56.P10.51/52

A series of studies trace the evolution of the interior bridge and associated double-height volumes of exhibition and jury room.

265. James Stirling, Michael Wilford, and Associates, School of Architecture Addition, Rice University, Houston: axonometric sketch, 1979–82 graphite on translucent paper; 59.5 x 84 cm (23 ⅜ x 33 ¹⁄₁₆ in); AP140.S2.SS1.D56.P3.59

This drawing is preparatory to the celebrated cut-away axonometric published in the "White" volume, p. 77. Each end of the bridge is marked by a conical skylight that penetrates the outer roof—one of the few evident signs of the modernism within.

Learning from Soane

There are in the archive a number of early photographs taken by Stirling—we have already seen those snapped during his visit to Le Corbusier's buildings in the mid-1950s. There are also a large number of photographs of Italian sites, and especially from Florence (the Palazzi Davanzati and Pitti and San Miniato al Monte), that seem to anticipate Stirling's later interest in striped façades. Among them, however, are a number of images of British neo-classical buildings, and notably of John Soane's Dulwich Picture Gallery, with its brick abstractions of classical orders, and its internal galleries with their unique systems of overhead indirect lighting. Many Soanian elements can be discerned in earlier projects, notably in the galleries for the Arthur M. Sackler Museum, Cambridge, MA, but it was in the commission for the Turner Gallery at the Tate (now Tate Britain), the Clore Gallery, that this reference was to come full circle, and with an almost over-determined associational relationship to its program.

266–268. James Stirling, photographer: views of Dulwich Picture Gallery, London (John Soane, architect) gelatin silver print;
10.6 x 7.3 cm (4 ⅛ x 2 ⅞ in) /
7.3 x 10.6 cm (2 ⅞ x 4 ⅛ in) /
7.4 x 10.6 cm (2 ¹⁵⁄₁₆ x 4 ¹³⁄₁₆ in);
AP140.S1.SS2.D2.P1.3 / .P1.4 / .P1.5

Stirling mentioned Soane in the Black Notebook as "perhaps" one of the few "great architects" of England, together with Mackintosh, Archer, Hawksmoor, Vanbrugh, and Inigo Jones. These photographs form part of the series of vernacular architecture he photographed in the mid-1950s.

266

267

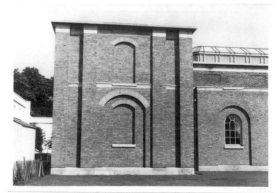

268

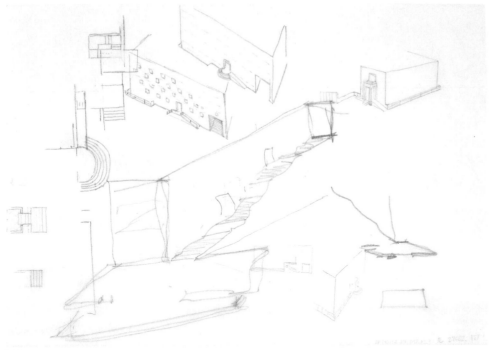

269

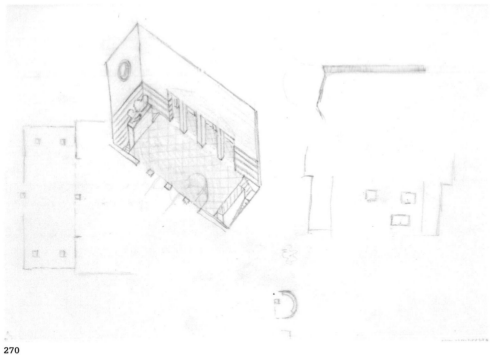

270

269. James Stirling, Michael Wilford, and Associates, Arthur M. Sackler Museum, Harvard University, Cambridge, Mass.: sketches, 1979–85
graphite on paper; 21 x 29.9 cm (8 ¼ x 11 ¾ in); AP140.S2.SS1.D58.P3.3

Adjoining the Fogg Museum and housing oriental, ancient and Islamic art, with offices for curatorial departments, and space for library collections, teaching rooms, and special exhibitions.

270. James Stirling, Michael Wilford, and Associates, Arthur M. Sackler Museum, Harvard University, Cambridge, Mass.: axonometric and plan, 1979–85
graphite and coloured pencil on paper; 20.9 x 29.9 cm (8 ¼ x 11 ¾ in); AP140.S2.SS1.D58.P3.4

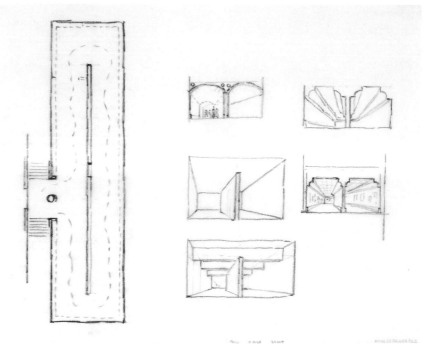

271

271. James Stirling, Michael Wilford, and Associates, Arthur M. Sackler Museum, Harvard University, analysis of Henri Labrouste's Bibliothèque Sainte-Geneviève, Paris, and alternative gallery sections, 1979–85
graphite on paper; 21 x 26 cm (8 ¼ x 10 ¼ in); AP140.S2.SS1.D58.P3.5

A study of reading rooms and galleries with double-bay top-lit vaulting, including the plan and section of Labrouste's Bibliothèque Sainte-Geneviève (1843–51).

272. James Stirling, Michael Wilford, and Associates, Arthur M. Sackler Museum, Harvard University, Cambridge, Mass.: sketches for top-lighting, 1979–85
graphite on paper; 29.5 x 41.9 cm (11 ⅝ x 16 ½ in); AP140.S2.SS1.D58.P3.1

Stirling experimented with top-lit, diffused natural lighting sections with evident memories of the galleries of Sir John Soane's Dulwich Picture Gallery (1811–17).

272

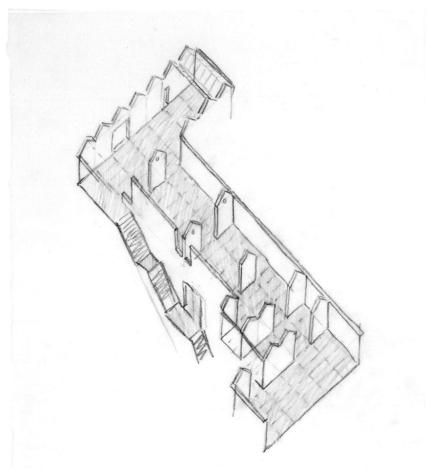

273

This gallery came under a great deal of criticism for its highly coloured interior and exterior, for its idiosyncratic entrance and foyer, and for its apparent postmodern frivolity beside the stern neo-classical lines of the Tate Gallery itself. And yet, judging from the archive, it was one of the most highly studied of the later commissions, with hundreds of options developed for the courtyard façade, and an equal number for the volumetric composition of the entry sequence, and studies for the exterior and interior colour schemes. Viewed now, the criticism itself seems entirely strident, in the face of a modest addition that works as a kind of garden pavilion (Stirling called it a "trellis") to the court, and as an equally modest entry sequence.

What offended the most was the apparently awkward way in which a visitor, having penetrated the revolving door set within a Boullée-like pyramidal arch, was forced almost immediately to move first to the left and then to the right up a long stair parallel to the front façade, before turning again to the left

273. James Stirling, Michael Wilford, and Associates, Arthur M. Sackler Museum, Harvard University, Cambridge, Mass.: axonometric, 1979–85 graphite and coloured pencil on paper; 31 x 28.4 cm (12 ¼ x 11 ⅛ in); AP140.S2.SS1.D58.P3.2

The long stair leading to the galleries was originally conceived as a termination of a circulation that led to the old Fogg Museum across a bridge at the top level. With the abandonment of the bridge, the stair now acts as the only access.

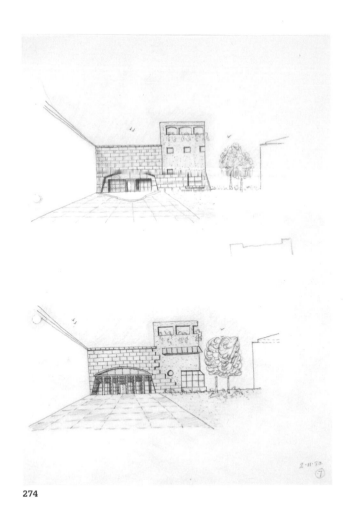

274

274. James Stirling, Michael Wilford, and Associates, Clore Gallery, Tate, London: perspectives, 2 November 1980
graphite and coloured pencil on paper; 29.9 x 21 cm (11 ¾ x 8 ¼ in); AP140.S2.SS1.D60.SD1.P4.8

The Clore Gallery, an extension for the exhibition of the J.M.W. Turner collection, included galleries, accommodation for paper conservation, and a meeting room for the Turner Society. In Stirling's report, the Clore Gallery was described as relating to the Tate and the old Queen Alexandra Hospital buildings, notably the brick Lodge, by virtue of its nature as a "garden pavilion," or "extension to the country house." The series of similar sketches explore this relationship, experimenting with transitions in material, scale, and detailing, with the aim of creating a "pergola" effect towards the terrace and pool in the Tate's garden.

to enter the first gallery. But of course, this was precisely the intention: to create a *promenade architecturale* against the movement of entry within a narrow space that otherwise would have provided little or no architectural experience. It was, indeed, very similar to that cross movement forced by Le Corbusier along the façade of the slab of the Salvation Army Building, which would if entered frontally on the axis of the corner site have had little "resistance" to accommodate the functions and sense of arrival. Once the visitor arrived at the galleries, however, the solid calm of a Soane-style space, with coved ceilings and light filtering down the edges, recomposed the experience. In the Clore, Stirling has been able to celebrate both the architecture of a neo-classical maverick and a modernist classic, with a simple but strong volumetric move. Turner was held between Boullée's dark funereal visions and his friend Soane's understanding of spatial complexity and aesthetic abstraction, all deployed for a contextual association that few were willing to recognize at the time.

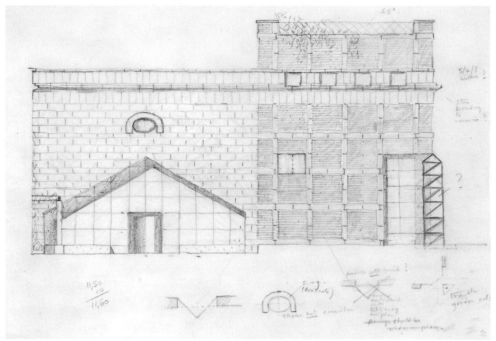

275

275. James Stirling, Michael Wilford, and Associates, Clore Gallery, Tate, London: elevation and sketches, 1978–86
graphite and coloured pencil on paper; 21 x 29.8 cm (8 ¼ x 11 ¾ in); AP140.S2.SS1.D60.SD1.P4.2

An elevation study approaching the final solution; in the built version, the revolving door is bright green, the brick panels on the left have been partially replaced with buff-coloured stucco, and the right corner structure has been removed in favour of a curved cut-away green glazed window. The drawing is signed "JS."

276. James Stirling, Michael Wilford, and Associates, Clore Gallery, Tate, London: sectional perspective, 1978–86
graphite on paper; 29.8 x 41.9 cm (11 ¾ x 16 ½ in); AP140.S2.SS1.D60.SD1.P5.2

With coved ceiling and diffused natural top-light along the centre gallery, and diagonally stepped diffusers to either side, the galleries retain a neo-classical sensibility for the Turner collection, derived from Stirling's early experience of Soane's Dulwich Picture Gallery. Stirling's approval of this scheme is signalled by a tick a the bottom of the drawing.

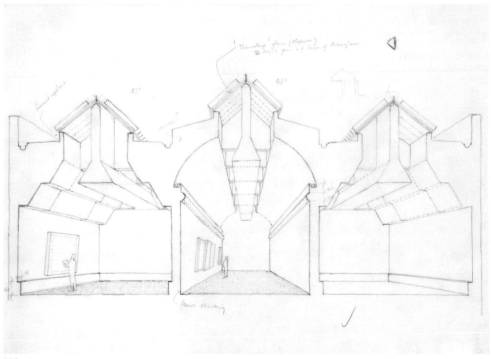

276

277. James Stirling, Michael Wilford, and Associates, Clore Gallery, Tate, London: section, 1978–86
graphite and coloured pencil on paper;
21 x 29.9 cm (8 ¼ x 11 ¾ in);
AP140.S2.SS1.D60.SD1.P4.11

The condensed section of the entrance foyer and apparently non-intuitive stair to the galleries—ascending in the opposite direction before turning and entering the galleries at right angles to their long axis—was the occasion of much criticism, as were the brilliant colours on the façades. Sir John Summerson, however, with his deep knowledge as curator of the Sir John Soane Museum, recognized the appropriateness of Stirling's spatial architectural promenade for a painter, Turner, who had been a close friend and colleague of Soane.

278. James Stirling, Michael Wilford, and Associates, Clore Gallery, Tate, London: perspective and plans, 1978–86
ink and graphite on paper;
42 x 29.8 cm (16 ½ x 11 ¾ in);
AP140.S2.SS1.D60.SD1.P6.4

Studies for the tightly controlled volumetric experience of the entrance foyer.

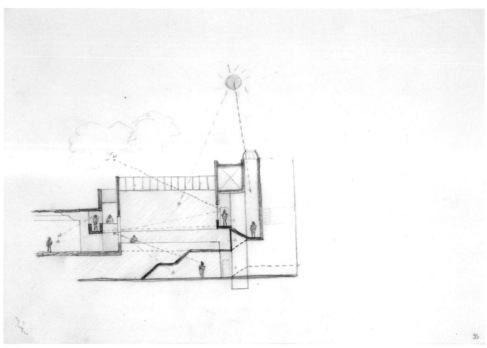

277

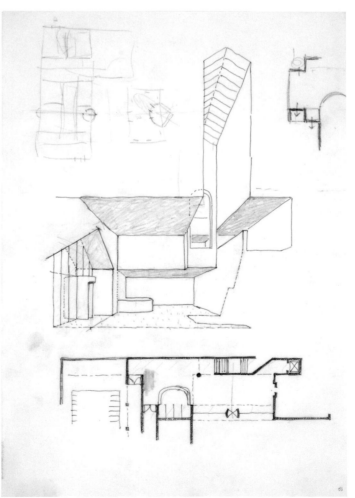

278

228

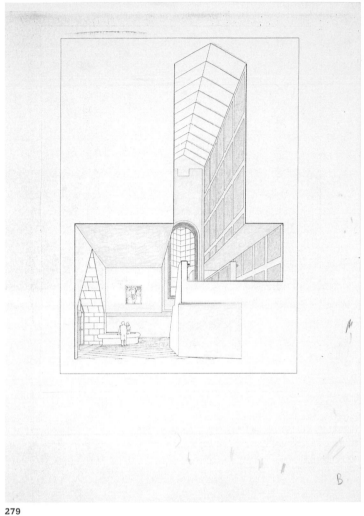

279

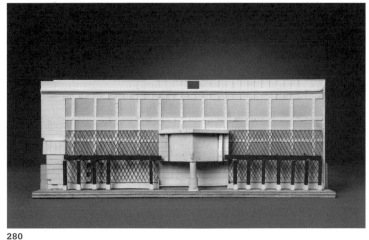

280

281

Cities in Microcosm

There were, however, many commissions for sites that were lacking in strong urban contexts, and gradually Stirling developed a strategy of composing the elements of these multi-functional programs into miniature cities in themselves. The discourse of urban renewal in the 1960s had given rise to proposals for what became known as "cities within cities," enclosed and self-sufficient developments that at once ignored their often dilapidated surroundings and were intended to act as spurs to development. Stirling, no doubt anticipating that such internalized developments would soon become escapist and as detrimental to their context as their modernist predecessors—indeed no more than aggrandized versions of urban renewal—began to explore the possibilities inherent in otherwise distinct institutional programs for their disaggregation, and reorganization as small urban contexts that could naturally receive extension and addition, expanding into their surroundings organically as needed: open-ended schemes for large-scale government centres—for Doha, Qatar (1976); for the Florence Administrative and Business Centre (1976); for the UNEP Headquarters in Nairobi, Kenya (1977); the Tehran Biology and Biochemistry Institute (1978); and the Headquarters for Bayer AG, Monheim, Germany (1978). Some of these projects, as in Doha, Florence, and Monheim, followed the precedent of the Siemens competition, with strict, centralized, or linear geometrical cores and extensions. Doha was extended along the shoreline of the corniche as a

282–283. James Stirling and Partner, Government Centre, Dawhah [Doha], Qatar: studies of alternative site strategies, 1976
graphite on paper / graphite and colored pencil on paper; 29.6 x 20.9 cm (11 ⅝ x 8 ¼ in) / 29.6 x 20.9 cm (11 ⅝ x 8 ¼ in); AP140.S2.SS1.D46.P3.13 / P3.14

In this project for a Government Centre and gardens for the Emir's palace, the ten twelve-storey ministry buildings are ranged along a mall fronting the sea, each with a courtyard and water garden.

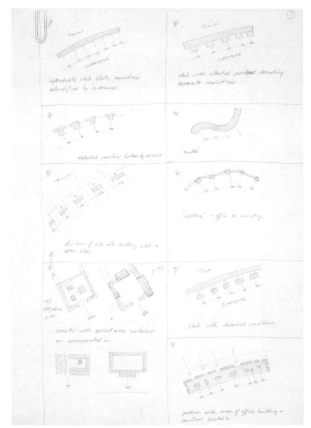

282

283

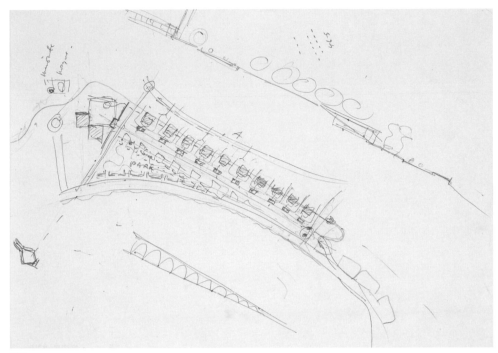

284

285

series of ministry office towers, and their services arrayed along a tree-lined boulevard, extending from the Emir's Palace. Each tower faced onto a courtyard with water gardens, and was shaded by arcades and rows of trees opening to the sea. The Tehran Biology Institute was similarly distributed as a linear organization of laboratory pavilions along a valley. Florence was conceptually joined to its "Roman" context by a "stone garden" connected axially to a cluster of four round hotel and service towers, and again to a miniature Roman city, formed by a group of public buildings—Law Courts, Government buildings, and shops around "piazzas, shopping streets, and colonnades" that "recall the traditional city."[193] The Headquarters for Bayer AG was even more formal, its central U-shaped park and administrative tower recalling the plans by Claude-Nicolas Ledoux for his Saltworks and Ideal City of Chaux (1771–1804), with laboratory complexes disposed radially around the park. The UNEP Headquarters in Nairobi, anticipating later "cities in microcosm" such as the Wissenschaftszentrum, Berlin, the Cornell Center for the Performing Arts, Ithaca, and British Telecom at Milton Keynes, was more freely distributed in the landscape.

It was, however, with the design of the Wissenschaftszentrum for Berlin that Stirling fully perfected the art of elemental combination of program units, absorbed within architectural typologies that, finally, had little or no relationship to their contexts. Through a process of iteration, explained in Part VII

193. *James Stirling, Michael Wilford and Associates: Buildings and Projects 1975–1992*, 42.

284. James Stirling and Partner, James Stirling and Partner, Government Centre, Dawhah: sketch plan, 1976 ink and graphite on paper; 20.9 x 29.6 cm (8 ¼ x 11 ⅝ in); AP140.S2.SS1.D46.P3.33

285. James Stirling and Partner, Administrative and Business Centre, Florence, Italy: sketches, 1976 ink on paper; 29.6 x 20.8 cm (11 ⅝ x 8 ¾ in); AP140.S2.SS1.D47.P2.1

The project included a new Regional Government Building, a new Palace of Justice, hotel, theatre, cinema, offices, and rapid transit connections.

286

below, Stirling developed a unique strategy—perhaps anticipated by the sharp break between exterior and interior at Rice—that moved away from his previous tactic of volumetric fusion, towards a looser combinatorial method. Now the functional units were equally isolated for identification, but then installed in iconographically distinct "shapes" that recalled earlier architectural types—castles, basilicas, theatres—and were joined together as if having grown up over time in related clusters.

The Center for the Performing Arts at Cornell University was perhaps the most elegant of these experiments in the miniature city, where a galleria overlooking the nearby gorge acts as a spine for the linear organization of theatres and auditoria behind. A small "baptistery" at the head, gives the whole composition, as Brendan Gill noted, the aspect of an Italian hill town—very much in keeping with the Italianate campanile on the main campus. The project for the Headquarters of British Telecom creates its own site, with a false "fortress" wall and moat posture as relics of former occupation, while a "castle," "theatre" and "basilica" demonstrated the potential for signifying shapes, with entirely differentiated content. Such autonomous "cities" were, so to speak, brought back home, in the project for the reconstruction of the Kaiserplatz at Aachen, where a galleria/stoa, a theatre, and a cubic pavilion not only refer to the old Roman centre of the city, but lead to the excavated Roman remains below.

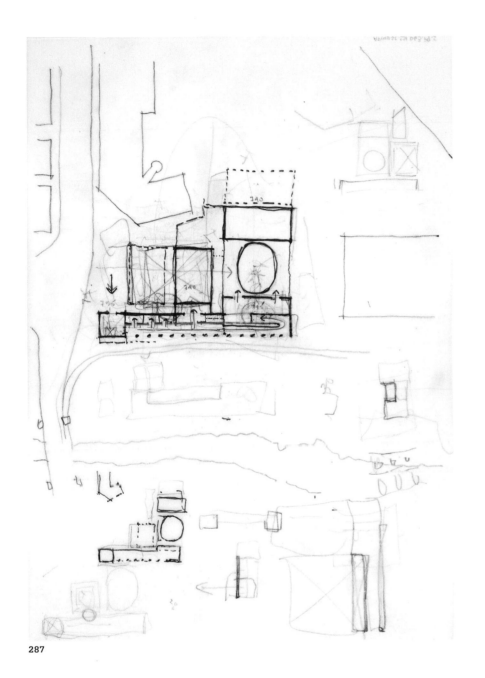

287

287. James Stirling, Michael Wilford, and Associates, Center for the Performing Arts, Cornell University, Ithaca, New York: site plan and sketches, 1982–89 graphite and ink on paper; 29.9 x 21 cm (11 ¾ x 8 ¼ in); AP140.S2.SS1.D63.P9.5

This program included a 450-seat proscenium theatre, a film forum, a dance performance studio, a flexible theatre, a black box studio, music studios, and cafeteria.

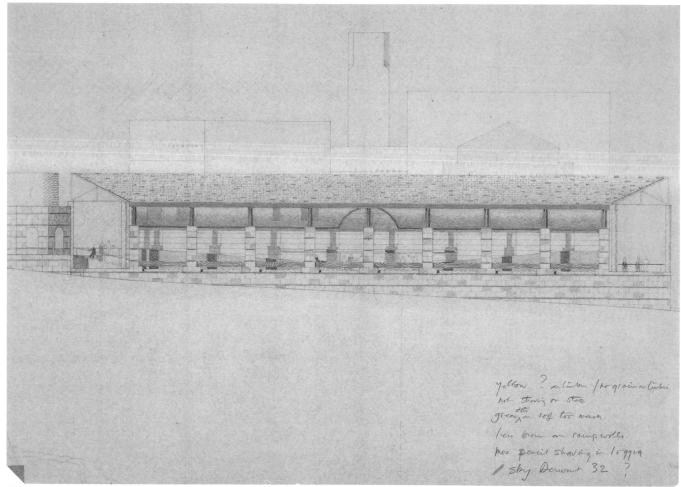

288

288. James Stirling, Michael Wilford, and Associates, Center for the Performing Arts, Cornell University: sectional elevation, 1982–89 colored pencil and graphite on reprographic copy; 29.9 x 42.1 cm (11 ¾ x 16 ⁹⁄₁₆ in); AP140.S2.SS1.D63.P16.24

The galleria at Cornell is one of many used by the firm to act as a kind of stoa, unifying disparate elements, as at the Wissenschaftszentrum and the Library at Latina.

289. James Stirling, Michael Wilford, and Associates, Center for the Performing Arts, Cornell University, Ithaca: presentation model for the first phase of construction, 1982–89 balsa wood and cork on wood base; 45 x 93 x 58 cm (17 ¾ x 36 ⅝ x 22 ⅞ in); AP140.S2.SS1.D63.P111

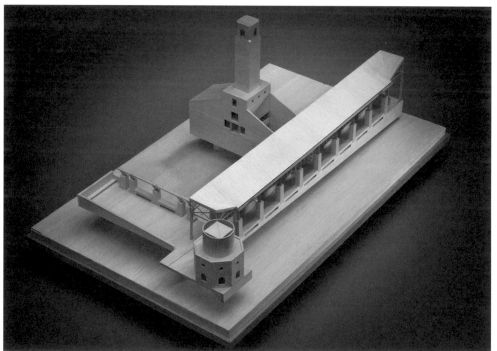

289

290. James Stirling, Michael Wilford, and Associates, Center for the Performing Arts, Cornell University, Ithaca: presentation site model (detail), 1982–89
wood and cork; 49 x 73 x 58 cm (19 ¼ x 28 ¾ x 22 ⅞ in) (largest); AP140.S2.SS1.D63.P116

291. James Stirling, Michael Wilford, and Associates, British Telecom National Networks Headquarters, Milton Keynes, England: presentation site model, 1983–84
painted cardboard over cork and wood base; 57 x 87 x 164 cm (22 ⁷⁄₁₆ x 34 ¼ x 64 ⁹⁄₁₆ in); AP140.S2.SS1.D66.P9

Planned as a "campus" with offices and ancillary services, according to the principles developed in the design of the Wissenschaftszentrum, Berlin.

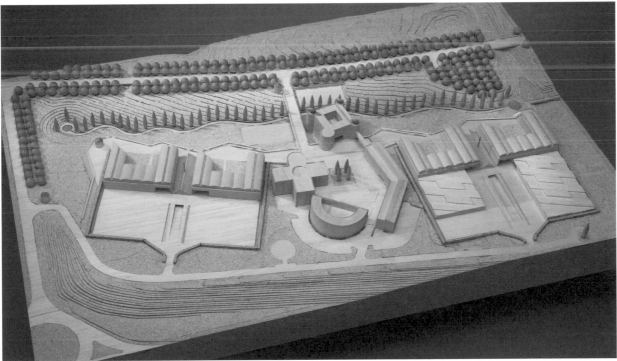

290

291

ANALYZ
ARC

ING THE
HIVE

Perhaps the most exciting experience of entering the archive during the past six years has been the discovery of a scene of drawing behind the elegant and all-too-finished presentations in the published work. This scene, in many of the projects after 1975, moves from the smallest thumbnail sketches in Stirling's stubby pencil, through what seem to be an endless series of alternative partis, to the working up of many of these partis into potential projects, and culminating in the analysis of each one and the comparison of many, and the selection of a scheme to present to the client, that will, in turn, be worked up and changed according to the response. Now this may, of course, seem to be similar to almost every architectural practice in the modern period, at least before the advent of digital iteration. But for Stirling this was a way of thinking architecture from the inside, avoiding prescriptive theory, and developing an idea or series of ideas in form and programmatic resolution. This development° was inevitably one conceived and extended in three dimensions; while many architects, after Le Corbusier, found the plan as generator, only later projecting perspectives and axonometrics for presentation purposes, for Stirling the axonometric ruled. It was, like Moretti's plaster models of spatial sequences as solid volumes, a truly volumetric way of working, and it showed the plan, sections, and elevation in true scale all at once. While perspectives were used, after the intervention of Léon Krier, as presentation devices, the axonometric was the preferred way of developing a design as a sketch scheme, after which it was to be resolved in plan, and then again, as shown by hundreds of small marginal drawings, rendered back into axonometric for study. The historical analysis of these design development drawings will take many scholars many years; here I have simply selected a few of the most arresting to give a sense of the internal dynamic of the archive, a dynamic that responds to the dynamic of making architecture itself.

VII: Content into Form

Drawing Content

A drawing has to be designed (viewpoint critical). Elimination of information is the crux and is achieved through a series of design decisions, often taken quickly in sequence; sometimes taking a lot of deliberation (more likely to be the less successful drawing). What is left on the image is the minimum required to convey the maximum information with the greatest clarity.

James Stirling, 1974[194]

In his introduction to *James Stirling, Michael Wilford and Associates. Buildings and Projects 1975–1992*, Michael Wilford, writing after the untimely death of Stirling, stresses the role that drawing played in the development of their projects. Beginning with a "series of alternative conceptual studies and schematic outline drawings," he wrote, carried out in felt-tip pen, graphite leads, and Stirling's favorite red Bic ballpoints, the plans, sections, and elevations were then drawn following discussions with the client. Drawn from different viewpoints—"up" or "down" axonometrics, isometrics, perspectives according to the demands of the scheme, these representations were "deliberately hard, spare, restrained, and scientific in character, meticulously to scale and as accurate as hand and eye can make them ... the absolute minimum necessary to convey the maximum amount of useful information." As many commentators have noted, the axonometric projection was a leitmotif of the office, enabling the setting out of "the spaces, surfaces, and volumes of a design in a single image which has no distortion, and gives an accurate reading of the building."[195]

It is not surprising, then, that the office archive contains thousands of these preparatory drawings, presenting a panorama of a working method that, while only described in 1992, was there, incipiently at least, from the beginning. As early as the House Studies drawn by Stirling and Gowan as a means of developing a *modus vivendi* for their design partnership, these formal

194. James Stirling "On drawing," in *James Stirling* (exhibition catalogue, RIBA, Heinz Gallery, London, 24 April–21 June 1974) (London: RIBA Publications, 1974), 16.

195. Michael Wilford, "Introduction," *James Stirling, Michael Wilford and Associates: Buildings and Projects 1975–1992*, 5.

exercises explore relationships between volumes, the means of juxtaposing and combining separate and formal elements and, when joined to the study of a brief, ways of exploring the articulations of a program as a series of semi-autonomous pieces. As Wilford explained, this was a consistent strategy "of breaking down each building into a number of discrete parts, each expressed separately and clearly."[196]

The first exhibition of Stirling's work in Britain, and the second after the Museum of Modern Art's "James Stirling—Three Buildings," of 1969, was appropriately enough held under the auspices of the Royal Institute of British Architects Drawings Collection in 1974. In his introduction to the catalogue, Reyner Banham assessed the nature and role of Stirling's drawn techniques. Against the generally popular assumption that Stirling was centrally committed to the axonometric, Banham argued that, in the first place, Stirling should be given credit for having introduced the application of Zip-A-Tone™, discovered in the United States during his visit of 1949, a technique that rapidly assumed the role of instant stand-in for the laborious vertical hatching by hand of Paul Rudolph and his school. Zip-A-Tone™ first appeared in the renderings for Sheffield, and then was liberally used in the presentations of his Thesis. Axonometrics, on the other hand, were important, but not as important as "the growing tribe of Stirlingologists" were proposing.[197]

Banham was responding to the enthusiastic analysis of Stirling's techniques by Charles Jencks in his recently published *Modern Movements in Architecture* (1973). Jencks assembled the axonometrics of Leicester, Cambridge History Faculty, Dorman Long and St Andrews, on a page, comparing them with a diagram of the Mariner 5 satellite.[198] Jencks traces what he sees as the evolution of the axonometric in Stirling from the project for Selwyn College, that combined a new kind of wrapped-glass-skin architecture with an "adhocist" treatment of standard industrial parts, and the use of the "axonometric technique." This was matured at Leicester where "instead of drawing in perspective, they switched to a birds-eye-view which could analyse and dissect the whole project showing its whole anatomy." This method, claimed Jencks, was not merely a presentation technique but "a method of designing", allowing the architects "to work out the space, structure, geometry, function, and detail altogether and without distortion."[199] As Jencks pointed out, many of the drawings in the publication *British Buildings 1960–64* were similarly presented as axonometrics that were especially pertinent to evoke "interest in the contrasting relationships between solids and voids" (i.e. between "mass" and "membrane").

Banham found this conclusion "shrewd" enough, but "over-elaborated." For the celebrated drawings of the cascading glass between the stair towers at Leicester, and of the entire composition, were of course perspectives, as were the aerial views of St Andrews and Siemens, the interior courtyard of the

196. Wilford, "Introduction," 5.

197. Reyner Banham, "Introduction," *James Stirling* (exhibition catalogue), 6.

198. Charles Jencks, *Modern Movements in Architecture* (London: Anchor Press, 1973), 266.

199. Jencks, *Modern Movements*, 263.

Florey Building and, equally important, the interiors of the Olivetti Training Centre and Headquarters and the galleria of Derby Civic Centre, all exhibited at the RIBA. If for Gowan the important question was the "style for the job," for Banham this variety of techniques indicated that Stirling was interested not in a fetishization of the axonometric, but in the right "technique for the job." "Lucid and explicit in its content," Banham concluded that a good Stirling drawing held the intellectual idea of the design and its technical materialization in balance, a salutary precision in the face of trophy-winning, client-oriented renderings. Axonometrics, perspectives, sections, and diagrams were all imbued with this demand, present in the instruction manuals of complex machinery in the Second World War.

The axonometric projection had, of course, as Jencks pointed out, been a favorite technique of many modernists—the Constructivist, Van Doesburg and the de Stijl movement—and in his own thesis, *Theory and Design in the First Machine Age*, Banham had traced its use back to the ahistorical depictions of Auguste Choisy's *Histoire de l'architecture* (1899). In these projections, the engineer Choisy had adapted an old stereometric projection used in the polytechnical schools since the early nineteenth century to describe the combination of structure and space, in an abstract formulation that allowed for comparison across time and geographical space. Le Corbusier had lifted some of them for his discussion of the relations of plan to volume in Santa Sophia. The technique was imported into Britain by the first generation of modernist exiles, the pages of the *Architectural Review* begin to publish axonometrics as early as the late 1920s, and an interest in the work of Choisy himself emerged in the 1950s and 1960s.

It is difficult to date the first appearance of the isometric and the axonometric in Stirling's work as so much was redrawn for exhibition and publication in 1974, with a good number of the drawings for the *Works 1950–1974* by Léon Krier, or in his signature style by others in the office. The perspective of the roof, and the axonometric view from below of the lobby and stairs at Sheffield are cases in point, that are retrospectively constructed to demonstrate affiliations with later projects. The archive too is ambiguous on this point. The Stiff Domino housing prototype is possibly the first in 1951, perhaps even polemically posed against the perspective view of Le Corbusier's initial Dom-ino system. Certainly the cut-away axonometric of the House in North London, 1953, and the structural diagrams of the Village Housing for CIAM, and the House Studies, both of 1955, are harbingers of the more advanced style to come. Dramatic, downward axonometrics of the interiors of Ham Common, the Isle of Wight House, and the House Conversion in Kensington, 1955–57, are also evidence of emerging experiments in representation. It is with the commission for an ideal "expandable" house, however, that the technique comes into its own, allowing the demonstration of the expanding house around its core, as if constructed out of a kit of parts—the instruction manual par excellence. After this, the birds-eye views of Preston, Churchill College, the Camberwell Assembly Hall, and finally Selwyn College bring the technique to what Jencks calls its "maturity."

Iterating Form

Throughout every stage of the design process we draw every probable
option for each part of the project.
Michael Wilford, 1992[200]

Following the publication of the "Black" volume in 1974, the archive preserves a vast quantity of preliminary drawings for each project—indeed it seems that the loss of such studies before 1974 led to an almost exaggerated desire to keep every line drawn in the office. A desire, however, that proves fruitful in studying the genesis, if the studies can be tentatively dated, of at least the alternative schemes that were brought to a level of conclusion before a project received its semi-final resolution. It has proved impossible to study each individual building in sufficient detail to correlate the "text" files, recording correspondence, memoranda and reports, with the drawing files in order to date the studies more precisely—this will occupy scholars over many years to come. But what emerges from a preliminary survey of a few major projects is a manner of working, a process of design that, while it might be paralleled in many offices of the period, seems to be unique in its approach towards the nature and role of what is called "iteration" and "reiteration" in a field that does not, and cannot of its nature, pretend towards "scientific" objectivity and single standards of assessment.

Many architects in the late 1960s and 1970s, disturbed by this lack of precise standards for the measurement of design success, sought to imitate and draw from more "scientific" fields of systems analysis and the emerging practices of computer-aided design. "Design Methods" courses were launched in many schools. Notably, the mathematician and architect Christopher Alexander spent many years attempting to develop a watertight method for analyzing a program, converting the analysis into mathematically translatable units, and devising systems of combination that would, so to speak, automatically result in a form that reliably fulfilled its given function. His *Notes on the Synthesis of Form*, published in 1964, became a source-book for the attempt to develop programming languages for design, and an initial step towards his invention of a "pattern language" for architectural composition (*A Pattern Language*, 1977). His own contribution to the PREVI project in Lima was an early experiment in developing a house prototype from such analytical procedures.

200. Wilford, "Introduction," 5.

Not surprisingly, Alexander and his followers and colleagues were regarded with suspicion, and not a little antagonism, by more "intuitive" architects concerned with a range of un-mappable values—history, tradition, cultural context, and formal invention—notably almost the entire generation of Team X. Stirling himself had little to say on the subject of "design method," and his laconic remarks on program and function seem aimed more at rationalizing his own formal moves than presenting any over-rigorous "functionalism." Yet one might in retrospect compare his insistence on continuous iteration through drawing to the more advanced computer approaches towards parametric design today; with one fundamental reservation: Stirling's iterations were always and without exception rooted in a sensibility that sought to "speak" to and learn from the entire history of architecture, globally considered, whether an architecture designed by "architects," or constructed within a guild or vernacular tradition. In this sensibility, Stirling was following in the line of name architects since the Renaissance, and especially those of the historically eclectic nineteenth century, as well as those from the "academic tradition" within modernism, from Butterfield to Le Corbusier, so to speak.

Derived from his Beaux-Arts/modernist training at Liverpool, with the added impetus of Colin Rowe's "abstract eclecticism," Stirling defined his approach to design early on, and was consistent thereafter. First, as he wrote in the Black Notebook under the portentous heading of "Process of Design (conception)," was a process of analysis—"from the conditions of the programme" looked at with an "unprejudiced" eye and "no preconceived ideas."[201] This analytical process was to be anything but scientific, even if it seemed to follow the logic of Locke's "association of ideas": "all factors," he opined, were to be "held in a formless state at the back of the mind." Only then could one begin the necessary "valuation of the functional and sociological importance of the various elements." In this "valuation," "elements" were engendered from the earlier "formless state" of the problem; from this arose the possibility of developing a "conception arising from a *partly intuitive* [my italics] perception of the plastic potentialities inherent in the accommodation and circulation." Here Stirling intimates what will become a central focus of his design approach—the combination of elements of *accommodation* with and through the diagram of *circulation*, a diagram that in turn becomes "plastic" and volumetric. The elements or "units" of accommodation are then ordered hierarchically: "hierarchical disposition of units all reflecting (suggesting) their function."[202] The subtle distinction between a "reflection" of a function— the modernist mantra—and "suggesting" a function would become for Stirling a way of distancing himself from a mechanistic functionalism, and leading instead towards a functionalism that was the purveyor of cultural, social, and, of course, architectural, associations.

201. Crinson, ed., *James Stirling: Early Unpublished Writings*, 28.

202. Crinson, ed., *James Stirling: Early Unpublished Writings*, 28.

Once ordered, the units are assembled according to necessary circulation. Indeed, Stirling wrote: "Having arrived at the germ or bones or mechanics of an architecture, the progress from this point can be quite automatic, such as questions of proportion, construction, material can now be considered." Always with the initial conception in mind, so as not to "disguise or obliterate" it, the analysis of every supporting move continues. Then Stirling considers the problem of simplicity and complexity. Disturbed by the programmatic simplicity of the International Style, he was concerned to develop a sufficient complexity in the solution (a concept he no doubt derived from his discussions with Rowe, who had always held that a complex problem demanded a solution that was complex enough to hold its own). "Before one can arrive at the sophistication of complexity," a "process of simplification" had to be developed: "How often one sees buildings which are just 'simple' or 'complicated' without having gone through a process of simplification." The final "process of complication" should guard against total disaggregation, for the design had perforce to be taken "to almost the point of total disintegration," at which point it had arrived at "the point of the greatest cohesion," which for Stirling meant the embedded "tension"—a dialectical moment that was exemplified in the work of Le Corbusier—or at least the work as it had been interpreted by Rowe in his first two essays on "The Mathematics of the Ideal Villa," and "Mannerism and Modern Architecture."[202] In the former Rowe had argued that the villas of Garches and Poissy owed their power to the formal transformation of Palladian prototypes, shifting their spatial order from Renaissance (centroidal) to modernist (peripheral) though the medium of the free plan. In the latter essay he had tried to demonstrate the fundamental recursivity of "mannerist" motifs and their inversion of Renaissance stereotypes in Modernism. For Stirling these were formal tools for the re-formulation of modernism itself. It was in the same pages of the Black Notebook that Stirling listed the antecedents of this reformulation, that had emerged, as it were, in the very beginning of the movement, led by the "superb plastician" Mackintosh. Before him loomed the great figures of former reformulators, all those who disturbed the reigning order to produce eccentric but enlivening openings: "Archer, Hawksmoor, Vanbrugh, Inigo Jones, and perhaps Soane."[203] These architects were, according to Stirling, "all sculpture or plastic school," and anticipated in their different ways a contemporary *renovatio* of architectural plasticity, suggesting that "it is in this aspect which our future architects will excel."[205] Written between 1953 and 1955, these remarks need little revision if applied to his later mature work.

203. Crinson, ed., *James Stirling: Early Unpublished Writings*, 28.

204. Crinson, ed., *James Stirling: Early Unpublished Writings*, 35.

205. Crinson, ed., *James Stirling: Early Unpublished Writings*, 34.

Spatial Narratives

In what follows I have selected three individual works in order to demonstrate the iterative process of Stirling's office. Without precise dating of each successive stage of design, and with the knowledge from former collaborators that many were options indeed developed in parallel, I have chosen to allow the drawings themselves to demonstrate their own logic of development. The result is, as might be expected, only an approximation of a process—close study will reveal that many drawings may in fact be in the wrong sequence—and further research will no doubt reconstruct the timeline for each project more accurately. Finally, this "panorama" of iterations represents only a very limited selection from the many folders for each project, each often containing over five hundred sketches and drawings.

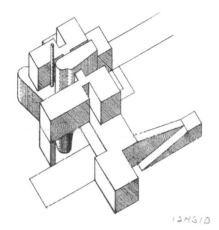

292

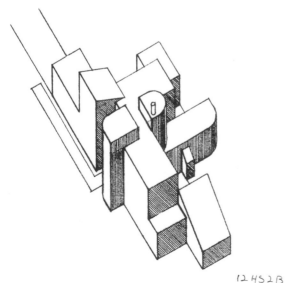

293

292. Stirling and Gowan, House Studies: view of an axonometric drawing, 1956 offset lithograph on transparent plastic film; 9.4 x 15.2 cm (13 11/16 x 6 in); AP140.S2.SS1.D13.P1.1

Perhaps the earliest evidence of Stirling and Gowan's collaboration as designers, these "studies" without rigid programs were drawn between the partners in order to explore their individual approaches to volumetric form and composition. Their traces can be followed throughout both architects' ensuing careers.

293. Stirling and Gowan, House Studies: view of an axonometric drawing, 1956 offset lithograph on transparent plastic film; 10.5 x 12.2 cm (4 1/8 x 4 15/16 in); AP140.S2.SS1.D13.P1.2

A City Within a City:
The Wissenschaftszentrum, Berlin, 1979–87

294. James Stirling, Michael Wilford, and Associates, Wissenschaftszentrum, Berlin: sketch site plan, 1979–87
graphite on reprographic
copy; 33 x 20.3 cm (13 x 8 in);
AP140.S2.SS1.D57.P4.9 (recto)

The Wissenschaftszentrum, or Social Science Research Centre, is built on the site of the former Social Services Administration, preserving the "Beaux-Arts"-style central pavilion. Site plan showing the Mies van der Rohe New National Gallery to the right and the Shell-Haus office building to the left. The preliminary scheme sought to extend the central block of the old Social Services building along the edges of the site to accommodate Institutes D, E, and C with centralized services in the centre. The plan of the original Social Services Institute is shown dotted in.

295. James Stirling, Michael Wilford, and Associates, Wissenschaftszentrum, Berlin: sketch site plans and perspective, 1979–87
ink on paper; 33 x 20.3 cm (13 x 8 in);
AP140.S2.SS1.D57.P4.9 (verso)

Sketches of possible *partis*. At the top, a plan to form an enclosed courtyard around the perimeter of the block, with a circular element in the centre, and access from the rear. In the centre, an axonometric showing the extension of the central pavilion to either side and a possible extension of each to the rear. The Mies National Gallery is to the right. Immediately below is a plan showing the block as a solid with a small central courtyard open to the rear of the site, and at the bottom is a plan showing the wings of the central pavilion with a U-shaped pavilion in the centre of the rear extension.

Of the three projects selected, one was built and two unbuilt. The first, the Berlin Wissenschaftszentrum (Social Science Research Centre) (1979–87), was required to incorporate the still standing front building of the former Prussian social services administration founded by Bismark in 1890. In the heart of the Kulturforum, it faces the Shell Haus canal, next to Emil Fahrenkamp's 1931 Shell-Haus office, close to Mies van der Rohe's New National Gallery (1968), and not too far from Hans Scharoun's Philharmonie (1956–63) in the centre of Berlin. The successive permutations of the project, the development of the final scheme, construct in microcosm both the vicissitudes and the potential successes of the iterative method. Along the bottom of a number of the plans, many prepared in the Berlin office, one can discern the little axonometric studies—whether drawn by Stirling or not—that mark his interventions into the process—together with the signature red pen ticks and crosses that indicate his opinions of the generated schemes.

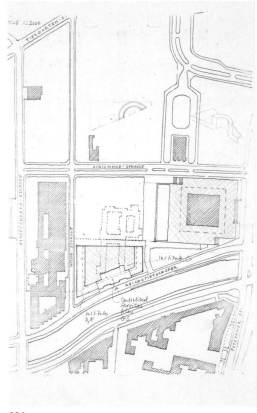

294

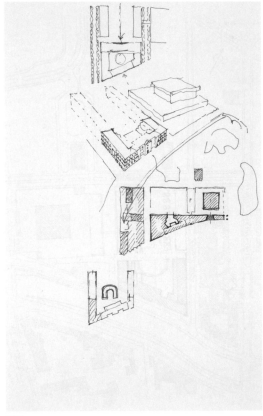

295

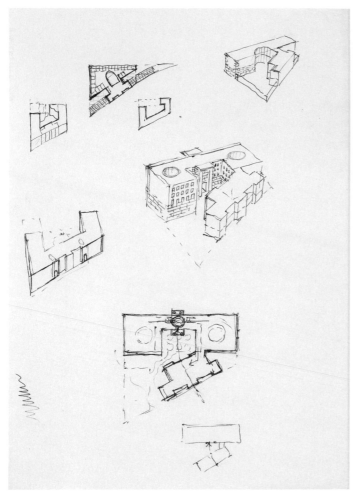

296

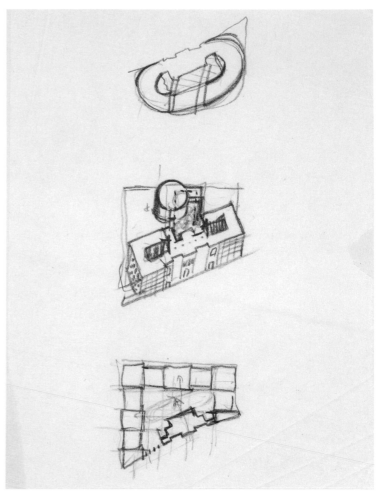

297

296. James Stirling, Michael Wilford, and Associates, Wissenschaftszentrum, Berlin: sketches, 1979–87
ink on paper; 29.7 x 21 cm (11 ¾ x 8 ¼ in); AP140.S2.SS1.D57.P4.11

Experiments with floating the central pavilion free of extensions, and building up the rear of the site with a single structure divided into two square blocks with central circular courts.

297. James Stirling, Michal Wilford, and Associates, Wissenschaftszentrum, Berlin: sketches, 1979–87
black pencil on paper; 25 x 18.9 cm (9 ⅞ x 7 ⁷⁄₁₆ in); AP140.S2.SS1.D57.P4.22

Three new variants of the *parti*: an ovoid extension of the central pavilion; a dense expansion of the central pavilion with a circular element to the rear; and a partial "nine-square" solution for the perimeter block.

298. James Stirling, Michael Wilford,
and Associates, Wissenschaftszentrum,
Berlin: site sketches, 1979–87
ink on paper; 29.8 x 20.9 cm
(11 ¾ x 8 ¼ in); AP140.S2.SS1.D57.P4.14

Elaboration of the scheme projected
in 279, with the introduction of a tower
element for the first time.

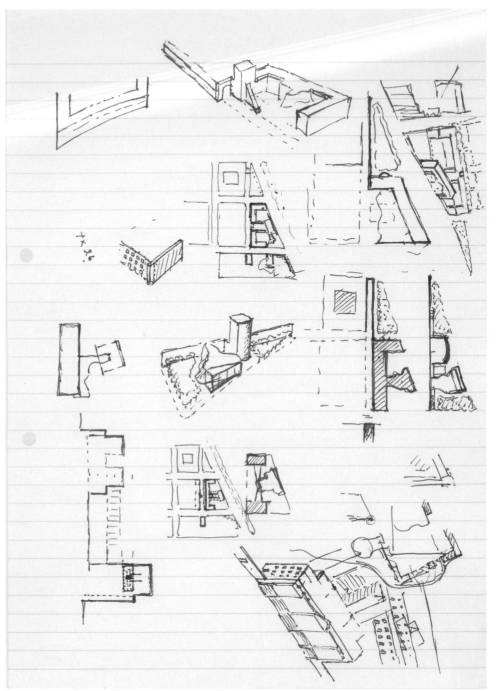

298

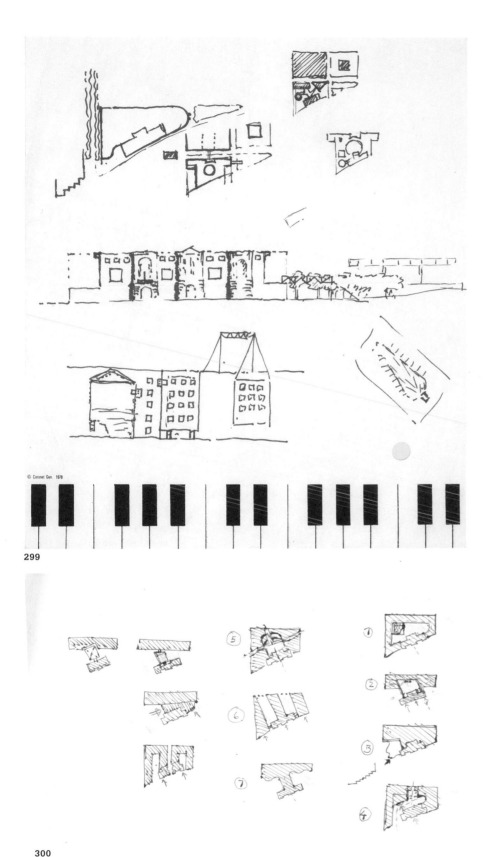

299. James Stirling, Michael Wilford, and Associates, Wissenschaftszentrum, Berlin: sketches, 1979–87
ink on pre-printed paper; 23.4 x 20.2 cm (9 ¼ x 8 in); AP140.S2.SS1.D57.P4.23

The beginnings of façade studies for the water front with reference to the classical front of the central pavilion and the Mies National Gallery to the right, sketched on a "music" notepad.

300. James Stirling, Michael Wilford, and Associates, Wissenschaftszentrum, Berlin: alternative plans, 1979–87
ink on paper; 30 x 48.6 cm (11 ¹³⁄₁₆ x 19 ⅛ in); AP140.S2.SS1.D57.P4.26

A sheet of drawings typical of the office, consolidating and comparing the range of five *parti*-types explored in the preliminary investigation of the project. Red arrows indicate entrances, and green the open courtyards.

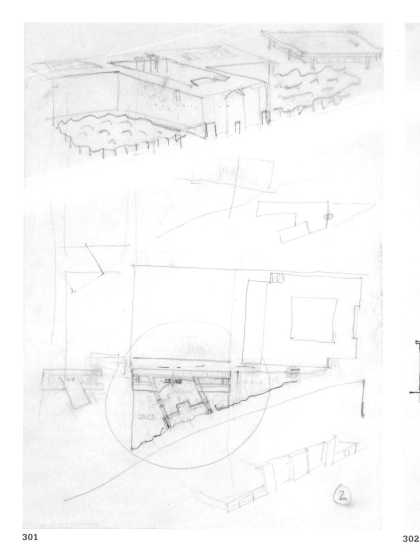

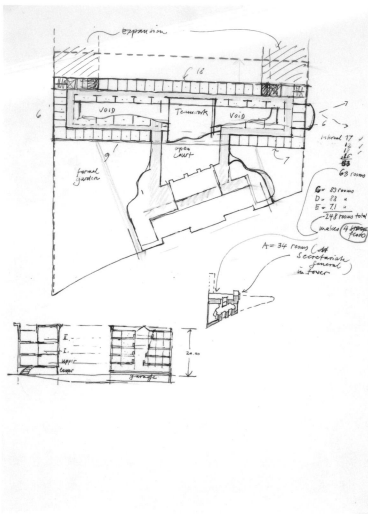

301

302

301. James Stirling, Michael Wilford,
and Associates, Wissenschaftszentrum,
Berlin: perspectives and plans, 1979–87
graphite, ink and coloured pencil on
paper; 29.5 x 21 cm (11 ⅝ x 8 ¼ in);
AP140.S2.SS1.D57.P6.201

Axonometric and plan of a scheme
that links the central pavilion to a rear
double-corridor office building with
courtyards to either side. The Mies
National Gallery is to the rear, right.

302. James Stirling, Michael Wilford,
and Associates, Wissenschaftszentrum,
Berlin: plan, section, axonometric, 1979–87
ink and coloured pencil on paper;
41.8 x 30 cm (16 ½ x 11 ¹³⁄₁₆ in);
AP140.S2.SS1.D57.P6.221

Development of the scheme in 283.
The central pavilion is expanded across
a glazed atrium and joined to a rear
building with a team room at the centre
and formal gardens to either side.

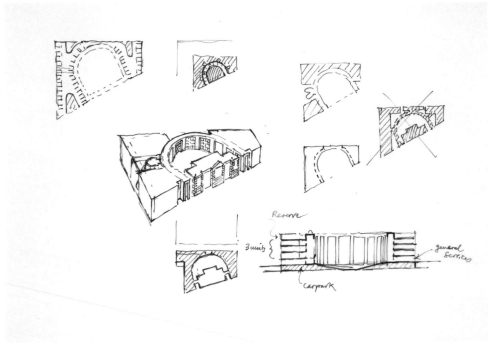

303

304

303. James Stirling, Michael Wilford, and Associates, Wissenschaftszentrum, Berlin: plans, perspective and section, 1979–87
ink on paper; 21 x 29.9 cm
(8 ¼ x 11 ¾ in); AP140.S2.SS1.D57.P6.160

Perhaps drawing on the experience of the Derby Civic Centre competition, the central courtyard is now seen as a U-shaped gallery joining the central pavilion on either side to two flanking blocks that fill the edges of the site. The result is a figure-ground plan that emulates a city square and urban gallery street.

304. James Stirling, Michael Wilford, and Associates, Wissenschaftszentrum, Berlin: perspectives and plan, 1979–87
ink, coloured pencil and graphite on paper; 21.1 x 29.9 cm (8 ⁵⁄₁₆ x 11 ¾ in); AP140.S2.SS1.D57.P6.165

Study for the layout of offices in the U-shaped *parti*, with a perspective of the corner entrance marked by a canopy reminiscent of the Staatsgalerie, Stuttgart.

305. James Stirling, Michael Wilford, and Associates, Wissenschaftszentrum, Berlin: plan and sketches, 1979–87
ink, coloured pencil and graphite on paper; 21 x 29.9 cm (8 ¼ x 11 ¾ in); AP140.S2.SS1.D57.P6.189

The U-shaped galleria is now open and tree-lined, giving onto a semicircular extension to the central pavilion and the perimeter offices, as if an extension of the canal footpath cut through the solid block of the building.

306. James Stirling, Michael Wilford, and Associates, Wissenschaftszentrum, Berlin: plan, 1979–87
ink, correction fluid and traces of graphite on paper; 18.9 x 30 cm (7 ⁷⁄₁₆ x 11 ¹³⁄₁₆ in); AP140.S2.SS1.D57.P6.181

The U-shaped galleria has now been transformed into a circular gallery with an open garden courtyard in the centre giving access to the perimeter block with double-loaded office corridor, and a central tower with the main staircase. Stirling has here indicated the circulation in his red pen.

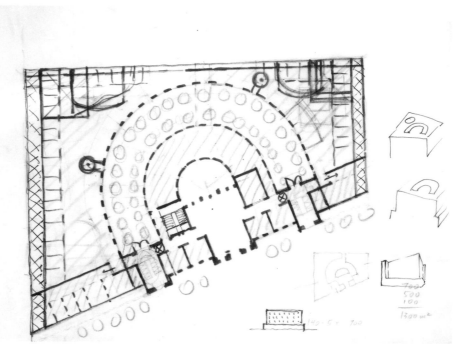

305

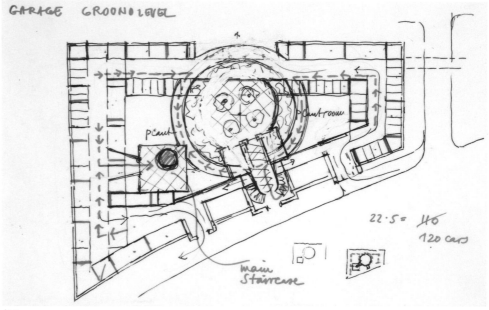

306

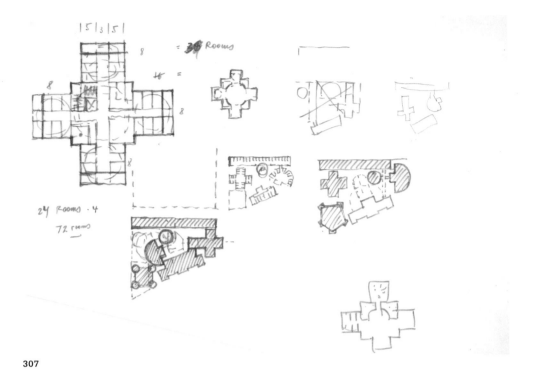

307

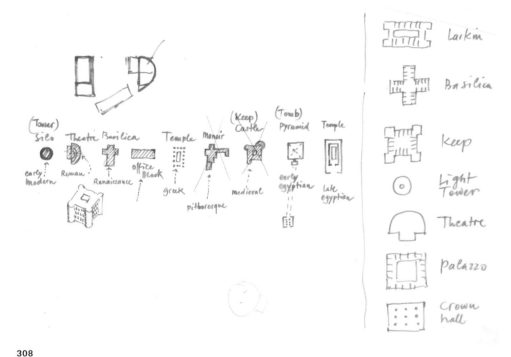

308

307. James Stirling, Michael Wilford, and Associates, Wissenschaftszentrum, Berlin: plans, 1979–87
ink and graphite on paper;
20.9 x 29.9 cm (8 ¼ x 11 ¾ in);
AP140.S2.SS1.D57.P6.4

The decision to disaggregate the different institutes into separate pavilions led to the exploration of diagrammatic shapes for each that would represent "history" through reference to the forms of architectural precedent and the "play" of these shapes as they took up varying positions on the site behind the central pavilion—cruciform, semicircular, square, circular, and pentagonal shapes jostle in different adjacencies, as if Le Corbusier's diagrams of Rome as an assemblage of primary forms had returned with new life.

308. James Stirling, Michael Wilford, and Associates, Wissenschaftszentrum, Berlin: typological study, 1979–87
ink and graphite on paper;
20.9 x 29.9 cm (8 ¼ x 11 ¾ in);
AP140.S2.SS1.D57.P6.15

Following the decision to separate the institutes and library into separate pavilions, this sheet categorizes the various historical plan-forms and "shapes" considered for each: together they display a diagrammatic panorama of the history of architecture from the early Egyptian (tomb, pyramid), through the late Egyptian (temple), Greek (temple), Roman (theatre/basilica), medieval (castle keep), picturesque (*manoir*), early modern (silo), and modern (office block). The precedents selected were ranged on the right of the sheet: Frank Lloyd Wright's Larkin Building, a cruciform basilica, a square keep, a circular light tower, a semicircular theatre, a square courtyard palazzo, and Mies van der Rohe's Crown Hall at the Illinois Institute of Technology.

309. James Stirling, Michael Wilford, and Associates, Wissenschaftszentrum, Berlin: plans, 1979–87
ink on paper; 20.9 x 29.9 cm
(8 ¼ x 11 ¾ in); AP140.S2.SS1.D57.P6.8

In a literal exercise in precedent use, the palazzo, the Larkin Building, the basilica, the theatre, and the silo take their places on the site—with the basilica and the theatre in contestation for the corner.

310. James Stirling, Michael Wilford, and Associates, Wissenschaftszentrum, Berlin: plans and axonometrics, 1979–87
ink and graphite on paper;
20.9 x 29.9 cm (8 ¼ x 11 ¾ in);
AP140.S2.SS1.D57.P6.11

In this iteration, Mies's IIT Crown Hall takes the corner, and the basilica, the theatre, and the palazzo are ranged across the rear of the site.

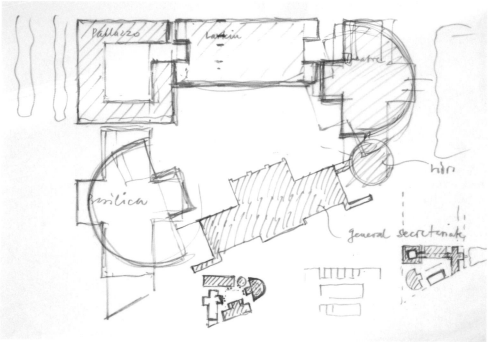

309

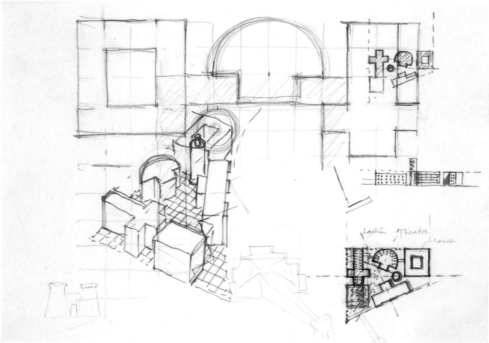

310

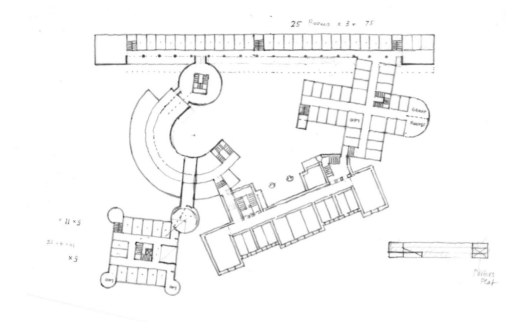

311

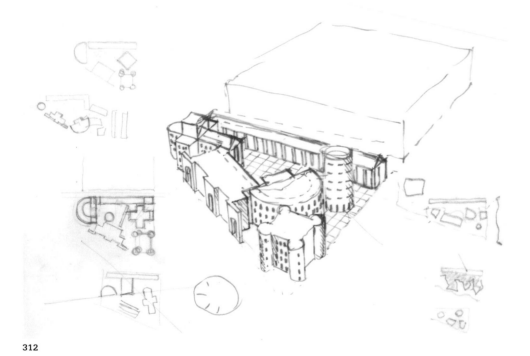

312

311. James Stirling, Michael Wilford, and Associates, Wissenschaftszentrum, Berlin: plan and section, 1979–87
ink and graphite on paper;
20.9 x 29.9 cm (8 ¼ x 11 ¾ in);
AP140.S2.SS1.D57.P6.13

The castle keep now takes the corner in this game of historical chess, with the theatre, basilica, and silo controlled by a long narrow block across the rear of the site holding the elements together as if seen as a Greek stoa holding the various buildings types of the agora together.

312. James Stirling, Michael Wilford, and Associates, Wissenschaftszentrum, Berlin: perspective and sketches, 1979–87
ink and graphite on paper;
21 x 29.9 cm (8 ¼ x 11 ¾ in);
AP140.S2.SS1.D57.P6.17

An axonometric study of the plan developed in 289 above.

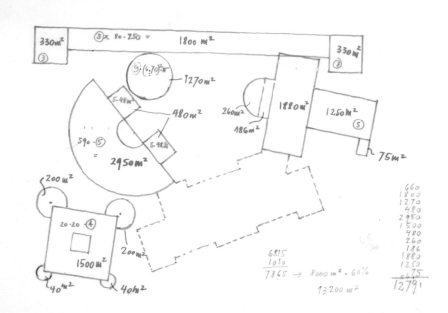

313. James Stirling, Michael Wilford,
and Associates, Wissenschaftszentrum,
Berlin: plan, 1979–87
ink on paper; 21.9 x 29.9 cm
(8 ⅝ x 11 ¾ in); AP140.S2.SS1.D57.P6.49

An analysis of the areas of each of the
pavilions.

314. James Stirling, Michael Wilford,
and Associates, Wissenschaftszentrum,
Berlin: study model, 1979–87
styrofoam; 2 x 22 x 45 cm
(¾ x 8 ⅝ x 17 ¾ in); AP140.S2.SS1.D57.P34

315. James Stirling, Michael Wilford,
and Associates, Wissenschaftszentrum,
Berlin: site plan, 1979–87
ink and coloured pencil on paper;
77.3 x 83.5 cm (30 ⁷⁄₁₆ x 32 ⅞ in);
AP140.S2.SS1.D57.P15.5

The final plan for the centre, with
hexagonal library, offices in the stoa,
theatre, and church, and the castle
keep marked only in the corner garden.

313

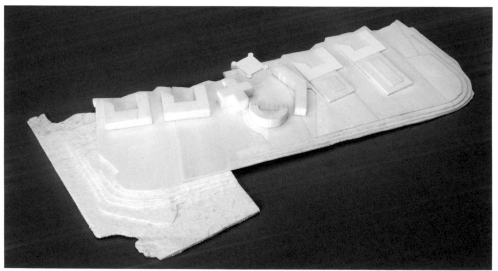

314

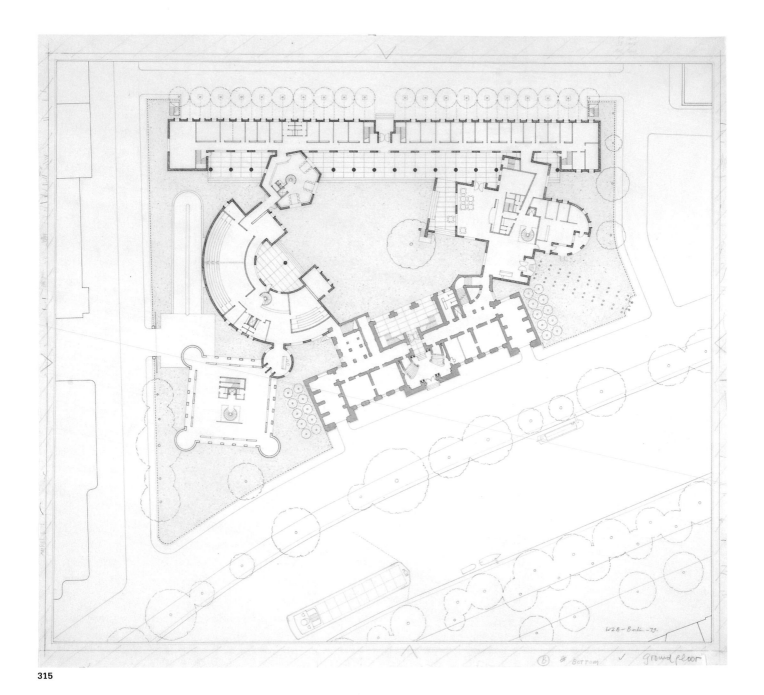

315

WZB – Berlin – 79.

Ⓑ Ⓑ bottom   ✓ ground floor

A Library in the City:
The Municipal Library, Latina, Italy, 1983

The second project, the Municipal Library for the town of Latina, in central Italy, was commissioned in 1983, but rejected in a change of local government. The town itself was founded by Mussolini in 1932 as Littoria, and designed in "neo-classical-modern" style by Marcell Piacentini and others. Stirling noted that it was "a city without a history," but of course it was precisely its history of foundation that had to be "forgotten" after 1945, and that led the left-wing government to sponsor a new library on a grand scale—200,000 volumes and accommodation for up to 500 readers at a time. The triangular site, with its two existing buildings, posed an interesting urban design problem for the office, and dozens of figure-ground sketches of alternative ways to block the library in relation to its surroundings survive in the archive. Early sketches, on the letterhead notepaper of the Latina Comune, envisage the library as a large rectangular block set on axis in the middle of the site. Others see the library ringing the triangular site; taking up an entire half of the site with a courtyard in the middle; free-standing as a pavilion in the site; running along one long side of the site; as two buildings split in the middle; as a central block with wings; as a main bock with various pavillionnate extensions; and finally, as a single unified building across the top side of the triangle symmetrically balancing the small librarian's house in the centre, and the existing commercial building at the tip. Accompanying these are studies for the layout of the public gardens. From the outset, as the notes on the Latina letterhead indicate, the library was envisaged as a "basilica," and its final form reflected this idea, as a continuous "hall" building with a steeply pitched roof entered from an upper-level portico along the garden side, and sheltering the two main library spaces (lending library and reading room) in cylinders that pierced the shed roof. With obvious reference to the main reading room of the British Museum library, and utilizing the unifying motif of a long gallery as at Cornell, the composition as a whole respected the symmetry of the modern neo-classical Latina style, while at the same time—as at Siemens—leaving no doubts as to the ultimately machine-age character of the institution.

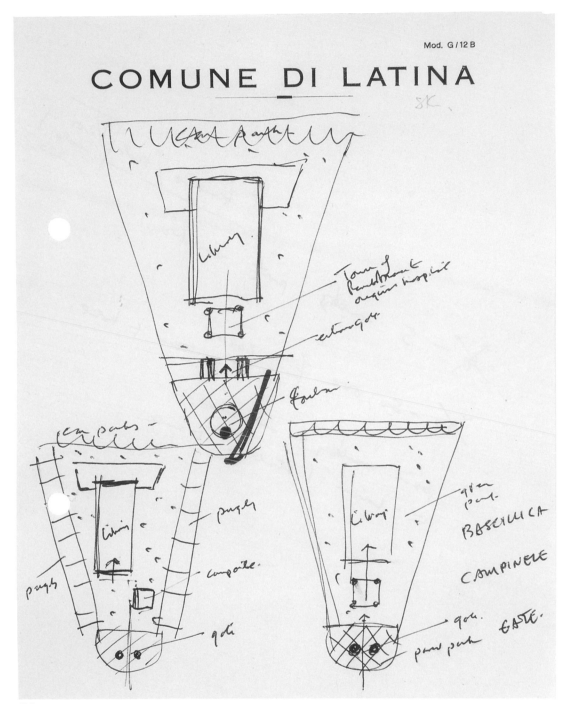

Mod. G / 12 B

COMUNE DI LATINA

316. James Stirling, Michael Wilford, and Associates, Biblioteca pubblica, Latina, Italy: plans, 1979–85
ink on paper; 20 x 15.8 cm
(7 ⅞ x 6 ¼ in); AP140.S2.SS1.D67.P6.2

Project for the Municipal Library with space for 200,000 books and 500 readers in two reading rooms with lending and reference libraries, a children's library, lecture theatre, and administrative offices. These sketches on the notepaper of the Comune were probably drawn during a preliminary meeting in Latina.

316

317

317. James Stirling, Michael Wilford, and Associates, Biblioteca pubblica, Latina: site plans, 1979–85 ink and graphite on paper; 21.1 x 29.9 cm (8 ¼ x 11 ¾ in); AP140.S2.SS1.D67.P6.6

Established by Mussolini in 1932 under the name of Littoria, Latina was built in the "modern" neo-classical style of Marcello Piacentini (architect of the E.U.R), Angiolo Mazzoni, and Duilio Cambellotti. Despite, or because of, this "history" it was thought by Stirling to be "a city without a history," and the figure-ground studies are an attempt to provide at least a spatial "history" or narrative for the proposed library, and explored the possible forms of the library on the site. This sheet is one of six similar drawings analyzing the urban consequences of varying plan-types.

318. James Stirling, Michael Wilford, and Associates, Biblioteca pubblica, Latina: sketches, 1979–85 ink on paper; 29.7 x 21 cm (11 ¾ x 8 ¼ in); AP140.S2.SS1.D67.P7.5

Studies for the roof forms and top-lighting of the two campanile library towers.

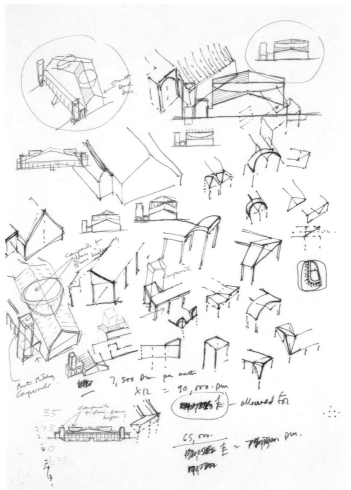

318

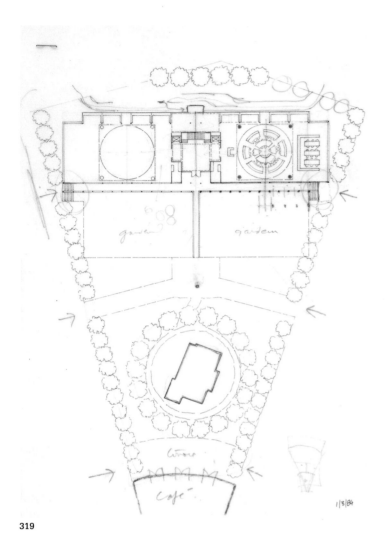

319

319. James Stirling, Michael Wilford, and Associates, Biblioteca pubblica, Latina: plan, 3 January 1984
ink, graphite and correction fluid on paper; 29.8 x 21.1 cm (11 ¾ x 8 ¼ in); AP140.S2.SS1.D67.P7.18

The triangular site is divided into two, with the library at the top end, the librarian's house set in a grove of trees in the centre, and an existing café at the point.

320. James Stirling, Michael Wilford, and Associates, Biblioteca pubblica, Latina: plan, 1979–85
ink, coloured pencil and graphite on paper; 21 x 29.9 cm (8 ¼ x 11 ¾ in); AP140.S2.SS1.D67.P7.12

Diagrammatic plan of the first floor with the circular reference and lending libraries flanking the entry and catalogue area.

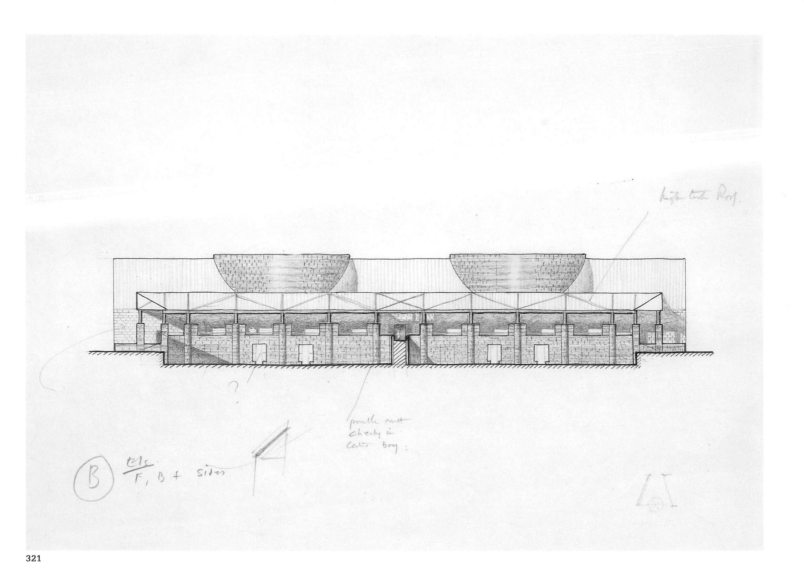

321

321. James Stirling, Michael Wilford, and Associates, Biblioteca pubblica, Latina: elevation, 1979–85
ink, coloured pencil, graphite and correction fluid on reprographic copy; 25.6 x 36.4 cm (10 ⅛ x 14 ⅜ in); AP140.S2.SS1.D67.P2.9

Façade study for the final scheme, with the glazed galleries across the entry front, and the "silos" of the library volumes piercing the deeply pitched shed roof. This project brings together not only references to classic libraries—the circular reading room of the British Museum and the stepped "Tower of Babel" within—but also joins the Latina library to a tradition of rural shed buildings in the Roman Campagna.

322

323

322. James Stirling, Michael Wilford, and Associates, Biblioteca pubblica, Latina: study model, 1979–85
wood; 4.2 x 33.6 x 21.9 cm
(1 ⅝ x 13 ¼ x 8 ⅝ in);
AP140.S2.SS1.D67.P24

323. James Stirling, Michael Wilford, and Associates, Biblioteca pubblica, Latina: presentation model, 1979–85
cardboard, wood and plastic;
20 x 97 x 64 cm (7 ⅞ x 38 ³/₁₆ x 25 ¼ in);
AP140.S2.SS1.D67.P26

A City of Books:
The Bibliothèque de France, Paris, 1989

The third example, the competition design for the Bibliothèque de France, designed over a period of a few months, represents a concentrated and "idealist" version of the iterative process. Announced in 1989, the year that France celebrated the 200th anniversary of the Revolution, as a culmination of the series of Grands Projets launched by President Mitterrand, this competition attracted a wide range of entries that spanned the spectrum of approaches to late twentieth-century architecture, from the radical reformulations of "library" by Rem Koolhaus and Future Systems, to the winning entry by Dominique Perrault that over-neatly parodied the postmodern and diagrammed the modern. Stirling's entry was one of three "selectionné" together with the entries of Future Systems and Pierre Chaix and Paul Morel. François Chaslin, a member of the jury, noted that Stirling's scheme was "directly inherited from the Enlightenment, notably from Boullée: a supple assemblage of monumental volumes, elegant and "informal," with an aspect of a still life where forms played in the light, with an impressive gravity and familiarity; a company of unusual and seemingly eternal objects, a miniature city."[206] With its overt references to the long 200-year tradition of national libraries, from the eighteenth-century project for a Bibliothèque Royale by Etienne-Louis Boullée (1785) to the mid-nineteenth-century Bibliothèque Nationale of Henri Labrouste (1862–68), the design was at once a pure example of the historical abstraction and typological exploration characteristic of the Stirling office, and an experiment in urban design; in this case, not a result of a contextualism responding to an existing context, but an attempt to develop a new context in itself as a "library city" in a barren area of eastern Paris beyond the tracks of the Austerlitz railroad station, and, significantly enough for Stirling, just northwest of Le Corbusier's Salvation Army Building. In honour of this site, the final project for the competition prominently included the moored barge designed by Le Corbusier for the Salvation Army, and still in existence on the Seine.

206. François Chaslin, "Souvenirs d'eclectisme," in *Bibliothèque de France. Premiers Volumes* (Paris: Institut Français d'Architecture, Editions Carte Segrete, 1989), 89.

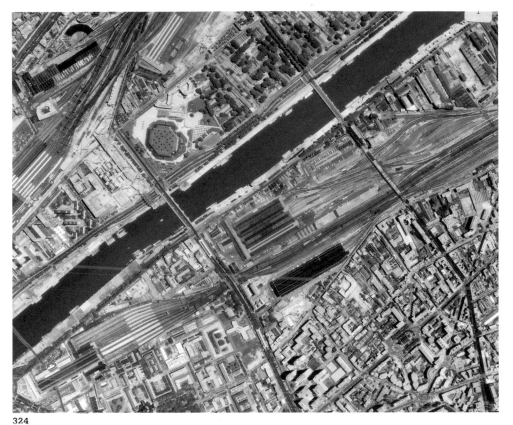

324

325

324. Bibliothèque de France, Paris: aerial photograph of site, from *Concours International d'Idées, Rules* (Paris: Ministère de la culture, de la communication, des grands travaux et du bicentenaire, 1989)
gelatin silver print; 20.8 x 23.8 cm; (8 ³⁄₁₆ x 9 ³⁄₈ in);
AP140.S2.SS1.D88.P4.1.1.1

Limited competition for the Bibliothèque de France, the new French National Library, with three main libraries— the Recent Acquisitions Library, the Reference Library, the Research Library, and Catalog Room. The twenty entrants were selected from 244 who responded to the call for qualifications. Among them were Future Systems and Stirling/ Wilford and Associates who were designated second, and Dominique Perrault, who won the competition and built the project.

325. Bibliothèque de France, Paris: diagrammatic site plan, from *Concours International d'Idées, Rules*, p. 11
AP140.S2.SS1.D88.P4.4.2

The site for the new National Library was to the east of Paris, opposite the recently constructed Hôtel des Finances (designed by Paul Chemetov and Huidibro), the sports palace and the American Center of Frank Gehry, and was east of the Austerlitz station between the bridge of Bercy and Tolbiac. A new pedestrian bridge was envisaged between the Parc de Bercy (on the site of the old wine markets of Bercy) and the new library.

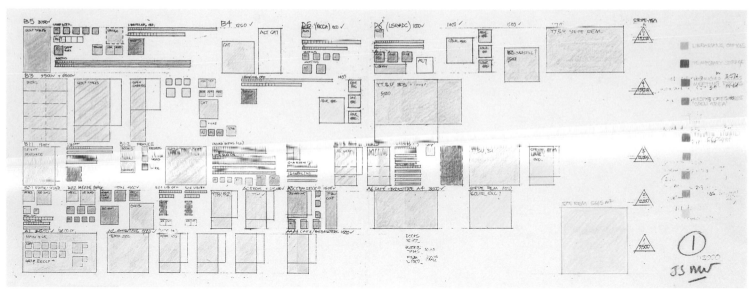

326

326. James Stirling, Michael Wilford,
and Associates, Bibliothèque de France,
Paris: analytical space plan, "1," 1989
coloured pencil, ink and graphite on
reprographic copy; 16 x 41.9 cm
(6 5/16 x 16 1/2 in); AP140.S2.SS1.D88.P13.1

The dossier containing the program,
plans and rules was sent to the contest-
ants on 21 April 1989, with a deadline
of 7 July for submission. The Stirling/
Wilford office analyzed the program
according to their practice in area and
colour coding. This drawing is numbered
"1" in the sequence that follows, all
signed "JS MW."

327. James Stirling, Michael Wilford,
and Associates, Bibliothèque de France,
Paris: plan, "2," 1989
coloured pencil, graphite and ink on
reprographic copy; 21 x 29.6 cm
(8 1/4 x 11 5/8 in); AP140.S2.SS1.D88.P13.2

One of many studies trying out the
program areas on the site.

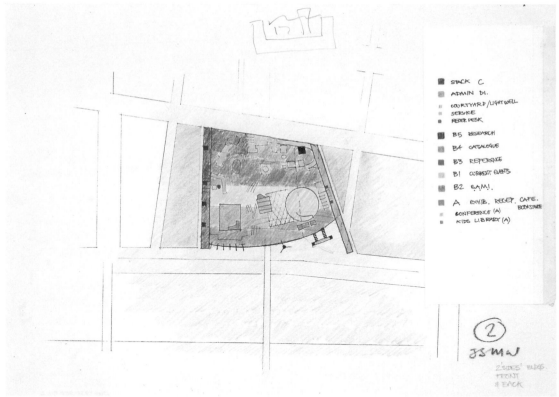

327

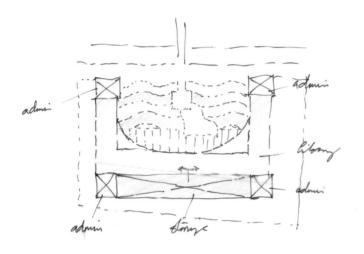

admin
admin
library
admin
admin
storage

328

300

③
js mw

1:4000
9-5-89

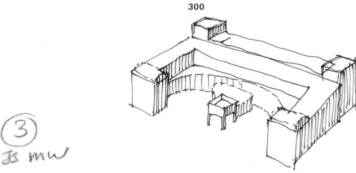

328. James Stirling, Michael
Wilford, and Associates, Bibliothèque
de France, Paris: plan and
axonometric, "3," dated 9 May 1989
ink and coloured pencil on paper;
29.6 x 20.9 cm (11 ⅝ x 8 ¼ in);
AP140.S2.SS1.D88.P13.3

A series of potential massing diagrams
were developed, this one bringing
all the functions into a single building
facing the Seine—much in the same
way as the Trocadéro to the northwest.

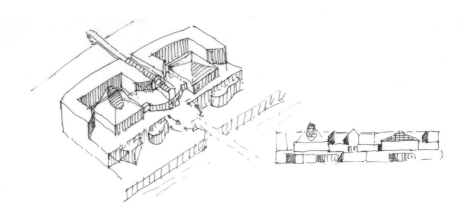

329. James Stirling, Michael Wilford, and Associates, Bibliothèque de France, Paris: axonometric and elevation, "4," 1989
ink on paper; 20.9 x 29.6 cm (8 ¼ x 11 ⅝ in); AP140.S2.SS1.D88.P13.4

An iteration of the "Trocadéro" type, with two pyramidal reading rooms flanking a central entrance hall.

330. James Stirling, Michael Wilford, and Associates, Bibliothèque de France, Paris: axonometric and plan, "5," 1989
graphite and coloured pencil on paper; 21 x 29.6 cm (8 ¼ 11 ⅝ in); AP140.S2.SS1.D88.P13.5

This scheme opens up a central courtyard giving onto the river with two major reading rooms to either side and the administration forming a perimeter block.

329

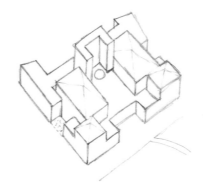

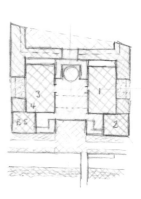

330

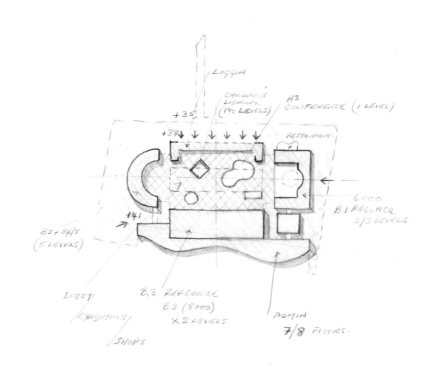

331. James Stirling, Michael Wilford, and Associates, Bibliothèque de France, Paris: annotated plan and section, "6," 1989
graphite and coloured pencil on paper; 29.7 x 21 cm (11 ¾ x 8 ¼ in); AP140.S2.SS1.D88.P13.6

The program is disaggregated with the main reference room in a block running east–west and facing the river.

331

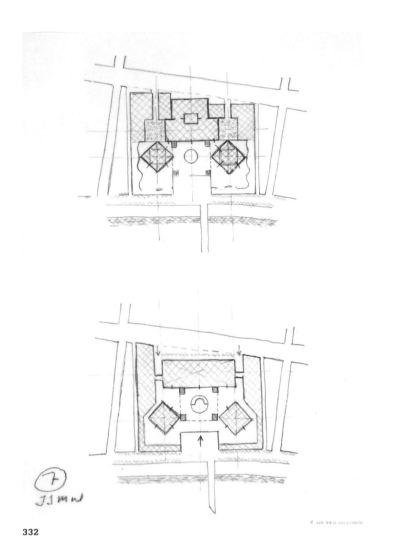

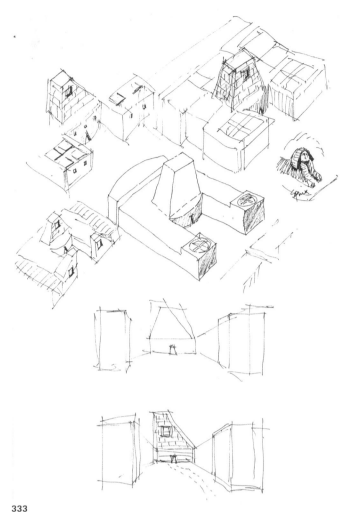

332

333

332. James Stirling, Michael Wilford, and Associates, Bibliothèque de France, Paris: plans, "7," 1989
graphite and colored pencil on paper; 29.7 x 21 cm (11 ¹¹/₁₆ x 8 ¼ in); AP140.S2.SS1.D88.P13.7

Two pavilionated schemes grouped in an informal U-shape towards the river. The three libraries are in purple with the reference library across the rear.

333. James Stirling, Michael Wilford, and Associates, Bibliothèque de France, Paris: axonometrics and perspectives, 1989
reprographic copy; 29.6 x 21 cm (11 ⅝ x 8 ¼ in); AP140.S2.SS1.D88.P14.120

Given the Egyptomania of 1989, with the renewal of the underground levels of the Louvre for the Egyptian collections, the glass pyramid, and the memory of Napoleon's expedition to Egypt, this perhaps not entirely serious proposal saw the library as an Egyptian monolith, if not as a Sphinx.

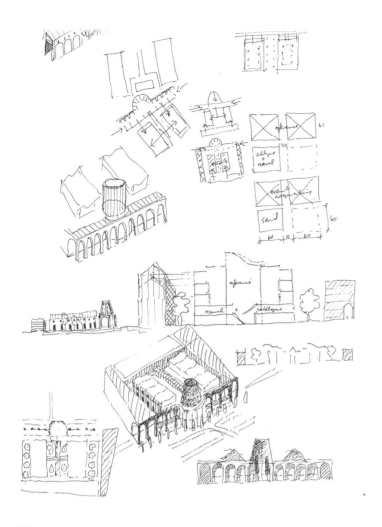

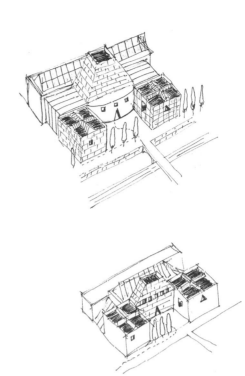

334. James Stirling, Michael Wilford, and Associates, Bibliothèque de France, Paris: plans, axonometrics, elevations, section, 1989
reprographic copy; 29.6 x 21 cm
(11 ⅝ x 8 ¼ in); AP140.S2.SS1.D88.P14.122

References to the "visionary" projects of the eighteenth-century architect Étienne-Louis Boullée abound in the sketches for the library—here the conical form of the entrance refers (perhaps unfortunately) to one of Boullée's cemeteries. By the 1980s Boullée was also filtered through the work of Aldo Rossi, who likewise used the form for his Cemetery at Modena.

335. James Stirling, Michael Wilford, and Associates, Bibliothèque de France, Paris: axonometrics, 1989
reprographic copy; 29.6 x 21 cm
(11 ⅝ x 8 ¼ in); AP140.S2.SS1.D88.P14.124

Here the cone becomes a truncated pyramid sandwiched between two square pavilions.

Content into Form

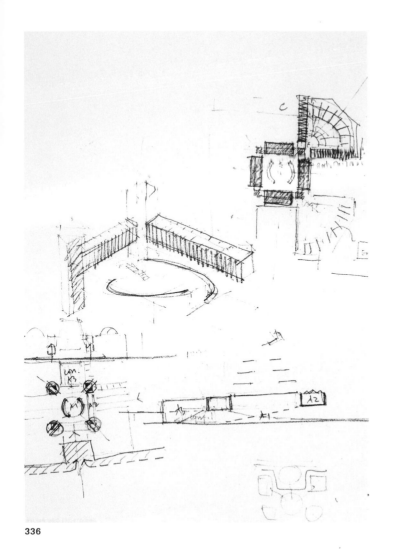

336

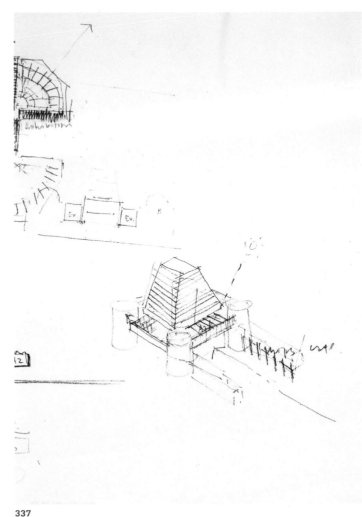

337

336. James Stirling, Michael Wilford, and Associates, Bibliothèque de France, Paris: axonometric and plan, 1989 reprographic copy; 29.6 x 21 cm (11 ⅝ x 8 ¼ in); AP140.S2.SS1.D88.P14.137

In this scheme the truncated pyramid takes over the entire library as a massive glass reading space.

337. James Stirling, Michael Wilford, and Associates, Bibliothèque de France, Paris: plans and axonometric, 1989 reprographic copy; 29.7 x 21 cm (11 ¹¹⁄₁₆ x 8 ¼ in); AP140.S2.SS1.D88.P14.138

Following the firm's reluctance to leave a precedent behind, this scheme forms the pyramid out of four Cambridge History Faculty buildings placed around an open square.

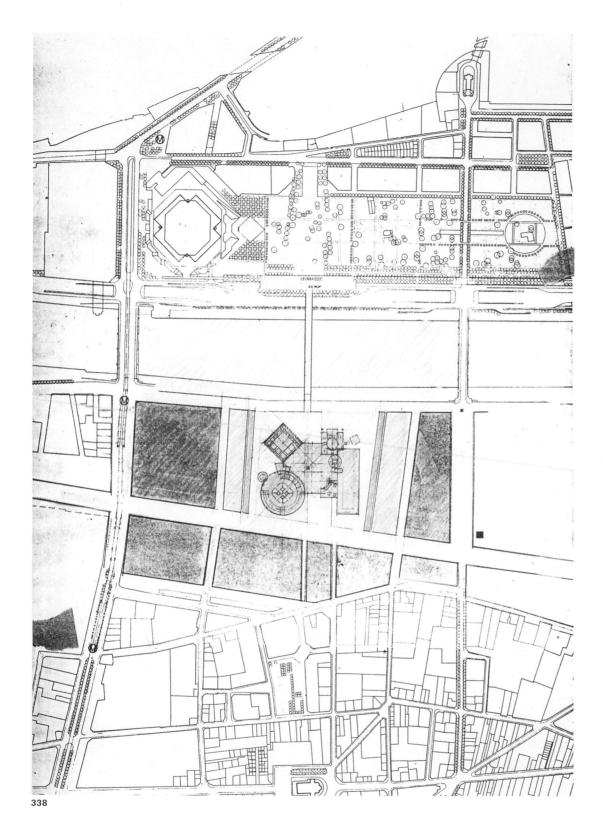

338

338. James Stirling, Michael Wilford, and Associates, Bibliothèque de France, Paris: site plan, 1989
coloured pencil on reprographic copy; 29.6 x 21 cm (11 ⅝ x 8 ¼ in); AP140.S2.SS1.D88.P12.11

The program elements have now been identified as geometric forms—square, circle, bar—and assembled on the site, with water let in from the river on either side.

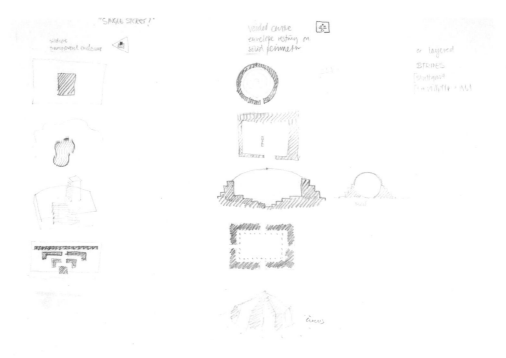

339. James Stirling, Michael Wilford, and Associates, Bibliothèque de France, Paris: conceptual diagrams, 1989
graphite on paper; 21 x 29.7 cm
(8 ¼ x 11 ¾ in); AP140.S2.SS1.D88.P12.32

Two fundamental compositional types—"solid core/transparent enclosure" and "voided centre/envelope resting on solid perimeter"—and the prototype of Boullée's Cenotaph to Newton (1784) adopted for a reading room section.

340. James Stirling, Michael Wilford, and Associates, Bibliothèque de France, Paris: annotated analytical diagram, 1989
coloured pencil, ink and correction fluid on reprographic copy; 48.7 x 34.2 cm
(19 ³⁄₁₆ x 13 ⁷⁄₁₆ in); AP140.S2.SS1.D88.P9.1

The functional breakdown now calculated according to the specific breakdown of the architectural elements: the blue children's library, the pink reference library, the purple research library, the green recent acquisitions library.

339

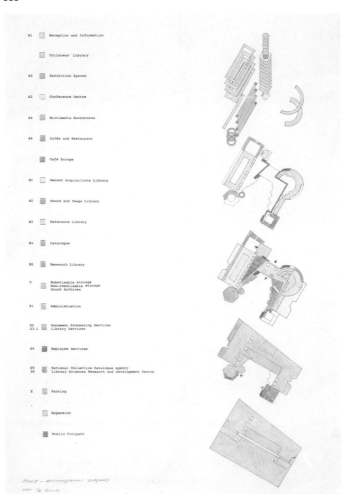

340

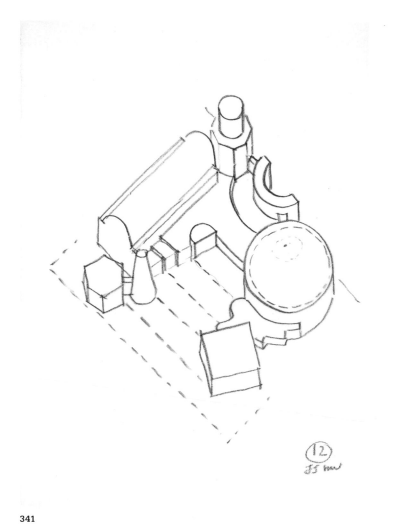

341

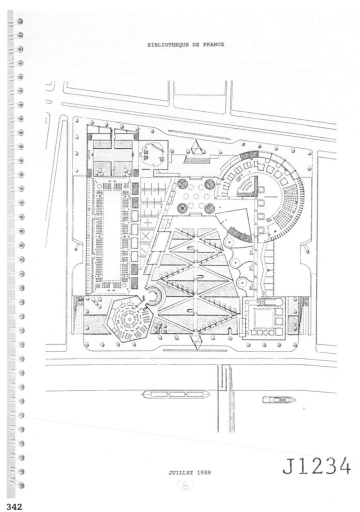

JUILLET 1989

J1234

342

341. James Stirling, Michael Wilford, and Associates, Bibliothèque de France, Paris: axonometric, "12," 1989 graphite on paper; 29.7 x 21.1 cm (11 ¾ x 8 ¼ in); AP140.S2.SS1.D88.P13.12

In the final scheme, Boullée's influence is even stronger, as the barrel-vaulted reference library takes the form of Boullée's Bibliothèque Royale of the mid-1780s, with the recent acquisitions library a domed circular volume drawn from Boullée's Newton Cenotaph.

342. James Stirling, Michael Wilford, and Associates, Bibliothèque de France, Paris: plan, July 1989, from "Library of France—Architect's Report" AP140.S2.SS1.D88.P4.2.1

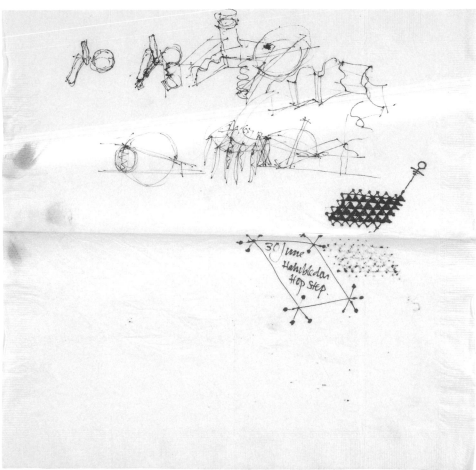

343. James Stirling, Michael Wilford, and Associates, Bibliothèque de France, Paris: conceptual sketches, 1989
ink on paper napkin; 33 x 33 cm (13 x 13 in) (unfolded; approx.); AP140.S2.SS1.D88.P12.18

From the time of Paxton, who was reputed to have drawn the system of the Crystal Palace of 1851 on a serviette, the table napkin has become a designer's tool—here is one found sandwiched among the drawings for the Bibliothèque de France competition—no doubt from the Café Flore …

344. James Stirling, Michael Wilford, and Associates, Bibliothèque de France, Paris: presentation model, 1989
paint, wood, moulded plastic and metal; 38 x 122 x 123 cm (15 x 48 x 48 ⅜ in); (largest); AP140.S2.SS1.D88.P20

343

344

Master Class

*The ultimate teaching achievement must be a Master Class. ... After twenty years
as a visiting teacher at Yale—and before that as part time critic at schools of
architecture in the UK—a Master Class would be a final accomplishment for me.*
James Stirling, 1987[207]

Stirling began to lecture soon after moving to London in the mid-1950s—first
at the Architectural Association School of Architecture, then at the ICA, then
for many years as a visitor to the Yale School of Architecture. His lecture notes
are found in various places in the archive—tucked into the pages of the Black
Notebook, written on the back of design studio assignments, jotted on postcards, index cards, and hotel stationery. His lectures were generally lapidary
and terse, offering little in the way of elaborated theory, preferring to quote lau-
datory or critical passages from critics—Charles Jencks (nicknamed "Charles
Junk" for the occasion), and Bob Maxwell were favorites. But when the notes
are examined, they exhibit a continuous exploration of themes from the critique
of modernist rationalism, the acknowledgement of a crisis following the death
of the heroes of the modern movement, the emergence of a regionalist sensibility, the relations between "context," "association," and "accommodation"
(program), and the consistent explanation of a project as a tight formal response
to the client's brief.

Speaking in the new School of Architecture building at Rice University,
within the pure modernist auditorium, its white, sculptural, two-storey "insert"
wrapped by the brick "neo-Cram" exterior, Stirling set out his manifesto for a
contextual modernism, one from which, in retrospect, he never deviated. From
the eclectic modernisms of his schoolwork, to the machine-age constructivisms
of the "red-brick" period, through to the contextual urban insertions of the
museums, and throughout the projects for cities in "microcosm" in the United
States and Europe, his message was one of continuity and reformulation. This
message was consistent in his lecturing and teaching from the outset, as is
revealed by a study of his lecture notes. Often jotted as a list of single words—
very much like his own style of lecturing—they trace an evolving sensibility,
as one by one projects are added over time, that reveals little in the way of
major shifts or radical breaks in approach, but rather a consistent search for the
appropriate expression, in context, of specific needs, and for an architectural
language that, with associations drawn from past building, whether "high" or
"low," expanded the vocabulary of modernism.

The following is a selection of these notes—written on the backs of hotel
stationery, postcards, and studio assignments. Often revised, and annotated for
reuse, they demonstrate that, despite his resistance to the "theoretical" and his

207. James Stirling, in Maxwell, *James Stirling Writings
on Architecture*, 275.

disinclination to put into words what could better be drawn or built, Stirling was continuously thinking through the principles of his practice, and, as with his thin-line axonometrics, reducing this thinking to its most economical expression.

345–349. James Frazer Stirling, lecture notes, *c.*1958
pen and ink and coloured pencil on postcard; 14 x 8.5 cm (5 ½ x 3 ⅜ in); AP140.S2.SS4.D7.P5.4.1-3

Written in pen on both sizes of small notecards this is perhaps the earliest set of lecture-notes—the talk finishes at Churchill and thus around 1958–9, it is centrally concerned with revealing precedents of a regional and vernacular nature.

345

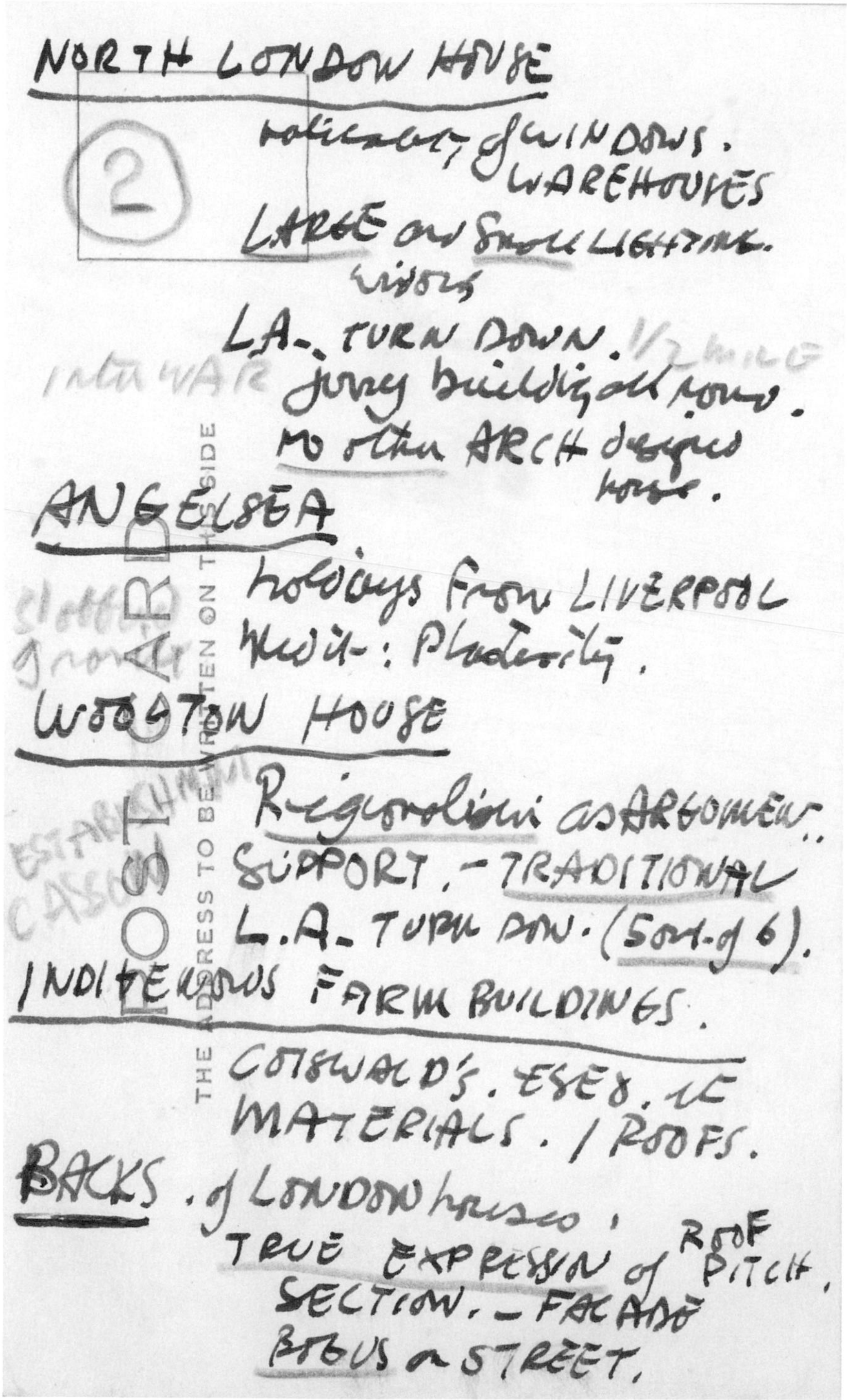

NORTH LONDON HOUSE

(2)

~~~~~~ of WINDOWS.
WAREHOUSES
LARGE ow SMALL LIGHTING.
windows

LA... TURN DOWN. 1/2 mile
jerry building all round.
no other ARCH designed
house.

ANGLESEA

holidays from LIVERPOOL
Nesbit : Photocity.

WOOTTON HOUSE

Regionalism as ARGUMENT..
SUPPORT. - TRADITIONAL
L.A. TURN DOW. (5 out of 6).
INDIGENOUS FARM BUILDINGS.

COTSWOLD'S. ESSEX. 1C
MATERIALS. / ROOFS.

BACKS. of LONDON houses.
TRUE EXPRESSN of ROOF
PITCH.
SECTION. - FACADE
BOGUS on STREET.

346

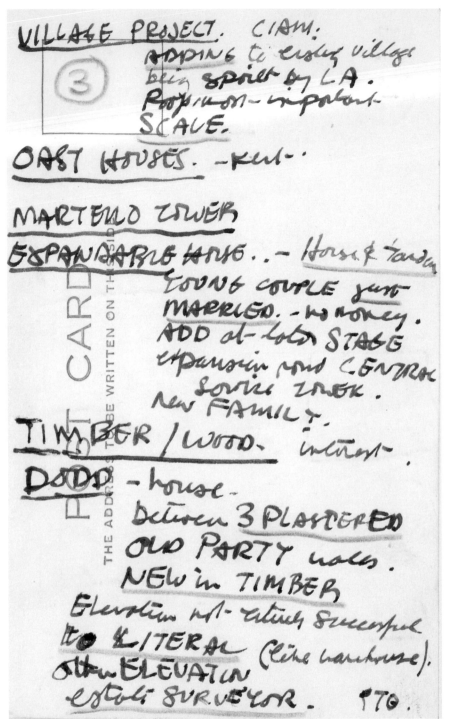

VILLAGE PROJECT.   CIAM.
③   ADDING to existing village
being spoilt by LA.
Proportion - important
SCALE.

OAST HOUSES. - Kent -

MARTELLO TOWER

EXPANDABLE HOUSE.. - House & garden
YOUNG COUPLE just
MARRIED. - no money.
ADD at later STAGE
expansion round CENTRAL
service track.
New FAMILY.

TIMBER / WOOD.   interest -

DODD - house -
between 3 PLASTERED
OLD PARTY walls.
NEW in TIMBER
Elevation not entirely successful
too LITERAL (like warehouse).
other ELEVATION
estate SURVEYOR -   970.

347

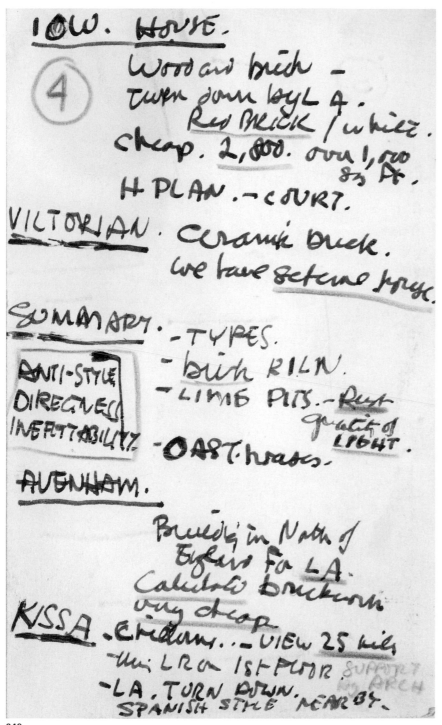

I.O.W. HOUSE.

④ Wood and brick —
turn down by L.A.
Red BRICK / white.
cheap. 2,800. over 1,000
83' Ft.
H PLAN. — COURT.

VICTORIAN. Ceramic brick.
we have setting pryce.

SUMMARY. — TYPES.
ANTI-STYLE — brick KILN.
DIRECTNESS — LIME PITS. — Rest
INEVITABILITY — quality of LIGHT.
— OAST. houses.

AVENHAM.

Building in North of
England For L.A.
Calculated brickwork
very cheap.

KISSA. Eveldam... — VIEW 25 miles
this LR on 1st FLOOR SUPPORT
NO ARCH
— LA. TURN DOWN. NEARBY.
SPANISH STYLE

348

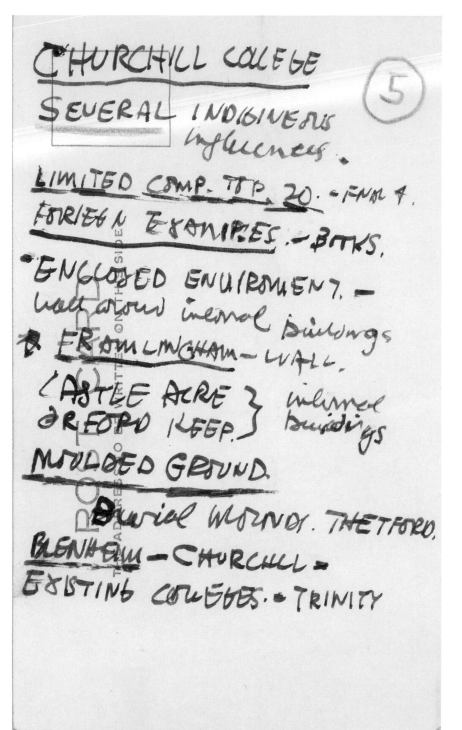

CHURCHILL COLLEGE

SEVERAL INDIGIVEOUS
influences.

LIMITED COMP. TOP 20. - FNOR 4.
FORIEGN EXAMPLES. - BOOKS.

*ENCLOSED ENVIROMENT. -
wall around inernal building
★ FRAMLINGHAM — WALL.

CASTLE ACRE ⎫ internal
ORFORD KEEP. ⎬ buildings

MOULDED GROUND.

★ Burial MOUNDS. THETFORD.
BLENHEIM — CHURCHILL -
EXISTING COLLEGES. • TRINITY

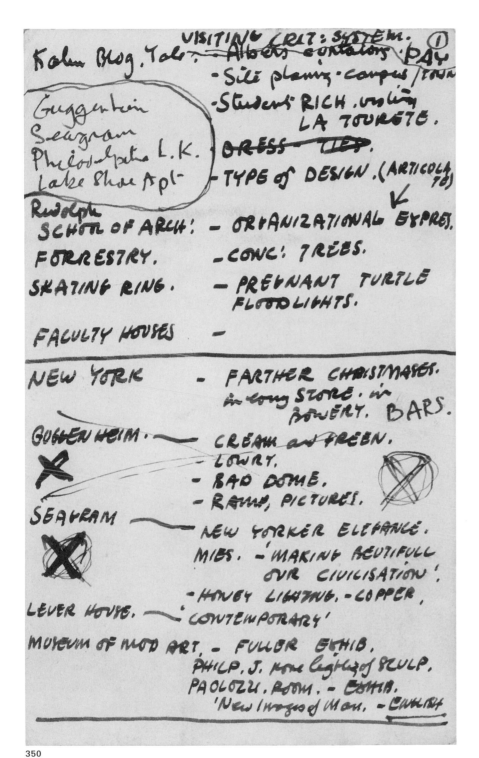

350–353. James Frazer Stirling, lecture notes, n.d.
pen and ink on postcard;
13.9 x 8.4 cm (5 ½ x 3 ¼ in) /
11 x 8.9 cm (4 ⅜ x 3 ½ in);
AP140.S2.SS4.D7.P5.1.1 /.2

Written on two postcards, one from the Cambridge University School of Architecture, this "Report from the US" was perhaps delivered on Stirling's return from his first visit to the United States and to Yale. He reports on the Kahn building at Yale.

350

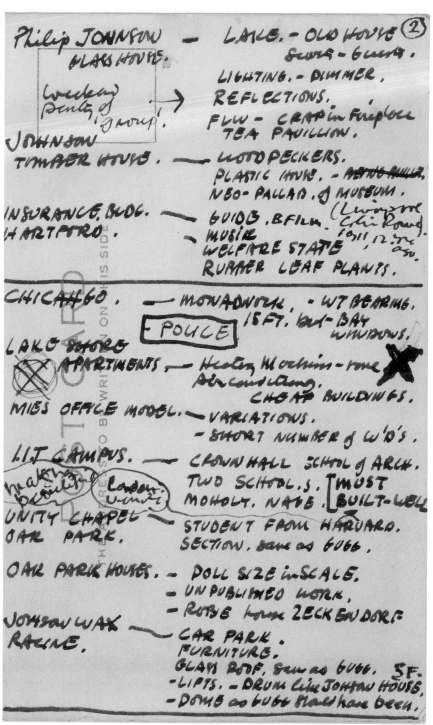

Philip JOHNSON — LA.C. — OLD HOUSE ②
GLASS HOUSE.   Slurk — Guests.
(weekly)   LIGHTING. — DIMMER,
Party of   →   REFLECTIONS,
'group'.   FLW — CRAP in Fireplace
JOHNSON   TEA PAVILLION.
TIMBER HOUSE. — WOODPECKERS.
                PLASTIC HOUSE. — ASTRO MILLS.
                NEO-PALLAD. of MUSEUM.
INSURANCE BLDG. — GUIDE. BFILM. (Liverpool
HARTFORD.   — MUSIC   Chi Row)
                WELFARE STATE   13,11,12 the
                RUBBER LEAF PLANTS.

CHICAGO. — MONADNOCK. - WT BEARING.
                          15 FT. but- BAY
                [POLICE]   WINDOWS.
LAKE SHORE
⊗ APARTMENTS, — Heating Machine — rone ✗
              Air conditioning.
                  CHEAP BUILDINGS.
MIES OFFICE MODEL. — VARIATIONS.
              - SHORT NUMBER of W'D'S.
L.I.T CAMPUS. — CROWN HALL SCHOOL of ARCH.
          London   TWO SCHOOL. S. [MUST
          Univ.   MOHOLY. NAGE. [BUILT- WELL
UNITY CHAPEL — STUDENT FROM HARVARD.
OAK PARK.   SECTION. Same as GUGG.
OAK PARK HOUSES. — DOLL SIZE in SCALE.
              = UNPUBLISHED WORK.
              - ROBIE House ZECKENDORF.
JOHNSON WAX — CAR PARK.
RACINE.   FURNITURE.
              GLASS ROOF. Same as GUGG. SF.
              - LIFTS. — DRUM Like JOHNSON HOUSE.
              - DOME as GUGG Should have been.

351

BOSTON. - SEVERUD HALL
- SCHOOL of ARCH. TYPE of WORK.
- GROPIUS. - influenced, but his EX-
STUDENTS few TOP MEN.
CAPE ～ SHERMAEFF week end house.
COD. TRADITIONAL. - EVOLVED.
CHEAP - MODEST.

─────────────────────────────

PHILADELPHIA.
LOB KAN ｜ ORGANIZATIONAL. EXPRESSION.
CHEM LABS not- STRUC: EXHIBITIONISM
TOWERS and LABS.
FEW
KAHN. - PIONEER type AMERICAN:
✗ not not - EUROPEAN.

─────────────────────────────

WELLSLEY. — swashing girls. - Books as Duties.
DECORATIVE GOTHASICISM
STYLA old Rudolph says no good.
LIBERTY. SHAPED COLUMNS.

─────────────────────────────

SAN :FRAN: - CHESTNAS. -TROPICAL
DRIVE from AIR PORT.
JUST - SLICK - DOWNTOW (MONTE CARLO)
Univ Ind and HOUSING. - (GREEK ISLAND).
FLW. MORRIS — same as 6066.
SHOP. - high class glass.
MAYBECK — S.F. EXHIB. FINE ARTS BUILDING.
CARDBOARD. /CREEK/ MILLIONAIRE.

HANNA HOUSE — FLW out of work on site ④
FLW. every other day.

STADIUM — new MOTOR SCALE. — future
New York city appearance.
Dodgers

LOS ANGELES. — 100 miles across. GREEN snow.
HILLS. | NEWSPAPER. REPORTER.

STURGES
HOUSE. — FLW.

ORCHE ELLWOOD HOUSE. — other crossing only YALE.
— OLDHAM GIRL. not
like MANCHESTER
— EARTHQUAKES (Ellwood
house)

GAMES HOUSE. — . not all out-of CATOLOGUE.
— Ellwood says DECORATIVE
cross bracing wires.

HOLLYHOCK HOUSE. — Los Ang MUSEUM.

ENNIS house. — Ennis house.
Top of hill taken off.
H.R.H. — TOO MONUMENTAL
— GETTING, BATING OF HOUND.

NEUTRA. — EMPTY.
ENT from TOP.
FLW - STOREY — GLASS in CONC: BLOCK.
houses.
MALIBU BEACH HOUSE. — UNDERSTRUCKTURE
SCHINDLER. — out via NEUTRA. — PLASTIC.
YALE awareness. ITALIAN.

353

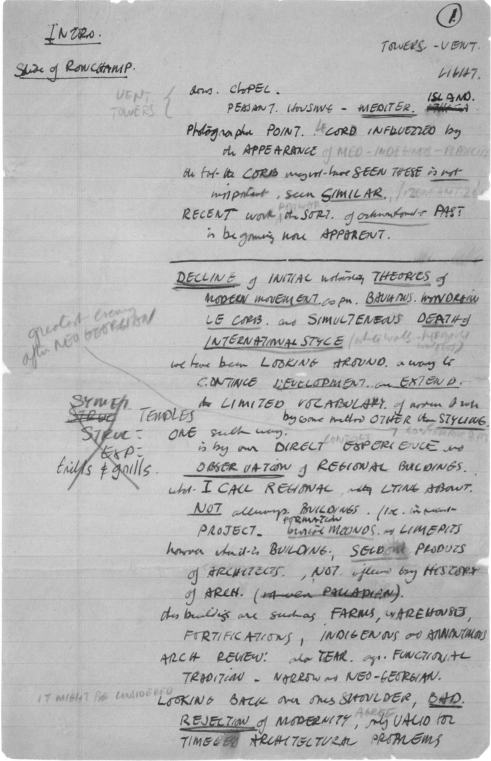

354–357. James Frazer Stirling, lecture notes for one of two talks, probably at Yale, 1959. This talk was used to prepare the article "The Functional tradition and Expression," published in *Perspecta* 6 in 1960
ink and coloured pencil on lined paper; 31.7 x 20.5 cm (12 ½ x 8 ⅛ in); AP140.S2.SS4.D7.P5.2.1-4

In this lecture, probably delivered to the Yale students in 1959, Stirling develops his thesis on the "Decline of the initial theories of the modern movement" and the "simultaneous death of the International Style."

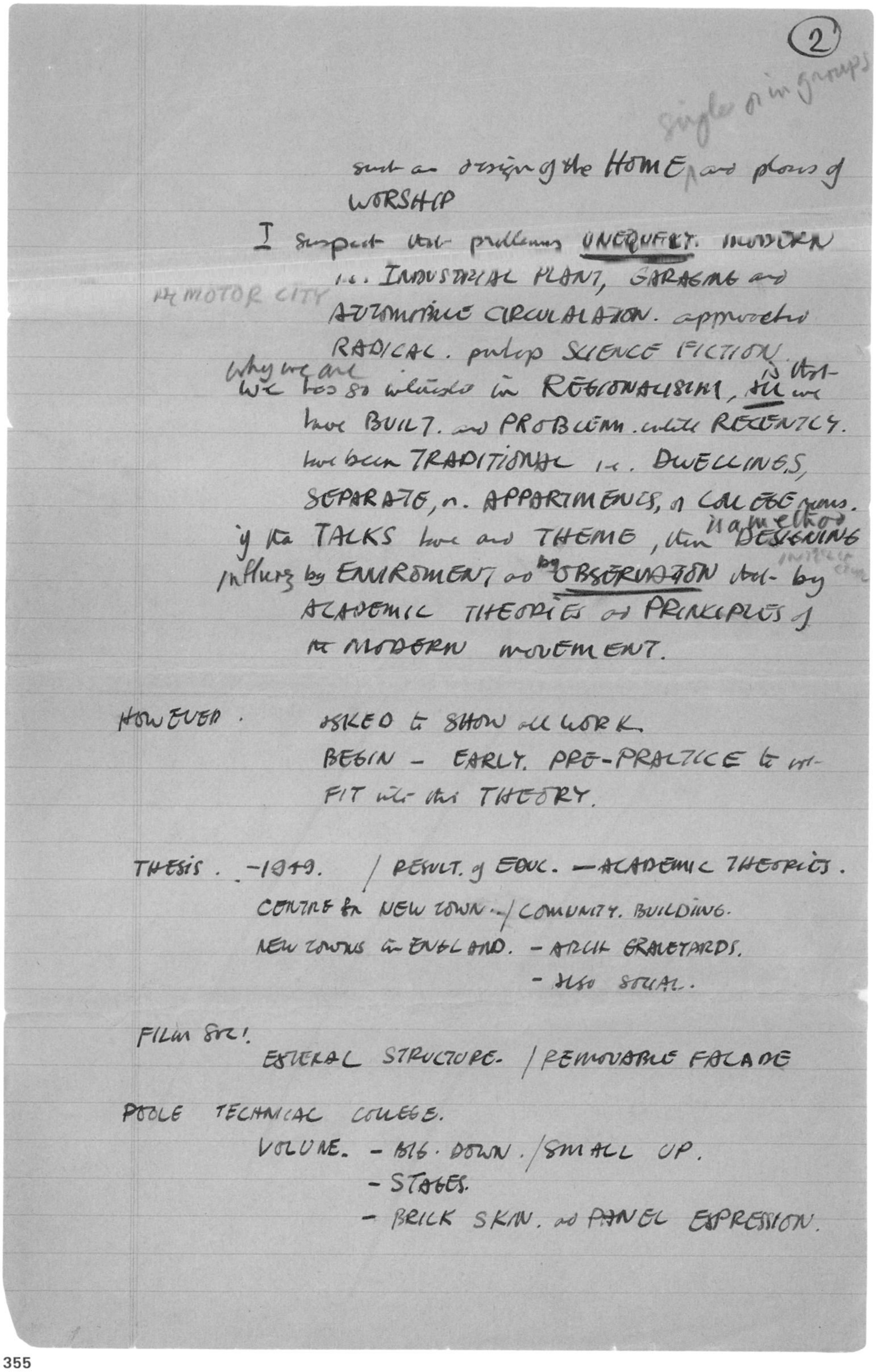

single or in groups

such as design of the HOME and plans of
WORSHIP

I suspect new problems UNEQUIPT. MODERN
i.e. INDUSTRIAL PLANT, GARAGING and
AUTOMOBILE CIRCULATION. approaches
RADICAL. perhaps SCIENCE FICTION.

At MOTOR CITY

Why we are
We has so interested in REGIONALISM, till we
have BUILT. no PROBLEM. until RECENTLY.
have been TRADITIONAL i.e. DWELLINGS,
SEPARATE, in. APPARTMENTS, in COLLEGE years.

a method
if the TALKS have any THEME, then DESIGNING
influenced by ENVIRONMENT and OBSERVATION not by
ACADEMIC THEORIES or PRINCIPLES of
the MODERN MOVEMENT.

intellectum

HOWEVER.   ASKED to SHOW all WORK.
                BEGIN - EARLY. PRE-PRACTICE to not
                FIT into this THEORY.

THESIS. -1949. / RESULT of EDUC. —ACADEMIC THEORIES.
        CENTRE for NEW TOWN -/ COMMUNITY. BUILDING.
        NEW TOWNS in ENGLAND. - ARCH. GRAVEYARDS.
                                - also SOCIAL.

FILM 8vz!
        EXTERNAL STRUCTURE. / REMOVABLE FACADE

POOLE TECHNICAL COLLEGE.
        VOLUME. - BIG. DOWN. / SMALL UP.
              - STAGES.
              - BRICK SKIN. and PANEL EXPRESSION.

355

288

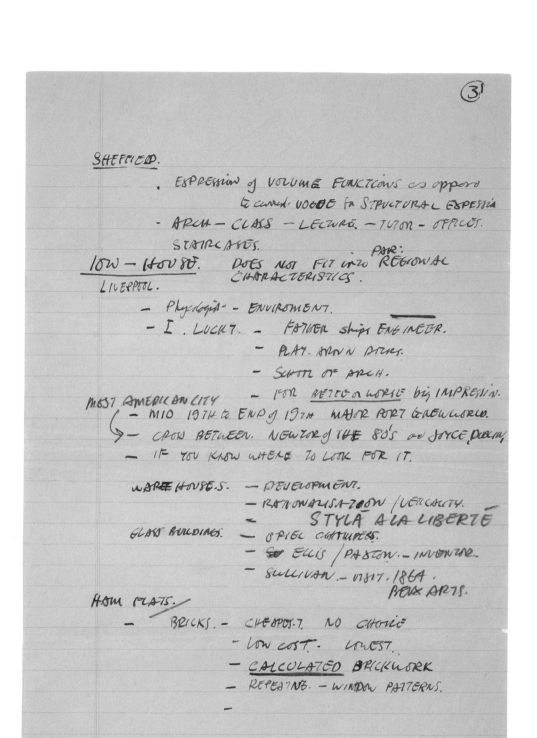

SHEFFIELD.

• EXPRESSION of VOLUME FUNKTIONS as oppose
to current VOGUE for STRUCTURAL EXPRESSIA

- ARCH - CLASS - LECTURE. - TUTOR - OFFICES.
  STAIRCASES.
PAIR:
10W - HOUSE. DOES NOT FIT into REGIONAL
CHARACTERISTICS.

LIVERPOOL.
- Physiogist - ENVIROMENT.
- I . LUCKY. - FATHER ships ENGINEER.
- PLAY. AROUN DERS.
- SCHOOL OF ARCH.
MOST AMERICAN CITY - FOR BETTER OR WORSE big IMPRESSION.
↳ - MID 19TH to END of 19TH MAJOR PORT G NEWWORLD.
↳ - CROSS BETWEEN. NEWYORK THE 80's and JOYCE, DUBLIN,
- IF YOU KNOW WHERE TO LOOK FOR IT.

WAREHOUSES. - DEVELOPMENT.
- RATIONALISATION /VERTICALITY.
STYLA A LA LIBERTÉ
GLASS BUILDINGS. - ORIEL CHAMBERS.
- ELLIS /PAXTON. - INVENTOR.
- SULLIVAN. - VISIT. 186A .
BEAUX ARTS.

HOM FLATS.
- BRICKS. - CHEAPEST. NO CHOICE
- LOW COST. LOWEST.
- CALCULATED BRICKWORK
- REPEATING. - WINDOW PATTERNS.
-

SOMETHING TODO. WITH WAREHOUSE. /DETAILS.
ALSO of COURSE. JAOUL.
MOD = ARCH DE STITL.
- UNE CONSOLE.

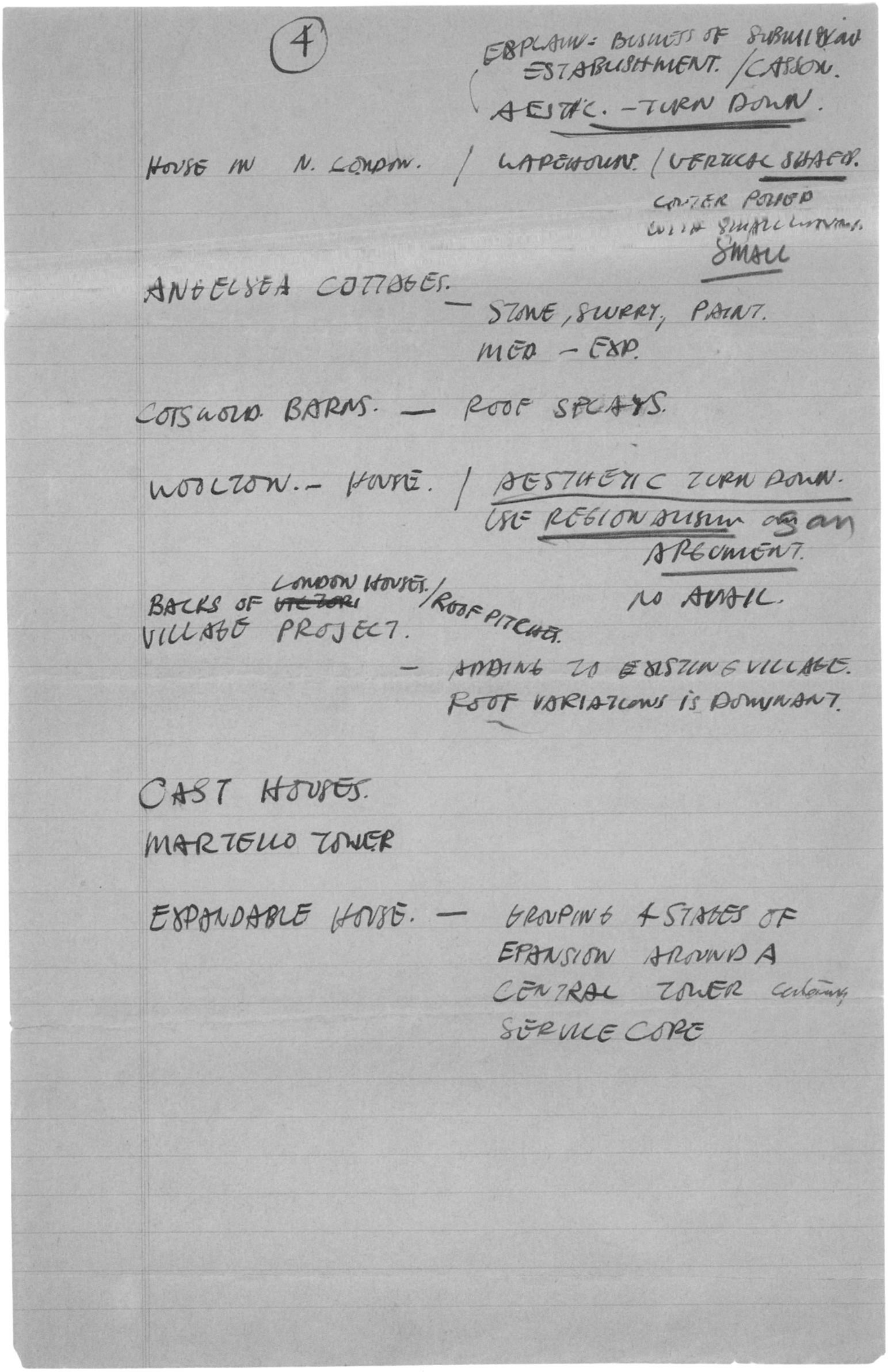

④

EXPLAIN: BUSINESS OF SUBURBAN
ESTABLISHMENT. / CASSON.
AESTIC. — TURN DOWN.

HOUSE IN N. LONDON. / WAREHOUSE. / VERTICAL SHAED.

CORNER PERIOD
WITH SMALL WINDOWS.
SMALL

ANGELSEA COTTAGES.
— STONE, SLURRY, PAINT.
MED — EXP.

COTSWOLD BARNS. — ROOF SPLAYS.

WOOLTON. — HOUSE. / AESTHETIC TURN DOWN.
USE REGIONALISM as an
ARGUMENT.

LONDON HOUSES. / ROOF PITCHES. NO AVAIL.
BACKS OF ~~VICTORI~~
VILLAGE PROJECT.
— ADDING TO EXISTING VILLAGE.
ROOF VARIATIONS IS DOMINANT.

OAST HOUSES.
MARTELLO TOWER

EXPANDABLE HOUSE. — GROUPING 4 STAGES OF
EXPANSION AROUND A
CENTRAL TOWER containing
SERVICE CORE

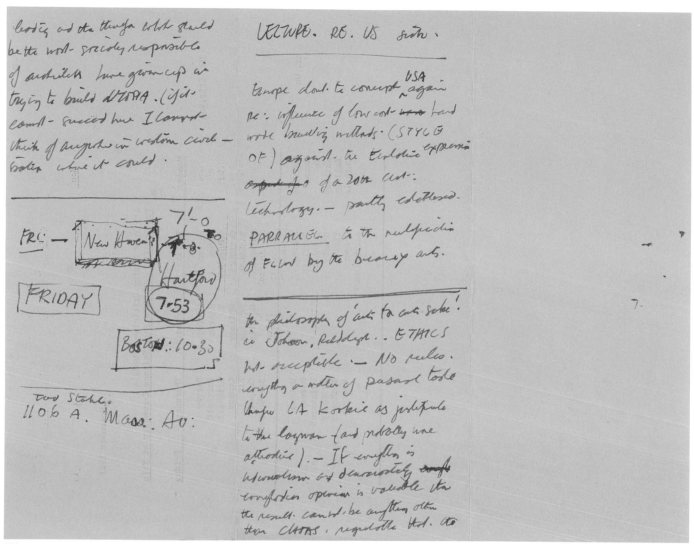

358

358. James Frazer Stirling, notes
written on the reverse of the Fourth
Year Design Criticism Schedule,
dated 10 November 1961
ink on yellow paper; 21.6 x 27.8 cm
(8 ½ x 10 ¹⁵/₁₆ in); AP140.S2.SS4.D7.P3.1

The Studio program, taught by
Professors Stirling and King-lui Wu,
was for the Pierson-Sage campus for
the Science Community at Yale.
Among the members of this studio
was Charles Gwathmey.

As written by Paul Rudolph, King-lui Wu
and E. William deCossy, the program
was "an urban problem … [and] also
the problem of the architect as planners
and developers have failed to rebuild
our cities." The "real challenge," they
concluded, "shall be the visual integration and unity of the new campus in
different stages."

Conclusion

I might like to think that the design of these buildings was influenced by nothing—and certainly not influenced by historic buildings. But nothing is conceived in a void. So if I'm looking for precedents, it might be from those of the "functional tradition"—which makes a connection back to the beginnings of the Modern Movement in architecture— and its rejection of history, which for some was like throwing out the baby with the bathwater. The fluctuation between modernity and tradition which has been so characteristic of this century is echoed in microcosm in the oscillation between functional abstraction and historical association in our own work. Here we hope we have achieved an unmonumental lightness of being.

James Frazer Stirling, opening day of the Braun Factory, Melsungen, May 27, 1992.

Out of the more than 40,000 objects in the James Stirling/Michael Wilford fonds, only some 5,000 have been examined for this introductory study; of these under four hundred have been reproduced. In this sense, these "notes" may be considered as only a very preliminary survey, and any conclusions must be provisional, dependent on the future work of scholars and critics. Individual case studies of built and unbuilt projects; thematic analyses of the development of typologies, programs, styles, and compositional strategies in the context of the larger issues confronting late modern architecture; and interpretations of Stirling's and Wilford's theoretical positions compared to those of their contemporaries, all may be accomplished through research in this archive.

Nevertheless, I have been able to propose certain important revisions to the generally accepted narratives of Stirling's career, narratives that were assembled moment to moment with the publication and construction of each successive project. First, there emerges a noticeable and fundamental continuity throughout his career—one based on compositional strategies, volumetric assemblages and dis-assemblages, programmatic responses, and, finally, stubbornly held personal preferences. Of course, it is only too easy to fabricate such

consistencies in retrospect, but the emphasis on the urban, whether in the form of new town development or the insertion of individual buildings into an urban context, was there from the outset, embedded in the totality of his Fifth Year Thesis: this represented his first experiments in the use of circulation to unify a scheme, the move away from the Corbusian free plan, the invention of personal motifs such as the weathervanes on top of the boiler-house chimneys, later to reappear in the Florey Building, and the overall concern to go beyond the norms of modern movement languages, by trying out their mingling and conjunction. Such themes, together with the formal signs of their presence, would be evident in all his future projects.

Similarly, and related to this, there is the obvious reluctance to leave a good invention behind and the continuing desire to build in one scheme what had had to be abandoned in a former. Thus the sweep of the office buildings proposed for the Olivetti Headquarters at Milton Keynes returns with even greater effect at Melsungen; the weathervane is ubiquitous; the projects for museums in Düsseldorf and Cologne are carefully dis-assembled and reassembled to form an even stronger *parti* for Stuttgart; and, in an equally artful manner, the "expandable House," invented by Stirling and Gowan for *House and Garden* in 1957, is introduced with social sensitivity in the framework and plan strategies for the PREVI housing in Lima some ten years later. Certainly the combinatory volumetric sketches by Stirling and Gowan for the "House Studies" of 1956 can be seen as generative of an inventive and productive compositional strategy that would be elaborated and refined throughout.

And what of the question of "language," a word avoided by the heroic modernists, but that by the 1950s had already been invoked to characterize what was an obvious heterogeneity of representative forms? Stirling's resolution in 1954 to enlarge the scope of modernism's expressive techniques, either by returning to the "functional tradition" or by the implied reference to the entire range of modern movements from Constructivism to Purism, was initially directed against the increasing normalization of the International Style. Subsequently, however, his deft handling of abstraction in spatial form marked by occasional signposts in the form of railings, canopies, technological elements, and materials, led him to develop a manner entirely different from that of his Team X contemporaries, with their resistance to any historical reference, or from that of the postmodernists, with their delight in literal quotation from historical sources. Stirling's independence from these movements, often leading to personal rivalries and broken friendships, was forged with a double edge.

Firstly, and following the early approach of Rowe, Stirling attempted to assimilate all of architectural history through compositional and *parti* analysis in a generative rather than a passive manner. Rowe's teaching method, which consisted of a seemingly endless evocation of potential organizations out of the plans and sections of history, accompanied by his insistence on drawing, over and over, on multiple sheets of tracing paper in thick pencil, was indelibly to mark Stirling's method. Secondly, Stirling's studied independence from, which did not preclude his intimate knowledge of, the academic theory common to his circle—Rowe, of course, but also Sam Stevens, Kenneth Frampton, Reyner Banham, and his closest friend Bob Maxwell—allowed him to avoid "authorizing" any of his projects with any single precedent, leaving it to the critics to track down, infer, and invent as many as needed. For in the end Stirling's "theory" was no less intellectual or theorized than that of his more verbal contemporaries—his early articles, notes, and lectures demonstrate his high degree of self-consciousness—but it was deeply embedded in the work itself. It was for the project to speak of its associations with its context, to exhibit its relations with the ongoing, and, for Stirling, unbroken tradition of architecture, high or vernacular. In this sense, Stirling's theory is the archive—not so much in the writings it contains (although a careful reading of the architect's reports and correspondence will evince a powerfully critical mind at work)—but in the tracing of the emergence of each design, its successive iterations, and the reiteration of one design in the next.

Finally, in one of his last talks, the "Birdwatcher" Stirling, who had been so assiduous in recording the birds of the Wirral in the early 1940s, and who had been delighted to see Le Corbusier providing bird nesting holes in the masonry of the Maisons Jaoul in the 1950s, returned to this theme on the opening day of the Braun Factory, Melsungen:

> I hope all who come to work in these new buildings will find them as easy to occupy as those families of falcons which have taken so readily to living in the bird houses we placed on top of the highest building.

The close relations between birdwatching and architectural design in modern society have yet to be explored in detail, but for Stirling the connection was obvious in the nature of close observation and the sensitive attention to both context and (all of) its inhabitants.

Selected Bibliography

The following bibliography lists James Stirling's major published articles and the principal monographic publications of the firm, supplemented by Mark Girouard's biography and Mark Crinson's transcription of the Black Notebook and various lectures. It does not take account of the multiple publications of Stirling's work in periodicals, catalogues, or any of the large secondary critical and historical literature.

Arnell, Peter, and Ted Bickford, eds. *James Stirling: Buildings and Projects*. Introduction by Colin Rowe. New York: Rizzoli International, 1984.

Crinson, Mark, ed. *James Stirling: Early Unpublished Writings on Architecture*. London: Routledge, 2009.

Foster, Norman, Mark Girouard and James Stirling. "Stirling Gold." *Architectural Design* 50, nos. 7–8 (1980): 1–58.

Girouard, Mark. *Big Jim: The Life and Work of James Stirling*. London: Chatto and Windus, 1998.

James Stirling, Michael Wilford and Associates: Buildings and Projects, 1975–1992. Introduction by Robert Maxwell, essays by Michael Wilford and Thomas Muirhead, layout by Thomas Muirhead, James Stirling and Michael Wilford. London: Thames and Hudson, 1994.

Maxwell, Robert. *James Stirling, Michael Wilford*. Basel: Birkhäuser Verlag, 1998.

___, ed. *James Stirling: Writings on Architecture*. New York: Rizzoli, 1998.

Stirling, James. "From Garches to Jaoul. Le Corbusier as Domestic Architect in 1927 and 1953." *Architectural Review* 118, no. 5 (September 1955): 145–151.

___. "Ronchamp. Le Corbusier's Chapel and the Crisis of Rationalism." *Architectural Review* 119, no. 711 (March 1956): 155–161.

___. "This is Tomorrow." In Theo Crosby, ed., *This is Tomorrow*. Exhibition catalogue. London: Whitechapel Art Gallery, 1956.

___. "Regionalism and Modern Architecture." *Architect's Year Book* 8, ed. Trevor Dannat (1957): 62–68.

___. "A Personal View of the Present Situation." *Architectural Design* (June 1958): 232–233.

___. "Packaged Deal and Prefabrication." *Design Magazine*, no. 123 (March 1959): 287.

___. "The Functional Tradition and Expression." *Perspecta* 6 (1960): 88–97.

___. "Seven Keys to Good Architecture." *Twentieth Century* (Winter 1962–1963): 145.

___. "An Architect's Approach to Architecture." Paper delivered at the Royal Institute of British Architects, 23 February 1965. *Journal of the Royal Institute of British Architects* 73, no. 5 (May 1965): 231–240. Also published in *Zodiac* 16 (1967): 160–169.

___. "Conversations with Students." *Perspecta* 11 (1967): 91–93.

___. "Anti-Structure." *Zodiac* 18 (1969): 51–60.

___. "Stirling in Tokyo," interview with Arata Isozaki. *Architecture and Urbanism*, no. 8 (August 1971): 4–7.

___. "On drawing." In *James Stirling*. Catalogue accompanying exhibition at RIBA, Heinz Gallery, London, 24 April–21 June 1974. London: RIBA Publications, 1974.

___. "Methods of Expression and Materials." *Architecture and Urbanism*, no. 2 (1975).

___. "Stirling connexions." An address by James Stirling to the second Iran International Congress of Architecture, Persepolis, 1974, *Architectural Review*, 157 (May 1975): 273–276.

___. *James Stirling: Buildings and Projects 1950–1974*. Introduction by John Jacobus, layout by Leon Krier and James Stirling (London: Thames and Hudson, 1975).

___. "Beaux-Arts Reflections." In Robin Middleton, ed., *Architectural Design* 48, nos. 11–12 (1978): 88.

___. "Royal Gold Medal for Architecture 1980." *RIBA Journal* 87 (March 1980): 35–42.

___. "Architectural Aims and Influences." *RIBA Journal* 87 (September 1980): 17–19.

___. "The Clore Gallery. Interview with Charles Jencks." *Architecture and Urbanism*, no. 4 (September 1987): 36–45.

Stirling, James, and James Gowan. "Afterthoughts on the Flats at Ham Common," *Architecture and Building* (May 1959): 167.

Index